The Study of Public Management
in Europe and the US

This book presents an overview of the scientific study of public management, gathering together some of the most authoritative experts in this area of study in Europe and the United States, writing specifically about their respective countries. These essays seek to present the national distinctiveness of the study of public management, in the context of specific state administration.

This book goes further than some previous books concerning public management by highlighting the underlying differences between Europe and the United States, and amongst European countries, in relation to their particular political-administrative circumstances. The aim of this book is to establish a dialogue between Anglo-American and European approaches to public management, to encourage readers to see their own national ideas and practices in contrast to others and foster learning by asking repeatedly, 'compared to what?'

This book will be of great interest to students and researchers engaged with public management, organisation and administration throughout Europe and the United States.

Walter Kickert is professor of public management at the Department of Public Administration at the Erasmus University in Rotterdam and scientific director of the Dutch national research school of administrative and political sciences, NIG.

Routledge studies in public management

The Study of Public Management in Europe and the US

A comparative analysis of national distinctiveness

Edited by Walter Kickert

 Routledge
Taylor & Francis Group

LONDON AND NEW YORK

First published 2008
by Routledge
2 Park Square, Milton Park, Abingdon, Oxon OX14 4RN

Simultaneously published in the USA and Canada
by Routledge
270 Madison Ave, New York, NY 10016

Routledge is an imprint of the Taylor & Francis Group, an informa business

Typeset in Times by Wearset Ltd, Boldon, Tyne and Wear
Printed and bound in Great Britain by TJI Digital, Padstow, Cornwall

British Library Cataloguing in Publication Data
A catalogue record for this book is available from the British Library

Library of Congress Cataloging in Publication Data
A catalog record for this book has been requested

ISBN10: 0-415-44386-5 (hbk)
ISBN10: 0-203-93617-5 (ebk)

ISBN13: 978-0-415-44386-9 (hbk)
ISBN13: 978-0-203-93617-7 (ebk)

Contents

Illustrations

Figures

Tables

Contributors

Xavier Ballart is associate professor of Political and Administrative Sciences at the Autonomous University of Barcelona. He has also taught at Indiana University (1999–2000) and the College of Europe (2000–2006). His main research interests and publications are in policy evaluation and innovation in public management and public administration in Spain and Europe. He has worked as a consultant for local and regional governments, the European Commission and the World Bank. He was the first editorial coordinator for the *Spanish Review of Political Science*.

Annie Bartoli is professor of Business Administration at the University of Versailles Saint-Quentin (France), where she holds the positions of co-director of the Centre of Research in Management, LAREQUOI, and director of the postgraduate Master in Strategic Management and Change. She is also visiting research professor at Georgetown University, Washington, DC. Professor Bartoli is author or co-author of 12 books and several dozens of articles in the fields of strategy, public management, piloting of change, information and communication. She is also a consultant in management for multinational companies and public organisations.

Tom Christensen is professor of Public Administration and Organisation Theory at the Department of Political Science, University of Oslo. His research interests include studies of central civil service and public reform, both nationally and comparatively. Among his recent books are *Autonomy and Regulation: Coping with Agencies in the Modern State* and *Transcending New Public Management: the Transformation of Public Sector Reform*, both edited with Per Lægreid, and a textbook, *Organization Theory for the Public Sector*, written with P. Lægreid, P. G. Roness and K. A. Røvik.

Gyorgy Hajnal is senior research fellow at the MKI/Hungarian Institute of Public Administration. His research interests are related to, among others, problems of public management reforms in transitional states, and the comparative study of administrative culture. He has served as a consultant to various domestic and international governmental, academic and corporate entities. He is the author of about 30 books, book chapters and journal articles, and numerous conference papers.

Gyorgy Jenei is professor of Public Policy and Management at the Corvinus University, Budapest. His research interests are in public management reforms, the functions of the modern state, and the role of civil society organisations in public policy-making and service provision. He has published books such as *Public Policy in Central and Eastern Europe*; *Institutional Requirements and Problem Solving in the Public Administrations of the Enlarged European Union and Its Neighbours*; *Challenges of Public Management Reforms: Theoretical Perspectives and Recommendations* and *East–West Co-operation in Public Sector Reform (Cases and Results in Central and Eastern Europe)*.

Walter Kickert is professor of Public Management at the Erasmus University, Rotterdam. His research interests are in management and organization of national administration, international comparative public management and administrative reform. He has published such books as *Managing Complex Networks* and *Public Management and Administrative Reform in Western Europe*. He has worked at the ministries of Education and Sciences, and Agriculture, Nature and Fishery, and has done research and consultancy for various public organizations. He is the deputy-editor of the *European Forum* of the international quarterly *Public Administration*. He is scientific director of the Dutch national research school for administrative and political sciences, NIG.

Per Lægreid is professor of Administration and Organisation Theory at the University of Bergen, Norway. He has published extensively on public sector reform and institutional change in comparative perspective. His latest publications include articles in *Governance, Public Administration,* the *Journal of Management Studies, Public Performance and Management Review, Financial Accountability and Management,* the *International Public Management Journal* and the *International Review of Administrative Sciences*. His recent co-edited and co-authored books are *Transcending New Public Management: The Transformation of Public Sector Reforms, Autonomy and Regulation: Coping with Agencies in the Modern State* and *Organization Theory and Public Organization: Instrument, Culture and Myth*.

Laurence E. Lynn Jr is Sydney Stein, Jr professor of Public Management Emeritus at the University of Chicago. His research interests include American and comparative public management, public administration theory and public sector governance. His most recent books are *Public Management: Old and New* and *Madison's Managers: Public Administration and the Constitution* (with Anthony Bertelli). He has held several senior planning and management positions in the US federal government and is past president of the Association for Public Policy Analysis and Management. He has received the H. George Frederickson, Dwight Waldo, Paul Van Riper and John Gaus

Awards for lifetime contributions to the literatures of public administration and management and to public service.

Kate McLaughlin is senior lecturer in Local Governance at the University of Birmingham. Her research interests include local governance, the voluntary and community sector and public services marketing. Until recently she was Director of the Public Services MBA at the University of Birmingham. She has worked extensively with UK government departments on research and consultancy projects around public management reform.

Marco Meneguzzo is professor of Public and Non-Profit Management at the University of Rome 'Tor Vergata' and contract professor at the Italian Swiss University of Lugano. His research interests include strategic planning, interorganisational networks, public sector modernization, helath-care management and management of cultural heritage agencies. He is Scientific consultant of the Italian Department of Public Administration and has been responsible for the national innovation award. He has coordinated several projects for international institutions (such as the EU and the World Bank) and public administrations at different levels in Italy and abroad.

Stephen P. Osborne is professor of International Public Management in the Management School at the University of Edinburgh. He worked for 13 years in local government in the UK before moving to Aston Business School in 1990. He is editor in chief of the journal *Public Management Review*, editor of several Routledge book series on public management (including *Critical Studies in Public Management* and the Routledge *Masters in Public Management)* and President of the International Research Society for Public Management. His research interests include public management reform, the voluntary and non-profit sector and public services, rural public service provision and innovation and change in public services.

Christopher Pollitt is professor of Public Management at the Catholic University of Leuven. His main research interests lie in comparative public management reform, public service quality improvement and programme evaluation. Author of many texts (including *The Essential Public Manager* and *Public Management Reform: A Comparative Analysis*), he has also undertaken consultancy for many international governmental organisations and national governments. He edits the *International Review of Administrative Sciences* and is past president of the European Evaluation Society.

Christoph Reichard is emeritus professor of Public Management at the University of Potsdam. He has worked primarily on public management reforms in the German-speaking countries but also with an international comparative perspective. He is also involved in issues of public personnel management, financial management and e-government. He is affiliated with several master's programmes in public management at the universities of Potsdam and Salzburg.

Kuno Schedler is professor of Public Management at the University of St Gallen in Switzerland. His main research interests lie in (new) public management reform, electronic government, and public financial and performance management. Author of many texts (including *New Public Management* and *Managing the Electronic Government*), he has also undertaken consultancy for many governmental organisations. He is a co-editor of the *International Public Management Journal*.

Foreword

This book is one of several that currently exemplify the emergence of a broad community of European scholars of public administration and public management that can rival, in breadth and diversity, the long-looked-up-to U.S. community. It is therefore both a pleasure and an honour to be asked by my colleague and friend Walter Kickert to contribute a brief foreword. As European editor of the leading journal *Public Administration*, and as a perpetually wandering, multi-lingual professor, he is well qualified to launch such a text. I share his hope that it will not only reinforce the sense of a European community of PA academics, but will also provide food for thought for our American colleagues, not all of whom have previously felt the need to look beyond their own capacious borders.

'Europe' is an ever-evolving concept, as Norman Davies's magnificent attempt at an overall history so clearly demonstrates (Davies, 1996). Even turning European maps through 90 degrees (as Davies does) so that Ireland appears at the top, can provoke radical new insights. In the present volume 'Europe' even seems to have reasserted its historical colonization of the New World (hence Chapter 11 on the United States). On the other hand, the book follows the recent enlargement of the EU only cautiously, with just one chapter on eastern Europe (Chapter 10 on Hungary). And there is no chapter on the study of EU institutions themselves. But whatever the precise boundaries, it is clear that we now have – to a far greater extent than 20 or 30 years ago – a group of public management academics who, while vigorously insisting upon their various national particularities, are nevertheless engaged on a common enterprise. This 'project' includes (although is not exhausted by) an extensively shared agenda and a considerable common pool of theories, concepts and techniques. It is enabled and lubricated by the advent of modern information and communication technologies, by the increased affordability and simplicity of long-distance travel, and by the ever-growing domain of the English language. (There is also the general increase in multi-lingualism within Europe – more academics of almost every country speaking not only their mother tongue plus English, but other European languages as well.) The number of European conferences and organizational platforms of one kind and another seems to grow almost weekly. The Bologna Agreement and other educational initiatives have made it less and less difficult for students and staff to move from one country to another, and to establish equivalences in qualifications. Within the field of public administration we have witnessed various schemes for the accreditation of public administration degrees on a European basis, and for co-operative approaches to doctoral study.

None of this means some crude 'convergence' of European thinking, and still less the ending of national differences (which several chapters in this book strongly reassert). But it does mean that sufficiently common agendas and vocabularies are emerging for the European academic community to talk across national boundaries. Even within the most traditional and nationally defined of public administration's many contributing disciplines – law – we have witnessed a marked growth in studies of European law and comparative law. And as more academics move across national boundaries, so do more of their students and more career public servants. In Europe, international networks are growing and growing, and this seems highly likely to have important long-term effects that are not merely institutional but also cultural and political.

One thousand or so years ago Europeans invented the idea of the 'university'. It was subsequently exported to every other inhabited continent. More than 200 years ago the study of public administration entered German universities with the foundation of chairs in 'cameralistics'. Twenty or so years ago European academics began to feel the impact of the Anglo-American doctrines now usually termed the 'New Public Management' (NPM). That particular tide has now faltered and is sliding back down the beach. Meanwhile, we have recently seen the 'European Administrative Space' expand enormously – mainly to the east (this year's lively conference of the leading eastern European association for the study of PA was held in Kiev). This is therefore a most appropriate moment for a reappraisal of the European study of public administration, and I commend Walter Kickert and his fellow authors for seizing the opportunity.

Christopher Pollitt
Catholic University of Leuven, Belgium

Bibliography

Davies, N. (1996) *Europe: a History*, Oxford: Oxford University Press.

1 Distinctiveness in the study of public management in Europe

An introduction

Walter Kickert

Introduction

This book presents an overview of the state of the art of the scientific study of public management in various European states and the United States, written by eminent, nationally renowned scholars from the various countries. Examples are presented of distinctive approaches to the study of public management in a variety of western European countries ranging from Norway up north in Scandinavia, the United Kingdom in the west, Germany, France, Switzerland and the Netherlands in the middle, Italy and Spain in the south, to Hungary in the east of western Europe. Most of the well-known textbooks and handbooks on public management are Anglo-American oriented. The North American and English-language audience is of course overwhelmingly large. Books written in German, French, Italian or Spanish, let alone in 'small' languages like Dutch, Norwegian or Swiss, only have a relatively small national market, and are hardly known across the border. In this book, authoritative experts in the study of public management in their respective countries, usually authors of standard public management textbooks in their countries, present the specific characteristics of the academic study of public management in their homeland, and place that in the context of their specific national state and administration. This book shows the national distinctiveness in the study of public management in a number of European countries, which, although probably well known to the inhabitants of those countries, is hardly known to the outside international, predominantly English-speaking, community. To them this book will, first of all, be highly informative.

This book seeks to introduce to an Anglo-American audience of public management scholars various European approaches to the study of public management, as well as to inform Europeans about the science of public management as practised by their neighbours and by America.

The relatively unknown and fairly recent European public management sciences are compared to the well-known, large and established field in the United States. Moreover a comparison is made between the various approaches in different European countries by relating the scientific characteristics to the specificities of the respective states and administrations.

This book can enhance self-understanding by encouraging readers to see their own national ideas on, and practices of, public management in contrast to others, fostering learning by asking repeatedly 'compared to what?'

Influence of national states and administrations

This basic question that this book addresses is: what is the influence of developments in different national states and administrations on the scientific study of public management within the respective states?

States and administrations in continental Europe strongly differ from the Anglo-Saxon ones and the United States, and they also considerably differ amongst themselves. That is reflected in the variety and specificity of the public management reforms that took place in different European countries (Kickert 1997). The belief in the early 1990s that the worldwide trend of public management reforms in Western administrations would tend to converge to one single, common, universal 'new public management' pattern (OECD 1995) has been refuted since in many comparative studies of public management reforms. The political-administrative context of a particular country does affect the form and content of the 'public management' reforms in that country. The well-known and comprehensive comparative analysis of public management reforms by Pollitt and Bouckaert (2004) provided impressive evidence.

In this book, that comparative line of thought is pursued one step further. The historical-institutional context of a particular state and administration affects not only the practice of public management reforms, but also the scientific study of public management in that country. Unlike the natural sciences, where the nationality of a researcher is irrelevant for his or her study, in the sciences of administration the nationality of the researcher does matter. The study of public administration is dependent on the object of study. The study of administration can never be detached from the particular national administration within a country. Because the world consists of many different types of states and administrative systems, diverse research styles and methods are inevitable. The administrative variety within Europe and between Europe and the United States is immense. That is why the study of public administration in different western European countries differs by country (Kickert and Stillman 1999). A survey of Public Administration education programmes in continental European countries (Hajnal 2003) showed three distinct clusters: continental European countries with a strong political-science component, Nordic countries with a stronger emphasis on business administration, and southern countries with a predominance of law in their curricula.

In this book we will show that the academic study of public management is also influenced by the particular institutional context of state, politics and administration in the country concerned. One might assume that the often-asserted convergence of administrative reforms in Western countries has led, by implication, to a likewise convergent common scientific approach to public management. And to a large extent this is indeed true. Managerial reforms were mainly caused by the underlying budgetary stress. Hence the need for more effectiveness and efficiency, more productivity, more value for money. Hence the emphasis on result orientation, performance indicators, and steering on outputs and results. The development since the early 1980s of a management science specific to the public sector has therefore also led to commonalities. Most mainstream Anglo-American textbooks on public management pay ample attention to output budgeting, steering on results, client orientation, competition and market testing, and to the usual facets of management: strategic, organisational, financial, personnel, and information management (see for example the well-known textbooks by renowned North American scholars like Bozeman (1989), Denhardt (1993), Lynn (1996), Rainey (1997) and Straussman (Bozeman and Straussman 1990), or by likewise well-known British scholars like Ferlie (*et al.* 1996), Flynn (1990) and Pollitt (1990), or by the Australian Hughes (1994)). Although French, German, Italian, Dutch, Swiss and Scandinavian textbooks on 'public management and organisation' at first sight show a remarkable similarity to the mainstream Anglo-American textbooks in paying ample attention to financial management, budgeting, client orientation, marketing and more, a closer look reveals important underlying differences that are related to their distinct political-administrative circumstances.

Distinctive national approaches

My inquiry into the differences and specificities of national approaches to the study of public management in Europe started with an analysis of France, Germany and Italy (Kickert 2005), three clear examples of countries with a distinctive, typical continental-European, strong legalistic state tradition. This tradition has its roots in the nineteenth-century history of state formation, particularly the establishment of the Liberal *Rechtsstaat* in continental Europe, and the legalistic tradition is still prevailing in these three countries. Legalism in the French, German and Italian administrations appeared to have a major impact on the managerial reforms in these countries, especially in the sense that these were hard to introduce and sustain. The legalistic paradigm fundamentally differs from the managerial one. Moreover, the national approaches to the study of public management also showed remarkable distinct characteristics.

In this book the inquiry is pursued by broadening up that international perspective to include more European countries, and above all by inviting authoritative scholars of public management in the respective countries to present their national case. Nationally renowned and authoritative experts in the study of public management were each asked to write a chapter on their country, following a common format to enable international comparison. As the objective of the book is to relate specificities in each country's approach to the study of public management to the national specificities of state, politics and administration, the common format which each author was asked to use in describing his or her country is:

-   a brief historical account of the state and its administration;
-   a survey of recent developments and reforms in state and administration;

- a state of the art of the study of politics and administration in both education and research;
- an overview of the specificities of the study of public management in the national context.

Selection of countries

The rationale for the selection of countries in this book was to include examples of different types of state traditions. In comparative politics and administration, three main European state types are usually distinguished. First, the Napoleonic type of state, with post-revolutionary France as the prime example. Spain and Italy are typically considered to belong to this type and so does Belgium. Second, the Germanic type with its Prussian and Habsburg roots, in which Germany and Austria can be placed. Third, the Anglo-Saxon type, with Great Britain as the main example. So, of course, the three large, exemplary countries France, Germany and Britain have been included in the book.

The smaller northern European states, such as the Netherlands and the Scandinavian countries, are usually considered a mixed form of the Anglo-Saxon and Germanic types of state. Elsewhere (Kickert and Hakvoort 2000) we have argued that this does not take into account that a whole range of smaller states from the far north to the middle of continental Europe – Finland, Norway, Sweden, Denmark, the Netherlands, Belgium, Switzerland, Austria – all have three characteristics in common: they all have a consensus type of democracy (Lijphart 1984); they all have a neo-corporatist type of state (Williamson 1989); and they have socio-political cleavages and fragmented political and social subcultures. So, three examples of these small continental-European states – Norway, the Netherlands and Switzerland – have been included in the book.

Although the southern European states Italy, Spain and Portugal are commonly considered as examples of the Napoleonic type of state, they have a number of economic, social and political characteristics in common that make them distinctive. A distinctive southern model of politics and administration might be discerned (Magone 2003). Southern European countries are often underrepresented in comparative studies of government and administration. Even after the end of the dictatorships (the military revolution in Portugal in April 1974, the fall of the colonels in Greece in July 1974, and the death of Franco in Spain in November 1975) and the transitions to democracy, the interest of the international political and administrative science community in the states, politics and administrations of such countries remains restricted, even in the field of comparative politics and government, let alone in public management. So two major southern European states – Italy and Spain – were included.

Another type of state that is becoming increasingly important in the future western Europe, are the 'new' European democracies, the former communist countries of middle Europe, the new member states of the European Union. The transition to free market economy and parliamentary democracy represented much more fundamental and urgent reforms of these states and administrations than the budget-driven efficiency reforms of public management. Moreover the modernisation and Europeanisation of these states (Goetz 2001) requires them first to restore the legalistic principles of the *Rechtsstaat* before embarking on the path of public management. So the example of the central European state of Hungary has been included in the book.

Finally we have invited a leading North American public management scholar, who is also well-acknowledged in the field of public management in Britain, France and Germany (Lynn 2006), to present his view on the study of public management in the 'New World' and to give a critical reflection from the other side of the Atlantic Ocean on the various European approaches.

Different state models in Europe

Before introducing the various authors and chapters, a brief further elaboration of the analytical rationale behind the country selection – the different traditions and types of states and administrations in Europe – seems appropriate. The vast literature on comparative politics and government contains many different typologies, which roughly speaking come down to the three categories: 'politics and society' (types of parliament, election systems, political parties, cultures, social movements, interest groups, etc.); 'state and government' (types of constitutions, governments, cabinets, parliaments, judiciary, etc.); and 'administration' (types of bureaucracies, politics-bureaucracy relations, organisation, recruitment, culture, etc.) (see e.g. Hague *et al.* 1992). Here, no attempt is made to carry out a comprehensive comparative analysis along all these dimensions. We will only briefly highlight a few features that are especially relevant to various country chapters, and that are often relatively neglected.

We begin with a historical account of the Napoleonic and Germanic *Rechtsstaat* traditions which shaped not only France and Germany but many other continental states as well. We then proceed by showing why the Mediterranean states, which are supposedly examples of the Napoleonic type, might be considered as a distinct southern European type. We then turn to the typical characteristics of a vast range of small continental European states, that is consensus democracy in a fragmented society, and corporatist state relations with interest groups. The Netherlands and Switzerland are typical examples. And although Scandinavia forms a somewhat deviant type, Norway is also an example of a consensual corporatist state.

Napoleonic and Germanic Rechtsstaat *model*

Many continental European countries have a strong legalistic state tradition, France and Germany being the prime examples. The Napoleonic state model, in which the nation state is united and the state serves the general interest, the administration is centralised, hierarchical, uniform, accountable and controlled, and state officials are highly trained and qualified, and organised in professional

'corps' (Wright 1990; Wunder 1995), also formed the foundation of Mediterranean states like Italy, Spain and Portugal. The Germanic *Rechtsstaat* tradition
can be recognised in countries like Austria. The main difference between the
legalistic Napoleonic and the Germanic *Rechtsstaat* model is that the Prussian
state formation was not based on a revolutionary abolishment of monarchy
by the bourgeoisie, but on the hegemony of the Prussian elite, in particular
the 'Iron Chancellor', Bismarck. The nineteenth-century German idea of
Rechtsstaat meant that the sovereign was to be bound by laws and rules (Benz
2001), which were to be equally and fairly applied to all state subjects, and that
judges and administrators were to be neutral. Contrary to the French *principe de
légalité*, in which the law is the expression of the *volonté générale*, of the people
(Ziller 2003), in Prussia and Habsburg Austria the emperors remained in
absolute power. Parliamentary democracy was only established in Germany
after the First World War.

The establishment of the Liberal constitutional *Rechtsstaat* became a fundamental turning point in the development of many European states (Finer 1954;
Heper 1987; Page 1992). It introduced the legalistic *Rechtsstaat* thinking about
state and administration. Legislation became the fundament of the state. Administration should be based on the primacy of the law. Constitution, laws and regulations became the exclusive source of administrative actions. Therefore the law
gained the monopoly of the only relevant expertise for the effective functioning
of the state. This led to the *Juristenmonopol* (monopoly of lawyers) in continental European administrations. State officials were predominantly (public)
lawyers. The establishment of the *Rechtsstaat* also marked the beginning of
modern professional bureaucracy. State officials transformed from personal servants of the king into servants of the impersonal state. They became properly
educated and trained professionals with the proper expertise, they fulfilled an
official, formally described task, held a formal and protected life-long position,
with regular salary and pension. The ideal-type 'bureaucracy' (Weber 1922)
was born.

The dominance of legalistic thinking in north-western European administrations like the Scandinavian ones and the Netherlands lasted broadly until the
Second World War and came to an end with the post-war expansion of the
welfare states. In Germany, Austria, France, Italy and Spain, however, the dominance of administrative law has not vanished.

Southern European model

The four southern European states Italy, Spain, Portugal and Greece have a
number of important cultural, social, economic and historical characteristics in
common, and their political systems are also often seen as similar (Magone
2003). They have failed to sustain stable democratic political systems in the
past, and have experienced authoritarian regimes. They used to be economically
less developed than most other western European countries. In (the southern
parts of) Italy, Spain and Portugal, agriculture was dominated by large farms

(latifundia). And unlike many other European countries where the Catholic–Protestant split was a major religious cleavage, in the south the politically important religious cleavage was a clerical–anticlerical one. Politics used to be dominated by the conflict between progressive Liberal and conservative patrimonial parties. The intense conflict between left and right political forces later formed a fertile ground for strong communist influences, such as in post-war Italy and in post-1974 Portugal. A distinctive southern European model of democracy might be discerned (Pridham 1982), even a distinctive southern model of bureaucracy (Sotiropoulos 2004).

Formalism and legalism strongly prevail in the Portuguese, Spanish, Italian and Greek administrations. The vast majority of civil servants in southern Europe are administrative lawyers. Legalism and formalism were historically introduced as a counterbalance against political interference, and in highly politicised southern administrations it still works so. Formalism and legalism are major reasons for the rigidity and inefficiency of southern bureaucracies. Management reforms are based on an economical frame of reference in terms of effectiveness and efficiency, which is contradictory to the legal frame of reference in terms of legal accountability. As management reforms have to be formulated in juridical language in order to become legally enacted, the legalistic monopoly remained unbroken (Kickert 2006).

In contrast to north-western Europe, where trained and qualified professionals run a rational, professional, 'neutral' administration, in Greek, Italian, Spanish and Portuguese administrations the factor of overriding importance is politicisation (Sotiropulos 2006). Political control of administration, relations between politicians and bureaucrats, political nominations of officials, party patronage and clientelism in southern European countries fundamentally differ from the political practice that is usual in western Europe.

Consensus and corporatism in small continental European states

Many of the smaller states in continental Europe are highly similar in three respects.

First, their type of state and politics. They all have a consensus type of democracy (Lijphart 1984). By contrast to the majoritarian Anglo-American two-party system of democracy, they have a multi-party system with proportional elections where governments consist of coalitions between several parties. The search for compromises and consensus is a main ingredient of their political culture. The search for consensus in the post-war *Große Koalition* in Austria, in the *Proporz* system of division of seats in government in Switzerland, in the coalition governments between the Flemish Christian Democrats and Walloon Socialists in Belgium, in the varying coalitions between the Social Democrats, Christian Democrats and conservative Liberals in the Netherlands, in the multi-party coalition cabinets in Denmark and Norway, which sometimes do not even have a parliamentary majority, these forms of consensus democracy explain the political stability in these societies.

Second, their type of state–society relations. They all have a neo-corporatist type of democracy. In contrast to the American pluralist type of democracy, in a neo-corporatist type of democracy, interest representation is undertaken by a few, well-organised groups, which are recognised by the state and to which many public tasks and state authority have been delegated (Williamson 1989). Sweden has a social-democrat type of corporatism, the Netherlands a typically confessional type, Belgium a linguistic, regional and confessional type, Austria again another type, but all are variations of the same basic type of neo-corporatism.

Third, their type of society. They all have socio-political cleavages and fragmented political and social subcultures. Austria has its Christian and Socialist *Lager*. Switzerland has its regional and linguistic fragmentation into *Kantons*. Belgium has the linguistic cleavage between Flanders and Walloon and the political cleavage between Socialists and Christians. The Netherlands has a *Verzuiling* (pillarisation) into protestant, catholic, socialist and liberal-neutral pillars.

The whole range of countries from the far north to the middle of continental Europe – Finland, Sweden, Norway, Denmark, the Netherlands, Belgium, Switzerland, Austria – all have these three characteristics in common, albeit to different degrees and in different variations. In Scandinavian states, no political fragmentation such as in Austria, Switzerland, Belgium or the Netherlands exists.

The three Scandinavian states – Denmark, Sweden and Norway – are examples of the model of consensual and corporatist democracy where political parties, officials and interest groups cooperate to produce public policy. Compromise, co-operation and consensus are its characteristics. Traditionally the social-democratic parties in the various Scandinavian countries were highly influential. A typical characteristic of the Nordic states is the intensive and formalised role that interest groups play in the preparation and formulation of public policies. The distinctive model of Scandinavian politics and government is related to the specific Nordic model of welfare, with Sweden as its typical example. The welfare sector is large, social rights of citizens are fundamental, most public services are provided by the state, and social-democratic, egalitarian values dominate (Arter 1999; Elder *et al.* 1982; Heidar 2004).

The authors and chapters

In this book, a number of outstanding public management scholars present the specificities of the various approaches to the study of public management in different European countries.

Professor Annie Bartoli of the university of Versailles St-Quentin, author of the French public management handbook *Le Management dans les Organisations Publiques* (Bartoli 2005), describes the relatively recent development of the study of public management in France in relation to the specificities of the French model of state and administration. For the long and rich history of the French state has led to many specificities that are crucial to understanding the functioning of its administration and its study – the special connotation of the public service, the different civil services, the special status of civil servants, the existence of professional bodies of civil servants, the educational system with its *Grandes Écoles*, recruitment by competitive examination, just to mention a few. Bartoli gives a highly informative overview of the very particular French system of administration, and teaching and research in public administration and management.

Professor Christoph Reichard of the university of Potsdam, author of the first German public management handbook *Betriebswirtschaftslehre der öffentlichen Verwaltung* (Reichard 1987), gives an account of the development of public management in Germany. The recent administrative reform patterns in Germany are related to the field of public management. Not surprisingly in the prototype example of the *Rechtsstaat*, the administrative law approach still dominates the academic study of public administration. A political-science-based approach of administration started only after the Second World War and is still having difficulties in getting a proper institutional position in academia. Reichard's conclusion is that public management as an academic field is poorly institutionalised and rather fragmented in Germany.

Professor Stephen P. Osborne of the university of Edinburgh, editor of the international journal *Public Management Review*, organiser of the annual *International Public Management Research Seminars* and author of numerous publications, together with his wife Kate McLaughlin of the university of Birmingham, presents a highly informative account of the development of the discipline of public administration and management, the more so because the tension between the political science and managerial roots of the discipline in Britain are now described by authors whose basis lies in management science. Their account differs refreshingly from the usual political science review of state, politics and administration and its study, and focuses much more on public service delivery and its management.

Professors Tom Christensen of the university of Oslo and Per Laegreid of the university of Bergen, co-authors of the Norwegian organization science handbook *Organisasjonsteori for Offenlig Sektor* (Christensen *et al.* 2004), illustrate the relationship between the study of public administration and management, and the development of the Norwegian state and administration over time. A typical characteristic of the Norwegian approach is the combination of organisation theory and political science focusing on empirical studies of decision-making and on institutional changes in organisations. This political and organisation science mixture is the internationally known Norwegian trademark, for which the basis has been laid by the long and close cooperation between Johan Olsen and Jim March.

The account of the study of public management in the Netherlands is presented by myself. Although the Dutch study of public administration and management during the first decades after its post-war beginnings more or less followed the North American example, since the 1990s some distinct approaches to public management have developed, such as those of 'managing complex networks' and of 'public governance'. These typical Dutch approaches of public management can be related to the historical characteristics of Dutch politics, government and governance.

Professor Kuno Schedler of the university of Sankt Gallen, European coordinator of the *International Public Management Network* and author of the first Swiss public management handbook *Ansätze einer wirkungsorientierten Verwaltungsführung* (Schedler 1995), outlines the basic principles of independence and neutrality that the Swiss cherished for centuries and still do. The underlying state traditions of federalism, non-professional political *militia*, direct democracy, and regional cultural and linguistic differences have an impact on both the functioning of the administration and its study. In Switzerland, as in Germany, the academic field of public management has to compete with the still-prevailing dominance of public law and the political sciences. The trend of 'new public management' reform in Swiss administration, in which Schedler has played an active role, has resulted in an increasing demand for research, teaching and executive education in public management.

Professor Marco Meneguzzo of the university of Rome Tor-Vergata, author of the Italian network management handbook *I Network del Settore Pubblico* (Meneguzzo 2001), describes the fairly recent development of public management research in Italy, which was the result of the administrative reforms that started in the early 1990s. The public uproar about corruption scandals led to a landslide in the political system that paved the way for state reform (decentralisation), privatisations and public management reforms. As the Italian administration is still dominated by lawyers and obsessed with legalism, no wonder that the study of administration continues to be dominated by public law. Public management is only gradually gaining some terrain, both in practice and in academia. A distinctive Italian approach to public management is the so-called *Economia Aziendale* approach, a kind of institutional economic theory of organisations.

After a brief historical review, Professor Xavier Ballart of the Autonomous University of Barcelona, co-author of the Spanish public administration handbook *Ciencia de la Administración* (Ballart and Ramio 2000), outlines the developments that took place after the death of Franco (1975), the transition to democracy and the constitution of 1978. Although the Opus Dei technocrats carried out some administrative modernisations under the Franco regime, and to some extent laid a basis for the scientific study of administration, that field only really developed after the establishment of democracy. The study of public administration and management in Spain is claimed by law, political sciences, economics and sociology. It is therefore an interdisciplinary and ill-defined terrain. Officially, political science and administrative science jointly form a university degree. Public management is also used to denote business-school programmes. Nevertheless Ballart manages to present an informative and systematic overview of the state of the art in Spanish public administration and management research.

Professors Gyorgy Hajnal and Gyorgy Jenie of the Corvinus University of Budapest, authors of Hungarian publications on public management, a language which I would not dare to pronounce, begin with a historical account of the development of the study of public management that starts in the middle ages, a remarkable sense of historical awareness. After the communist era, Hungary underwent a radical transition to market economy and liberal democracy. From the 1990s on, the most important task was to restore the democratic *Rechtsstaat* tradition. Joining the free Western world was also symbolised by EU membership, which was attained in 2004. The fundamental reforms of economy, society and state were of course much more important and urgent than managerial efficiency reforms. Legalism and managerialism have a tense relationship.

Professor Laurence E. Lynn Jr is professor of Public Management Emeritus at the University of Chicago, the internationally renowned North American public management scholar and author of handbooks on public management such as *Public Management as Art, Science and Profession* (Lynn 1996) and *Public Management: Old and New* (Lynn 2006), was given the last word in this book to present his view from the other side of the Atlantic. His historical account of the study of public management in the 'New World' certainly makes clear that the stereotypical simple prejudice against Anglo-American 'managerialism' as a narrowly defined intra-organisational matter of effectively and efficiently 'running the business of government' definitely does not coincide with his view on the American approach to public management. His concluding remarks from the American viewpoint on European developments in public administration and management are equally reflective and critical. A refreshing and thoughtful last word.

Bibliography

Arter, D. (1999) *Scandinavian Politics Today*, Manchester: Manchester University Press.

Ballart, X. and Ramio, C. (2000) *Ciencia de la Administración*, Valencia: Tecnos.

Bartoli, A. (2005) *Le Management dans les Organisations Publiques*, 2nd edn, Paris: Dunod.

Benz, A. (2001) *Der moderne Staat*, München: Oldenbourg Verlag.

Bozeman, B. (1989) *All Organizations are Public*, San Francisco: Jossey-Bass.

Bozeman, B. and Straussman, J. D. (1990) *Public Management Strategies*, San Francisco: Jossey-Bass.

Christensen, T., Laegreid, P., Roness, P. G. and Rovik, K. A. (2004) *Organisasjonsteori for Offenlig Sektor*, Oslo: Universitetsforlaget.

Denhardt, R. B. (1993) *Theories of Public Organizations*, Belont: Wadsworth.

Drewry, G. and Butcher, T. (1988) *The Civil Service Today*, Oxford: Blackwell.

Elder, N., Thomas, A. H. and Arter, D. (1982) *The Consensual Democracies: The Government and Politics of the Scandinavian States*, Oxford: Martin Robertson.

Ferlie, E., Ashburner, L., Fitzgerald, L. and Pettigrew, A. (1996) *The New Public Management in Action*, Oxford: Oxford University Press.

Finer, H. (1954) *The Theory and Practice of Modern Government*, London: Methuen.

Flynn, N. (1990) *Public Sector Management*, New York: Harvester Wheatsheaf.

Goetz, K. H. (2001) 'Making sense of post-communist central administration: modernisation, Europeanization or Latinization', *Journal of European Public Policy*, 8: 1032–51.

Hague, R., Harrop, M. and Breslin, S. (1992) *Comparative Politics and Government: An Introduction*, Houndmills: MacMillan.

Hajnal, G. (2003) 'Diversity and Convergence: A Quantitative Analysis of European Public Administration Education Programs', *Journal of Public Affairs Education*, 9: 245–58.

Hartung, F. (1950) *Deutsche Verfassungsgeschichte*, Stuttgart: Köhler Verlag.

Heidar, K. (ed.) (2004) *Nordic Politics: Comparative Perspectives*, Oslo: Universitetsforlaget.

Heper, M. (ed.) (1987) *The State and Public Bureaucracy: A Comparative Perspective*, New York: Greenwood Press.

Hughes, O. E. (1994) *Public Management and Administration: An Introduction*, Houndmills: Palgrave.

Kickert, W. J. M. (ed.) (1997) *Public Management and Administrative Modernisation in Western Europe*, Cheltenham: Edward Elgar.

Kickert, W. J. M. (2005) 'Distinctiveness in the study of public management in Europe: a historical-institutional analysis of France, Germany and Italy', *Public Management Review*, 7: 537–63.

Kickert, W. J. M. (2006) 'Distinctive characteristics of state and administrative reforms in Southern Europe', Milan: EGPA conference.

Kickert, W. J. M. and Hakvoort, J. (2000) 'Public Governance in Europe: a historical-institutional tour d'horizon', in O. van Heffen, W. Kickert and J. Thomassen (eds) *Governance in Modern Society*, Dordrecht: Kluwer Academic Publishers.

Kickert, W. J. M. and Stillman, R. J. (eds) (1999) *The Modern State and its Study*, Cheltenham: Edward Elgar.

Lijphart, A.(1984) *Democracies: Patterns of Majoritarian and Consensus Government in Twenty-one Countries*, New Haven: Yale University Press.

Lynn, L. E. (1996) *Public Management as Art, Science and Profession*, Chatham: Chatham House.

Lynn, L. E. (2006) *Public Management: Old and New*, New York: Routledge.

Magone, J. M. (2003) *The Politics of Southern Europe*, Westport: Praeger.

Meneguzzo, M. (2001) *I Network del Settore Pubblico*, Milan: EGEA.

OECD (1995) *Governance in Transition: Public Management Reforms in OECD countries*, Paris: PUMA/OECD.

Page, E. (1992) *Political Authority and Bureaucratic Power*, New York: Harvester Wheatsheaf.

Pollitt, C. (1990) *Managerialism and the Public Services*, Oxford: Blackwell.

Pollitt, C. and Bouckaert, G. (2004) *Public Management Reforms: A Comparative Analysis*, 2nd edition, Oxford: Oxford University Press.

Pridham, G. (1982) 'Comparative Perspectives in the New Mediterranean Democracies: a Model of Regime Transition', *West European Politics*, 7: 1–29.

Rainey, H. G. (1997) *Understanding and Managing Public Organizations*, San Francisco: Jossey-Bass.

Reichard, C. (1987) *Betriebswirtschaftslehre der öffentlichen Verwaltung*, 2nd edition, Berlin: De Gruyter.

Schedler, K. (1995) *Ansätze einer wirkungsorientierten Verwaltungsführung*, Bern: Paul Haupt Verlag.

Sotiropoulos, D. A. (2004) 'Southern European public bureaucracies in comparative perspective', *West European Politics*, 27: 405–22.

Sotiropoulos, D. A. (2006) 'Patronage in South European bureaucracies in the 1980s and

1990s: the politicization of central public administrations in Greece, Italy, Portugal and Spain', Nicosia: ECPR workshops.

Thuiller, G. and Tulard, J. (1984) *Histoire de l'Administration Française*, Paris: Presses Universitaires de France.

Weber, M. (1922) Wirtschaft und Gesellschaft, Tübingen: Mohr (reprint 1972).

Williamson, P. J. (1989) *Corporatism in Perspective*, London: Sage.

Wright, V. (1990) 'The administrative machine: old problems and new dilemmas', in P. A. Hall, J. Hayward and H. Machin (eds) *Developments in French Politics*, Hound-mills: MacMillan.

Wunder, B. (ed.) (1995) *The Influences of the Napoleonic 'Model' of Administration on the Administrative Organization of Other Countries*, Brussels: IIAS-cahier (in French and English).

Ziller, J. (2003) 'The continental system of administrative legality', in B. G. Peters and J. Pierre (eds) *Handbook of Public Administration*, London: Sage.

2 The study of public management in France

La spécificité du modèle français d'administration

Annie Bartoli

Introduction

The study of public management in France is presently advancing at a strong pace. Just as academic teaching and research in this field has made headway, continuing education for civil servant managers and professional studies in the field have flourished. As for initial training in the French higher educational system, it is gradually incorporating – though still modestly – the topic of public management in the curricula.

To understand the reasons behind this movement, it is necessary to consider the historical development of the French public sphere, as well as the particularities of its context from the social, legal, economic and political points of view. Indeed, the French public system seems to differentiate itself from most other Western countries by numerous specificities pertaining to its history, to the cultural, social and political context within which it evolves, to its missions, rules, stakeholders, institutions (D'Iribarne 2006). Moreover, generally, different countries' conditions are so differentiated that any scope for comparison gives rise to problems of method and terminology such that it is preferable to identify general trends rather compare different national systems via detailed analysis (Lallement 2003).

Moreover, the use of an appropriate vocabulary is not easy from international viewpoints. Thus, for instance, the simple phrase 'civil servant', which takes on a significant importance in France, as it relates directly to almost five million people under the specific status of public employment, is not used in the same sense in other countries. In Germany, for instance, out of a workforce of public officials globally equivalent to that of France, less than two million people have the status of civil servants. In addition, civil servants in England would correspond in the French system only to the civil service of the central Administration, whereas officials of local authorities would be identified rather as 'public servants', i.e. people in charge of public activities in the English local communes.

We must therefore be careful in the descriptions and translations to avoid misunderstandings which could be deep. The first of these precautions, therefore, is the need to place the public systems in their historical and cultural context, before going on to the identification of current major trends.

In France, the historical roots of the state in fact go back more than two centuries, and have witnessed several developments. After presenting an outline of the history of the state and of the administration, we will describe the civil servant status, as well as the main rights and duties resulting from it. Then we will analyse the present characteristics of the French public system, both in quantitative and in structural terms. From there, we will highlight the processes of modernisation and reform of public services, as well as the study of their impact on public management. Finally, we will carry out an appraisal of the current development in teaching and research relating to the public sphere, which mostly use the traditional field of political and legal sciences as a base for management sciences.

History of the French state and administration

The development of the public sector in France is characterised by strongly engrained traditions and values. The traditionally pronounced distinction between the public world and the world of private transactions is several centuries old. The republican administration was put into place to strengthen efforts to unify France.

Strong roots dating back to the eighteenth and nineteenth centuries

The legal origins of the French 'public service' are quite ancient. The decision of the Court of Conflicts (Tribunal des Conflits) of 8 February 1873 (Blanco judgment) constitutes the base of French administrative law (Chevallier 1991). The notion of public service covers all activities of general interest carried out directly or indirectly by the public powers, both national and local. In fact, public service refers to political choices and to cultural dimensions, two aspects which are closely linked in France and which are subject to numerous debates and frequent heated social conflicts. In certain countries, such as the United States and the United Kingdom, labour relations in the public sector fall under the jurisdiction of the private sector. In contrast, from the nineteenth century on, French civil service law has been subject to progressively emerging special status.

As regards the organisation of the French public administrative system, its centralist design goes even further back in time, since it is generally associated with the *Ancien Régime* and with the setting-up of a strong monarchical state. The French Revolution, whilst bringing about significant upheavals, would not break away from this centralist organisational base (Le Roy Ladurie 2001). According to the terminology of the time, at the end of the eighteenth century there existed two categories of public officials: civil servants and 'employees' (Fons and Meyer 2005). The civil servant was elected (which is no longer the case today) and he was at the top of the public employment hierarchy; as regards the public sector employee, he was appointed by the government and carried out executive tasks. This distinction into two large categories came about under the Empire. At the beginning of the nineteenth century, Napoleon I abolished the election system for senior civil servants and established the principle of central appointment for them; this was particularly reflected in the introduction of 'prefects', who were bound by obedience to the government. Only one term remained, that of civil servant (*'fonctionnaire'* in French).

The reinforcement and structuring of the administration came about during the nineteenth century, under Napoleon's reign. During that period, the civil service workforce grew significantly. The centralist state became structured and was organised into ministries, so as to ensure a concentration of the knowledge that was required to carry out the different missions. The *grands corps d'État* (main state bodies) were set up by the creation of the *grandes écoles* (higher-education schools) designed to impart the said knowledge. Thus was born the principal of an elite within the top civil service of the French state, which still exists today, and which constitutes one of the main specificities of the French system. Its role was considered as essential and was based on the values of loyalty, discipline and devotion to the public interest. In all the ranks of the administration, the rules and procedures set up were supposed to create links between the thinkers (the main bodies) and the doers, with the common objective of ensuring and preserving equality in public service provision across the national territory. Gradually, the situation of civil servants improved, salaries were paid regularly, and job security was ensured. It was later, with the Second Empire, as was the case in Victorian England, that public regulations were introduced; they imposed the principle of an entrance examination (*'concours'* in French) and the requirement of degrees for the recruitment of civil servants. The notion of a civil service status developed throughout this period, till the 1940s.

The establishment of a general civil servant status

At the beginning of the twentieth century, civil servants' associations demanded the creation of a status to guarantee the rights of officials throughout their career. But not everybody shared this opinion; for a long time in France, the notion of a civil servant status was in fact opposed by some of their own organisations, even at the cost of very tough strikes, especially in the postal services in 1899 and in 1909. 'We do not want a status, since we do not want to be inferior citizens,' said someone in charge of post office employees at the time (quoted by Rigaudiat 1995). It is true that at the time, the notion of status was seen as synonymous with the absence of union rights, and it is no accident that the first general civil servant status dates to 1941 and was the one imposed by the Vichy regime. In September 1941, the first general civil servant status was therefore set up, establishing not only certain rights, but also duties and constraints, such as prohibition of the right to strike and of freedom of association. After the Second World War and the period of economic difficulties and social unrest which accompanied it in France, a new civil service organisation was set up, and the general status was updated and made more flexible in 1946. Since then, the French civil service status has formalised the rights of officials (freedom of speech, union rights, protection, participation, right to strike) and the duties (hierarchical obedience, neutrality, responsibility, exclusivity of duties). It was at that time that the École Nationale d'Administration (National School of Administration), or ENA, was created, as well as the interministerial body of 'civil administrators', a major *grand corps d'État*, still very strong today in the functioning of the French public sector (Gaillard 1995).

The main developments in the last 50 years

The first in-depth analyses of the French bureaucratic malfunctioning date back to the beginning of the century with the study on 'Postal Services – Telegraphs – Telecommunications' by Henri Fayol, which led him to conclude that 'The State needs to be industrialised'. Since this recommendation was not implemented, the French public system continued to function on the same bases. Its shortcomings and its negative side effects were later strongly highlighted through the works of the sociologist Michel Crozier (1963), who described a 'blocked society' due to the static nature of its bureaucratic administration. However, the author also showed, through several case studies, that even within a restrictive and regulated system, the public official always had room to manoeuvre, which often led to changes that were not properly managed.

Yet, although rules and procedures were at the heart of the functioning of the French civil service during the entire twentieth century, it would be wrong to believe that administrative and 'managerial' principles are recent within French public bodies, as demonstrated by the methods implemented from the years 1960 and 1970.

A decision-making method was implemented as of 1960 (Rationalisation of Budget Choices – in French 'RCB', inspired by the 'Planning Programming Budgeting System' (PPBS) of the American army. It was based on a system of objective and resource planning with control over budget operations (Le Duff and Papillon 1988). The RCB was accompanied by management control tools, as well as a system of 'Management by Objectives' (MBO) aiming at making the decision-makers at senior and intermediary management levels aware of their responsibilities (Huet and Bravo 1973).

The enterprise mode did not appear until the 1980s, in the guise of the admin- istration – enterprise fad. From that period on, the subsequent governments offi- cially adopted the long and difficult movement toward the modernisation of the state.

Throughout the twentieth century, the French public sector underwent signific- ant development from a quantitative point of view, today counting approximately five million civil servants, as well as from a qualitative point of view, with the emergence of new missions for the state. Up until 1980, French public adminis- tration had been characterised as strongly centralised, due to the 'Jacobinism' doctrine (centralised governance advocated by Robespierre and others at the end of the eighteenth century) dating back to the Revolution.[1] Since 1982, as we will see hereafter, decentralisation has strongly changed the situation, by establishing a local civil service, complementary to and distinct from the central civil service (Bodineau and Verpeaux 1996).

Present characteristics of the French public system

A quantitatively significant public sector

The public sector in France is characterised by its quantitative importance:

> there are approximately five million civil servants, and the manpower con-tinues to increase year after year. Moreover, all employees of public enter-prises, who are part of the civil service according to specific rules (Nora 1967), particularly in the fields of transport and energy, should be added to these figures; these personnel are not civil servants but fall under particular status specific to each relevant enterprise. The public expenditures exceed 53 per cent of the interior production and the employees with a public status represent 20 per cent of the working population.
>
> CNFPT and Dexia 2006

Numerous organisms make up the public scene in France:

- the state civil service is composed of different civil ministries (notably com-prising Finance, Justice, Education, Police, Infrastructure, Environment and Culture);
- the territorial service is composed of municipalities, general councils (for Departments), regional councils (for Regions), etc.;
- the public hospital service comprises 1,000 public hospitals of various sizes and vocations;
- finally, public enterprises, public institutions and public institutes represent a heterogeneous category, including a wide range of statutes, histories, man-agement modalities, and legal structures; a broad variety of organisations ranging from utilities and public transport companies to the postal service and universities, with very different degrees of dependency on the state.

Indeed, the size, diversity and organisational complexity of the French public realm are very great.

The three 'civil services'

In contrast to the German or English cases, most officials of the French civil ser-vices are employed under the civil servant status. However, there are also 15 per cent of the personnel said to be contractual, i.e. employed by the government on contract under private law, generally for a fixed term.

The French civil service is both homogenous and diversified; it is in fact made up of three major sectors, regulated by different laws, since the 1980s:

- state civil service;
- local government civil service;
- hospital civil service.

While each of these three sectors has a distinct historical background, there are still many points of convergence in the employment status among the three sectors.

Thus, the entire management of public officials in France is still supported today by an overriding principle, which is of a national, administrative and regulatory nature. It is based on texts and statutes which structure the centralised system, said to be career-oriented, which has been well established for some 50 years now, and whose foundations date back, as we have seen, many centuries.

A career-oriented civil service

Like some other countries (such as Spain, Greece, Japan), France has chosen a career-oriented civil service, whereby civil servants are governed by statutes for specific personnel. Under this system, the French civil servant is an employee of the public service. His position is obtained through competitive examination and is secured for life.

The career system is based on the principle of specificity of public administration, whose functioning implies that the personnel are endowed with particular skills, and are normally at the service of the public body for their entire professional life. The civil servant is considered as a generalist and chalks out a career in accordance with promotion mechanisms based on seniority and meritocracy.

The 1958 Constitution states that 'The government has the administration at its disposal', which fully illustrates the situation of dependency and execution of the civil servant with regard to politicians. In return, placed in this statutory and regulatory situation, he enjoys job stability and is shielded from all economic problems which could affect his employment situation.

Many other OECD countries have instead adopted what can be considered employment-oriented systems, where the selection of civil servants is done by looking for the best match between the profile and the post, as in Australia, New Zealand, Canada and, to a lesser extent, the United Kingdom (Pilichowski 2005). The choice of the employment system reflects in principle the desire to place the civil service close to the civil society, while the career-oriented system reflects the desire to have a clearer separation between the private and the non-private, guided by care for public interest and public service. This separation between public and private is very strong in the mindsets and in the regulations in France.

However, on the international level, the distinction between the career-oriented system and the employment system is not always clear: 'Analysis of the different public services in Europe immediately leads to the observation that no state practices in an integral and purist manner either of these two organisational systems but that all offer a very rich array of mixed systems' (Crema 2003). Moreover, many systems have recently changed; thus nearly half of the OECD countries have modified rather fundamentally their rules since the end of the 1990s, by making them more flexible and moving them closer to the private sector. Let us give as an example the very radical reform of public employment in Italy, a country which has, for 15 years, established contracts under private law for its public officials, thus privatising work relations and establishing equality of rights and of rules between private and public employees.

These fundamental changes in the system have not taken place in France, where the public service is still regulated by statutes dating back many decades. Often considered as cumbersome and complicated, but sometimes also presented as major assets, these texts define the general and centralised rules relating to the management of the personnel, particularly dealing with recruitment through competitive exam, marking systems, right to continuous training, union rights and right to strike, pay scales, disciplinary procedures, leave, and conditions of occupational health and safety. They also include the fundamental distinction between the grade and the job; in France, the grade of a civil servant corresponds to a qualification earned in competitive examinations. This grade determines his salary, regardless of the position he holds. French public service status is also based on the so-called system of 'bodies' (*'corps'* in French).

The system of 'bodies'

The French public service is divided into 'bodies' of civil servants. Earlier we mentioned the major state bodies or *grands corps d'État*, i.e. the civil service directors, most of whom are graduates of the *grandes écoles* or higher-education schools. However, the notion of *'corps'* is broader and includes all civil service personnel categories. To give a few examples, there are the corps of nurses, and of librarians, as well as primary school teachers, administrative assistants, technical agents and so on – several hundred different corps all told.

Within the same body, there are one or several grades. The holder of a position remains the owner of his grade and occupies a job chosen by the administration; the two notions of 'grade' and of 'employment' are thus totally distinct. The body constitutes the support structure of the French state public service and hospital public service. In the local government civil service, the employment framework has been established instead; wider than the body, it groups together various local government jobs by professional categories (administrative, technical, medico-social, etc.). Beyond the general public service status (common provisions, specific provisions for each public service), there is a particular status for each body which determines the internal regulations thereof (recruitment conditions, appointment, promotion system, special provisions where appropriate).

Some particularly well-known and influential bodies are known as the 'main state bodies' (*grands corps d'État*): the main administrative bodies, normally recruited through the École Nationale d'Administration (ENA), and the main technical bodies, traditionally recruited through the École Polytechnique (engineering school). The final rankings from these schools are crucial for obtaining jobs at the top of the French civil service; this makes up the elite charged with promoting and ensuring respect for the public interest and the independence of administration from politics. This public elite therefore also displays the characteristic of having been trained according to relatively uniform national standards, within the state's public *grandes écoles*. In particular, the *Énarques* (graduates from the ENA) form the large majority of members at the top of the state public service, and also of politicians (ministers, elected members, etc.).

The system of bodies illustrates a very strong social stratification which many deem, at least with regard to some aspects, relatively rigid, and sometimes too homogenous.

Competitive exams and career path

For the incumbents, recruitment through competitive exam (*concours*) is a basic principle of the French civil service, inscribed in the general statute. The goal of this system is to ensure objectivity in recruitment and equality of chances. Although they are generally considered as an unavoidable mechanism, competitive exams are today regularly criticised. Criticisms generally relate to their content and less to their principle, which shows the strong attachment of politicians and civil servants to them. 'The contents of competitive exams are often not in line with work practices, forcing those who want to progress in their career to work for their exams at the expense of the duties of their post' (Louart 2003). In particular, the subjects on which they are based do not seem to be in line with work practices; they therefore seem hardly compatible with the principle of modern human-resource management, particularly because they do not favour the best match between the profile of the persons and the content of the posts (Eymeri 2003). However, at present, changes in the competitive examination system are planned, particularly in the local government public service (which concerns officials of communes, municipalities, departments, regions); they aim at facilitating the access to it, in particular by lightening the content of the exams and by giving value to professional experience.

As regards the career path, it is also very much codified. Grade promotion is achieved through registration on an aptitude list, professional selection examination, or by complementary competitive exams during one's career.

Human-resource management in the French public service is therefore characterised by a strong administrative and bureaucratic heritage, which does not always facilitate the dynamics of change. These mechanisms, particularly nowadays, raise the issue of the limited room for manoeuvre given to the hierarchy for the management of the career paths of their teams (Bartoli 2006). This creates paradoxical situations with respect to the numerous incentives to develop a managerial culture in the civil service, which is contained in all the state modernisation policies in France over the last 20 years or so.

The modernisation process of French public services

The need to update and reform the functioning modes of the French public system has been underlined for many decades. De facto, many and sometimes profound transformations have taken place, even if they have never been led by radical disruptive measures. In this regard, France differentiates itself from other European countries like the United Kingdom or Italy, which have witnessed some significant modifications of their public systems. Generally, France carries out studies and analyses underlining the problems, and then proceeds to the reforms by playing both on innovation and on continuity.

In 1989, the Prime Minister Michel Rocard's circular on the 'Renewal of the public service' formalised the idea of the modernisation of the French public sector, with fields of action linked to computerisation, human-resource management and management control. Since then, all the governments in power, irrespective of their political inclination, have implemented state reform policies to meet the important challenges faced by the French public system.

Important challenges to be met

The new challenges are obviously linked to turbulences in the national and global environments. French public organisations are facing a few specific challenges:

- economic crises and state budget restrictions;
- alternating between nationalisations and privatisations, depending on the political trend;
- European policies concerning open competition between European states and calling into question traditional French monopolies (telecommunications, transportation, energy, etc.); world competition that has created the move toward transnational partnerships;
- the wide diffusion of new technologies in different sectors of activity (with increasing intertwining between the public and private sectors, or between crown/state and market economies);
- broad development of electronic administration;
- new demands of client-users;
- wider press coverage of political life;
- wage claims and expectations of civil servants and public agents;
- and the continuing strong influence of French civil servant unions.

Furthermore, the last 25 years have been characterised by significant and multiple restructuring movements and legal and political reforms. Decentralisation as of 1982, launched again in 2003, the slimming of statutes in the 1980s, and the great accounting and financial reform (LOLF, Organic Law relating to the Financial Laws) in 2001 count among the most outstanding events.

We now burn to these two major reforms, which have greatly affected the traditional functioning modes of the French public service since the 1980s.

Decentralisation

In France, decentralisation undertaken a quarter of a century ago has profoundly modified the general landscape of the public system. The 1982 law has thus led to the transfer of some missions formerly undertaken by the state to local authorities (solidarity, i.e. help for the needy) and rural development for the department, professional training and local development of the region, land use and town planning for the commune). This first decentralisation Act is reflected in employment transfer for only about 23,000 people, since many have been assigned to the local authorities by the state. However, the second Act, undertaken in 2003, which includes many other fields of expertise (social, roads, education), assumes the transfer of a workforce of about 130,000 officials of the state civil service to the local government civil service. This constitutes, as one can imagine, a very specific challenge in terms of strategy, organisation and human-resource management, as the status, regulations, policies and practices are different in the two public sectors.

Decentralisation has had many rapid consequences for the management of public organisations; therefore, some state administrations see their prerogatives largely diminished (for examples, the Ministries of Equipment and of Health and Social Affairs), and they must fit into the contractualisation processes with the local communities (particularly departments) for transfers of activity and of personnel, if necessary.

Organisations that did not formerly exist develop and are rapidly structured. Sometimes these suddenly available resources are incoherently used, provoking severe criticism. This situation has occurred in some departmental and regional councils. Globally, the manpower of the local authorities increases significantly. As for the communes, while they still tend to believe that compensations in terms of resources (manpower and budgets) have not matched the transfers of expertise, they are strongly reorganising themselves around their new missions (particularly town planning) and around their management activities. The second decentralisation Act, as from 2003, brings back numerous questions of a political, organisational, social and financial nature. In addition to a constitutional revision, the Act has been subjected to different legislative measures. They relate to different areas including the social field, roads and education. Three organic laws relating respectively to experimentation, local referendum and financial issues illustrate the decentralising principles. By pursuing the transfer of state expertise towards local authorities, French public governance thus continues to change, looking for new balances, which are not always easy to establish.

The LOLF (Organic Finance Law)

The Organic Law relating to the Finance Laws (LOLF), promulgated on 1 August 2001, profoundly updated the architecture of the state budget. It led to the transition from a budgetary structure based on type of expenses (without any real link with objectives) to a budgetary structure based on purpose of expenses linked to missions, which were detailed into programmes or actions (Trosa 2002). This modification aimed at an in-depth questioning of the principle of functioning at all levels of public service, since it implied the setting of performance objectives for all heads who would have relative freedom in the use of resources allocated to them.

It is too early to know if the ambition behind the reform is realistic or misplaced, given the strength of existing traditional cultures and structures. But it is undeniable that this text, which swept away the 1959 ordinance, set up a framework where the spirit of French public sector administration was more managerial. Yet, the risk of losing the managerial spirit through the adoption of a technocratic and procedural implementation instead of a real change management is very real and may require reconsideration of the anticipated results.

More generally, the increased importance of the culture of results (represented by the LOLF in France, but which can be found in other systems and in most developed countries) has brought to the forefront – at least theoretically – the need to develop a real human-resource management, which is a major performance factor, and to give more autonomy and responsibilities to managers. (IGPDE 2006). The initial philosophy of the LOLF in fact provided for some decentralisation of management actions and responsibilities towards operatives. Moreover, new responsibility chains appeared, in parallel with the usual organisation of public structures; this is how heads of the BOP (Programme Operational Budgets) have been created, reflecting a more or less successful linkage with the pre-existing structures, depending on cases. Today, most analyses of the LOLF emphasise the challenge of this linkage and the need to manage the organisational incidents that it causes (Cannac and Trosa 2007).

Quality and flexibility objectives

In many countries, policies for the modernisation of administrative systems and reform of public organisations have been in place for some 15 years; they often bring up a major flexibility objective, and are usually accompanied by the willingness to develop a managerial administrative culture. We then find the themes of contractualisation, establishment of objectives, evaluation and performance measurement.

A definition of the concept of flexibility developed in these reforms is put forward in the OECD report of 1993 on changes in public management; it would thus concern 'all the resources used to improve the efficiency of public bodies by using a results-oriented approach, and of all the human and financial resource management methods based on decentralisation of responsibilities and adaptation to the market rules'.

Thus, the OECD study of human-resources management carried out in 2004 shows a general trend of the vast majority of countries towards more and more individualisation and delegation of management processes. However, this trend is more easily seen in countries which have opted for a public service based on the employment system than in those which, like France, have opted for a career-oriented system. Nevertheless, the effects of these developments towards more individualisation are not always positive, since we would also observe a drop in collective values and in ethical behaviour.

The policies of modernisation of public administration are often related to the movement called 'New Public Management' (NPM) (Ferlie *et al.* 1996), which appeared during the years 1980–1990. The general idea was to develop administrative and management methods (as were prevalent for a long time in the private sector, but without necessarily transposing them as is) and to decrease the importance of the application of rules, of administrative procedures and of bureaucratic functioning. In this context, the search for performance and for the satisfaction of citizens is considered as the major objective of public service. However, today the expression New Public Management reflects various, indeed heterogeneous, designs which lead to great confusion in the analyses and the evaluations that are carried out on this matter. In particular, while the main actions which concern efficiency or the privatisation of some departments have been quite largely undertaken in many Western countries, the procedures set up in France seem to have remained globally more moderate. Reforms implemented in the French public sector therefore depend much more on the creation of an ad hoc public management, deemed to improve overall quality and performance (Cannac 2004), while respecting the values of public service, and by avoiding the blind transposition of techniques from the private sector. The issue of the compatibility of such combined principles is thus raised, leading to the co-existence of different principles and to serious culture shocks both for officials and for citizens.

The present co-existence of different principles in French public service

As regards the functioning of the French public sector, we can observe at present the co-existence of various principles:

- the purely legal principle, inherited from rules and traditions;
- the political principle, in terms of politics and choice of public actions, which depend in the first place on national and local elected members;
- the administrative principle, which sets up an array of tools and systems that tend to be better at knowing and dealing with the social, local or national realities;
- the managerial principle, driven by middle and top management, which aims at mobilising officials, in the dynamics of participative and strategic changes.

In everyday life, this co-existence sometimes creates tensions, disturbances and misunderstandings, often criticised by the officials and the users; administrative red tape is still present, management tools are abundant and participative dynamics of change are innumerable. Some are near saturation level and are losing their landmarks! It is true that changes undertaken or likely to be undertaken are numerous, particularly in the field of management.

This multiform reality can also be found in teaching, study and research areas in public institutions and organisations. We thus notice the maintenance of traditional fields such as public law and political science, and the emergence of new academic disciplines linked to public management. However, as we will see below, these different fields still often remain isolated.

The studies and research on the public sector

The major founding disciplines

Ambiguity exists with respect to the meaning and boundaries of the expression 'public management'. The term was often used in France and in the United States during the 1970s when referring to public policy administration, as opposed to the operational management of public organisations.

Which scientific disciplines is public management derived from? In France, the academic sphere is strongly divided into distinct scientific disciplines. This distinction can also be found in teaching, studies and research which concern the operation of the public organisations and institutions. Thus, when one tries to locate the great disciplines which are at the source of what we call public management today, we discover various scientific fields.

Public Management is a multidisciplinary field of study combining public law, economy, the sociology of organisations, political science and management sciences.

Public law

The French scientific tradition sees a clear distinction between private law and public law. The latter concerns all the relationships between public organisations (government, local authorities) and other individual and collective bodies; it also governs the regulations specific to the functioning of public sector (status, etc.) units and the organisation of government (constitutional law).

However, while any company manager needs to know the minimum basics of corporate law, labour law, etc., this need seems even more obvious for a public sector manager. Indeed, the very context of his task depends on regulated choices and directions, and the impact of his activities on society is also highly controlled. Moreover, the internal functioning of public organisations is based on particular statutes and procedures that he must know, if not abide by. Finally, the revenues and the methods of financing of public organisations being extremely supervised, practitioners and experts have also had to specialise in this field. It is also striking to note that in France most reforms of the state and its functioning are the object of a judicial text.[2] This is nothing new, and was already in fact the case in Montaigne's day (Montaigne 1995).

We can thus understand that a considerable number of specialists today in public management in France are publicist lawyers who, interested in the methods of use of the said regulations, are able to look into the management of the bodies applying them. It is, moreover, generally within this discipline of public law that the works and programmes in political and administrative science have been born, thus remaining an essential reference base for issues and training in public management (Chevallier 2002).

Political science

Political scientists are also directly interested in public management insofar as the subject studies the way in which society is collectively organised and governed and analyses the activities of the decision-making authorities as well as public policies.

Originating from Anglo-Saxon countries (particularly American and British), political science in France has witnessed strong developments from the administrative science mainstream in the 70s, then with the contribution of the political sociology of public action as from the end of the 80s.

This discipline specifically focuses on public and political organisation, and on the role played by organisation members and institutions. In France, there has been significant public management research work done recently on the issues and impact of tools and instruments used in piloting governmental and political organisms (Lascoumes and Le Galès 2004). Also, managerial reflection on political governance in general has been enriched by insights of political science researchers into the political profession (Poirmeur and Mazet 2000).

Public economy

This section of political economy (or of economic science) deals with themes as varied as public finances, optimisation of political choices, the role of the state, organisation of public policies, price determination for public goods, etc.

In France, while the university section of management sciences emanates (in 1974) from the economic sciences section, we can at the same time consider that a large part of public management comes from public economy and was often driven by former economists (Le Duff and Papillon 1988). French economic researchers have analysed the state's role in the economy in particular detail. Furthermore, since the 1970s, the widely known work on the revelation of preferences for public goods (Green and Laffont 1977), and on the existence of free-riders is in part rooted and further developed in the work carried out in France by Jean-Jacques Laffont, recognised worldwide (Laffont 2002).

Furthermore, the study of various possible scenarios of production and consumption of public goods and collective services, whether they are public or mixed, constitutes an essential macro context for the micro strategic decisions of public entities.

Moreover, the bases of national accounting (concerning the follow-up of flows and stocks resulting from the activity of the whole nation) constitute references of public economy which are based at the same time on statistics of public accounts, intermediate accounts and private accounts. Questions relating to price determination of public services depend on economic calculations of optimisation, and lead to management practices impacting, for example, the marketing of public services. Economic techniques of budgetary organisation and rationalisation were adopted by the French public sector at the end of the 1960s in a major reform of administrative functioning, the rationalisation of budgetary choices (French acronym 'RCB') based on the US's Planning Programming Budgeting System (PPBS).

These examples illustrate the strong overlapping that can exist between economic science and management science, and can explain why for a long time there has been a confusion between the concept of public management and the economy of public policies.

Sociology of organisations

The role of sociologists has been fundamental in the development of knowledge in public management. Thus, while Mr Weber was not a pure sociologist (because of his opening on other disciplines such as history), his works have nonetheless a strong sociological connotation. In addition, many major topics in public management (such as decision-making processes, power, the role of stakeholders, organisational systems) depend largely on the sociology of organisations.

In France, the works of Michel Crozier and Erhard Friedberg and of their teams (the Centre for the Sociology of Organisations) largely contributed to the understanding of the functioning of public institutions. Michel Crozier's study of the inner workings of French administrations has shown that in the most heavily bureaucratic organisations, where decision-making is the most constrained, individuals maintain independence vis-à-vis the organisation. Their strategy consists primarily of defending or improving their place in the system. The organisation is perceived by its members as too great a constraint, and is therefore diverted from its conformity, leading to mission-creep, away from its theoretical objectives towards functioning notably according to individual strategies in reaction to organisational regulation.

The work of Michel Crozier initiated the development of the idea of a blocked society (Crozier 1971), hampered by the immobility and dysfunction of its administration. In the 1960s and 1970s, these analyses were timely indeed for the French: on the one hand, they denounced bureaucratic dysfunction without questioning the underlying validity of the public system; on the other hand, these analyses appeared in a new socio-political environment characterised by broader acceptance of the concept of competitiveness and the rise of more liberal economic thought. There was more emphasis on the human dimension of organisational functioning at a time in France when the 1968 worker and student movements were focusing on the social dimensions.

From the 1980s on, other French researchers made an impact on the study of public organisation, notably by revealing the system's drift and dysfunction (Dupuy and Thoenig 1985).

The role of the sociology of organisations in public management has been fundamental on two accounts: first, this has given an internal view of the functioning of public entities; second, it has helped in the development of ideal theoretical reference systems (economic optimisations and legal rules) to study the day-to-day reality of public practices, in particular through clinical analyses.

Management sciences

Strangely, it is the subject of management sciences which has remained for a long time the poor relation of public management in France. Faced with many hesitations due to the profit taboo, management researchers have, until the mid-80s, largely neglected the public sector or have got themselves expelled from it! Administration and management consultants managed to step into the public sector before the scientists, for better and for worse. In particular, this is the phase of keen interest (and of rejection) with regard to the private sector that public institutions have experienced towards the end of the 1980s.

Yet public management, as the science of the action of public organisations, can fundamentally be management-oriented, while developing strong interactions with related fields. Indeed, let us recall that management relates to a choice, to the combination and the use of resources (human, physical and financial) within a finalised work unit, in the context of specific objectives and constraints. Consequently, public management is based on administrative practices and techniques, within a framework of specific political orientations. It is interesting to note that a French precursor, the engineer Henri Fayol, was studying company and state management early in the previous century (Fayol 1916).

Management can be defined as that which relates to the processes of planning, organising, leading and controlling (Thiétart 1979), whatever the field, be it public or private. These processes are in any case a key focus of current French public management researchers, many of whom are university or *grande école* professors in Business Administration. The legitimacy of this discipline's contributions to the public sphere is still occasionally questioned, but the debate is more or less closed, in light of the acknowledged quality of the research done in the field over the last few decades (Burlaud and Laufer 1980).

Traditionally, management sciences are organised in functional components (finance, marketing, production management, human resource management) supplemented by interdisciplinary dimensions such as strategy or information systems. Obviously, terms which, in the private sector, are associated with some of these functions (primarily the first two, in particular with the concepts of profitability, profit, customer and market) are very poorly suited to the French public context and are the source of many ambiguities and hindrances. Their use, some-times excessive and without undertones, had at the end of the twentieth century largely contributed to the activation of the question of the legitimacy of public management and, probably, to delay or compromise in the modernisation of public institutions. The question of the relevance of business concepts to the public field was in addition all the more delicate since the public sector is, in France as in many other countries, very heterogeneous. More and more, it combines commercial activities with non-commercial services, and, moreover, it is currently undergoing significant transformations.

However, these multiple interrogations and ambiguities did not constitute sufficient reasons to hinder studies and researches of a management nature relating to the public sector. On the contrary, real scientific works in the field of public management have clearly developed since the end of the twentieth century in France, helping to limit the traps of the pure and simple transposition of private sector management tools, which prove to be prejudicial both for knowledge and for practical operations.

The development of teaching

Training in civil administration and action was for a long time the exclusive domain of France's *grandes écoles*, one of the most famous being the École Nationale d'Administration (ENA). It has however gradually spread to universities, first associated with political science and public law disciplines, and increasingly with management sciences.

It is not possible to present here all the French institutions which contribute to training, studies and research in public administration and management, because there are many of them, both at the national level and the regional or local level.

However let us recall first that the French higher educational system is based on a distinction between:

- the universities, which are public and depend on the Ministry for National Education;
- the *grandes écoles*, with varied status, which can be either public and under various ministries, or attached to Chambers of Commerce, or private.

Studies and training in public administration and management are also subject to this distinction, with a few hybrid institutions such as Sciences Po Paris. As for the *grandes écoles*, some are specialised in various main professions, with a public purpose. They are spread across the country (the National School for the Judiciary – École Nationale de la Magistrature (ENM),[9] the National School for Public Health – École Nationale de la Santé Publique (ENSP),[10] etc.).

Here, we will choose to centre our discussion on:

- two *grandes écoles* of interdisciplinary application: one for the state (the ENA), the other for local government (the INET);

- Institutes of Political Studies (IEP), including 'Sciences Po Paris', which has a special status; it is neither a *grande école* nor an *université;*
- the university degrees, notably numerous masters and doctorates in diverse academic disciplines, concerning public management.

The ENA

Top civil servants of the state have for 60 years been trained mainly at the ENA, whose mission is to be a school applied to the field of public administration.

Traditional training

Since the creation of the school, approximately 5,600 French graduates and 3,000 foreign graduates form part of those commonly referred to in France as the '*Énarques*'. Most occupy management positions in the central or the decentralised administration – indeed political mandates in some cases. Until recently, when the training schemes were totally reformed, the initial training of civil administrators, obtained through competitive examination, lasted 30 months and was based on two fields, one in administration and one in economics. One international-relations field also existed for the long cycle of foreign students. Generally, the teaching mostly dealt with the methodology for drafting legal or economic texts and executive summaries to support decision-making, as well as the knowledge and the expertise of procedures and public channels. From the beginning, it was decided to entrust 80 per cent of the conduct of courses to top civil servants of the state, in order to ensure a perfect alignment with the social, economic and political realities of the country. In the late 1980s, each batch had 150 students; this figure has decreased to 90 at the time of writing (2007).

Until the 1980s, business administration and management were totally absent from training programmes. In the light of the turbulence which took place in the French state's environment with the political changeover of 1981 and decentralisation as from 1982, some changes have gradually been introduced. Some private-sector accounting courses were first introduced some 20 years ago, but without any real connection with the new needs of public management. Then, as from the 1990s, the students themselves asked for changes, and in the light of the thinking that had been taking place for some time within the management teams of the school, teaching in public management was gradually brought into the curricula over the last ten years. These minor changes were, however, often regarded as largely insufficient by comparison with the need for major transformation that was felt by many. This is why a major change in the training offered by the ENA was thought out as from 2002 and was implemented very recently.

Recent transformations

In 2003, the decision was taken to carry out a reform of the ENA and training of the French top public administrators, under the impetus of the Minister for the

Civil Service at that time, Jean-Paul Delevoy, for implementation beginning in 2006. As regards the development of training in public management, a test of the new models was carried out in permanent training two years before, on students already working in the public sector and having passed the administrative competitive examination for a career promotion.

The new initial training curriculum, which started in January 2006, lasts 27 months and is based on revised principles. 'A new schooling has been developed. . . . It will be organised around three training modules, namely Europe, administration of the territories and State reform' (Senate 2004). This new schooling thus starts in January, and now includes four main periods of four to eight months each, which takes students to an end of schooling in March of their third year:

- Period 1: European issues, with training alternating between studies and work placements of four months fully based in a European institution;
- Period 2: territorial issues, based on a common curriculum with students from the local authorities of the National Institute for Local Government Studies, and work placement in a local authority or in the central administration;
- Period 3: public organisation and management, with training covering the major aspects of management (strategy, social dialogue, negotiation, human resource management, organisation, management control, evaluation, etc.), and a work placement in a company or in the central administration;
- Period 4: choice between law, economy, social issues, management, local government.

While the legal aspect is, of course, always present in this programme, we can observe the strong integration of public management, which becomes a central subject.

This change also relates to continuous training, since any new director of the central administration now undergoes a four-day training in public management at the ENA, normally within six months following his appointment. Lastly, the ENA now intends to develop its research activities in public administration and management. Administrator of the *Revue Française d'Administration Publique* since 2002, it has started to reinforce its scientific activity, in conjunction with academia.

The INET

The National Institute for Local Government Studies (INET) provides, at national level, initial and continuous training for leaders of the main local authorities (cities of more than 40,000 inhabitants, inter-community structures, departments, regions). The INET has been in existence since 1984, and has achieved great importance, being now considered equivalent to the ENA for local government public service.

Training of administrative students is carried out over nine months, alternating between theoretical sessions and work placements in local authorities, within a personalised schedule. These students join the INET after passing a national entrance examination. This training also applies to the management cadre of local authorities, already in employment and recently appointed through internal promotion or through competitive exam; depending on employment conditions, these trainee civil servants also follow a training alternating between theoretical sessions and practical work placements.

In addition, long cycles of continuous training are also offered to managers and executives of local authorities. Among these, the most significant are the Cycle Supérieur de Management (CSM) (post-graduate training in management) and the Direction Générale (DG) cycle (training for top executives), which are actual training processes in the field of strategic management.

All training programmes at INET include management modules. This choice was made very early, almost from the beginning, as a complement to traditional subjects, which are law, political science and economy. Moreover, this school is presented as the 'pole of competences in the strategic management of the local government mission', and has played a pioneering role in this field.

Lastly, every December since 1998 the INET has organised the 'Strasbourg Conference on Local Government', a national conference of executives of local authorities with over 20,000 inhabitants. More than 1,500 executives in employment come to present their managerial experiences by participating in some 40 workshops over three days. This event largely contributes to the diffusion of managerial culture and to research applied to local government administration.

The IEP

The Institutes of Political Studies (IEP) are nine public institutions for higher studies whose objective is to disseminate knowledge and develop research on modern political issues. Their official task, as defined by dcecree, is to

> contribute, both through initial training and though continuous training, to training top executives of the public, para-governmental and private sectors of the country, and particularly of the state and local government public services . . . and to develop, particularly with institutions for higher studies . . . research into political and administrative sciences.

The oldest of the IEPs is that of Paris, created in 1872 under the name of the Private School of Political Sciences and nationalised in 1945. The eight others, located in the large provincial cities, were created on this model between 1945 and 1991.

However, the Paris IEP occupies a special place in this sector, in particular in terms of its legal status; indeed, it is the only big establishment that is independent of universities. This institute, familiarly known as 'Sciences Po Paris' has gained great renown for its teaching and its research centres. The latter include the

CEVIFOP – Centre de Recherches Politiques – and the CSO – Centre de Sociologie des Organisations – known worldwide for their work in the sociology of public organisations and their political studies. Unlike the IEP de Paris, the other IEPs operate within universities. The Strasbourg IEP is an internal institute of a university; the seven others are public establishments of an administrative nature attached to a university.

The IEP provides multidisciplinary training of four to five years, including law, economy, history, political science, geography, sociology and modern languages. Some also provide courses for the competitive examination of the top civil service. The majority of those admitted at the ENA are thus graduates of an IEP, generally that of Paris.

University degrees

Bachelor's degrees (called '*Licences*' in France) in Public Administration, offered by French universities for many decades, are now completed in six semesters following the baccalaureate. They are generally meant for students who wish to embark on administrative careers and middle- or top-management jobs in the public service. The given training is thus based on subjects included in the public service competitive exam: public law (constitutional law and political institutions, administrative law and administrative institutions), European Union law (institutional law and community law), knowledge of the modern world and economics (economic policies), sociology, political science, and increasingly today some introductions to business administration and management.

The master's degrees in Public Administration are more recent, but tend to develop, keeping pace with the need for better-qualified candidates for public service positions. They are generally driven by the faculties of law, and generally constitute a continuation of the bachelor's degree in Public Administration.

The master's degrees in Public Management are much more recent, the oldest being a maximum of ten years old, and most having been developed since 2004. Around 12 French universities offer this type of training today, under various specialised titles (the title 'public management' being sometimes expanded to make it more specific). Their objective is to prepare for senior positions in the state public service or in the local government civil service (through competitive examination or on a fixed term contract), or in private organisations working in the public sector (management consultancy, financial institutions, etc), or they way even lead to high-level teaching and research.

This type of master's degree in Public Management is offered much more widely now, due to national and territorial administrations' great need for competent managers. Law graduates are still necessary, but no longer suffice. Recruitment of this type of manager is still held back by the omnipresent civil service examinations, which remain in most cases indispensable to obtain a permanent position. The problem is that these exams remain little changed, still largely legal-based, with little managerial content. However, it appears that there will be changes in coming years with the modification of the examinations and the development of contracts for private sector law graduates in the civil service.

Doctorates in Public Law, Political Science, Public Economy, Sociology of Public Organisations and Public Management have traditionally been offered by French universities. Their specific characteristics with regard to research in these fields are detailed below.

Continuous training in public management

Increasingly, university master's degrees in public management are designed as continuous training for senior officials who are keen on completing their knowledge and know-how in new fields of management, in order to match the current challenges in their line of work, and to better understand the developments which they have to face. Similarly, the *grandes écoles* and institutions which provide training in public administration are developing their offerings for continuous training in these areas.

But one should note the pioneer quality, in France, of two significant initiatives for continuous training of senior officials in management, which started in the years 1984/1985, at a time when such practices and such themes were completely absent, and could even seem subversive since they related to the business world of the private company. They are:

- the Cycle Supérieur de Management Territorial (CSM) (Postgraduate Course in Management of Local Authorities) of the *INET*, a long training programme spread over 18 months, for executives of local authorities, carried out alternatively in relation to their professional duty;
- the Cycle Supérieur de Management de l'Équipement, (CSME) (Graduate Course in Equipment Management), a long programme of training-practice, spread over a period of about one year, for the top executives of the departmental or regional bodies of the Ministry of Equipment. The CSME has gradually been opened to other ministries (Interior, Agriculture, Environment).

These two programmes, which still exist today, are models of their kind for the other French, and even foreign, public institutions, and are recognised for their valuable contributions to the improvement of performance and capacity to adapt of the authorities and administrations concerned.

Similar cycles of continuous training in public management developed later in sectors like public hospitals and horizontally in all public administrations.

Development of studies and research in public management

In just the last 15 years, research activities, scientific colloquiums, researcher networks and laboratories have developed to a point where today they represent quite a significant contribution. Scientific reviews also exist and often with a rich multidisciplinary character.

In political science and public law, many French researchers are interested in public administration and have been publishing in these fields for a long time. One finds in particular several examples of these scientific works at the faculties of law and political science of French universities.

At the same time, research in public economy and the sociology of public action has also been conducted for several decades (at least half a century), either individually or collectively at university research centres or teams of the National Scientific Research Centre (CNRS), a large, well-known public research institution in France.

Researchers in management science have started investigating this field only very recently (mainly since the 1980s); their almost exclusive preoccupations had till then been the world of the private enterprise. However, over the last 20 or 30 years, the movement, at first hesitant, has transformed itself into a significant trend in France, and research in public management is now very visible (Gibert 2004; Cliquet and Orange 2002). For example, the annual 'Politiques et Management' public colloquium regularly brings together several hundred researchers in this field from different countries.

Several recognised scientific journals have worked for many years in the field of public administration and management; let us quote in particular, among the oldest, the *Revue Française d'Administration Publique* (now managed by the ENA) and *Politiques et Management Public*, managed by the Institute of Public Management in Paris. The IDMP is considered one of the first and most ancient academic networks independent of the French language on public management and political analysis. It organises annual conferences and publishes a quarterly journal, 'Politics and Public Management'. Moreover, academic networks have been formed since the mid-90s, like RECEMAP, the network of researchers and teachers in public management, created in 1996, or the Ville-Management (City-Management) network, which organises seminars for research and conferences every year, and publishes analytical works. For example, the City-Management network is particularly interested in trends in territorial public administration, and has collaborated with academics, territorial leaders and local officals in its research (Le Duff and Rigal 2004). RECEMAP is also known for encouraging young public management researchers via doctorate student seminars tutored by senior researchers, and an annual prize is awarded to the best master's dissertation in public management (the Jean-Baptiste Colbert Prize). These programmes exemplify the target to develop French research in public management for future generations.

Doctoral dissertations in public management

In management sciences, the 'public management' specialisation is not yet formally recognised among the academic standards providing the basis for career progression in France, which has consequently hampered the development of the discipline.

Indeed, while more and more doctoral students and research advisors carry out research in public management, they sometimes do not explicitly label it as such, not wanting to venture on as-yet unstable terrain.

Nevertheless, since the end of the 1990s, 20 public management doctoral dissertations have been produced each year in the field of management sciences, in parallel with doctoral dissertations on private company management. This work demonstrates that genuine study and research is being carried out in the field. The research themes developed in these doctorate theses are various, but we can identify a few major interests (Bartoli, 2004):

- The most popular theme is unmistakably the one which revolves around the eternal issue of 'performance' and its evaluation. The key words used in the titles of the theses are very evocative: effectiveness, performance, quality, control, management control, evaluation, etc. The treatment of these themes is regular, several theses dealing with them appearing every year and reminding us clearly, if we needed reminding, of the advantage of approaching research in public management through the field of management science;
- The second theme is from the field of public organisation strategy, studied with a classical terminology around the key words: strategy, policy, objectives, project, planning;
- The field of power and decision-making is also very present in French doctoral researches in public management, and often relate to current concerns and issues: governance, decision, power, obbying, decentralisation;
- Finally, the field of organisation remains an important subject; it is particularly a question of structure, processes, networks, information systems. These terms seem to show that the approaches developed today have gone beyond the traditional bureaucratic and administrative analysis.

Other studies and analyses in public management

France is also supported by a long tradition of studies carried out by work groups commissioned by the government or by official public institutions. Most of these official reports are published by the very famous Parisian publisher La Documentation Française, and represent an immense wealth of diagnoses, discussions and recommendations on the functioning of the public sector, with an increasing emphasis on the meaning of public management (see for example the Vallemont 1999 and Cannac 2004 reports).

Think tanks directed by high-ranking civil servants are also created, for perspective on practices and in order to define avenues to improve the functioning of public sector organisation structures. A good example is the 'Sociology-Management Club' set up several years ago by the Civil Service Ministry (ministère de la Function publique), bringing in researchers and academics to think about trends in public action from a sociological and management viewpoint.

Another significant example is the 'Circle of Reflection on State Reform', presided over by Yves Cannac. Its objectives are – on the basis of the experience of its members – to produce analyses and concrete propositions to facilitate the adaptation of the state to current challenges – new needs and expectations of society, the new international context, transformations in the public sphere and the imperative need for financial recovery and better-quality services. In November 2006 this circle organised a major colloquium at the Conseil Économique et Social, and published a work on specific French avenues for modernising the state (Cannac and Trosa 2007).

Moreover, many reports and dissertations are produced by students and trainees of universities and the *grandes écoles* (like the ENA and the INET, mentioned above), and constitute priceless material for the analysis of the life of French public institutions.

Conclusions

The concept of management has long remained absent from the vocabulary and practices of the French public service. For many, it evoked too directly the business world of enterprise, because it was linked (wrongly, in our opinion) to objectives of profitability and performance of a purely financial nature.

Over the years, ideas changed, and many government organisations and French authorities clearly made the distinction between the end and the means. They thus realised that management could represent a range of initiatives appropriate for their environment, provided that there was no attempt to transpose them from the business world, and that the mission–methods differentiation was kept consistent. Thus, a specific public management, tailor-made and respecting the outcomes of general interest, has proved to be completely appropriate, and has gradually shown its usefulness.

Development of public management study and research in France still has deep historical, cultural and institutional roots. Projected measures needed or required to improve public sector performance are strongly influenced by already existing structures and their legal and cultural bases.

Elitism in French public sector recruitment is potent, via the *grands corps* and examination system, with its tendency towards a uniform view of the public system due to the long-term persistence of certain types of training.

Finally, research work is restricted by French academic standards, especially by compartmentalisation of disciplines. Regard for this compartmentalisation has a direct impact on the careers of academics and researchers. This runs against the multidisciplinary approach that in fact appears to be a driving force behind development of public management.

Therefore the current French systems are contradictory to the specific needs for creation and transmission of public management knowledge. However, this is all undergoing radical change, though not always at a rapid pace. Concepts, value systems and choices of action in France are leaning towards more innovative, horizontal approaches while trying to maintain the advantages and strengths of a recognised and appreciated socio-cultural system.

This cultural transformation has partly been achieved thanks to research, studies and training in public management which have been developed in France since the 1980s. Still insignificant some 20 years ago, they are today very present and recognised.

The study of public management in France today is thus undergoing great change. It is largely surpassing (without ignoring) its legal roots, and benefiting from various disciplinary approaches while experiencing an interesting development from the quantitative and qualitative points of view. Such evolutions are more than useful for furthering understanding and steering in an area marked by significant transformations.

Acknowledgements

We thank Françoise Camet, director of permanent training and research at the ENA, and Gérard Moreno and Alain Screve, in charge of training at the INET, for their help on the contents of the paragraphs on ENA and INET respectively .

Notes

1 Some historians trace decentralisation back to the first years of the French Revolution and the quarrel between the Jacobins, partisans of a highly unified republic, and the Girondins, who advocated decentralisation.
2 This trend, often considered typically French, is the case throughout the public service administration. The 2006 report of the Conseil d'État notes, moreover, that the number of general texts in force is still growing: since 2000, when 9,000 laws and 120,000 decrees were on record, an average of 70 more laws and 1,500 additional decrees has been handed down annually.

Bibliography

Bartoli, A. (2004) 'Etat des thèses en management public', paper presented at 17èmes Journées Nationales des IAE, University of Lyon, September 2004.
Bartoli, A. (2005) *Le management dans les organisations publiques*, 3rd edn, Paris: Dunod.
Bartoli, A. (2006) 'Les nouvelles perspectives de la GRH dans la fonction publique', in *Les Cahiers Français* nr. 333, July–August, Paris: La Documentation Française.
Bodineau, P. and Verpeaux M. (1996)*Histoire de la décentralisation*, Paris: Editions PUF.
Burlaud, A. and Laufer, R. (1980) *Management public: gestion et légitimité*, Paris: Dalloz.
Cannac, Y. (ed.) (2004) 'La qualité des services publics', report to the prime minister, Paris: La Documentation Française.
Cannac, Y. and Trosa, S. (eds) (2007) *Pour un nouveau management public, par la confiance et la responsabilité*, Paris: Dunod.
Chanut, V. (1998) *La formation continue de l'encadrement supérieur de l'Etat. Bilan des pratiques et perspectives*, Paris: La Documentation Française.
Chevallier, J. (1991) *Le service public,* Que sais-je? collection, 2nd edn, Paris: PUF.
Chevallier, J. (2002) *Science administrative*, Thémis collection, 3rd edn, Paris: PUF.
Cliquet, G. and Orange, G. (eds) (2002) 'Organisations privées, organisations publiques', miscellanies in honour of Robert Le Duff, Rouen: Presses Universitaires de Rouen.

CNFPT and DEXIA (2006) *Les fonctions publiques locales dans les 25 pays de l'Union européenne*, Lilicampanule: Presses de IMP Graphic.

Conseil d'Etat (2006) 'Rapport public 2006. Sécurité juridique et complexité du droit', *Etudes et Documents* nr. 57, Paris: La Documentation Française.

Crema, G. rapporteur (2003) 'Conseil de l'Europe: Les réformes de la fonction publique en Europe', Doc. 9711, 19 February 2003.

Crozier, M. (1963) *Le phénomène bureaucratique*, Paris: Le Seuil.

Crozier, M. (1971) *La société bloquée*, Paris: Le Seuil.

Crozier, M. (1991) *Etat modeste, Etat moderne*, Paris: Editions du Seuil.

D'Iribarne, P. (2006) *L'étrangeté française*, Paris: Editions du Seuil.

Dupuy, F. and Thoenig, J. C. (1985) *L'administration en miettes*, Paris: Fayard.

Eymeri, J. M. (2003) *Les administrateurs issus du 3ème concours de l'ENA et des IRA: fonctionnaires du 3ème type ou cadres nouveaux de l'administration de demain?*, report for the Minist of the Civil Service, Paris: DGAFP.

Fayol, H. (1916) *Administration industrielle et générale*, reprint Paris: Dunod, 1979.

Ferlie, E., Ashburner, L., Fitzgerald, L. and Pettigrew, A. (1996) *The New Public Management in Action*, Oxford: Oxford University Press.

Fons, J.-P. and Meyer, J.-L. (2005) *La flexibilité dans les fonctions publiques en Angleterre, en Allemagne, et en France. Débats, enjeux, perspectives*, Paris: DGAFP, La Documentation Française.

Gaillard, J.-M. (1995) *L'ENA, miroir de l'Etat – De 1945 à nos jours*, Paris: Editions Complexe.

Gibert, P. (2004) 'Le Management Public', in *Les Cahiers Français* nr. 321, Paris: La Documentation Française.

Green, J. and Laffont, J.-J. (1977) 'On the Revelation of Preference for Public Goods', *Journal of Public Economics*, 8: 79–93.

Huet, P. and Bravo, J. (1973 *L'expérience française de la RCB*, Paris: Editions PUF.

IGPDE (2006) '2005, l'année des RH . . . Perspective Gestions Publiques', published by IGPDE/Recherche–Etudes–Veille, nr. 17, Paris, January 2006.

Lacasse, F. and Verrier, P.-E. (ed.) (2005) *Trente ans de réforme de l'Etat: expériences françaises et étrangères*, Paris: Editions Dunod.

Laffont, J.-J. (2002) 'Public Economics Yesterday, Today and Tomorrow', *Journal of Public Economics*, 86: 327–34.

Lallement, M. (2003) 'Pragmatique de la comparaison', in M. Lallement and J. Spurk (eds) *Stratégies de la comparaison internationale*, Paris: CNRS Editions.

Lascoumes, P. and Le Galès, P. (eds) (2004) *Gouverner par les instruments*, Paris: Presses de la Fondation Nationale des Sciences Politiques.

Le Duff, R. and Papillon, J.-C. (1988) *Gestion publique*, Paris: Editions Vuibert.

Le Duff, R. and Rigal, J.-J. (eds) (2004) *Démocratie et Management Local – 1ères rencontres internationales*, Paris: Dalloz.

Le Roy Ladurie (2001) *Histoire de France des Régions: la périphérie française des origines à nos jours*, Paris: Seuil.

Louart, P. (2003) 'GRH dans les fonctions publiques. Sur les pas du privé', *Revue personnel* nr. 433, ANDCP, October 2003.

Montaigne, M. de (1995) *Essais: Livre 3*, Paris: Flammarion, chapter 13: 1580–8.

Nora, S. (ed.) (1967) *Rapport sur les entreprises publiques*, Paris: La Documentation Française.

Pilichowski, E. (2005) Etude OCDE (direction de la Gouvernance Publique et du développement territorial), Evolution des politiques de gestion des ressources humaines dans les pays de l'OCDE: une analyse des résultats de l'enquête de sur la gestion stratégique des ressources humaines, Paris: OECD.

Poirmeur, Y. and Mazet, P. (2000) *Le métier politique en représentations*, Paris: L'Harmattan.

Rigaudiat, J. (1995) 'Gérer l'emploi public: Quelles fonctions publiques pour quel service public?' *Dossier Métiers et formations*, BBF, t.40, 6: 8–10, http://bbf.enssib.fr.

Santo, V. M. and Verrier, P. E. (1993) *Le Management Public*, Que sais-je? collection, Paris: PUF.

Senate (2004) 'Projet de loi de finances pour 2005: Fonction publique', Rapport législatif déposé par Jacqueline Gourault–Avis nr. 79–Fonction publique (2004–2005), tome 9, Paris: Espace Librairie du Sénat.

Thiétart, R. A. (1979) *Le management*, Que sais-je? collection, Paris: PUF.

Trosa, S. (2002) *Le guide de la gestion par programmes. Vers une culture du résultat*, Paris: Les Editions d'Organisation.

Vallemont, S. (1999) *La gestion des ressources humaines dans l'administration*, official report, Paris: La Documentation Française.

3 The study of public management in Germany

Poorly institutionalized and fragmented

Christoph Reichard

Introduction

This chapter presents information about the development of public management as a field of teaching and research in Germany. Starting with a short historical review, the paper provides an overview of specific features of the state perception and cultural traits in Germany. It also traces some trajectories of administrative reforms and their consequences for public management, and tracks the academic field from the broader administrative sciences to the emergence and rise of public management. At the core of the chapter, the author presents important issues and institutions of public management research and teaching in Germany. The chapter concludes by stating that public management as an academic field is poorly institutionalized and rather fragmented in Germany.

Specific features of the German state and administration

Historical development of German statehood

The first elements of German statehood emerged in the early Middle Ages around 900, based on the Holy Roman's Empire traditions of the German nation. Over the centuries, the Reich developed to an ever-increasing extent. Its powers were based on a strong and closely connected church, on influential dukes of the different regions and on quite independent cities (e.g. the Hanse cities in the north). After about 1250, the regional dukes gained more power and, over 400 years, the Reich remained a corporative state with strong regional rulers and a fairly weak emperor (Heyen 1982, 1984). Over time, both the dukes and the cities established some first administrative structures, whereas on the whole, the Empire did not develop a great deal of administrative apparatus. After the Thirty Years War (1648), with its endless religiously motivated struggles, as in some other European states, absolutist regimes replaced the old corporative regime structures. Due to the disastrous destruction of infrastructures and economy as a result of the war, the governments in Germany engaged in active economic and population policies. This marked the beginning of an active involvement of the state in infrastructure development and industry promotion in Germany (mercantilism). In the seventeenth and eighteenth centuries, the dualism between Austria and Prussia became more intense and caused several conflicts and wars. During this time, but particularly following the triumphal victories of Napoleon after 1806, the principles and structures of a modern government and administration emerged (Ellwein 2001). The administrations of the royal court and of the state were more strictly separated from each other. The administration was also separated from the judiciary. Administrative capacities became increasingly developed, e.g. with regard to tax collection or to the establishment of regional governments.

Administrations increasingly recruited employed professionals on a full-time basis. All of these elements, which were influenced to some extent by the 'Napoleonic model', constituted the building blocks of an emerging administrative state in Germany, which in turn was considered to be an important prerequisite of the *Rechtsstaat*.

During the nineteenth century, some consolidation and integration took place, although the so-called German revolution of 1848 failed. From 1870/71, the German Reich emerged under the strong leadership of Prussia. Coinciding with the state integration, the absolutist states in the nineteenth century were increasingly superseded by the liberal constitutional state and – after the First World War – by the democratic welfare state of the Weimar Republic. From 1933 to 1945, the Nazi regime radically interrupted this development; state and administration were formed according to the autocratic and racist rules and ideologies of the National Socialist Party. Soon after the Second World War, Germany was split up into two different states: the Federal Republic (FRG) and the Democratic Republic (GDR) of Germany. These two states were built upon highly divergent principles: whereas the FRG followed the basic ideas of Western democracy, the welfare state and social market economy, the GDR was structured along the building principles of a socialist statehood, with a one-party system, a strong ruling politburo, the principle of democratic centralism, etc. The co-existence of the two German states remained in place for about 40 years, ending with the fall of the Berlin Wall in 1989. With reunification, the Western system of statehood has been transferred to the East; since this time, the federal state of Germany has consisted of 16 *Länder* and comprises some 80 million inhabitants. Interestingly, the German administration showed a high level of continuity over the centuries (Ellwein 2001). It adjusted its structures and procedures only very slowly to new requirements and challenges. Even in times of political disruptions – 1918, 1933 or 1945 – the bureaucratic apparatus was stable and continued its business as usual. The dark side of such an attitude was the willingness of bureaucrats to collaborate with all kinds of governments, regardless of their political values and ethical principles (example: collaboration of bureaucrats with Nazi politicians).

Perceptions of state and administration

German society has long been characterized by a strong etatism; citizens believe in a powerful state and expect a great variety of tasks and services to be provided to them by the state. This was fuelled as early as the eighteenth century by cameralism and mercantilism (for more details on the emergence of the German administration, see Heyen 1984; Rosenberg 1958; Lynn 2006: 43). The German philosopher Hegel also influenced the thinking of the role of the state in relation to society, by placing the state above (civil) society (Kickert 2005: 548). Etatism became particularly strong during the nineteenth century, when more and more services to the general public that had previously been provided by private suppliers were transferred to the state (eg infrastructure, water, energy, education, health and social care and much more).

The debate regarding the separation of powers, which is related to scholars such as Hobbes or Montesquieu, and which came into practice in several states, was fairly late to develop in Germany, even though thinkers such as Kant or Hegel disputed this (Becker 1989: 45). However, during the nineteenth century, the basic foundations of the *Rechtsstaat* emerged, together with the evolution of the liberal constitutional state (Jann 2003: 98; Kickert 2005: 540; Lynn 2006: 52). The rise of the rule of law in Germany emerged as a specific mix of the protection of civilian rights on the one hand and of the dominance of regulations and bureaucratic mechanisms against the citizens on the other (the German authority state or *Obrigkeitsstaat*). Rules and regulations began to play a strong role in the German state and society, particularly from the early nineteenth century onwards. As is the case in some continental European countries, in Germany bureaucracy is older than democracy. This sequence has had severe consequences for the role and position of democracy against bureaucracy in Germany (König 1997: 56).

To maintain the etatist expectations of society and to support the power and influence of the ruling classes, a specific system of civil service evolved at the beginning of the nineteenth century. Practically in parallel in Bavaria and Prussia, the absolutist rulers established a professional civil service (*Berufsbeamtentum*), the basic principles of which are still in operation today (Becker 1989: 816; Derlien 1991; for a comparison between France and Germany, see also Proeller and Schedler 2005; more generally Raadschelders and Rutgers 1996). The principles of the German system of *Beamte*, which can also be found in the structural elements of the Weberian model of bureaucracy (see next section), were, and indeed remain, the following: neutrality, devotion to the state, lifelong tenureship, compensation according to the social status of the servant.

Based on the traditional features of etatism, *Rechtsstaat* and civil service, the specific patterns of the German state and administration evolved over time. The rule-bound and bureaucratically structured public administration emerged from the beginning of the nineteenth century, perceiving its role in a rather pre- or undemocratic manner as the agent of the state or of the rulers. With the rise of the welfare-state doctrine, the administration assumed an increasing number of tasks, both in the Weimar Republic and in the early years of reconstruction after the Second World War. However, as in other countries, after the peak of welfare orientation and with several fiscal crises and excessive demands to the state, the actual values and visions of a more neoliberal perception of the state also arrived in Germany. Current debates on the Lean State, the Ensuring State or the Regulatory State are a symptom of these developments (Jann 2003).

Core features of the present public sector of Germany

Germany has a Western-type democracy, following the common guidelines such as division of powers, equality, rule of law, etc. It is a federal state, consisting of the federal government and 16 *Länder* governments (for an overview, see e.g. Pollitt and Bouckaert 2004; König and Siedentopf 2001; Wollmann 2001a; Wollmann and Bouckaert 2006; Lynn 2006: 33). The German federalism may be called 'administrative federalism' because the implementation and execution of tasks is primarily the duty of the *Länder*. The federal government itself is relatively small (only about 10 per cent of the total public sector workforce), with very limited executive tasks of its own (e.g. military defence and customs). The federal level is primarily responsible for policy-making, legislation and overall policy coordination. Integration of the different government levels is also maintained by central rules and regulations of the administrative system: all governmental units have to follow common regulations set by federal government with regard to public finance and budgeting, civil service and formal procedures. All in all, the German public administration shows a more unified pattern than, for example, the Swiss governmental system.

The governmental system consists of a parliament with two chambers (the Bundestag as the House of Representatives and the Bundesrat as a representation of the *Länder*). Elections are based on a proportional voting system. The executive branch is a cabinet system with the Chancellor as head of government. Governments are usually based on coalitions of two parties. Within the three-level macro structure of the administrative system, there are some typical substructures. Most of the larger states are subdivided into territorial districts (*Regierungsbezirke*), which are responsible for several tasks such as police or economic development, and which coordinate and oversee the provision of local and regional services. Local government itself consists of two different layers: the county and the municipal administration.

Another characteristic is the principle of local self-government; local government is relatively strong in Germany, at least from a legal point of view. All local affairs are to be managed autonomously by the communes themselves. In reality, however, this principle is less strong, primarily because of dependence on state funding and strict federal and state regulations.

Although there is a vertical division of powers among the different levels of government, the amount of joint policies and of vertical policy linkages has considerably increased in the last decades. In many policy sectors, federal and state governments fund tasks on a mutual basis; this has caused inefficiencies and unclear responsibilities. Very recently, the federal and state governments undertook a reform of the multilevel interrelations, aiming for a decoupling of responsibilities of the different layers within the federation.

Although recent reforms have made some limited changes towards manageri-alism, German public administration still shows clear patterns of a classical bureaucratic and rule-bound administrative culture. As a result of education and socialization, administrators – primarily at the operative level – perceive them-selves as executors of regulations. After reunification of the two German states, some cultural differences can still be observed between West and East-German administrators, although the cultural diversity will decrease over time (see e.g. Schröter and Röber 1997 for details).

Trajectories of public sector reforms

German administration has, as previously stated, shown a remarkable con-tinuity over the last two centuries. It was, and continues to be, an example of classical Weberian bureaucracy. Its central features have not changed a great deal over time: hierarchy is still the dominant structural principle. Steering with precise regulations and with the classical cash-based and detailed budget is still the standard. The principles of the civil service changed little over that time. On the other hand, both the contexts and the tasks of administration have changed considerably. After the Second World War and the establishment of the federal republic, German public administration underwent several distinct phases of development (Bogumil and Jann 2005: 183; see also Wollmann 2001b):

1   Phase of reconstruction, re-hierarchization and consolidation (1947–63): establishment of federal government, restructuring of the *Länder*, re-establishment of the traditional civil service system, first attempts to achieve administrative simplification;

2   Phase of active policies and of local territorial reforms (1964–75): public finance reforms, some functional task reforms (devolution to local level), some experiments with programme budgeting; attempts to achieve compre-hensive administrative reforms and civil service reforms, amalgamation of municipalities;

3   Phase of debureaucratization and citizen orientation (1978–89): extensive reform attempts to reduce bureaucratic burdens and to improve services to the citizens; additionally, some privatization programmes;

4   Phase of reunification and of transformation of Eastern administration (1990–??): technical and administrative assistance to East German adminis-trations, restructuring of the Eastern *Länder* and local governments, intro-duction of the (traditional!) West German system of administration; in parallel, moving of parts of the federal government from Bonn to Berlin;

5   Phase of managerialization (1991–??): experiments with NPM-type reforms (new steering model), particularly at local level; and later with e-government approaches;

6   Phase of reorientation of state functions (1998–??): debating on new percep-tions of the state (activating, enabling or ensuring state), rearrangement of

labour and social policies, more emphasis on civic society, liberalization and deregulation of utilities.

The reforms in Germany have not, in general, proved to be a sweeping and sustainable success (Seibel 2001). Most of the reforms of phase 2 yielded only limited results; the public finance reforms were partly successful, as macroeconomic targets became part of the budgeting process. On the other hand, experiments with programme budgeting in line with the international trend towards PPBS failed. The ambitious programme of modernizing the German civil service by harmonizing the different types of employment and by introducing modern incentive systems ended with practically no success. The only administrative reform to succeed was the amalgamation of counties and municipalities: between 1968 and 1976, the number of municipalities was reduced from about 24,000 to 8,800. Although the amalgamation showed only modest efficiency gains and reduced the accessibility of authorities for citizens, the general administrative capability of German local government was strengthened. The many attempts in phase 3 to reduce bureaucracy and to introduce new concepts of steering and coordination did not prove to be successful and sustainable. The major features of a bureaucratic administration survived. There were, however, some modest improvements regarding citizen orientation. Various municipalities began to introduce one-stop shops (*Bürgerbüros*) and trained their staff to provide a greater customer orientation.

Phase 4 (reunification) was an exception in the reform trajectories. This unpredictable project of transforming the state and local administration in the East arose under strong time pressure and did not allow for a great deal of reflection and conceptual development. In the end, the transformation of the East to a Western-type democracy succeeded to a great extent. After a couple of years, the Eastern authorities were working according to the principles and procedures of the (West) German politico-administrative system. However, the price of such a forced transformation programme was that it was nearly impossible to combine the transformation with reform attempts. The West exported the old Weberian models and structures to the East, but there was no opportunity to implement modern concepts (Reichard and Röber 1993). As a result, East German administrations are still much more reluctant to implement elements of the new steering model compared with the West (Bogumil *et al.* 2006).

The still ongoing phase 5 (managerialization*)* has so far shown some modest positive results. Some elements of the new steering model have been widely practised in operative government for several years. At the local and partly at the state level, several managerial instruments have proved to have positive effects (eg budgeting, performance measurement, cost accounting). On the other hand, many expectations have not been met and some critical side effects of NPM have been observed (more details in section 3 of this chapter or Reichard 2003a; for empirical results of German NPM reforms, see Bogumil *et al.* 2007). With regard to phase 6, it is too early to assess concrete results. So far, most of the reform programme consists of rhetoric.

Comparing the current status of German administration with the situation some 50 years ago, there are doubtless also some positive results of change: the responsiveness and the orientation towards effectiveness and efficiency have increased over time. The bureaucrats are friendlier, the procedures are quicker, and most actors behave in a more cost-conscious and economic way. The expectations towards the welfare state have been reduced, and more emphasis on the markets and the self-regulation of society can be observed.

As can be seen, there have been numerous reform attempts in the German administration during the last 50 years. The trajectory of administrative reform in Germany – as in most other countries – has certainly not been straightforward or well planned. The authorities at the different government levels have reacted to various impulses with reform declarations (talk) and sometimes also with substantial reform activities. However, they have done so in an incremental way (Benz 2005: 659). The reform impulses have come from quite different external and internal angles. The reconstruction phase was the logical consequence of the complete destruction of the German politico-administrative system after the Second World War. The phase of active policies was a result of a political change from conservative to social-democratic government, but also a result of mainstream thinking in economics and political sciences (Keynesianism, belief in rational policy-making). After the disillusionment of this phase, the reform pendulum swung back to focus on simpler steps of reducing bureaucracy and – because of the respective demands – on measures to strengthen the citizen orientation of authorities. But again, the debureaucratization activities proved to be inadequate for changing the deeply rooted patterns of German rule-based administration. Thus, German administrators followed, with some delay, the worldwide fashion of NPM and introduced – at least at the local level – the new steering model, believing in the positive effects of managerialism.

After about ten years of managerialism, ultimately, the administrators once again felt disillusioned with the meager results and turned to new, fashionable reform topics; e-government and issues of governance arrived as the latest reform trends. Altogether, the focus of administrative reforms has turned around quite considerably in Germany during the last few decades. Internal and external pressures, but also international fashions, seem to have been the main driving forces for reforms (Bouckaert 2004: 25).

Consequences for public management

The historical developments, the legacies and the characteristics of the German statehood and administration have distinct consequences for the perception and design of the discipline of public management. The etatism, the legalism and the related cultural patterns do not represent a very fertile climate for a management approach. Interpreting administration as a management problem is not common in this country. Thus, the preconditions for applying management concepts and instruments to public sector structures are not very positive.

The legalistic culture of the civil servants seems to be a major hindering factor for strengthening managerial thinking in public administration. Rule-based steering is a deeply rooted practice in all public sector organizations. It is still a major issue of education and training and the respective practices are handed down from one generation of bureaucrats to the next. The legalistic and specialized education of mid-level civil servants in the internal staff training colleges and the preferred recruitment of lawyers to senior civil service classes contribute to this perpetuation of the legalistic culture as well as the traditional socialization mechanisms of day-to-day work routines. Thus, to think and to behave in managerial categories is by no means a relevant value or attitude for most of the public sector personnel.

The 200-year-old German civil service system maintains these patterns. Its structures and incentive mechanisms are highly inflexible and demotivating. They do not provide attractive incentives for well-performing or reform-oriented employees. Furthermore, the system does not allow the rotation of staff between public and private sector and thus perpetuates a bureaucratic subsystem that is isolated from the rest of society.

Nevertheless, there have been some reforms and innovations in the field of public management. Most local authorities and several *Länder* governments have introduced NPM-related concepts and instruments in the last 10–15 years (see phase 5 above). The design of the concepts and the implementation strategies of public management reforms have been affected by the institutional particularities of the German public sector. The concept of the new steering model for municipalities was shown to have a rather narrow and one-sided structure (see Reichard 2003a for details). It emphasized a naïve 'product' orientation and cost-cutting tendency, but it neglected strategic steering aspects and market mechanisms. Thus, the concept was unable to exploit the potential of a modern public management concept.

The process of implementing public management elements in Germany was also influenced by institutional particularities. The federal structure, with large administrative bodies at the *Länder* level, explains why there have been very different approaches of public management reforms. Each state aimed to design and implement its own specific public management reform concept. The strong principle of local self-administration in Germany points in the same direction: despite the integrative role of the KGST as a local government think tank and innovator of the new steering model, local governments have had the freedom and opportunity to implement quite diverse public management reform elements (Banner 2006). Unlike in other countries, there has been no integrative support of reform initiatives from central (federal) government. As a result, there is a wide variety of public management approaches in the German public sector. The style of implementation also showed some particular characteristics; several reform elements were introduced in a rather perfectionist way (e.g. the product concept). Pragmatism was not a common trait of German public management reforms. As may be expected in a legalistic system, several governments enacted specific reform laws to provide the necessary regulations for practising the new instruments.

Public-sector-related teaching and research in Germany

A short historical review

The study of state and administration in Germany has a centuries-old tradition. A particularly strong phase was the *Policey-Wissenschaft* in the seventeenth and eighteenth centuries (Becker 1989: 138; Heyen 1982; Bogumil and Jann 2005: 18; Lynn 2006: 46). This discipline followed a comprehensive policy approach (*policey* = policy) and intended to provide legalistic, governmental and administrative advice to the absolute rulers of those times. Johann von Justi was one of the most prominent scholars during this phase (Justi 1760). The dominant aim of this academic field was the economic and social reconstruction and development of the states after the Thirty Years War by employing and mobilizing legal and technical means of the state. This also included a strong economic activity of the state (mercantilism). In the early eighteenth century, the *Policey-Wissenschaft* and *Kameral-Wissenschaft* played an important role at most universities in Germany. Whereas the former dealt with general welfare issues, the latter focused more on economic and managerial affairs. Both were prominent and very influential disciplines, which provided not only legal knowledge but also necessary economically and technically oriented practical skills to the emerging professionalized *Beamte* of the German states. The first chair of *Kameralistik* was founded in 1727 at the University of Halle. With the growth of academic knowledge, the *Kameralistik* split up in the early nineteenth century into three different branches: public finance and accounting, public economics (particularly trade and agriculture) and state sciences (*Staatswissenschaft*). This last branch had a particular impact on the emergence of the disciplines of state law and administrative law, which became increasingly important with the rise of the liberal *Rechtsstaat*. Scholars like Robert von Mohl and Lorenz von Stein were prominent representatives of this branch (Maier 1980).

The other two branches lost their relevance in the nineteenth century. Public economics, however, gained a new momentum in the second part of the nineteenth century and established itself as economics (*Nationalökonomie* or *Volkswirtschaftslehre*) at university level. The normative and positivist orientations of *Staatswissenschaft* and law became increasingly dominant in the study of the public sector in Germany. The empirically and practically oriented public administration disciplines disappeared to a greater or lesser degree. Even political sciences did not play a major role during these times. State activities proved to be primarily a matter of law and not of policy-making.

The theories of the famous German sociologist Max Weber in the early twentieth century regarding bureaucratic organization did not bring about a great deal of change. The features of his ideal type of bureaucratic organization – e.g. professional civil service, specialization, hierarchy, rule-orientation and impersonal and formal actions – coincided to a large extent with the already-existing administrative patterns (Weber 1921). His perception of administration as a rational, well-calculable and controllable type of organization was in line with the dominant understanding of public administration as being based on laws and regulations with a clear hierarchical structure and an undivided chain of accountability.

After the Second World War, there were a small number of attempts to reintegrate administrative law and administrative science (e.g. Peters 1949 or Morstein Marx 1959). However, the functional divide between normative law studies and descriptive or explanatory administrative studies could not be overridden. Public law remained the most influential discipline in the public sector.

Administrative sciences in Germany

Administrative sciences – as the sum of all public-sector-related disciplines – are not interrelated and integrated to a high degree in Germany. They primarily represent the following four basic disciplines:

- law disciplines, particularly public law (with many subdisciplines dealing with specific aspects of administrative law, e.g. organizational law, civil service law, budgetary law, procedural law, plus sectoral laws such as social law or police law, etc.);
- political sciences, particularly policy analysis and institutional theories (Scharpf 1971);
- economics and public-sector-oriented business administration (public management);
- public-sector-related sociology; well-known scholars such as Niklas Luhmann or Renate Mayntz are examples of a sociological approach to public administration (e.g. Luhmann 1966; Mayntz 1997).

These basic disciplines shed light on different, albeit one-sided points regarding the subject of public administration, each of which has its own, independent scientific interest. These different viewpoints have not yet been integrated and this considerable lack of scientific integration is stronger than in other countries, particularly the Anglo-Saxon domain. Furthermore, there is a fundamental, unsolved conflict between the normative and prescriptive disciplines (law, public management) and the empirical-analytical disciplines (political science, sociology). Administrative sciences in Germany are an additive concept and can rather be interpreted as a plurality of single disciplines (sciences) and not as one integrated scientific paradigm.

Derived from the basic disciplines of German administrative sciences, several state-focused variants have emerged in the last decades (see also Bogumil 2005):

- a law-based and primarily normative concept of theories of the state (*Staatslehre;* see for example Herzog 1971);
- a political-science-based analytical concept of government studies (*Regierungslehre*; see for example Ellwein 1963);

- a more pragmatic, partly law-based concept of administrative studies (*Verwaltungslehre*; see for example Thieme 1984);
- and, some years later, the public sector variant of business administration, public management studies (*Öffentliche Betriebswirtschaftslehre*; see for example Eichhorn and Friedrich 1976; Reichard 1977).

Not surprisingly, the law-based disciplines of constitutional, state and administrative law, with their manifold variants, have been the dominant field of administrative sciences in Germany over the last two centuries. The social-science-oriented and management-related disciplines have played only a marginal role. Only in the last 20 years have public policy and public management gained more momentum. However, we can still observe an asymmetric multidisciplinarity in the German administrative sciences (Benz 2005: 662).

A similar picture can be drawn with regard to public sector research. Traditionally, administrative research in Germany concentrated greatly on legal issues and applied the typical juridical concepts and methods of hermeneutics and normative interpretation. In the last two or three decades, greater emphasis has been placed on empirical-analytical research from the perspective of political science or sociology. Additionally, in line with the recent move towards managerialism, research has also dealt with the analysis and design of appropriate management concepts for public sector organizations.

What are the consequences for the education and training of civil servants in Germany? For many decades, civil servants at different levels of bureaucracy have been educated in a legalistic way (Dose 1999; Reichard 1998). Administrators for senior positions (administrative class, or *höherer Dienst*) have traditionally held a law degree, and this remains the case today. The *Juristenmonopol* is still observable: about 65 per cent of senior positions in ministries are held by lawyers (Benz 2005: 663). Only professionals for technical, medical or educational services have their respective academic degrees. The education of middle and lower civil service classes is in accordance with this pattern. The executive class (*gehobener Dienst*) is usually trained by internal staff colleges in a legalistic manner. Employees for operative tasks predominantly learn the application of rules and regulations as preparation for their jobs. Thus, the majority of the general administrative staff of German public authorities have undergone a thorough legal training and are equipped to deal with norms and regulations. Their dominant values and attitudes are related to the execution and application of laws and regulations.

There have been only a small number of educational exceptions and experiments during the last three or four decades. A prominent reform initiative was the implementation of a completely new study programme of public administration in terms of public policy at the University of Konstanz in 1973 (Esser *et al.* 1977): For over 20 years, this programme was the only fully fledged study of public administration from a social-science-based perspective in Germany (in 1994, the University of Potsdam started the second programme of this kind in Germany). However, the number of Konstanz graduates recruited by German public administration has remained fairly low over the years; most were employed in private business or the non-profit sector. In a similar way, some polytechnic universities (*Fachhochschulen*) in Germany tried to change the curricula for civil servant training from a dominant law focus to a broader, interdisciplinary perspective, also covering public policy and management. Some of these have been partly successful (Reichard 1998), but the major recruitment strategy of German public administration – at least at state level, less so at local level – has remained focused on law degrees.

The institutionalization of administrative sciences in Germany is rather weak compared with other countries. Referring to the above-mentioned four basic disciplines, teaching and research positions are distributed quite unequally:

- public law, with its many subdisciplines, is by far the most widespread discipline because it is taught in nearly every German university with a law faculty;
- public policy, government studies and other public-sector-related areas of political sciences can also be found in numerous German universities, although a specific public administration focus of research is of only modest relevance in the German political sciences (for the relationships between public administration and political science, see Bogumil 2005);
- administrative sociology (*Verwaltungssoziologie*) is a rather rare academic field in Germany; only a small number of sociologists have a major interest in public-sector-related topics;
- the same is true for economics and business administration; some economists deal with public finance; and relatively few scholars concentrate on public management issues (see below for more details).

The institutional landscape of German administrative sciences is highly fragmented. The main reason for this is the disciplinary differentiation and the extremely low tendency to collaborate between the disciplines. Law scholars collaborate only marginally with public policy or public management scholars. Scholars belong to their home disciplines, i.e. to law, business administration or political science. For example, law-oriented scholars are affiliated in the highly prestigious Vereinigung der Deutschen Staatsrechtslehrer (Association of German University Teachers of State Law); political-science-related scholars are professionally associated in the Deutsche Vereinigung für Politische Wissenschaften (DVPW; German Association of Political Sciences), public management scholars in a section of the Verband der Hochschullehrer für Betriebswirtschaft (Association of University Professors of Business Administration). So far, the various scholars have not established an integrative joint professional network or association for administrative sciences, as is the case in many other countries (eg the NASPAA in the USA). Moreover, scholars are used to publishing their research results in the scientific journals and book series of their home disciplines. As a consequence, well-known interdisciplinary scientific journals do not exist in the field of public administration. The journals

are either law-based (e.g. *Die Verwaltung* or *Verwaltungsarchiv*) or else originate in the political sciences (e.g. *Politische Vierteljahresschriften*) or are related
to economics and business administration (e.g. *Zeitschrift für öffentliche und
gemeinwirtschaftliche Unternehmen*).

Furthermore, public administration teachers and researchers are highly dispersed in regional terms. As individuals in large faculties, they are marginalized
to some extent. There are only a small number of centres for public-sector teaching and research in Germany where some capacities have been concentrated: the
Deutsche Hochschule für Verwaltungswissenschaften Speyer (DHV), with its
Research Institute for Public Administration, the Faculty of Administrative Sciences at the University of Konstanz and the Potsdam Centre for Policy and Management at the University of Potsdam.

A further reason for the fragmentation is the divided German academic
system. For about 35 years, there has been a distinction between universities
and polytechnic universities (*Fachhochschulen*). Universities usually educate
lawyers and thus are responsible for providing young academics for the superior
level – the administrative class – of the civil service. *Fachhochschulen* educate
mid-level administrators (executive class) for the German civil service. A
special variant of these, the civil service staff training colleges, have a quasi-
monopoly on preparing the graduates for the general administrative service.
Altogether, there are about 20 *Fachhochschulen* in Germany with a clear focus
on public administration teaching (and to some extent also research). The degree
of collaboration between universities and *Fachhochschulen* is very low; university teachers sometimes hold a fairly arrogant attitude of superiority over their
colleagues from the second league. This also explains the extreme fragmentation
of the German administrative sciences.

Compared with other countries, the German institutional position of administrative sciences is weak, fragmented and not very visible (for a critical assessment, see also Benz 2005 and Bogumil 2005). Apart from public law, the amount
of public-sector-oriented research is quite modest, particularly if it is related to
the still-high relevance of the state in society and in citizens' expectations.

The (inter)-discipline of public management in Germany

Emergence of public management

The study of public management is not new. Issues dealing with planning,
coordination and control of, and within, public administration have been a
subject of academic studies for centuries (e.g. of the cameralist sciences of the
eighteenth century). Attempts at public management have also been a theme of
the law-oriented administration studies (*Verwaltungslehre*) since the late nineteenth century. A major issue was the rationalization of procedures, e.g. during
the times of the Weimar Republic, promoted by a newly established association
that is still in action: the Association of Economy and Administration (Ausschuß
für Wirtschaft und Verwaltung). Since the Second World War, administration

studies under the umbrella of law faculties has became more influential. This has resulted in several textbooks on the subject (e.g. Thieme 1984; Püttner 2000).

The study of public management in a more current sense in Germany began in the 1960s. In its early days (in the late 1950s and early 1960s), it also received contributions from administration studies (e.g. proposals for improving structures and procedures of administration) as well as from business administration (extension of general management knowledge to the public sector). In the phase of the active state during the late 1960s, scholars from political science also contributed to topics of public management, e.g. relating to public planning and budgeting and to new patterns of coordination (Mayntz and Scharpf 1973).

In the late 1960s, a specific subdiscipline of business administration emerged in Germany: public business administration (*Betriebswirtschaftslehre der öffentlichen Verwaltung*; presented by authors like Chmielewicz 1971; Eichhorn and Friedrich 1976; Oettle 1976; Reichard 1977). One of the first important publications was by a Swiss author, Bischofberger 1964. During those first days, scholars in this first phase of public management dealt with what were the current practical topics of administrative reforms: comprehensive planning and coordination concepts and goal- and performance-related steering (Reinermann 1975). In the late 1960s, the German as well as many other governments imported rational methods of planning and coordination, for example the well-known 'Planning–Programming–Budgeting–System' (PPBS), from the US. However, these concepts were not very successful and mostly disappeared after some years. Public management scholars were also involved in transferring private sector management concepts and instruments to the public sector, e.g. management by objectives or motivational concepts (Wild 1973; Reichard 1973). It can be said that in the late 1960s and early 1970s, there was a first phase of public management debate in Germany, nearly 30 years before the new public management entered the stage (see below).

The emergence of public management thinking in the late 1960s and early 1970s was a result of an increased openness of the German government to innovations in the public sector. It was the phase of active policies, in which the government and many authorities experimented a great deal with new concepts and instruments. Some well-known issues on the reform agenda were:

- elaborated concepts of planning and efficiency analysis (PPBS, cost-benefit analysis, multicriteria analysis);
- management by delegation (decentralizing competencies and responsibilities to lower levels of hierarchy);
- management by objectives (introducing concepts of goal-setting and performance measurement);
- incentive systems (introducing intrinsic incentives in the civil service system).

The main aims of NPM were anticipated to some extent, although the innovations focused primarily on intra-administrative reforms and followed a quite technical and naïve method of knowledge transfer from the private to the public sector. The ideological framework of that time was less receptive to such messages because there was still a belief in the omnipotent welfare state.

In the 1970s and 1980s, public management in Germany became more established, although it remained a marginal subdiscipline of business administration. Research topics dealt again with the pressing practical issues of those times: with debureaucratization, with increasing citizen orientation and with personnel management issues.

The rise of NPM in Germany

New Public Management (NPM) as a reform concept for public sector organizations arose fairly late in the day in Germany. In the early 1990s, the KGST, a local-government think tank, developed a concept called the New Steering Model (NSM; for details see Jann 1997; Reichard 1997, 2001 and 2003a). The elaboration of the concept was purely driven by practitioners, mainly by city managers. The involvement of academia was very limited. The author was member of the working group that elaborated the NSM; he was the only academic in the whole group. The basic ideas of NSM were imported from the Dutch city of Tilburg, which at the time was operating a concept of corporate management that impressed the German practitioners (see Hendriks and Tops 2003 for the trajectories of the Tilburg model). Later on, some impulses came from the academic field, particularly from public management scholars (e.g. Budäus 1994; Budäus and Finger 1999; Eichhorn 2001; Reichard 1994; Reichard and Röber 2001). Political sciences were fairly late to react and were in part rather sceptical. Among the political-science-related authors dealing with the NSM development were Bogumil (2001), Jann (1997), Kropp (2004), Naschold (1995), and Wollmann (1996).

The law disciplines were even slower to react to the NPM discourse. They dealt primarily with issues of legal compatibility of certain NSM-elements (e.g. with the legal status of internal management contracts; see, e.g. Hill 2002). Only a small number of law-oriented authors took up the whole concept of NSM (e.g. König 2000; Mehde 2000). It was a long time before the first empirical studies came out, which evaluated the implementation and the results of NSM reforms in Germany (see Jaedicke *et al.* 2000; Bogumil *et al.* 2006).

Although the public management scholars' influence on the development of NPM in Germany has been modest, the general movement of NPM, by contrast, has had a positive effect on the acceptance and visibility of the discipline of public management. Its academic position has been much more stable since the mid-1990s and its research results seem to be of greater relevance and influence, at least concerning the practice of public sector management.

Perceptions of the 'field' of public management

Public management as a field of study is perceived from two different perspectives in Germany (Reichard 2003b: 498–9): either a   as the public-sector-related subdiscipline of business administration: public management equals public business administration (*Öffentliche Betriebswirtschaftslehre*), which means that public sector problems are treated like business management problems, with a clear focus on efficiency; or

b   as the managerial part of administrative sciences: public management has a broader interdisciplinary focus here, not only on efficiency but also on effectiveness and legitimacy; it looks not only at single public sector organizations, but is also interested in issues of steering and control of the whole public sector.

So far, the first perspective is more relevant in the German academic system. The majority of scholars in public management originate from and still belong to the field of business administration. Only a limited number of political-science-related scholars and a very small number of law-oriented scientists conduct research and publish in the field of public management. Compared with other countries, only a small number of public management researchers perceive their position as a true interdisciplinary one.

The inclination of public management towards business administration has consequences for the design and results of research; public management researchers in Germany usually follow a dominant prescriptive and praxeological research orientation. They deal with managerial improvements and are less interested in analytical or explanatory studies. The analysis of political or sociological problems does not play a major role. This can be clearly seen in a retrospective analysis of the major research issues of the past decades. Since the 1960s, there has been a strong emphasis on the development of management instruments and on the transfer of concepts and instruments from the private to the public sector (e.g. goal-setting techniques, accounting and budgeting concepts). This also continued during the phase of NPM.

Among the business-administration-related studies of public management are two major fields of research. Some of the scholars concentrate largely on the public sector within a narrow understanding of governmental or state-run organizations. They deal with management issues of central, subnational or local governments and of public utilities and public enterprises. Other scholars have a broader view of the public sector and also include the non-profit sector, although non-profit organizations are private entities rather than state-owned. Some of them even concentrate on this sector and leave out the governmental sector (e.g. Witt *et al.* 2004; Helmig and Purtschert 2006). Only a small number of contributions to NPO management come from political-science-oriented authors (e.g. Nährlich and Zimmer 2000).

The rather one-sided perception of public management in Germany does not seem to be adequate for the complexity of the field. The narrow focus on efficiency, the underlying assumption of economic rationality in public (and political) activities, the preference for prescriptive and normative research findings and the poor foundation in empirical research – all of these shortcomings represent restrictions on German scholars taking part in international comparative research on public management issues.

Major issues of public management research

Research activities in the past 20 years have dealt primarily with the conceptualization of management systems and instruments for single public sector organizations. With regard to publications, the following topics have been particularly relevant:

- tools and techniques for managerial functions, e.g. for planning, decision-making, steering and coordination, and supervision or overview;
- restructuring of public sector organizations: efficiency effects of different structural variants, improvement of business processes;
- better utilization of public resources, particularly regarding financial resources, human resources, or information resources;
- efficient methods of production and distribution of public goods and services.

During the last ten years, public management research has dealt with the well-known top issues of NPM and followed the mainstream debates of the international public management community. Besides the usual topics of NPM, German public management publications have primarily focused in the last few years on financial management, particularly the introduction of resource-based, commercial-type accounting concepts and lump-sum and result-based budgeting systems. This occurred because the German government decided in 2003 to reform the local governments' accounting and budgeting system (with some extension to the *Länder* level). Other prominent topics were HRM issues (personnel development, incentives), e-government and new institutional arrangements of public service provision such as autonomization, PPP, contracting out and privatization.

Public management research takes place in the same academic institutions that are involved in teaching (see below). Some universities with chairs in public management are active in public management research: the DHV Speyer, with its own research institute for public administration (*FÖV*), and the universities of Hamburg, Konstanz, Mannheim and Potsdam. A few political science departments also conduct research with a focus on public management (e.g. the universities of Bochum, Hagen, Duisburg-Essen, Hanover and, very recently, the Zeppelin University in Friedrichshafen). Some polytechnic universities are also quite active, e.g. the FHTW Berlin. Some consultancy firms and think tanks (e.g. *KGST*) are also occasionally involved in public management studies.

Results of public management research are usually published in books. Some publishers offer well-known book series. Reputable public-sector-oriented publishing houses are, e.g., Nomos Verlag, Edition Sigma, and VS-Verlag. Scientific journals are bound to their home disciplines, e.g. to law, political science or business administration. So far, there is no true scientific journal that covers the entire field of public management. Two journals are focused on public management: *Verwaltung und Management* and *Innovative Verwaltung*. However, both deal primarily with practical issues and do not have a clear scientific focus. Academic journals that publish articles on public management quite frequently are *Zeitschrift für öffentliche und gemeinwirtschaftliche Unternehmen, Die Verwaltung, Verwaltungsarchiv, Die öffentliche Verwaltung and Politische Vierteljahresschriften*. Almost all publications are in the German language, with only a small number of contributions in English. This is one reason why German public management research is not very visible in the international community.

Teaching public management

Different elements of public management at university level are offered in the following disciplines of administrative sciences:

- in several German law faculties where administration studies (*Verwaltungslehre*) are offered;
- in about a dozen business administration departments with a specialization in public management (widely known are, for example, Hamburg, Mannheim and Potsdam); some of the departments concentrate on specific sectors like hospital or transportation management;
- in some political science departments dealing with public policy or government studies.

In all university programmes, public management modules have only a supplementary role; they constitute a rather small part of the curriculum. Fully fledged public management programmes do not exist at the German university level. This may change with the emergence of master's programmes in the near future; a first example is the Master in Public Management and Governance of the Zeppelin University. Up to now, the modules are part of diploma degrees, e.g. of the Diplom-Kaufmann as the traditional German university degree in business administration. Following the Bologna treaty, German universities are currently transforming their programmes into the two-tiered approach of bachelor and master's degrees.

Example 1: the Major in Public and Nonprofit Management of the MSc in Business Administration of Potsdam University. The major consists of two lectures with integrated exercise courses, a seminar and a study project, altogether 40 ECTS (European Credit Transfer System). The courses cover a broad selection of public management issues concerning the management functions of public and non-profit organizations;

Example 2: the Public Policy and Management master's programme of the University of Konstanz. This two-year programme, which is mostly taught in English, offers four main areas: public policy and governance, administrative reform and organizational change, European integration and international organization, and management of conflict and peace. Each of these areas is organized in four modules: methods, theories, applied methods and theories, and related programmes and related disciplines. Courses also offer some public management contents, primarily related to managerial change and project management.

Public management contents can also be found at the polytechnic level: some *Fachhochschulen* offer specific public management degrees, e.g. in Berlin, Osnabrück, Wernigerode and in several internal staff training colleges. Public-management-related modules are also part of programmes of business administration or of social work.

> Example 3: the BA in Public Management of the Berlin University of Applied Sciences (FHTW) and the Berlin Polytechnic University of Administration and Justice (FHVR). The three-year BA contains various compulsory courses from public law, political sciences, economics, statistics, ICT and accounting to international public management reforms, organization, HRM and governance. The electives cover financial management, marketing, organization and personnel.

At the level of professional training and continuing education, the situation is comparable. In contrast with other countries, in Germany there is as yet only a limited offer of specialized public management degree programmes. Potsdam University offers an English-language Master of Public Management, the University of Kassel a distance-learning variant of public management. The private Hertie School of Governance in Berlin has, since 2005, offered a postgraduate master's degree in Public Policy, which also includes a course in public management. In addition, there are some degree programmes at the polytechnic level. By contrast, the supply of short-term training programmes plays a much larger role; numerous training institutes – both government-owned and private providers – are offering short courses and seminars about public management topics.

> Example 4: the mid-career master's degree in Public Management of Potsdam University. The one-year, full-time master's programme in the English language offers five broad modules, each consisting of compulsory and optional courses: public management, public administration/government, public policy, methods and skills, and supplementary studies.

So far, students of public management in Germany do not have a great deal of choice available to them when drawing on public management textbooks for their learning. There are two textbooks that offer excellent and reflective insights into (new) public management, but not a complete overview of all managerial functions and issues. Both are by Swiss authors: Schedler and Proeller (3rd edn

2006) and Thom and Ritz (3rd edn 2006). Additionally, there are a few text-books offering a more business-administration-related view: Brede (2005), Schmidt (2004), Steinebach (1998). From the author of this chapter, there is a rather outdated textbook (Reichard 1987).

Public management as a profession

It has not been common to recruit management professionals to managerial posi-tions in the German public sector. In both administrations and utilities, leader-ship functions were traditionally administered by lawyers or legally trained amateurs. Since the arrival of the NPM wave in Germany, the demand for staff with managerial skills has grown, particularly at the local level. However, the number of educated management personnel is still much lower than the expecta-tions. In view of the strong fiscal pressure and the need for more effective man-agement, this tendency can be assessed as dangerous (Budäus 2006: 14). There seems to be a kind of a vicious circle behind the recruitment strategies of German public administration. Federal and state administrations tend to recruit legally trained personnel. Coupled with the current budget crisis and the conse-quent hiring freeze, the result is a low demand for staff with managerial qualifi-cations. Consequently, students are only marginally interested in studying public management. This, in turn, leads to a reduction in teaching capacities in the field of public management (some of the few chairs of public management have been cancelled and earmarked for more fashionable fields of business management in the last years), which ultimately results in a poor supply of adequately trained management personnel for the public sector.

Several public sector organizations in Germany have expressed criticism based on their experiences in recruiting professionals with a business adminis-tration background. These managers were educated with a private sector orienta-tion and were not sufficiently familiar with the particular cultural patterns of public administration. They were unable to collaborate with typical bureaucrats or to understand the specific rationale of politicians. Finally, many of those private-sector-trained managers quit the civil service after a short time, thus sub-stantiating the existing prejudice that management qualifications are not really necessary for public administration.

A different, but also critical, development has occurred in the public utility sector of Germany in the last few years. Public utilities came under competitive pressure due to national and EU liberalization strategies. They were forced to compete with private providers for their survival on the opened markets. Con-sequently, many utilities recruited professionals with a business administration degree. But again, utilities were not interested in personnel with a specific public management qualification, but rather in strong private sector manage-ment skills and attitudes. To some extent, this recruitment tendency can be explained through the growing cultural distance between utilities and their public owners. There is clear evidence that utilities are hiving off from their own parent municipalities (Edeling *et al.* 2004). The top managers of these utilities no longer feel committed to the public interest of their parents, and are primarily interested in sales and profits. Their values have changed considerably. Why, then, should they recruit public managers?

The picture in the German non-profit sector is not very different from public administration. Management positions are usually occupied by amateurs, e.g. medical doctors or social workers. Although the competitive pressure has increased due to shrinking state funding and deregulation, the awareness of NPOs in terms of investing in specifically educated management staff is as yet fairly limited.

As a result, the overall demand for professionals who are specially trained in public management is below the expectations and generally disappointing in Germany. This again weakens the academic field of public management.

Institutionalization of public management

Quite similar to the situation of the whole of administrative sciences, the institutional position of public management in Germany is rather weak. If we concentrate on capacities in the fields of business administration and political science and leave out the – rather differently focused – capacities in law and in specialized sectors like health care, there are less than a dozen professors of public management at the university level and about 20–25 professors at the *Fachhochschule* level. This is surprisingly low compared with about 1,300 university professors in business administration in around 50 German universities with a business administration degree, particularly if we consider that the public and non-profit sector in Germany is fairly large and accounts for roughly 50 per cent of the ratio of public spending to GDP.

However, not only is there a very low number of professors, but the positions in the academic system are also highly fragmented. First, professors are firstly divided into the two classes of higher education (university and polytechnic); second, they belong to different home disciplines (law, business administration and political science); and third, they are regionally dispersed. Altogether, this adds up to a poorly visible institutional landscape with only very few centres and poor opportunities to mobilize critical masses and to collaborate in research.

A poor degree of institutionalization can also be observed with regard to research. Public management as a discipline has not been very successful in mobilizing research funds. It cannot often be found in large research programmes, e.g. in specialized PhD schools or research programmes funded by the German Research Foundation. And finally, as mentioned above, the lack of scientific journals focusing specifically on the subject is also a result of poor institutionalization.

Public management in Germany today – and into the future

Comparing public management in Germany with other countries, the overall impression is that the scientific focus of the field in Germany is rather narrow and one-sided, that there have been only weak tendencies to conceptualize public management as an interdisciplinary subject and that the field is poorly institutionalized. By contrast, public management in several other European countries is better off than in Germany; the field is well established and institutionalized, particularly in the Anglo-Saxon sphere. The discipline is more relevant and visible in research and teaching, and is also widely accepted as a professional field by public employers. From a scientific point of view, public management in most of the other countries has a broader and more interdisciplinary perspective and concentrates less on prescriptive and normative research findings.

What are the reasons for the quite dissatisfying state of public management in Germany? The current situation can be partly explained from a historical-institutional point of view. For about 150 years – since the phasing-out of the cameralist *Policey-Wissenschaft* – the dominance of law has been very strong in public-sector-related disciplines in Germany. The different subdisciplines of law have occupied large parts of the study of Germany's public sector – and have viewed it through the normative lens of legality. Other disciplines arrived late in the day and had to work hard to get a 'piece of the cake'. Thus, there was some academic competition and only limited interest in collaborating. Competition and the trend to define separate disciplinary territories caused a domain-oriented pattern of scientific analysis of public sector problems. The result of this is a poor ability of the different disciplines to collaborate and conduct joint research. Each discipline has been unable to break free from its narrow disciplinary boundaries and restrictions. This applies particularly to public management. This field always refers to its roots in business administration. Researchers are less willing to collaborate in an interdisciplinary manner.

A further reason for the underdeveloped condition of public management is the weak demand side. Unlike other countries, the recruitment of civil servants in Germany is still concentrated either on lawyers or on specific technical professions like engineers or social workers. Due to the dominant bureaucratic culture, the need for well-functioning rule-executors was always greater than the need for public managers.

Future challenges

The German public sector faces several challenges in the future, which make it more likely that the demand for public managers will increase. The following incomplete list gives a rough picture (Budäus 2006):

* handling of the enduring fiscal crisis, particularly reduction of national debts;
* introduction of the new resource-based accounting and budgeting system, not only at the local but also at state and federal level;

- management of highly fragmented state and local governments with all the many autonomized separate entities;
- handling of the increasing market competition, also including regulatory issues;
- Management of complex policies in multi-level governance structures, including EU policies;
- handling of the future demographic challenges, also regarding the shrinking civil service;
- utilization of the new potential of ICT and e-government;
- handling of new ethical challenges due to increasing corruption risks.

The topics mentioned in the list signify that there will be a considerable need for professionals with specific public management qualifications in the future. Thus, there will be an increasing demand concerning public management, both in teaching and in research. However, the topics will change to some extent; the classical managerial issues will probably become less relevant, and new topics will emerge.

In Germany – as in other countries – some changes in the research object should be expected. Issues dealing with state-owned institutions will become less relevant, while issues regarding services to the public – regardless of ownership of the providing institution – will gain in importance. As we will have a more colourful mix of different institutions in the future, we will have to employ aspects and concepts of governance, i.e. of steering complex arrangements or networks of organizations. This is an opportunity for the German researchers dealing with the concept of the ensuring state (*Gewährleistungsstaat*) to further develop their ideas about the new roles and responsibilities of the state in the times of governance (Schuppert 2004, 2005; Reichard 2006). As the debate on the ensuring state seems to be a rather unique German topic, it is now time to introduce it to the international community.

In terms of the ensuring state and of the governance debate, it is likely that public management will converge to some extent with the policy-related administrative sciences. The object of both is similar, but the focus is different; public management will also, in the future, analyze its problems from the perspective of efficiency and effectiveness. And it will continue to follow a dominant prescriptive orientation, with the intention of providing recommendations for practice. However, we can expect some convergence between public policy and public management. From an institutional point of view, this may have the consequence that German universities will become more willing to initiate joint centres of public policy and management, as is already the case in some other countries.

To meet these trends and challenges, the German public management community has to broaden the disciplinary focus and to engage in more interdisciplinary research and teaching. Furthermore, German scholars have to collaborate more intensively with international research partners and to stimulate exchange between students, junior researchers, etc. The field has to be intensively connected with international counterparts. And third, the German public management community must overcome the fragmentation of its field. There is a strong need to concentrate on powerful centres in order to undertake visible and relevant research programmes and to use existing synergies.

However, some open questions remain. How will the recruitment policies of public administration develop in the future? Will the traditional *Juristenmonopol* continue? Or is some cultural change to be expected? Will the field of public management be able to escape from the irrelevance trap? And will it become more influential? What will be the role of German language – with regard to research publications and perhaps also to teaching? What will be the impact of the adjustments of academic degree programmes after the Bologna reforms on the demand for public management? Some of these questions may also be relevant in other European countries – but they are extremely important for the future of public management in Germany.

Bibliography

Banner, G. (2006) 'Local Government – A Strategic Resource in German Public Management Reform', in V. Hoffmann-Martinot and H. Wollmann (eds) *State and Local Government Reforms in France and Germany. Divergence and Convergence*, Wiesbaden: VS-Verlag, 125–64.

Becker, B. (1989) *Öffentliche Verwaltung*, Percha: Schulz.

Benz, A. (2005) 'Public Administrative Science in Germany: Problems and Prospects of a Composite Discipline', *Public Administration*, 83: 659–68.

Bischofberger, P. (1964) *Durchsetzung und Fortbildung betriebswirtschaftlicher Erkenntnisse in der öffentlichen Verwaltung*, Zurich: St Gallen.

Bogumil, J. (2001) *Modernisierung lokaler Politik*, Baden-Baden: Nomos.

Bogumil, J. (2005) On the Relationship between Political Science and Administrative Science in Germany, *Public Administration*, 83: 669–84.

Bogumil, J. and Jann, W. (2005) *Verwaltung und Verwaltungswissenschaft in Deutschland*, Wiesbaden: VS-Verlag.

Bogumil, J., Grohs, S. and Kuhlmann, S. (2006) 'Ergebnisse und Wirkungen kommunaler Verwaltungsmodernisierung in Deutschland – Eine Evaluation nach zehn Jahren Praxiserfahrung', in J. Bogumil, W. Jann and F. Nullmeier (eds) *Politik und Verwaltung*, Wiesbaden: Politische Vierteljahreszeitschrift Sonderheft 37: 151–84.

Bogumil, J., Grohs, S., Kuhlmann, S. and Ohm A. K. (2007) *10 Jahre Neues Steuerungsmodell – eine Bilanz kommunaler Verwaltungsmodernisierung*, Berlin: Ed. Sigma.

Bouckaert, G. (2004) 'Die Dynamik von Verwaltungsreformen. Zusammenhänge und Kontexte von Reform und Wandel', in W. Jann *et al. Status-Report Verwaltungsreform. Eine Zwischenbilanz nach zehn Jahren*, Berlin: Ed. Sigma, 22–35.

Brede, H. (2005) *Grundzüge der Öffentlichen Betriebswirtschaftslehre*, 2nd edn, Munich, Vienna: Oldenbourg.

Budäus, D. (1994) *Public Management*, Berlin: Ed. Sigma.

Budäus, D. (2006) 'Notwendigkeit eines Forschungs- und Ausbildungsschwerpunktes "Informations-, Struktur- und Finanzmanagement öffentlicher Verwaltungen (Public

Management)" an den wirtschafts- und sozialwissenschaftlichen Fakultäten deutscher Universitäten', in R. Schauer, D. Budäus and C. Reichard (eds) *Public and Nonprofit Management*, Arbeitsberichte und Forschungsergebnisse aus Deutschland und Österreich, Linz: Trauner, 7–17.

Budäus, D. and Finger, S. (1999) 'Stand und Perspektiven der Verwaltungsreform in Deutschland', *Die Verwaltung*, 32: 313–43.

Chmielewicz, K. (1971) 'Überlegungen zu einer Betriebswirtschaftslehre der öffentlichen Verwaltung', *Zeitschrift für Betriebswirtschaft*, 41: 583–610.

Derlien, H. U. (1991) 'Historical Legacy and Recent Developments in the German Higher Civil Service', *International Review of Administrative Sciences* 57: 385–401.

Dose, N. (1999) 'Teaching Public Administration in Germany', *Public Administration*, 77: 652–6.

Edeling, T., Stölting, E. and Wagner, D. (2004) *Öffentliche Unternehmen zwischen Privatwirtschaft und öffentlicher Verwaltung. Eine empirische Studie im Feld kommunaler Versorgungsunternehmen*, Wiesbaden: VS-Verlag.

Eichhorn, P. (2001) *Öffentliche Dienstleistungen. Reader über Funktionen, Institutionen und Konzeptionen*, Baden-Baden: Nomos.

Eichhorn, P. and Friedrich, P. (1976) *Verwaltungsökonomie I*, Baden-Baden: Nomos.

Ellwein, T. (1963) *Das Regierungssystem der Bundesrepublik Deutschland*, 5th edn 1983, Opladen: Westdeutscher Verlag.

Ellwein, T. (2001) 'The History of Public Administration', in K. König and H. Siedentopf (eds) *Public Administration in Germany*, Baden-Baden: Nomos, 33–45.

Esser J., Fach, W., Simonis, G. and Väth, W. (1977) 'Verwaltungsstudium in Konstanz', in G. Voegelin (ed.) *Sozialwissenschaften. Berufsorientiertes Studium?* Frankfurt: Campus, 100–26.

Helmig, B. and Purtschert, R. (eds) (2006) *Nonprofit-Management*, 2nd edn, Wiesbaden: Gabler.

Hendriks, F. and Tops, P. (2003) 'Local Public Management Reforms in the Netherlands: Fads, Fashions and Wind of Change', *Public Administration*, 81: 301–23.

Herzog, R. (1971) *Allgemeine Staatslehre*, Frankfurt a.M: Athenaum.

Heyen, E. V. (ed.) (1982) *Geschichte der Verwaltungsrechtswissenschaft in Europa. Stand und Probleme der Forschung*, Frankfurt a.M: Klostermann.

Heyen, E. V. (ed.) (1984) *Wissenschaft und Verwaltung seit dem Ancien Régime. Europäische Ansichten*, Frankfurt a.M: Klostermann.

Hill, H. (2002) 'Zur Rechtsdogmatik von Zielvereinbarungen in Verwaltungen', *Neue Zeitschrift für Verwaltungsrecht*, 9: 1059–63.

Hoffmann-Martinot, V. and Wollmann, H. (eds) (2006) *State and Local Government Reforms in France and Germany. Divergence and Convergence*, Wiesbaden: VS-Verlag.

Jaedicke, W., Thrun, T. and Wollmann, H. (2000) *Modernisierung der Kommunalverwaltung. Evaluierungsstudie zur Verwaltungsmodernisierung im Bereich Planen, Bauen und Umwelt*, Stuttgart: Kohlhammer.

Jann, W. (1997) 'Public Management Reform in Germany: A Revolution without a Theory?', in W. Kickert (ed.) *Public Management and Administrative Reform in Western Europe*, Cheltenham and Northampton: Elgar, 81–100.

Jann, W. (2003) 'State, Administration and Governance in Germany: Competing Traditions and Dominant Narratives', *Public Administration*, 81: 95–118.

Jann, W. et al. (2004) *Status-Report Verwaltungsreform. Eine Zwischenbilanz nach zehn Jahren*, Berlin: Ed. Sigma.

Justi, J. v. (1760) *Die Grundfeste zu der Macht und Glückseligkeit der Staaten – oder ausführliche Vorstellung der gesamten Polizeywissenschaft*, Königsberg, Leipzig.

Kickert, W. (2005) 'Distinctiveness in the Study of Public Management in Europe. A historical-institutional analysis of France, Germany and Italy', *Public Management Review*, 7: 537–63.

König, K. (1997) *Zur Kritik eines neuen öffentlichen Managements*, Speyerer Forschungsberichte, nr. 155, 2nd edn, Speyer: FÖV.

König, K. (2000) *Zur Managerialisierung und Ökonomisierung der öffentlichen Verwaltung*, Speyerer Forschungsberichte, nr. 209, Speyer: FÖV.

König, K. and Siedentopf, H. (eds) (2001) *Public Administration in Germany*, Baden-Baden: Nomos.

Kropp, S. (2004) 'Modernisierung des Staates in Deutschland: Konturen einer endlosen Debatte', *Politische Vierteljahresschriften*, 45: 416–36.

Luhmann, N. (1966) *Theorie der Verwaltungswissenschaft*, Cologne: Heymanns.

Lynn, L. E. (2006) *Public Management: Old and New*, New York, London: Routledge.

Maier, H. (1980) *Die ältere deutsche Staats- und Verwaltungslehre*, 2nd edn, Munich: Beck.

Mayntz, R. (1997) *Soziologie der öffentlichen Verwaltung*, 4th edn, Heidelberg: UTB.

Mayntz, R. and Scharpf, F. (1973) *Planungsorganisation: Die Diskussion um die Reform von Regierung und Verwaltung des Bundes*, Munich: Piper.

Mehde, V. (2000) *Neues Steuerungsmodell und Demokratieprinzip*, Berlin: Duncker & Humblot.

Morstein Marx, F. (1959) *Elements of Public Administration*, 2nd edn, Englewood Cliffs: Prentice Hall.

Nährlich, S. and Zimmer, A. (eds) (2000) *Management in Nonprofit-Organisationen. Eine praxisorientierte Einführung*, Opladen: Leske & Budrich.

Naschold, F. (1995) *Ergebnissteuerung, Wettbewerb, Qualitätspolitik. Entwicklungspfade des öffentlichen Sektors in Europa*, Berlin: Ed. Sigma.

Oettle, K. (1976) *Grundfragen öffentlicher Betriebe*, 2 Bände, Baden-Baden: Nomos.

Peters, H. (1949) *Lehrbuch der Verwaltung*, Berlin: Springer.

Pollitt, C. and Bouckaert, G. (2004) *Public Management Reform. A Comparative Analysis*, 2nd edn, Oxford: Oxford University Press.

Proeller, I. and Schedler, K. (2005) 'Change and Continuity in the Continental Tradition of Public Management', in E. Ferlie, L. Lynn and C. Pollitt (eds) *Handbook of Public Management*, Oxford: Oxford University Press.

Püttner, G. (2000) *Verwaltungslehre*, 3rd ed, Munich: Beck.

Raadschelders, J. C. N. and Rutgers, M. R. (1996) 'The Evolution of Civil Service Systems', in H. Bekke, J. L. Perry and T. A. J. Toonen (eds) *Civil Service Systems in Comparative Perspective*, Bloomington: Indiana University Press, 67–99.

Reichard, C. (1973) *Managementkonzeption des Öffentlichen Verwaltungsbetriebes*, Berlin: Duncker & Humblot.

Reichard, C. (1977; 2nd edn 1987) *Betriebswirtschaftslehre der öffentlichen Verwaltung*, Berlin: De Gruyter.

Reichard, C. (1994) *Umdenken im Rathaus. Neue Steuerungsmodelle in der Kommunalverwaltung*, Berlin: Ed. Sigma.

Reichard, C. (1997) 'Neues Steuerungsmodell – Local Reform in Germany', in W. Kickert (ed.) *Public Management and Administrative Reform in Western Europe*, Cheltenham and Northampton: Edward Elgar, 61–82.

68   *C. Reichard*

Reichard, C. (1998) 'Education and Training for New Public Management', *International Public Management Journal*, 1: 177–94.

Reichard, C. (2001) 'New Approaches to Public Management', in K. König and H. Siedentopf (eds) *Public Administration in Germany*, Baden-Baden: Nomos, 541–56.

Reichard, C. (2003a) 'Local Public Management Reforms in Germany', *Public Administration*, 81: 345–63.

Reichard, C. (2003b) 'Public Management im deutschsprachigen Raum', E.-B. Blümle, H. Pernsteiner, R. Purtschert and R. Andeßner (eds) *Öffentliche Verwaltung und Nonprofit-Organisationen. Festschrift für Reinbert Schauer*, Wien: Linde, 496–518.

Reichard, C. (2006) 'Öffentliche Dienstleistungen im gewährleistenden Staat', in GÖW (ed.) *Öffentliche Dienstleistungen für die Bürger – Wege zu Effizienz, Qualität und günstigen Preisen, Symposium der GÖW 2005*, Berlin: GÖW, 53–79.

Reichard, C. and Röber, M. (1993) 'Was kommt nach der Einheit? Die öffentliche Verwaltung in der ehemaligen DDR zwischen Blaupause und Reform', in G.-J. Glaeßner (ed.) *Der lange Weg zur Einheit*, Berlin: Aufbau, 215–46.

Reichard, C. and Röber, M. (2001) 'Konzept und Kritik des New Public Management', in E. Schröter (ed.) *Empirische Policy- und Verwaltungsforschung*, Opladen: Leske & Budrich, 371–92.

Reinermann, H. (1975) *Programmbudgets in Regierung und Verwaltung – Möglichkeiten und Grenzen von Planungs- und Entscheidungssystemen*, Baden-Baden: Nomos.

Rosenberg, H. (1958) *Bureaucracy, Aristocracy and Autocracy: The Prussian Experience 1660–1815*, Boston: Harvard University Press.

Scharpf, F. (1971) 'Verwaltungswissenschaft als Teil der Politikwissenschaft', *Schweizerisches Jahrbuch für polit, Wissenschaften*: 7–25.

Schedler, K. and Proeller, I. (2006) *New Public Management*, 3rd edn, Bern: Haupt.

Schmidt, H.-J. (2004) *Betriebswirtschaftslehre und Verwaltungsmanagement*, 6th edn, Heidelberg: Deckers.

Schröter, E. and Röber, M. (1997) 'Regime Change and Administrative Culture – Role Understandings and Political Attitudes of Bureaucrats from East and West Berlin', *American Review of Public Administration*, 27: 107–32.

Schuppert, G. F. (2004) 'The Ensuring State', in A. Giddens (ed.) *The Progressive Manifesto*, London: 71–85.

Schuppert, G. F. (ed.) (2005) *Der Gewährleistungsstaat – Ein Leitbild auf dem Prüfstand*, Baden-Baden: Nomos.

Seibel, W. (2001) 'Administrative Reforms', in K. König, and H. Siedentopf (eds) *Public Administration in Germany*, Baden-Baden: Nomos, 73–89.

Steinebach, N. (1998) *Verwaltungsbetriebslehre*, 5th edn, Regensburg-Bonn: Walhalla.

Thieme, W. (1984) *Verwaltungslehre*, 4th edn, Cologne: Heymanns.

Thiemeyer, Th. (1975) *Wirtschaftslehre öffentlicher Betriebe*, Reinbek: Rowohlt.

Thom, N. and Ritz, A. (2006) *Public Management*, 3rd edn, Wiesbaden: Gabler.

Weber, M. (1921) *Wirtschaft und Gesellschaft*, Berlin (5th edn, Tübingen: Mohr, 1980).

Wild, J. (1973) 'MbO als Führungsmodell für die öffentliche Verwaltung', *Die Verwaltung*, 6: 283–316.

Witt, D. Purtschert and R. Schauer, R. (eds) (2004) *Funktionen und Leistungen von Nonprofit-Organisationen*, Wiesbaden: Gabler.

Wollmann, H. (1996) 'Modernization of the Public Sector and Public Administration in the Federal Republic of Germany – (Mostly) A Story of Fragmented Incrementalism', in M. Muramatsu and F. Naschold (eds) *Public Policy and Administration in Japan and in Germany*, Berlin: De Gruyter.

Wollmann, H. (2001a) 'Germany. Länder and Local Diversity', '*Disputació Barcelona 2001*', online, available at: www.diba.es/innovacio/fitxers/germany.pdf (accessed 29 August 2006).

Wollmann, H. (2001b) 'Germany's Trajectory of Public Sector Modernisation: Continuities and Discontinuities', *Policy and Politics*, 29: 151–69.

Wollmann, H. and Bouckaert, G. (2006) 'State Organisation in France and Germany between Territoriality and Functionality', in V. Hoffmann-Martinot and H. Wollmann (eds) *State and Local Government Reforms in France and Germany. Divergence and Convergence*, Wiesbaden: VS-Verlag, 11–37.

4   The study of public management in Great Britain

Public service delivery and its management

Stephen P. Osborne and Kate McLaughlin

Introduction

This chapter explores the evolution of the discipline of public administration and management in the UK. It focuses in particular upon the dynamic tension between the political science and managerial roots of the discipline and how these have been played out in the struggle for hegemony between the contributory disciplines of public administration and public management.

The chapter opens by reviewing the history of the academic study of public administration and management in the UK and by relating this to the current state of managerial practice. It then relates this context to the evolution of the academic discipline and considers what issues will frame its development over the coming decades.

An important note on terminology

At the outset, it is important to be clear about the terms to be used in this chapter. 'Public Administration and Management' (PAM) is used to denote the overall academic discipline in the UK that is concerned with the nature of the British state, the policy formulation and implementation process and the management of public services. 'Public Administration' (PA) is the discipline that is most concerned with the relationship between the state and society and with the policy process. It has its roots in the 'traditional' discipline of political science. 'Public Management' (PM) is the discipline that is most concerned with the implementation of public policy and the management of public services. It has its roots in the 'traditional' discipline of management. 'Public services management' (PSM) is a term used to denote the practice of public management in the provision of public services. Finally the term the 'New Public Management' (NPM) is somewhat more complex. It arose originally as a descriptor for the managerial changes in PSM that occurred in the UK during the 1980s. Subsequently it has evolved to stand as a somewhat confusing 'crossover' term. Dawson and Dargie (1999) argue that it has actually has three possible definitions – as a set of political beliefs about how public services should be organised and managed in the UK, as an academic discipline that commentates upon the practice of PSM and as a set of managerial practices concerned with the provision of public services. Finally, 'public service organizations' (PSOs) is used here to denote organizations that deliver public services irrespective of their sectoral base – they may be governmental (public sector), voluntary and non-profit or commercial organizations.

In this chapter, we will commence by considering the history of PSM in the UK before going on to consider the evolution of the academic disciplines of PA and PM in the UK. A key theme is the empirical, rather than theoretical, basis of PAM (and of its subdisciplines of PA and PM) in the UK. The discipline has evolved in a grounded sense, on the basis of the study of practice and the derivation of theory from this practice, rather than from theoretical principles and core scientific disciplines as might be said to be the case in mainland Europe. This empiricism is deeply embedded as a defining element of the discipline in the UK and goes back to its early founders, such as Robson (1928), discussed further below.

Public services management in the UK: a brief history

In order to understand the evolution of the discipline of PAM in the UK, it is necessary to understand two points. First, the provision of most public services has historically been coordinated at the local level – usually by local authorities or health authorities, whilst policy-making has taken place largely at the national level. This bipolar mode has set up inevitable tensions between national government and the local level – the national government being concerned that the letter (and spirit) of their legislation was carried out and the local level being concerned to mediate and adapt (or even ignore) this legislative framework to local needs (John 1990; Wilson 2003). This tension was seen at its most extreme in England[1] during the Conservative government of 1979–1997, during which time a state of almost guerrilla warfare existed between national and local government. The (Conservative) national government would introduce a policy initiative, such as the compulsory competitive tendering for the provision of public services. Policy-making and implementation at the local level, within the (mostly Labour) local authorities, was then concerned how to mediate, and often negate the impact of such policies on local public services. This tension is essential to the nature of PSM in the UK.

Second, there is a local tension between local government and the voluntary and community sector in the local provision of public services. It is this tension that has been central to the provision of these services in the UK over the nineteenth and twentieth century (Osborne 1998a). It is returned to in detail below.

PSM in the nineteenth century

During the late nineteenth century, public policy was dominated by the belief that both the state and government involvement in society was,[2] at best, a necessary evil. It was the charitable and philanthropic organizations of the time that consequently took the lead in developing many services that have subsequently become the backbone of public services in the UK, such as health, education and many social services. There was thus

> a well understood if tacit agreement between private charity and the statutory authorities as to the sphere in which each properly operated .... The main responsibility for social welfare lay with the voluntary agencies. The function of the state was largely supplementary.
>
> (Owen 1964: 211)

The emphasis of these charitable organizations was invariably upon the individual, who was perceived as flawed in some way, rather than upon societal needs; for example they would focus upon the needs of a particular deprived child or parent, rather than upon childcare as a social issue. This approach was best summed up in the title of the classic study and critique of children's services in the period, *The Child Savers* (Platt 1969).

Important as these charitable organizations were, both in providing important public services and in laying the foundations for the future development of the public sector in the UK, they suffered from five failures of philanthropy (Owen 1964; Prochaska 1988):

* philanthropic insufficiency (the inability of philanthropic funds to deal with the extent of social need);
* philanthropic gaps/duplication (the inability of philanthropy to deal with unpopular needs and the overprovision in relation to popular needs);
* philanthropic amateurism/corruption (the lack of professional/managerial skills in dealing with complex social needs and the misuse of philanthropy as a way to avoid the already minimalist government regulation and taxation system);
* philanthropic parochialism/paternalism (the concentration of philanthropy in the more wealthy areas of southern England and the over-dominance of the views of the philanthropist upon organizational practices – however inappropriate or downright bizarre they might be);
* philanthropic limitations (the fact that philanthropy was often based upon the concept of the 'undeserving poor' – as was the then Poor Law – and that it dealt with individual blame rather than societal needs).

The rise of Fabianism

The turn of the century, however, saw an ideological shift in societal values in England, away from the 'Victorian [anti-state] values' that had dominated the late nineteenth century and towards the more statist view encapsulated within Fabianism (Cole 1932). This was the early precursor of the municipal socialism that came to dominate in the UK in the second half of the twentieth century. It sought to develop socialism in the UK through reformist rather than revolutionary means. Its more famous proponents included George Bernard Shaw, H. G. Wells, Sidney and Beatrice Webb, Emmeline Pankhurst, Bertrand Russell and John Maynard Keynes.

Alongside this shift came two things – a recognition of the limitations of the philanthropic sector as the appropriate conduit through which to meet social needs (precisely because of the 'failures' detailed above) and a new focus on societal issues (such as childcare, above) rather than individual failings.

This societal shift became known as the 'new philanthropy' and was given voice in the work of Elizabeth Macadam (1934). She argued that the philanthropic sector needed the guidance and support of government to deal with these philanthropic failures. She thus first acknowledged the need for partnership between the state and what became known as the voluntary sector in the UK. However, this was very much an unequal partnership; the voluntary sector was unambiguously the junior partner in this evolving relationship, with an explicitly formulated role around its potential for meeting newly discovered needs and/or developing new forms of public service. Sidney and Beatrice Webb had codified this role in their seminal study of social welfare at the turn of the century:

> Looking back on the social history of the last hundred and fifty years, we must recognise that nearly all our successful developments ... have been preceded, or rendered practicable, by private experiments .... It is the first, the highest, and in many ways the most useful duty of the voluntary agencies to perform this indispensable service of invention and initiative and purposeful experimenting.
>
> Webb and Webb 1911: 240–1

This expression of the innovative role of the voluntary sector subsequently became the accepted wisdom in public policy circles and was embedded in the foundation of the welfare state by Beveridge (1948).

This period also saw the first growth of governmental funding of the voluntary sector as an instrument of public services delivery; one estimate is that governmental funding accounted for 37 per cent of the income of registered charities in 1934 (Braithwaite 1938). To give just one example, the National Council of Social Services (the forerunner of the National Council for Voluntary Organisations) in England received grants from the Ministry of Labour in 1936–1937 in excess of £100,000. Owen (1964) estimates that during the 1930s '[a]ltogether [it] must have received from government sources not less than £1 million' (p. 531). Finally, this period also saw the first strategic document about working with the voluntary sector issued by a local authority, London County Council (Davis Smith 1995). Taken together with the prior financial changes in the profile of the sector, these developments presaged the growth of the more formal relationships between local government and the voluntary sector that have dominated the last third of the twentieth century.

State dominance: the era of the welfare state

The foundation of the welfare state in post-Second World War Britain led to another seismic shift in public policy and public services provision. This was with the foundation of the welfare state. Implicit in this was the belief that voluntary and philanthropic action had had their day as a significant force in addressing social needs. This is not to say that the political leaders of the time were implacably opposed to the sector. They were not. Davis Smith (1995) points out that Attlee had worked in Toynbee Hall (if only for a year), whilst Beveridge continued to believe that there was a role for the voluntary sector in experimenting with new forms of public service:

> The capacity of voluntary action inspired by philanthropy to do new things is beyond question. Voluntary action is needed to do things which the state should not do ... It is needed to do things which the state is most unlikely to do. It is needed to pioneer ahead of the state and make experiments.
>
> Beveridge 1948: 301–2; see also Bourdillon 1945

Moreover, one significant authority argued that

> It is a great mistake to suppose that as the scope of state action expands, the scope of voluntary social services necessarily contracts. Its character changes in conformity both with changing views of the province of the state and with the growth of the spirit and substance of democracy.
>
> Cole 1945: 29

Nonetheless, voluntary provision of public services was increasingly criticised as being 'inefficient and ineffective' and many philanthropic leaders of the day did fear for the future of the sector (Deakin 1995). However, this period did not see strong government action to dismantle the voluntary sector as a provider of public services. In quasi-Marxist terms, it was assumed that it would 'wither away', as the welfare state increasingly assumed responsibility for all social needs 'from the cradle to the grave'.

This period did also see the high point of the influence of the academic discipline of PA upon PSM in the UK. Public services became customarily provided through large central or local government bureaucracies based around a predominating profession (such as social work, teaching or medicine). The dominant mode of service provision was quasi-professional, with the users of public services often denoted as 'clients' who relied upon the professional judgements of public service workers to define their needs and expectations. The allocation of scarce public resources was through administratively controlled bureaucracies where rules all too often dominated at the expense of the exercise of judgement. One critic (Mischra 1984) has suggested that this period of PSM can only be understood by understanding its roots in the rationing mentality of post-war Britain, when equality of service delivery between citizens (ensuring that citizens received a basic minimum entitlement) took precedence over equity of service delivery (ensuring that citizens received a level of service delivery commensurate with their needs).

The assumption of the withering-away of the voluntary sector was never fulfilled. Quite the opposite happened, in fact. Even in the early 1960s, during the high point of the hegemony of the welfare state, the role of the voluntary sector in service provision was reborn – and on the back of significant government funding. Moreover, this rebirth also saw a change in the nature of the sector, with smaller, local, community groups coming to assume importance in local government – voluntary sector relationships, alongside the more formal voluntary organizations. This new combined 'voluntary and community organization' (VCO) sector became in the 1960s and 1970s a significant instrument for public policy implementation, and particularly in the policy areas of employment and area regeneration (for example in the Youth Opportunities Programme, the Manpower Services Programme (MSP) and the Urban Programme).

This period latterly became known as the 'grant economy', when VCOs received one-off grants (though with the potential for annual renewal) from government in return for the delivery of public services. Little was specified in terms of the nature of the services, beyond their purpose. At its best, this 'benign paternalism' offered the development of flexible and cost-efficient services, with low managerial costs, because of the low level of accountability required from such grants. However, it could also lead to the growth of poorly focused services, with little actual account of need and no mechanisms for the accountability of public money. The governmental sector also retained control of the public policy process. And it continued to be a one-way relationship, with little ability for the VCO sector to influence the direction of public policy or its content. At its worst, these grant regimes produced extreme insecurity amongst VCOs, as their continued work (and possible existence) became dependent upon the paternalism of local government and often on an annual grant round that made medium- or long-term planning impossible. This process produced a distrust of local government by the VCO sector that was to colour future relationships (see for example Addy and Scott 1988 on the MSP).

These developments had little impact upon such mainstream areas of local public services as social and health care, however. These continued to be provided by local authority departments and district health authorities in a unitary fashion. The pattern of provision could still be complex, though, with a panoply of differing local government departments involved and a lack of co-terminosity between local government and health authorities. This issue has continued to dominate the coordination of local services delivery in the UK.

The rise of the New Public Management and the contract state

The election of the first Thatcher Conservative government in 1979 presaged a third major paradigmatic shift in the nature of PSM in the UK,[3] with the rise of what has become known as the 'new public management' or NPM (Hood 1991). As has been well analysed elsewhere, this was part of a much wider political agenda to redraw the nature of the public sector in the UK, based upon disillusionment with the effectiveness of hegemonic state action to date; as Gladstone

(1979: 22) noted at the time, mistrust of government intervention in society 'has swollen to a flood' (see also Mischra 1984 for a broader analysis of this period). This disillusionment led ultimately to the introduction both of managerial approaches to the delivery of public services (McLaughlin *et al.* 2002) and of the concept of 'the plural state', where a plurality of actors are involved in the service delivery process (Osborne 2002).

For local public services this transition had three core elements. First, it began the process that disaggregated the role of local government as the core provider of these services and that has subsequently propelled the VCO sector from the periphery to the mainstream of public services delivery. In particular, the development of what became known as the 'mixed economy of welfare' led to the expansion of the role of VCOs as the providers of an increasing range of local social care services, with the role of the local authority becoming that of the purchaser of these services (Wistow *et al.* 1996). This was the birth of what became known as the 'plural state' in England.

Second, this transition introduced the mechanisms of the market and of competition into the provision of public services, ostensibly as a way in which to allocate scarce resources. However, within this model, relationships were structured so that government maintained control of the policy-making process, with the role of the VCO sector being restricted to that of the service agent (Gutch 1990). Some critics have argued further that such partnerships were not at all concerned with genuine partnership between local government and the VCO sector, but rather were about the introduction of market disciplines to local public services as a means by which to emasculate local government as a stakeholder within the British state (Mackintosh 1992).

Third, the 'service contract' (or sometimes 'service level agreement') became the key governance mechanism of this relationship. The contract state was born. Moreover the emphasis initially was upon classical and neo-classical modes of contracts as the governance mechanisms, which were oft times ill suited to the complex and changing nature of public services, and that led to the imposition of significant transaction costs (Williamson 1988) upon the government departments responsible for the management of these contracts. Only latterly did more 'relational' forms of contracting become established, a trend which is still continuing (Bovaird 2006).

It is undoubtedly true that the growth of the NPM in England both improved the focus and efficiency of local public services and clarified roles and relationships between local government and the VCO sector to a far greater extent than before. Whatever its benefits, though, the NPM model had four definite drawbacks. First, it undermined the wider role of VCOs in society. It was not uncommon in this period, for example, to hear either central or local government 'warn off' any VCO that exercised its role as critic of the local state, with the threat of withdrawal of service funding. Second, it led to the growth of a managerialist culture inside PSOs that many saw as undermining their distinctive organizational features and public service ethos (for example, Landry *et al.* 1985 in relation to the VCO sector).

Third, as detailed above, it led to the growth of the transaction (or managerial) costs of managing public services for all PSOs. The service specification and tendering process was especially expensive to manage for local authorities, as was their subsequent monitoring of the performance of PSOs. The PSO sector also saw increased transaction costs arise from the demands made upon them by their governmental funders.

Finally, as a result of this latter point, and mirroring the distrust of local government engendered within the VCO sector by the previous grant economy, local government now began to develop a culture of distrust of service providers from other sectors, and especially of VCOs. Principal–agent problems in monitoring performance (Vickers and Yarrow 1988) meant that local government was often suspicious of them in delivering public services, fearing that they were being not as efficient as they could be, or else were making a surreptitious profit from local government contracts.

Partnership and community governance

The election of the new Labour government in 1997 (and its subsequent re-election in 2001 and 2005) marked a fourth shift in the public policy framework for PSM. A key theme in the early years of this government was the pursuit of joined-up government as a response to complex local social and economic issues (for example, DETR 1998). Government departments at the national and local level were increasingly expected to work collaboratively in dealing with complex social and economic issues. VCOs had also previously been identified by the Labour Party as having an important contribution to make to such a pursuit, because of their potential to identify unmet needs in a way that transcended both the traditional departmental boundaries of central government and the professional specialisms of local government officers (Labour Party 1997).

This meant that from the outset, the involvement of VCOs in delivering local public services became the cornerstone of what became known as 'community governance' (Clarke and Stewart 1998). For the first time, this model of PSM actively encouraged the involvement of VCOs in the policy formulation process, rather than just its implementation. This process was epitomised by the development of the Voluntary Sector Compact. This was a national – and subsequently a series of local – agreements that sought to establish a value-based relationship between government and VCOs that would later frame the policy-making and implementation process at both the national and local levels in the UK (Stowe 1998; Osborne and McLaughlin 2002).

Community governance in itself was part of a broader agenda of the Labour government to modernize local government (Cabinet Office 1999). Whilst the previous Conservative government had chosen the economic (and market) approach to local government reform, the Labour government adopted an explicitly political approach that sought to change the institutional architecture of local government, and which included such reforms as cabinet government and elected mayors for local authorities.

Whilst community governance remained an opaque and ill-defined aspiration, though, mostly honoured more in the exception rather than the generality, the broader concept of 'partnership' became central to the vision of PSM espoused by the Labour government. This involved partnership with the VCO sector in the field of public service provision and also with the private sector, both for service provision and also for capital investment (such as through the Private Finance Initiative or PFI – see Ball *et al.* 2003 for a discussion of this initiative and the management of risk within it).

As the system of local partnerships grew ever more complex in England, the government urged the integration of individual partnerships within 'Local Strategic Partnerships' (LSPs) for area regeneration at the local level and through 'Local Area Agreements' (LAAs) on local public spending. These attempted to provide a strategic framework for relationships between the key actors in local services provision. Whilst it is too early to judge the success, or otherwise, of LAAs, the execution of LSPs has been flawed. They have struggled to balance the joint production of public services alongside their joint management and governance. The emerging evidence is that, all too often, co-governance, as this latter activity has become known in the UK, has lost out to co-production and coordination (Johnson and Osborne 2003; for a more detailed treatment of co-governance and associated terms, see Brandsen and Pestoff (2006) and Pestoff *et al.* (2006)).

Partnership has, however, brought a range of new roles and relationships to the practice of PSM, though organizational learning has been slow. In part, this learning process has been hindered by the legacies of distrust, on behalf of both local government and the VCO sector, inherited from previous relationships. To stretch a metaphor, if your partner has repeatedly stood on your toes in a dance, you may be less willing to engage in future dances with them, especially if it involves a high degree of trust in their performance!

However, there have also been more fundamental pressures on this approach to PSM. First, the economic imperative for the cost-efficient production of local services has not gone away; if anything it has became stronger. Further, many of the staff in both sectors learned their 'trade' under the previous Conservative government. There has been evidence that many have found it hard to discard the more adversarial approach of that prior period for the complementarity required by the partnership approach to PSM. Finally, there is increasing concern, within the VCO sector in particular, that such close partnership will lead to the assimilation of VCOs into a neo-corporatist local state, with their subsequent loss of both organizational distinctiveness and independence (Osborne and McLaughlin 2002, 2004).

PSM in the early twenty-first century

The emerging evidence is that the above pressures are undermining the commitment of the Labour government to a pure model of partnership in public services delivery. This is an increasing concern to routinise and rationalise the operation of the partnership, the process being ever more orchestrated by central government in London.

The central elements of this latest evolution of PSM have been well laid out in the recent cross-cutting review of the role of the VCO sector in public services delivery by the Treasury (HM Treasury 2002). This review is positioned within the context of a radical programme of public service investment and reform, the goal being the delivery of 'world-class public services'. VCOs are articulated as having a key role to play in this process (p. 5). Whilst the tone of the review is still very much committed to partnership, this is explicitly a partnership related primarily to the delivery of public services rather than to a broader role either of policy formulation or of sustaining civil society; that is, the focus is firmly upon coordination and co-production rather than upon co-governance:

> Our aim must be to build a new partnership using the [VCO] sector's strengths to challenge and stimulate new ideas, complement our shared objectives and take forward the development of social policy generally. This partnership is about fresh ways of thinking through the role and structure of government and the voluntary sector and the way we deliver public services.
>
> HM Treasury 2002: 3

Elsewhere, we have argued that the cross-cutting review represents two important trends in British PSM (Osborne and McLaughlin 2004). First, the service delivery role for VCOs, in terms of 'world-class public services', looks destined to be focused increasingly on a small number of, presumably larger, VCOs, working in relational contracts with government as its preferred suppliers, and with a further diminution in the role of local government as a provider of public services.

Second, from having been a vehicle for the modernisation of local government, those VCOs engaged as 'preferred suppliers' are likely to be themselves the subjects of a modernisation programme for the VCO sector (McLaughlin 2004). Discussing the Futurebuilders fund (a central government initiative to develop the infrastructure of the VCO sector, with an explicit intention of equipping it for the delivery of 'world-class public services'), the cross-cutting review declaims explicitly that this fund will provide 'strategic investment to modernize the sector' (p. 32). Current research upon the experience of local government in the UK in terms of the modernization agenda (for example Ball *et al.* 2002; Hartley *et al.* 2002; McLaughlin 2002; Martin 2002) has suggested that this challenges not just the capacity but also the politics and performance of organizations subject to this agenda.

Finally, it is worth making the point that the NPM within the UK is quite distinct from other national variants. In the US, for example, privatization has not been such a core element of the practice of NPM as in the UK, primarily because there were comparatively few public services to privatise (Borins 2002).

Moreover, influenced by the work of Ostrom and Ostrom (1971), it has had far more of a focus on interorganizational, and not solely intra-organizational, relationships than in the UK. Similarly, the UK variant of the NPM is quite distinct from the version that has developed many parts of continental Europe, which often emphasizes contractual mechanisms within rather than without government (for example, Schrijvers 1993).

In the years since it first emerged as a model of PSM, the NPM has become questioned increasingly on a range of grounds (see, for example, Farnham and Horton 1996; Ferlie *et al.* 1996; McLaughlin *et al.* 2002). Critics in the UK and elsewhere have argued, *inter alia*, that

- the NPM and PM are not one phenomenon or paradigm, but a cluster of several (Ferlie *et al.* 1996);
- the NPM has a number of distinct personae, dependent upon the audience, including ideological, managerial and research-oriented personae (Dawson and Dargie 1999);
- the nature of the NPM is geographically dependent, with, for example, the British and American variants actually being quite distinct from each other in their focus and locus (Borins 2002); Kickert (1997) has also argued that the reach of NPM is limited to Anglo-American, Australasian and (some) Scandinavian arenas, whilst the managerial tradition of public administration continues to remain dominant elsewhere;
- the benefits of the NPM are at best partial and contested (Pollitt and Bouckaert 2004);
- at its most bleak, the NPM is a failed paradigm (Farnham and Horton 1996).

The NPM has been criticized most devastatingly for its introspective intra-organizational focus in an increasingly plural world, as discussed above, and for its adherence to the application of outdated private sector techniques to PSM, in the face of evidence about their inapplicability (Metcalfe and Richards 1991). Hood and Jackson (1991) concluded that the NPM was 'a disaster waiting to happen'.

Conclusion: lessons for the future of PSM in the UK

Four lessons emerge from this 'history lesson' for the future of PSM in the UK. First, PSM has been inextricably linked with the relationship between government and the VCO sector – and relationships do have history. It is not possible to understand the present state of PSM without understanding the past. Thus, for example, one needs to understand the legacy of distrust between local government and the VCO sector from previous relationships in order to understand quite why it has been so hard for them to work in partnership.

Second, there are three parties in this relationship – not only local government and the independent (VCO and business) sector, but also central government. The trajectory of local relationships cannot be understood without understanding either the place of central government in the relationship and the agenda(s) that it is pursuing, as was discussed at the outset of this chapter, or the complexity of central–local government relationships in the UK.

Third, national policy-makers often ignore at their peril the complexity and diversity of actors at the local level. Arguably, progress on local LSPs has been hampered precisely because of a failure by central government to recognize this factor. It assumed that the corporate approach adopted by central government and the national independent organizations would be replicated at the local level. This has not been the case. Diverse agendas exist both within local authorities and within the diversity of other local stakeholders.

Finally, the plural state as presently constituted has costs for its multiplicity of actors, both in terms of the economic transaction costs of such relational working and in terms of the opportunity costs for PSOs. These opportunity costs include the danger of independent organizations being incapacitated from acting independently, being subject to isomorphic pressures that might undermine their organizational distinctiveness, and being incorporated into a local state, wholly losing their identity and distinctive contribution to society.

PAM as an academic discipline in the UK

If the practice of PSM in the UK has been dominated by inter-sectoral relationships, the defining element of PAM as an academic discipline has been the dichotomy between Public Administration (PA) and Public Management (PM) as (often competing) subdisciplines. In contrast to the situation across much of continental Europe, constitutional or administrative law have been significantly less influential in these disciplines, perhaps reflecting the lack of a written constitution in the UK.

More than a decade has passed since the publication of Christopher Hood's influential piece that codified the nature of the New Public Management (NPM) (Hood 1991). This is often seen as the start point for the evolution of PM as an academic discipline, though actually its roots go back prior to this time. At that juncture it seemed likely in the UK that PM would sweep all before it in its triumphal recasting of the nature of the overall PAM discipline – in theory and in practice. One hundred-odd years of the hegemony of PA in the discipline seemingly counted for nothing in this momentous shift. Since then, though, the debate upon the impact both of the NPM and of PM upon PAM, and indeed about whether either constitutes a discipline at all (Gow and Dufour 2000), has become rather more contested.

Public administration

The key elements of PA as an academic discipline in the UK can be defined as

- the dominance of the rule of law;
- a focus on administering set rules and guidelines;
- a central role for the bureaucracy in policy-making and implementation;

- the politics–administration split within public organizations;
- a commitment to incremental budgeting;
- the hegemony of the professional in the service delivery system.

In the research community, this has led to a focus on the policy-making and implementation cycle, which work has often been located within public policy and political science departments (and latterly with an especial concentration in the 'new universities' of the British higher education system). Its seminal theorist was William Robson (1928) and it has at its core a concern with the unitary state, where policy-making and implementation are vertically integrated within government. It focuses precisely upon this policy-making and implementation system, or cycle, with an assumption that effective PAM is comprised of the successful implementation by public managers of policies decided upstream in this system by democratically elected and accountable politicians (Parsons 1996). Because of its vertically integrated nature, hierarchy is the key governance mechanism for PA, with a focus upon vertical line management to ensure accountability for the use of public money, whilst its value base is strongly that of an explicit public sector ethos (see for example Day and Klein 1987; Simey 1988). Some writers, of course, have long recognised the fallibility of the PA paradigm without entirely dismissing it as a framework for the design and delivery of public services. The American theory of 'street level bureaucrats' (Lipsky 1979), for example, has long held substantial currency in the UK. This seeks to explain the breakdown of the policy-maker–administrator divide in conditions of resource shortage, but without dismissing in its entirety the framework of PA for the provision of public services.

As outlined above, then, PA as a discipline developed out of the early years of the provision of public services in the late nineteenth century, and reached its peak of influence (both academically and upon PSM practice) in the UK in the 1945–1979 era of the welfare state, when the state was confidently expected to meet all the social and economic needs of the citizenry, 'from the cradle to the grave'. PA was to be the academic discipline that underpinned this brave new world. Predictably, perhaps, such a vision was doomed to failure and, in the latter days of their hegemony, both the welfare state and PA came under increasing fire – first from their academic critics (for example, Dunleavy 1985) and eventually from the political elite (see Mischra 1984 for an overview of these critiques). Most damagingly, Chandler (1991) argued that PA had now entered terminal decline as a discipline, whilst Rhodes (1997) later asserted that it had become a 'bystander' to the practice of PAM. This paved the way for the rise of PM.

Public management

The spread of the managerial practices within PSM that subsequently became known as the NPM, from the late 1970s onward, saw the growth of a new discourse within PAM as an academic discipline. In its most extreme form, this asserted the superiority of private sector managerial techniques over those administrative procedures embodied within PA, with the assumption that the application of such techniques to public services would automatically lead to improvements in the efficiency and effectiveness of these services (Thatcher 1995). The key elements of the NPM can be summarised as

- an attention to lessons from private sector management;
- the growth both of hands-on management – in its own right and not as off-shoot of professionalism – and of 'arm's length' organizations where policy implementation is organizationally distanced from the policy-makers (as opposed to the interpersonal distancing of the policy–administration split within PA);
- a focus upon entrepreneurial leadership within public service organizations;
- an emphasis on inputs and output control and evaluation and upon performance management and audit;
- the disaggregation of public services to their most basic units and a focus on their cost management;
- the growth of use of markets, competition and contracts for resource allocation and service delivery within public services (based on Hood 1991).

Within the academic field this led to the study of PSM as an explicit managerial discipline. Thus, for example, study of policy implementation, with its links to the policy formulation process, became subsumed within a discourse of change management (Osborne and Brown 2005). Similarly the issues of accountability and needs identification increasingly became viewed within a marketing framework (Walsh 1991, 1994). Underlying all of this, PM as a discipline became concerned with the production process for public services, with a central focus on the relationship between economy, efficiency, effective and equity and between the inputs, outputs and outcomes of public services (Knapp 1984; Osborne *et al.* 1995). Thus the policy formulation process became one of a range of inputs into the production of public services, rather than the mainspring of scientific attention.

In the PM research community, this led to a focus upon public management as a discipline in its own right – distinct and in counter-position to PA and usually located within management and business schools. PM was very much a child of neo-classical economics and particularly of rational/public choice theory. Despite its origins in the UK, its seminal influences are transatlantic primarily, with Tiebout (1956) and Niskanen (1971) making key contributions. It is concerned with a disaggregated state, where policy-making and implementation are (at least) partially articulated and disengaged, and where implementation is through a collection of independent service units, ideally in competition with each other. Its focus is almost wholly upon intra-organizational processes and management and the managerial and economic relationships identified above. It assumes competitive relationships between the independent service units inside any public policy domain, taking place within a horizontally organized market place, and where the key governance mechanism is some combination of competition, the price mechanism and contractual relationships, depending upon which particular variant of the PM one chooses to expound. At its extreme, the argument is made the marketplace, and its workings provides the most appropriate place for the production of public services (for example, Pirie 1988) – though there are other, more gentle versions of this that combine the managerial concerns of PM with some of the issues of accountability of traditional PA (for example, Flynn 2002).

The state of the art

Increasingly, then, both PA and the PM have begun to look like partial disciplines within the overarching academic discipline of PAM in the UK. The strength of PA has been in its exploration of the essentially political nature of PAM and of the complexities and nuances of the public policy-making process. The extent to which the implementation studies literature in PA has been able to unpackage the differential influences upon public policy implementation has been disappointing, however. There is a tendency for implementation to be seen simply as a black box, with no apparent will to explore the complex sub-processes of the management of the outputs and outcomes of the policy process – public services and the meeting of social and economic needs (Schofield 2001; Hill and Hupe 2003). At worst, public managers and management are portrayed as the villain(s) of the piece, thwarting the resolve of their political masters and often subverting the intentions of new policy to their own ends.

By contrast, the strength of PM as a discipline has been in its ability to address precisely the complexities of this black box of implementation, though with an equally frustrating tendency to see the public policy process as simply a context within which the essential task of public management takes place. In its most extreme form, PM has even questioned the legitimacy of public policy as a context for public management, arguing that it imposes unreasonable democratic constraints on the management and provision of public services. Most damaging, though, is that PM has become perceived as limited and one-dimensional in its ability to capture and contribute to the management and governance of public services and of PSOs, whether situated in the public, private or voluntary sector, in an increasingly plural and pluralist world (Rhodes 1997).

This debate has led the discipline of PAM to a crossroads. Whilst the more fundamentalist supporters of both PA and PM continue to assert their hegemony, many in the wider PAM community, including these authors, have begun to wonder aloud if there might not be a third option. This would need

- to integrate the scientific insights of both PA and PM;
- to move beyond the sterile analytic dichotomy of administration versus management;
- to allow a more comprehensive and integrated approach to the study, and practice, of PAM.

Whilst it is beyond the scope of this current chapter, one of these authors has suggested elsewhere that this need may well be met by the growth of the 'New Public Governance'[4] as an integrative theory and academic discipline within PAM (Osborne 2006). This would look far more towards organizational sociology and network theory for its inspiration (for example, Ouchi 1979 and Powell 1990). It would perforce focus both upon the relationship between public policy-making and implementation and public services management and upon the governance of interorganizational relationships in the plural state. Table 4.1 sketches out the key elements of PA and PM in the UK, and what a third option (called here the New Public Governance) might look like in contrast to them.

PAM and the research community in the UK: what are we writing about?

One important way to explore the extent of the differentiation of the PA and PM communities in the UK is to explore what they are writing about. One of these authors recently undertook a survey of articles published over the last seven years in the journals *Public Administration* and *Public Management Review*, as representative journals of the respective traditions of PA and PM. The results of this survey are presented in Tables 4.2–4.7. Before embarking on our analysis of these tables, it is important to note some important caveats:

- it is probably a caricature to portray these two journals as wholly representative of the PA and PM traditions in the UK; however it is legitimate device for the purpose of this chapter;
- a proportion of the articles, whilst published in a UK-based journal, are in fact from other nations;
- the survey itself was very much a 'quick and dirty' one; as a consequence, it is a good indicator of trends but would need a deal more deliberation to count as definitive;
- the articles were classified on the basis of their abstract and key words only, and against only one subject matter or locus.

Despite these self-imposed limitations, the survey does reveal a fascinating portrait of the nuances of the discipline of PAM in the UK at the start of the twenty-first century.

Tables 4.2 and 4.3 provide an overview of all the articles published in the journals. Four points stand out from this overview. First, five topics account for 82 per cent of the papers published in these journals over the past seven years. These are the policy process and policy networks (19 per cent), partnerships and governance (18.5 per cent), managerial activity and skills (18 per cent), public management reform (16 per cent) and audit, performance management and scrutiny (10.5 per cent). Second there is surprisingly little on either e-government/governance or procurement. Third, in terms of locus, almost half (48 per cent) are located within the traditional domains of national or local/subnational government, rather than within

Table 4.1 Three paradigms of PAM in the UK

Paradigm / key elements	Theoretical roots	Nature of the state	Focus	Emphasis	Relationship to external (non-public organizational partners)	Governance mechanism	Value base
Public Administration	political science and public policy	unitary	the policy system	policy implementation	potential elements of the policy system	hierarchy	public sector ethos
(New) Public Management	rational/public choice theory and management studies	disaggregated	intra-organizational management	service inputs and outputs	independent contractors within a competitive market place	the market and classical or neo-classical contracts	efficacy of competition and the market place
New Public Governance	organizational sociology and network theory	plural and pluralist	inter-organizational governance	service processes and outcomes	preferred suppliers, and often interdependent agents within ongoing relationships	trust or relational contracts	neo-corporatist

Table 4.2 Overview of PAM articles by locus, 1999–2005 (September)

Year	National government	Local or subnational government	Non-governmental bodies, Quangos	Health	Voluntary or NGO sector	European Union	Non-specific or cross-government	Total
2005	10	18	1	7	0	1	17	54
2004	16	15	4	10	3	0	23	71
2003	10	19	4	2	3	4	24	66
2002	10	19	4	11	3	2	16	65
2001	17	16	3	4	2	2	28	72
2000	19	26	3	5	2	2	16	73
1999	12	19	3	5	3	5	17	64
Total	94 (20%)	132 (28%)	22 (5%)	44 (10%)	16 (3%)	16 (3%)	141 (31%)	465 (100%)

Table 4.3 Overview of PAM articles by subject, 1999–2005 (September)

Year	PAM as discipline	Policy process and networks	Public managment reform	E-government	Partnerships and governance	Procurement	Audit, performance managment and scrutiny	Managerial action	Other	Total
2005	5	8	11	0	14	2	4	10	0	54
2004	6	14	11	1	11	0	5	17	6	71
2003	7	15	9	1	14	2	9	9	0	66
2002	2	16	7	3	15	8	3	9	2	65
2001	2	13	13	0	9	4	14	13	4	72
2000	0	12	10	0	17	3	8	18	5	73
1999	1	12	12	1	7	6	6	10	9	64
Total	23 (5%)	90 (19%)	73 (16%)	6 (1%)	87 (18.5%)	25 (5.5%)	49 (10.5%)	86 (18%)	26 (6.5%)	465 (100%)

the more newly emergent plural state. Finally, there is very little in either journal on the EU, the VCO/NGO sector or on Quangos.

Moving on to a comparison of the journals, Tables 4.4 and 4.5 compare them across the locus of the papers published therein. Reinforcing the third point above, this found 79 per cent of papers from both journals focusing upon a governmental setting. However, whilst *Public Administration* had a greater focus on national government (28.5 per cent of papers compared to 9 per cent), *Public Management Review* had a greater focus on local and subnational government (36.5 per cent compared to 22.5 per cent). At the margins, an interesting pattern emerged. *Public Administration* had no papers on VCOs or NGOs over this period, but a limited number on Quangos (7 per cent) and on the EU (5 per cent). In contrast, *Public Management Review* had only limited papers on Quangos (2 per cent) or the EU (1 per cent) but a more emergent focus on VCOs and NGOs (8 per cent).

Finally when the subject of these articles is analysed, a shade of emphasis rather than a stark contrast is found. In *Public Administration*, 81.5 per cent of the articles are accounted for by five subjects – the policy process and policy networks (27.5 per cent), partnerships and governance (17 per cent), managerial action and skills (14 per cent), public management reform (12 per cent) and audit, performance management and scrutiny (11 per cent). In *Public Management Review*, 83.5 per cent of its papers were accounted for by the same five subjects, but in quite different proportions – managerial action and skills (24.5 per cent), partnerships and governance (21 per cent), public management reform (20 per cent), audit, performance management and scrutiny (10 per cent) and the policy process and policy networks (8 per cent). Revealingly, neither journal had a significant focus on the development of PAM as a discipline or on its pedagogy.

It is possible to draw out three emergent conclusions from this 'quick and dirty' analysis. First, the majority of work within both the PA and PM communities in the UK continues to be statist in focus; the emergent plural state is only slowly being included in these mainstream PAM journals. Second, whilst there is a lack of focus on these developing plural actors in PAM, there is an important strand of work that looks at issues of partnership and governance, though from primarily a governmental point of view. Third, whilst there is a great deal of commonality between the journals, an administration–management dichotomy does emerge, but again as a difference of emphasis rather than dissimilarity. *Public Administration* does have a greater focus on the policy process and policy networks and upon the formal pluralism of the EU and Quangos, whilst *Public Management Review* has a greater focus on managerial action and skills and upon public management reform strategies and an emergent focus on the new pluralism of VCOs and NGOs.

Some blue-skies thinking on the future of the discipline

It would be an opportunity missed if we did not close with some thoughts about where we feel the discipline of PAM should be heading in the next decade.

Table 4.4 Public Administration articles by locus, 1999–2005 (September)

Year	National government	Local government	Non-governmental bodies, Quangos	Health	Voluntary or NGO sector	European Union	Non-specific or cross-government	Total
2005	9	11	1	3	0	0	10	34
2004	13	4	4	8	0	0	16	45
2003	8	7	2	0	0	4	15	36
2002	8	7	4	4	0	2	10	35
2001	14	10	2	3	0	2	10	41
2000	16	11	3	4	0	2	8	44
1999	8	10	2	2	0	4	6	32
Total	76 (28.5%)	60 (22.5%)	18 (7%)	24 (9%)	0 (0.0%)	14 (5%)	75 (28%)	267 (100%)

Table 4.5 *Public Management Review* articles by locus, 1999–2005 (September)

Year	National government	Local or subnational government	Non-governmental bodies, Quangos	Health	Voluntary or NGO sector	European Union	Non-specific or cross-government	Total
2005	1	7	0	4	0	1	7	20
2004	3	11	0	2	3	0	7	26
2003	2	12	2	2	3	0	9	30
2002	2	12	0	7	3	0	6	30
2001	3	6	1	1	2	0	18	31
2000	3	15	0	1	2	0	8	29
1999	4	9	1	3	3	1	11	32
Total	18 (9%)	72 (36.5%)	4 (2%)	20 (10%)	16 (8%)	2 (1%)	66 (33.5%)	198 (100%)

Table 4.6 Public Administration articles by subject, 1999–2005 (September)

Year	PAM as discipline	Policy process and networks	Public managment reform	E-government	Partnerships and governance	Procurement	Audit, performance Managment and scrutiny	Managerial action	Other	Total
2005	3	8	6	0	10	2	1	4	0	34
2004	6	12	7	1	6	0	2	6	5	45
2003	1	13	6	0	8	0	4	4	0	36
2002	1	13	2	3	5	3	3	4	1	35
2001	0	9	4	0	5	2	11	7	3	41
2000	0	9	6	0	6	3	5	11	4	44
1999	1	10	2	1	5	4	3	2	4	32
Total	12 (4.5%)	74 (27.5%)	33 (12%)	5 (2%)	45 (17%)	14 (5%)	29 (11.%)	38 (14%)	17 (7%)	267 (100%)

Table 4.7 *Public Management Review* articles by subject, 1999–2005 (September)

Year	PAM as discipline	Policy process and networks	Public managment reform	E-government	Partnerships and governance	Procurement	Audit, performance managment and scrutiny	Managerial action	Other	Total
2005	2	0	5	0	4	0	3	6	0	20
2004	0	2	4	0	5	0	3	11	1	26
2003	6	2	3	1	6	2	5	5	0	30
2002	1	3	5	0	10	5	0	5	1	30
2001	2	4	9	0	4	2	3	6	1	31
2000	0	3	4	0	11	0	3	7	1	29
1999	0	2	10	0	2	2	3	8	5	32
Total	11 (5.5%)	16 (8%)	40 (20%)	1 (0.5%)	42 (21%)	11 (5.5%)	20 (10%)	48 (24.5%)	9 (5%)	198 (100%)

In the most recent call for proposals of the Economic and Social Research Council (ESRC) Public Services Programme in the UK (ESRC 2006), Christopher Hood noted the following four areas as gaps in this programme. They are, we would argue, ongoing gaps in the development of the PAM discipline in the UK:

- theoretical modelling of performance management and performance metrics;
- work on the unintended consequences of social interventions and public services;
- rigorous cross-national and comparative studies of the UK experience of PAM in the global context;
- methodological development for the study of PAM.

Based on our experiences within the PAM academic community, we would add four trends that we expect to characterise this community over the early decades of the twenty-first century:

- a continued dichotomy between PA and PM, setting a focus on the policy process and policy networks against one on managerial action and skills;
- both will continue to have a core concern with public management reform and with partnerships and governance, though perhaps from different perspectives;
- a growing emphasis on the study of three PSM issues – the 'metrics' of audit and performance management, e-government/governance, and the evolution of the plural state;
- the development of new subject areas, such as risk management, knowledge transfer and innovation and citizen engagement.

Finally we would also argue that there is a need for much greater pluralism in the PAM research community and much less concern for the ageing PA–PM dichotomy. In particular, we would echo the call of Hood, above, for methodological development in the community. This might include

- the cross-fertilisation of conceptual and theoretical approaches from political science, management theory and organizational sociology, rather than their continued use in isolation;
- the growth of structured comparative research, historical and longitudinal studies, anthropological studies and other methodological developments;
- an industry focus not just upon the 'usual suspects' of social care and health, but also upon new industries – the environment, arts and regeneration, for example;
- the development of cross-industry studies;
- the exploration of the impact of targets, performance measurement and audit upon organizational performance itself;

- a shift away from the overwhelmingly statist focus of our work and towards the embracement of the other elements of the plural state;
- the need for rigorous development and testing of new theoretical perspectives, such as of the concept of the 'new public governance' outlined above.

Notes

1 To confuse the picture even more, there are significant differences in the practice of public services management across the national regions of the UK – and especially between England, Scotland and Northern Ireland. Osborne *et al.* (2003), for example, have shown how PSM in England is produced within a plural state, where local government is one of many actors, how in Scotland it is still dominated by a strong service-delivering state and how in Northern Ireland it is the voluntary and community sector (with significant funding from the now defunct EU Peace and Reconciliation Programme) that takes the lead in public services delivery.

2 It is at this point that the trajectories of PSM in England and Scotland begin to diverge significantly, with the managerialist and institutional reforms of public services having far less impact in Scotland than in England. The trajectory discussed here is primarily that experienced in England.

3 This trend was captured at the time in the satirical phrase that characterized public officials as 'jobsworths'. This itself was a contraction of the phrase 'more than my job's worth' to denote the hegemony of rule following over individual judgement in the public bureaucracies).

4 Osborne (2006) makes the point that the term 'governance' is itself open to widely varying theoretical formulations. The use here is rooted within the work of Kickert (1993) and Rhodes (1997) that conceptualizes it as the machinery of 'self-organizing, inter-organizational networks' that function both with and without government to provide public services.

Bibliography

Addy, T. and Scott, D. (1988) *Fatal Impacts? The MSC and Voluntary Action*, Manchester: William Temple Foundation.

Ball, A., Broadbent, J. and Moore, C. (2002) 'Best Value and the control of local government: challenges and contradictions', *Public Money and Management*, 22: 9–16.

Ball, R., Heafey, M. and King, D. (2003) 'Risk transfer and value for money in PFI projects', *Public Management Review*, 5: 279–90.

Beveridge, W. (1948) *Voluntary Action*, London: Allen & Unwin.

Borins, S. (2002) 'New Public Management, North American style', in K. McLaughlin, S. Osborne and E. Ferlie (eds) *The New Public Management. Current Trends and Future Prospects*, London: Routledge.

Bourdillon, A. (1945) *Voluntary Social Services*, London: Methuen.

Bovaird, T. (2006) 'Developing new forms of partnership with the "market" in the procurement of public services', *Public Administration*, 84: 81–102.

Braithwaite, C. (1938) *The Voluntary Citizen*: London: Methuen.

Brandsen, T. and Pestoff, V. (2006) 'Co-production, the third sector and the delivery of public services: an introduction', *Public Management Review*, 8: 493–501.

Brenton, M. (1985) *Voluntary Sector in British Social Services*, London: Longman.

Cabinet Office (1999) *Modernising Government*, London: HMSO.

Chandler, J. (1991) 'Public administration: a discipline in decline', *Teaching Public Administration*, 9: 39–45.

Clarke, M. and Stewart, J. (1998) *Community Governance, Community Leadership and the New Labour Government*, Tork: YPS.

Cole, G. (1932) 'Fabianism. An Essay', in E. Seligman (ed.) *Encyclopaedia of the Social Sciences*, New York: Macmillan.

Cole, G. (1945) 'A retrospect of the history of voluntary social services', in A. Bourdillon (ed.), *Voluntary Social Services*, New York: Macmillan.

Davis Smith, J. (1995) 'The voluntary tradition: philanthropy and self help in Britain 1500–1945', in J. Davis Smith, C. Rochester and R. Hedley (eds) *An Introduction to the Voluntary Sector*, London: Routledge.

Dawson, S. and Dargie, C. (1999) 'New Public Management: an assessment and evaluation with special reference to health', *Public Management Review*, 1: 459–82.

Day, P. and Klein, R. (1987) *Accountabilities*, London: Tavistock.

Deakin, N. (1995) 'The perils of partnership: the voluntary sector and the state 1945–1992', in J. Davis Smith, C. Rochester and R. Hedley (eds) *An Introduction to the Voluntary Sector*, London: Routledge.

Department of Environment, Transport and the Regions [DETR] (1998) *Community-Based Regeneration Initiatives: A Working Paper*, London: DETR.

Dunleavy, P. (1985) 'Bureaucrats, budgets and the growth of the state', *British Journal of Political Science*, 15: 299–328.

Farnham, D. and Horton, S. (eds) (1996) *Managing the New Public Services*, Basingstoke: Macmillan.

Ferlie, E., Ashburner, L., Fitzgerald, L. and Pettigrew, A. (1996) *The New Public Management in Action*, Oxford: Oxford University Press.

Flynn, N. (2002) *Public Sector Management*, London: Prentice Hall.

Gladstone, F. (1979) *Voluntary Action in a Changing World*, London: Bedford Square Press.

Gow, J. and Dufour, C. (2000) 'Is the New Public Management a paradigm? Does it matter?', *International Review of Administrative Sciences*, 66: 573–97.

Gutch, R. (1990) *Partners or Agents?* London: NCVO.

Hartley, G., Butler, M. and Benington, J. (2002) 'Local government modernization: UK and comparative analysis from an organizational perspective', *Public Management Review*, 4: 387–404.

Hill, M. and Hupe, P. (2003) 'The multi-layer problem in implementation research', *Public Management Review*, 5: 471–90.

HM Treasury (2002) *The Role of the Voluntary and Community Sector in Service Delivery. A Cross Cutting Review*, London: HM Treasury.

Hood, C. (1991) 'A public management for all seasons?', *Public Administration*, 69: 3–19.

Hood, C. and Jackson, M. (1991) 'The new public management: a recipe for disaster', *Canberra Bulletin of Public Administration*, May: 16–24.

John, P. (1990) *Recent Trends in Central-Local Government Relations*, London: PSI.

Johnson, C. and Osborne, S. (2003) 'Local Strategic Partnerships, neighbourhood renewal and the limits to co-governance', *Public Money and Management*, 23: 147–54.

Kickert, W. (1993) 'Complexity governance and dynamics: conceptual explorations of public network management', in J. Kooiman (ed.) *Modern Governance*, London: Sage.

Kickert, W. (1997) 'Public governance in the Netherlands: an alternative to Anglo-

American "managerialism" ', *Public Administration*, 75: 731–52.

Knapp, M. (1984) *The Economics of Social Care*, Basingstoke: Macmillan.

Labour Party (1997) *Building The Future Together: Labour's Policies for Partnership Between Government and the Voluntary Sector*, London: Labour Party.

Landry, C., Morley, D., Southwood, R. and Wright, P. (1985) *What a Way to Run a Rail-road: an Analysis of Radical Failure*, London: Comedia.

Lipsky, M. (1979) *Street Level Bureaucracy*, New York: Russell Sage Foundation.

Macadam, E. (1934) *The New Philanthropy*, London: Allen & Unwin.

Mackintosh, M. (1992) 'Partnership: issues of policy and negotiation', *Local Economy*, 7: 210–24.

McLaughlin, K. (2002) 'Lesson drawing from the international experience of moderniz-ing local governance', *Public Management Review*, 4: 405–10.

McLaughlin, K. (2004) 'Towards a "modernized" UK voluntary sector: emerging lessons from government–non-profit relationships', *Public Management Review*, 6: 555–62.

McLaughlin, K., Osborne, S. and Ferlie, E. (eds) (2002) *The New Public Management. Current Trends and Future Prospects*, London: Routledge.

Martin, S. (2002) 'The modernization of UK local government: markets, managers, mon-itors and mixed fortunes', *Public Management Review*, 4: 291–308.

Metcalfe, L. and Richards, S. (1991) *Improving Public Managemen*, London: Sage.

Mischra, R. (1984) *The Welfare State in Crisis*, Brighton: Wheatsheaf.

Niskanen, W. (1971) *Bureaucracy and Representative Government*, Chicago: Aldine-Atherton.

Osborne, S. (1998) 'Partnership. A bridge too far for the voluntary sector?', *Local Economy*, 12: 290–5.

Osborne, S. (2002) 'Public Management across the twentieth century: a review of prac-tice and research', in S. Osborne (ed.) *Public Management: Critical Perspectives*, Volume I, London: Routledge.

Osborne, S. (2006) 'The New Public Governance?', *Public Management Review*, 8: 377–87.

Osborne, S. and Brown, K. (2005) *Managing Innovation and Change in Public Service Organizations*, London: Routledge.

Osborne, S. and McLaughlin, K. (2002) 'Trends and issues in the implementation of local "Voluntary Sector Compacts" in England', *Public Money and Management*, 22: 51–63.

Osborne, S. and McLaughlin, K. (2004) 'The cross-cutting review of the voluntary sector: where next for local government–voluntary sector relationships?', *Regional Studies*, 38: 573–82.

Osborne, S., Beattie, R. and Williamson, A. (2003) 'The national context of local gover-nance: does it matter? Evidence from rural regeneration initiatives in England, North-ern Ireland and Scotland', *Local Governance*, 29: 1–13.

Osborne, S., Bovaird, A., Martin, S., Tricker, M. and Waterston, P. (1995) 'Performance management and accountability in complex public programmes', *Financial Account-ability and Management*, 11: 19–38.

Ostrom, V. and Ostrom, E. (1971) 'Public choice: a different approach to the study of public administration', *Public Administration Review*, 31: 203–16.

Ouchi, W. (1979) 'Markets, bureaucracies and clans', *Administrative Science Quarterly*, 25: 129–41.

Owen, D. (1964) *English Philanthropy 1660–1960*, Cambridge, Mass: Belknapp Press.

Parsons, W. (1996) *Public Policy*, London: Edward Elgar.

Pestoff, V., Brandsen, T. and Osborne, S. (2006) 'Patterns of co-production in public services: some concluding thoughts', *Public Management Review*, 8: 591–5.

Pirie, M (1988) *Privatization: Theory, Practice and Choice*, London: Wildwood House.

Platt, A. (1969) *The Child Savers*, Chicago: University of Chicago Press.

Pollitt, C. and Bouckaert, G. (2004) *Public Management Reform – A Comparative Analysis*, Oxford: Oxford University Press.

Powell, W. (1990) 'Neither market nor hierarchy: network forms of organization', *Research in Organizational Behaviour*, 12: 295–336.

Prochaska, F. (1988) *The Voluntary Impulse*, London: Faber & Faber.

Rhodes, R. (1997) *Understanding Governance*, Buckingham: Open University Press.

Robson, W. (1928) *Justice and Administrative Law*, London: Macmillan.

Schofield, J. (2001) 'Time for a revival? Public policy implementation: a review of the literature and an agenda for future research', *International Journal of Management Reviews*, 3: 245–63.

Schrijvers, A. (1993) 'The management of a larger town. Outcome related performance indicators and organizational control in the public sector', *Public Administration*, 71: 595–603.

Simey, M. (1988) *Democracy Rediscovered: a Study in Police Accountability*, London: Pluto Press.

Stowe, K. (1998) 'Compact on relations between government and the voluntary and community sector in England and Wales', *Public Administration and Development*, 18: 519–22.

Thatcher, M. (1995) *Downing Street Years*, London: Harper Collins.

Tiebout, C. (1956) 'A pure theory of local expenditures', *Journal of Political Economy*, 64: 426–4.

Vickers, J. and Yarrow, G. (1988) *Privatization. An Economic Analysis*, Great Yarmouth: MIT Press.

Walsh, K. (1991) 'Citizens and consumers: marketing and public sector management', *Public Money and Management*, June: 9–16.

Walsh, K. (1994) 'Marketing and public sector management', *European Journal of Marketing*, 28: 63–71.

Webb, S. and Webb, B. (1911) *The Prevention of Destitution*, London: Longman.

Williamson, O. (1988) *Economic Organization*, Brighton: Wheatsheaf.

Wilson, D. (2003) 'Unravelling control freakery: redefining central–local government relations', *British Journal of Politics and International Relations*, 5: 317–46.

Wistow, G., Knapp, K., Hardy, B., Forder, J., Kendall, J. and Manning, R. (1996) *Social Care Markets: Progress and Prospects*, Buckingham: Open University Press.

5 The study of public management in Norway

Combination of organization theory and political science

Tom Christensen and Per Laegreid

Introduction

In this chapter we will illustrate that the study of public administration and management in Norway has to be understood in relation to the particular context of the Norwegian state and the administrative reform and administrative policy that have been conducted over time. The study of public administration and management in Norway represents a combination of organizational theory and political science focusing on empirical studies of decision-making and institutional changes in formal organizations. This special mixture of democratic theory, organization theory and a strong empirical focus has given the Norwegian research on public administration and management a strength and innovation that is internationally acknowledged. There has not been any long-standing and distinct public management study tradition in Norway, partly because most studies of public management reforms has been conducted inside political science/public administration departments, with a political-democratic focus.

We will first give an overview of the history of state and administration in Norway by using four different state models, the centralized state model, the institutional state, the corporatist state model and the super market state model (Olsen 1988). We will have a special focus on recent administrative reforms and policies from the mid-1980s onwards. Second, we will give a brief overview of the development and state of Norwegian academic study of public administration and management. Third, we will address more thoroughly the Norwegian characteristics of the development of research on Norwegian public administration and management by distinguishing between three periods of research. Finally, we will sum up some of the main features and challenges for the future.

History of state and administration[1]

Historical development of the central Norwegian governmental apparatus

The centralized state model is built on a structural view of governance, emphasizing central control by political and administrative leaders and public structures consciously designed and redesigned to further collective goals (Egeberg 2003; March and Olsen 1983; Olsen 1992). It covers both the constitutional design of public powers and the internal organization of public bodies.

The Norwegian Constitution of 1814 was built on a Montesquieu-like concept of public governance. It marked the finish of Norway's 400 years of subordination to Denmark and the start of about 90 years of subordination to Sweden in a union. The king and his advisers formed the executive. The Storting – or parliament – was relatively weak, elected by only a small sector of the population and dominated by a class of civil servants; until 1884, the Storting was not based on political parties. From the beginning, judicial power was relatively weak and it has remained of low political significance. In 1814 the central administrative apparatus changed from a collegial structure to a hierarchical structure dominated by seven ministries and by judicial expertise (Christensen 2003).

Two major changes occurred in the central political-administrative system during the nineteenth century. In the 1830s, professional groups began demanding independent administrative bodies outside the ministries. The breakthrough came in the 1850s, when there was a rapid increase in the number of such bodies, with a second wave in the 1870s (Christensen 2003). These central agencies grew faster than the ministries and imitated the Swedish model with its relatively autonomous bodies. Second, there was organized opposition to the king in the Storting by a coalition of urban radicals and nationalist-minded farmers. This opposition established the parliamentary principle in 1884 and coincided with the birth of the first two parties, the Conservatives and the Liberals. After 1884, executive power was based on parliamentary parties and had a neutral and professional civil service at its disposal that prepared and implemented public policy.

This loss of the king's personal power potentially created an alliance between the Storting and the cabinet. The increasingly close connection between the executive and the legislature consolidated and increased the strength of the central state. When the union between Norway and Sweden was dissolved in 1905, Norway had a well-established centralized state tradition. The period between 1884 and 1940 was characterized by greater reluctance to accept independent agencies for fear of undermining central control.

After World War II the Labour Party stood at the forefront of a strong build-up of the centralized state, and the party had a majority in parliament from 1946 to 1961. It maintained close connections with the new group of key civil servants – the economists – based on a shared belief in technical rationality and strong central capacity and central planning to solve societal problems (Slagstad 1998). This led to the introduction of more laws, the delegation of authority from the legislature to the executive, and delegation by the political leadership in the executive to the administrative leaders and to various ranks of the civil service. It also led to increased specialization and complexity inside the central administrative apparatus (Olsen 1983). There was a rapid growth in the number of central agencies and directorates from the mid-1950s until the early 1970s, stemming from the new administrative doctrine that technically oriented tasks and institutions should be hived off in order to take the burden off the political executive. Overall the changes in the central administrative apparatus since World War II have led to the elaboration and growth of the central state, despite some delegatory features.

The institutional state emerges

Features of an institutional state model, with a gradual development of cultural identities, loyalties and informal shared norms and values in political and administrative institutions, can be discerned quite early in the development of the centralized Norwegian state. In his analysis of the national strategists, Slagstad (1998) describes not only their programs and support for the central state but also the parallel development of the institutional state. Central politicians tried to channel cultural and collective interaction into furthering public goals. The state was important for creating a good society and enhancing moral progress.

Central actors saw state institutions as creating and supporting norms in an integrative way, forming a social consensus. United by a common commitment to the political-democratic process, different cultural elites formed a reformist coalition, which integrated a broad range of popular groups into the political-administrative system and later furthered the integration of the labor movement into the same system. The idea of political identity formed the cultural basis of the Labour Party state after World War II. The state was seen as a powerful cultural body encompassing the dual identities of nationalism and class, and the latter was mobilized to support the national project. This project aimed at expanding the welfare state and the educational system after World War II (Slagstad 1998: 202).

Other more general cultural features can also be found. Norway is historically a homogeneous society with many shared norms and values and a low level of conflict. This is reflected in the political-administrative system (Christensen and Peters 1999). The cabinet in Norway has comparatively strong collegial features, favoring consensus and working as a team (Christensen and Lægreid 2002; Eriksen 1988). Politicians and central civil servants have a long tradition of sharing values and mutual trust. The Storting has strong norms of consensus and collectivity, and its relationship to the executive has traditionally been good and built on trust. Most citizens trust both central political and administrative institutions and individual political and administrative actors (Listhaug and Wiberg 1995) and the system is traditionally characterized more by meta-rules, strong norm-building and socializing institutions than by detailed formal rules and incentive systems (Christensen and Peters 1999).

The corporatist state after World War II

Historically, the corporatist state model, with formal, extensive, integrated organizational participation in government, and with the state as an arena for bargaining and conflict resolution, is primarily relevant for understanding governance in Norway after the Second World War (Olsen 1983). After World War I, the intensity of the relationship between the public sector and interest groups grew, but it remained informal. Following World War II, this relationship increased substantially in intensity and became more and more formal. It arose out of dependence, from the need for expertise and the right of participation. This feature fostered homogeneity and strengthened the centralized state. Interest groups were seen as important actors in the collective effort to build the welfare state and they not only influenced policy development and represented special interests but were also major partners in policy implementation.

The mixed or negotiated economy tradition for interest groups and the political control of companies is different from the Anglo-American tradition. It has become one of the most comprehensive national consultative and bargaining communities in the world and today encompasses nearly 3,000 national interest groups (Christensen 2003). Consultation and bargaining take place in various ways: via the organizational public committees, boards, the hearings system, the delegation of public authority, wage negotiations and informal contact. Although the system incorporates many interests, it is nonetheless dominated by large interest groups like the big trade unions and the employers' organizations because these have many administrative resources and members. The system links the civil service and interest groups, while politicians are less frequently involved (Olsen 1983).

The central state since the 1980s – a period of gradual transformation

The last two decades of the twentieth century brought challenges to the centralized state model, primarily through structural devolution. The creation of more independent agencies and state-owned companies meant that subordinate organizational units were moved further away from political executive leaders (Christensen and Lægreid 2003). Nevertheless, Norway for some time continued to be labeled a 'reluctant reformer' (Olsen 1996). In the period 2001–2005, however, the new Centre-Conservative government has adopted some major ideas from the neo-liberalist doctrine and the supermarket state model (Self 2000). In addition, the institutional and corporatist models, which have historically supported the centralized state, have been modified. The election in 2005 brought a Red–Green coalition into government, but its administrative policy is ambiguous and conflict-ridden. In the following, we will outline some of these developments and ask whether they have in fact transformed the centralized state.

Structural devolution

In the 1970s, devolution came about mainly as a response to the capacity problems posed by new tasks and policies at the central level. Decentralization to the regional level was re-established, and some tasks were assigned to the local level. In the 1980s, however, devolution went a step further, with the introduction of structural devolution in the central administrative apparatus. One element was internal structural devolution – ordinary agencies were given more autonomy and new independent regulatory agencies were established (Christensen and Lægreid 2003). A more formalized performance-assessment regime has been established. This development has not aroused much controversy among political and administrative leaders (Christensen and Lægreid 2002). Another development has been the autonomization of regulatory agencies, often giving them more formal autonomy than ordinary agencies mentioned above. This has been combined with an increase in horizontal differentiation of the roles and tasks of agencies, according to the principle of 'single purpose organisations'. This has been much more contested and ambiguous. What we see is a parallel process of 'agencification', autonomization and re-regulation, where the main picture is that agencies/regulatory agencies are given more autonomy, but also exposed to more control and scrutiny systems (Christensen and Lægreid 2006).

The second element of structural devolution was external structural devolution, comprising the establishment of new autonomous state-owned companies (SOCs). Until 1992, major public domains, like the railways, telecommunications, airport administration, road construction, the power supply, postal services, forestry, grain sales and public broadcasting, were organized as central agencies or more integrated government-administrated enterprises. Since then, the commercial parts of these enterprises have been corporatized, i.e. established as various types of SOCs, while the regulatory parts have retained their agency form. This development began when the Labour Party in the 1980s gradually began to accept more of the central ideas of New Public Management (Christensen and Lægreid 2003), i.e. attending more to market forces. This constituted a break with Norwegian public tradition, which emphasizes equality and standardization (Brunsson and Olsen 1993; Christensen 2003). The last and most controversial development in this direction, partly privatising Statoil and Telenor in 2000, created much conflict within the Labour Party.

These changes undermined central political control over state-owned companies. The formal instruments of control were weakened and the ownership and regulator roles made more passive (Christensen and Lægreid 2001c). The result is that actors in SOCs now pay less attention to political signals (Christensen and Lægreid 1998a) and there is a tendency to define political involvement in public enterprises as 'inappropriate' interference in business matters. When the political executive has lost influence, the parliament has stepped forward, trying to fill the gap (Christensen *et al.* 2002), but administrative leaders have also gained influence, like directors of agencies and state-owned enterprises (Christensen and Lægreid 2002). The principle of ministerial responsibility is still firmly supported, even though the political leadership has less control than before (Christensen and Lægreid 2001c). Conversely, the actors gaining influence are not any more accountable than before, which may be seen as a challenge to democracy.

Increased control by the parliament

The NPM-inspired reforms of the 1990s also strengthened the Office of the Auditor General, thus allowing the Storting to exert more control, power of scrutiny and oversight over the executive. The increased emphasis on perform-ance auditing and the revitalization of the Standing Committee on Scrutiny and Constitutional Affairs led to more focus on oversight (Gunvaldsen and Karlsen 1999). This also takes the form of open committee hearings, spontaneous ques-tion time with ministers, and more active parliamentary investigations. This policy is new. Traditionally the Storting has been passive in its control of the executive (Christensen and Peters 1999). It could further effectiveness in the control function, but also create more conflict between the legislature and the executive, because their relationship is now more formally and adversely defined and no longer seen primarily as a close relationship based on a shared culture (Christensen and Lægreid 2002). There may also be more tension between political and administrative leaders inside the civil service, because there may be more blame-avoidance and risk-averse behavior (Christensen *et al.* 2002).

Accountability and the institutional state model

The institutional state model is relevant for analyzing the changing role of civil servants under NPM. Under NPM, accountability is based on output or results, competition, transparency and contractual relations and thus represents a depar-ture from public administration of the old school, where various forms of accountability were based on process and procedures, hierarchical control, trust and cultural traditions (Christensen and Lægreid 2001c). There has been a shift from simple to complex models of accountability.

In administrative reforms like NPM, much attention has been paid to man-agerial accountability and very little to political responsibility on a cultural basis. By managerial accountability we mean the obligation to account for one's actions 'to' those in superior positions of authority. Responsibility, on the other hand, is accepted 'for' the actions of oneself or others and is a more subjectively felt sense of obligation. To be responsible connotes the ability to act as well as simply to report and implies a concern for the consequences of this action. There is a moral flavour, as emphasized in the institutional state model, missing from managerial accountability (Martin 1997). The main concern in the institutional state model is following rules and the assumption is that the moral element is embedded in the rules. So accountability under NPM seems to reflect a shift from traditional cultural norms of integration and trust to a more instrumental and formal way of defining the role the civil servants, building more on distrust.

NPM, interest groups and the consumer focus

NPM can be seen as a reaction to the corporatist state model (Olsen 1988: 244), which is perceived by its critics as too rigid, sectorized, expansive and expen-sive, and special interests are considered to be too powerful in public policy-making. According to this view, the state needs to maintain a certain distance and independence from the various interests in order to govern. Integrated organizational representation in public decision-making is seen more as a threat to democratic governance than as an extension of democracy. The corporate state implies a non-transparent process of negotiation in which responsibility for the final outcome is often unclear. In Scandinavia, interest groups have traditionally had a high standing in public decision-making processes and civil service unions are seen as vital participants in reform processes (Lægreid and Roness 2000; Olsen 1983). This tradition came under pressure in the 1990s.

In 1982 the Conservative government, drawing on the findings of the first Power Study, a trail-blazing large research project initiated by the government, proposed a substantial cut in the number of public committees (Nordby 2000). These features led to less contact with the civil service and a slight change in the role of interest groups (Christensen 2003). One effect of such a change has been an increase in lobbying of the Storting by interest groups, partly helped by professional lobbying firms (Christensen and Rommetvedt 1999).

NPM has also brought variety in the strategies of interest groups. Some of the unions connected with the Labour Party have continued to defend traditional values and have opposed any changes in the public sector inspired by an increased market orientation. Others have adjusted to the new values, or at least tried to reach some compromise with the modernizers.

Towards a supermarket state?

Historically speaking, Norway has adopted few features of the supermarket state model. Economic norms and values have traditionally counted for less than political control, professional expertise, institutional rights and participation by affected groups. Introducing the rule of the market has not been compatible with the Norwegian public tradition, which emphasizes equality and standardization (Brunsson and Olsen 1993). On the contrary, Norway has been characterized by strong regulation of the private sector – the so-called mixed or negotiated economy system (Christensen 2003).

The supermarket state of the 1980s was introduced rather reluctantly and encompassed many different strands. The main supporters of the supermarket state reforms have been liberal and conservative politicians, supported by business leaders, leaders of state companies and business economists. They have argued that a leaner state is more efficient and effective and offers better and more transparent political control. The supermarket state, in their view, must respond to environmental-deterministic pressures (Olsen 1992), such as economic globalization, adaptation to the EU and international institutional pressure from Anglo-American countries and the OECD. Traditionally, the socialist and social democratic parties in Norway have opposed the supermarket state reforms, and they have been supported in this opposition by the trade unions and civil servants' unions connected with the Labour Party. Their arguments emphasized their determination to retain control over the economy and to resist market principles that undermine democracy and create inequality. The key element in the changes stemming from the supermarket state tradition has been the Labour Party's gradual acceptance of some its elements. This is seen by some as controversial but by others as a political necessity.

The NPM reforms in the Norwegian civil service started slowly in the late 1980s and gained momentum from the mid-1990s onwards (Christensen and Lægreid 2001b; Olsen 1996). These reforms are not identical to the neo-liberal and political-ideological supermarket reforms, but they have some common features. The Norwegian way of adopting NPM reforms is more pragmatic and leans more towards the managerial tools of NPM than towards the market tools. They are primarily confined to management by objectives (MBO); increased structural differentiation of the roles and functions of the government to cater to the need for increased market competition and contracting-out; the structural devolution of agencies and state-owned companies; and increased managerial autonomy and the use of leadership contracts. There have also been client-oriented changes in service contracts and the introduction of one-stop shops. However, over the last five to ten years some more controversial changes have been implemented, including the partial privatization of major SOCs, the government takeover of the hospitals, turning them into health enterprises and adoption of the 'money-follows-the patient' principle, a partly market-oriented reform of the higher education system and the reform and relocation of regulatory agencies. Whether these reforms symbolize the breakthrough of the supermarket state tradition in Norway is unclear. If we look at the history of reforms it appears likely that the more radical changes will be modified and packaged in a 'Norwegian' way. Norwegian civil servants tend to stick to traditional norms and are skeptical about radical NPM reforms because of political and professional considerations, even though their role is gradually becoming more complex as they begin to accept some modernist values. NPM is more widely accepted among administrative executives than among civil servants, particularly those with judicial backgrounds working on individual cases. Most of the political executive leaders seem to be either traditionalists or cautious modernizers, and few of them support radical reforms (Christensen and Lægreid 2002). SOE directors are the most keen and radical modernizers.

The Red–Green alliance coming to power in 2005 ran pretty much on an anti-NPM ticket, arguing that NPM reforms should be stopped or modified because of their negative consequences, such as reduced political control and more fragmentation. This view was particularly interesting coming from the Labour Party, which had previously been seen as supporting NPM. The crucial question is whether the anti-NPM rhetoric will result in major changes. The government has already started to modify or stop some of the NPM-style reforms, but there are doubts about whether the Labour Party will really pursue anti-NPM measures or simply continue with NPM-inspired reforms at a somewhat slower pace. The best example of a policy confronting the NPM-inspired reforms is that the government has tried to modify the effects of the new competition law by saying no to some decisions from the competition agency, thereby attending more to wider political concerns.

Summing up, this analysis has shown the interweaving of different state models and traditions and how the tradition of the centralized state has developed in a dynamic relationship with the institutional state and the corporatist state. History shows that new ideas have been adapted to the long-standing traditions of Norwegian government. A crucial question is, therefore, whether this will also be the case for the supermarket state. Up till now, the supermarket state elements have been incorporated as an elaboration of the central state, without threatening its basic values and ideas.

Study of public administration

In Norway there is not a strong distinction between political science and public administration, and the latter is not a separate discipline. Neither is public management a separate discipline or distinct field of study. The study of public administration is one of four subfields of political science. The other three are political theory, comparative politics and international politics. It is a rather new discipline. In 1965 Knut Dahl Jacobsen became the first professor of political science to be appointed in Norway, at the University of Oslo. He came to Bergen in 1969 to establish the field of 'Public Administration and Organization Theory'. He was one of the key entrepreneurs and institution builders in the field until his death in 1998.

In contrast to many other countries, organization theory in Norway has not moved into the business schools. What is unique about the study of public administration founded by Dahl Jacobsen is the combination of political science and organization theory. Such a combination of general political science theory with an emphasis on public administration and public policy and theories on organizational behaviour was an important academic innovation when the field emerged. It was unusual both in Norway and internationally (March 1997). However, it has been a fruitful fusion, which several universities and colleges in Norway have since imitated. Unlike what has happened in many other countries, the development of Norwegian political science has been marked by the fact that organizational theory soon received a relatively central position in the multitude of approaches used. In universities, organizational theory has been closely tied to the different academic fields, and the study of public administration has not been singled out as an individual speciality, academically and organizationally independent of political science, in the way it usually has in other European countries and in the US.

Johan P. Olsen has been one of the most influential researchers in the field of administration and organization theory since the beginning of the 1970s. He became a professor in Bergen in 1972 and he was a leader of the Study of the Distribution of Power in Norway, which was the most important individual research project on the generation of empirical knowledge on the political-administrative system of governance in Norway. In the 1980s, Johan P. Olsen also served as a research director on the Swedish Power Project, and he played an important part in the establishment of the Norwegian Research Centre in

Organization and Management in Bergen in 1987. In 1993, Johan P. Olsen established ARENA at the University of Oslo, which is a research program on Europeanization of the national state. He has contributed more than anyone else to the international reputation of the Norwegian public administration research. He has made a number of important contributions to concept- and theory-formation in the fields of organization theory and public administration. Examples include the 'garbage can' model (March and Olsen 1976) and neo-institutionalism (March and Olsen 1989, 1995).

Today's public administration research is rooted in a Norwegian organizational-theoretical political science tradition. This program integrated Herbert Simon's organizational-theoretical approach, based on the notion of bounded rationality, with empirical studies of the Norwegian public administration's structure and actual mode of operation. Decision-makers have limited time, attention and analytical capacity in relation to the tasks and problems with which they are confronted, and their attitudes and actions are influenced by the organizational structure within which they work and by the external environment to which they are connected (Simon 1957).

Key to the development of this direction in Norway is Johan P. Olsen's cooperation with James G. March and their combination of organizational theory, democratic theory and the study of decision-making behavior in formal organizations (Egeberg and Lægreid 1999). Their particular contribution over the later decades has been to introduce institutional perspectives in analyses of the political-administrative system's organization and functioning. Over the last years, we have witnessed an increasing pluralism in theoretical perspectives and frames of reference in the study of public organizations and institutions in Norway. Today's public administration research and its theoretical basis constitute an interdisciplinary field of research. It is still dominated by people trained in the combination of organization theory and political science, but historians, business economists, sociologists and people coming from other disciplines are also studying public administration. The study of public administration still has a stronghold at the universities but has spread to colleges, external research institutes and also to business schools focusing especially on public management issues.

The study of public administration and management in Norway has attracted many students who have moved into the civil service, and has resulted in many research projects that have developed new theoretical and empirical insight in how the political-administrative system in Norway works in practice and changes over time.

Research on public administration and public management[2]

The research tradition of studying public administration in Norway paints a picture of a public administration integrated into complex political and societal networks (Olsen 1983). It is a story of interplay between competing contexts, logics, loyalties and influences, demanding competing models of decision-making and change that can elaborate on the insight given by the Weberian ideal model. It shows how a strong theoretical tradition based on bounded rationality and studies of political and administrative leadership are supplemented first by theories and empirical studies of heterogeneity, and later by different types of institutional theories. Norway has a strong empirically oriented tradition of independent research, studying the functioning, change and reforms of public administration through large research programs. The knowledge obtained through these programs has been channeled back to the public apparatus, reflected in terminology, new insight and reforms.

Three periods may be distinguished in public administration research in Norway. The pioneer period, the breakthrough period, and the last 15 years that has been characterized by continuity, growth and variation.

The pioneer period

Political science in Norway is rooted in the disciplines of law and history, but gradually the field gained more independent features throughout the 1960s. Organization theory gained a central position in public administration research, and a transition occurred from constitution analysis to organization analysis. After World War II, Norway was more societal and scientifically oriented towards the US than before, a development that was amplified by the behavioral revolution, and this also led to more emphasis on the seminal organizational works of people like Simon (1957). This theoretical basis of future public administration research also had a practical potential – to contribute to the education of means-end-oriented political scientists who could challenge the rule-oriented jurists that had long dominated the civil service (Eckhoff and Jacobsen 1960). It has also had a lasting impact on the practice of public administration through the increasing role of people educated in public administration and policy in the civil service, particularly from the 1970s. Jacobsen was a trail-blazer in researching the role of civil servants, and his doctoral thesis of 1964 on the development of the central agricultural administration was very advanced at the time (Jacobsen 1964).

Jacobsen was also concerned with the development of the value basis and cultural norms in public administration, inspired by Simon's distinction between value and factual premises. He emphasized variety, complexity and conflicting loyalties in the administrative role, but also general mechanisms, norms and values in the relationship between politicians and civil servants. He put public bureaucracy in an explicit political-democratic context, with dynamic and active relations to the political leadership and actors in the civil society. The focus was on how tensions and inconsistency between the problem structure and organizational structure, between the demands of the society and the professional administration's answer, created a potential for change. He also provided insight into the relations between the internal administrative condition, professions, political leadership and external client interests, and this has later led to many empirical studies of the interest of clients, partly with a normative edge.

The pioneer period emphasized theoretical ideas about complexity of the administrative role in a democratic context, and how these ideas could be carried out in specific sector-oriented case studies. Norwegian public administration research during these founding years was built on a tradition of theoretically oriented and empirically based studies of decision-making in formal organizations, which in general have shown that rational decision-making models must be elaborated and modified, and is thereby connected to an important line of theory development.

The great leap forward

The great leap forward in Norwegian public administration research was the Power Study in the period 1972–1982, which examined the central administration and the corporative system. The focus was on actors who represented formal organizations, and how their models of thought and action, their decision premises and decision behavior are formed by the organization and the organizational context they belong to. The Garbage Can model also contributed to the theoretical basis of the Power Study (March and Olsen 1976). It implied a more general analytical scheme and central concepts for analyzing public decision-making processes that were widely used in the study and later on. But it was also a more specific decision-making model that established a basis for the study of loosely coupled organizations and non-routine decision-making situations. The role that simultaneity, ambiguity and symbols might play for decision outcome was highlighted.

Also an interest in a prescriptive approach to administrative research emerged, and the question was raised whether political science could be regarded as an 'architectural discipline', i.e. giving new insight into the relationship between the formal governmental structures and their effects, and thereby a potential for conscious design by political and administrative leaders based on this knowledge (Olsen 1982). This prescriptive line has been further developed into a design model, which elaborates the knowledge base for decision-making and professional working practices (Egeberg 1994 and 2003). This type of theory has been applied to studies of administrative-political processes and their effects, and has also focused on normative questions (Roness 2006).

Empirically, the Power Study focused on the factors that shape administrative structures, changes and effects. A broad empirical program was outlined, and was followed up by case studies of the public administration and its relations with the environment. A number of surveys of individual decision-makers in the ministries and the interest organizations were also carried out. The broad survey of the civil service was the basis of a study of the organization of knowledge, beliefs, authority and interests in the ministries (Lægreid and Olsen 1978). The relative explanatory power of two analytical models – the responsible and the representative bureaucracy – for the beliefs and the contact and control patterns of the civil servants was analyzed. This study not only showed the importance of the organization structure for decision-making, but also modified the conception of a uniform administrative apparatus and argued that the civil service was characterized by heterogeneity and institutional pluralism.

The civil service survey was repeated in 1986, 1996 and 2006, now also including the central agencies. Adding to the continuity from the former surveys, new trends were also discussed, for example through studies of the 'Europeanization' of the public administration and of New Public Management reforms in the civil service (Christensen and Lægreid 1998b). Supplementing the surveys, a long tradition of case studies of reorganization and reform processes in the central civil service was continued in this period, showing the considerable significance of the political and administrative leadership in the processes of reorganization.

Analyses of organizational demography and personnel policies, adding to the understanding of organizational structure, can also be traced back to the Power Study. One study of how demographic and organizational factors influence decision-making in administrative agencies characterized by considerable mobility was conducted in the public petroleum bureaucracies (Lægreid 1988). The research on recruiting and mobility patterns, workplace democracy and other aspects of salary and personnel policy in public administration has shown that these aspects of administrative policy cannot be reduced to technical/administrative questions.

The Power Study did not focus so much on the political leadership, but there was a study on how the content of the cabinet's decision-making was influenced by the organizational frameworks within which it was operating (Olsen 1983). The study showed that the political leadership is confronted with problems of capacity, understanding and authority, which are managed through increased specialization and negotiation, both within the administrative apparatus and with organized interests in society. Further studies showed that various organizational models of the relation between ministries and directorates have different implications for political governance and professional autonomy (Christensen and Lægreid 2002). The balance between political and professional premises in the administrative role has been analysed by using the concept of loyalty, neutrality and professional autonomy (Jacobsen 1960). The conclusion is that a certain ambiguity in their role enables civil servants to handle complexity and to integrate opposing values in the decision-making process.

Regarding the more specific external networks of the central administration, a main argument in the Power Study was that parliamentary power in relation to the civil service is characterized by cycles (Olsen 1978). The relationship between the Storting and the civil service goes through phases of detraction and contraction, emphasizing different trade-offs between political control and administrative discretion and autonomy. Studies of later periods appear to support the view that the power relationship has not necessarily been displaced to the disadvantage of the Storting, something that reflects decades of minority governments (Hernes and Nergaard 1990; Nordby 2000).

The pattern of contact between the civil service and the interest organizations was given considerable attention in the Power Study and in subsequent studies (Egeberg 1981; Olsen 1983). Surveys showed that the interest organizations were closely integrated into public policy and that the pattern of participation in the various forms was biased towards large interest groups. The 'segmented state' was advanced as a concept to characterize decision arenas consisting of specialized politicians, civil servants and interest group representatives (Egeberg *et al.* 1978). Later studies questioned the relevance of the segmentation thesis to the Norwegian administrative system today (Rommetvedt 2002).

The Power Study had different effects, theoretically, empirically and professionally. First, it developed and showed the empirical relevance of a systematically theoretical framework based in bounded rationality and theories focusing on the importance of formal organization structure in public administration. This influenced a whole new generation of then-young scholars who later took up positions in universities and colleges, furthering these theoretical ideas. Second, it participated, through new textbooks and expanded public administration education opportunities, in producing a whole new generation of civil servants. The last two decades have seen political scientists as the fastest-growing group in the central civil service. Third, by introducing new concepts and approaches to the study of the political-administrative system, it influenced the political and administrative leaders' vocabulary, and the image of public administration more generally. Through these processes, the practice of the political-administrative system has also been affected. More emphasis was put on the challenge from corporative arrangements on political governance; on the consequences of designing the public administration in certain ways; on the complexity of interests and considerations of doing so; and on institutionalizing an administrative policy. The Power Study was rather focused both theoretically and empirically, but this feature gives a background for the 'opening up' of public administration research in the next period.

Continuity, growth and pluralism

The last two decades have been characterized by continuity, growth and variety in public administration studies in Norway. The growth in the number of administrative studies has been substantial. There is, however, also a tendency toward theoretical pluralism and more variety in methods, analytical foci and empirical areas studied.

The theory development in this period is mostly related to different types of institutional theory. March and Olsen (1989) have outlined a broad institutional perspective on analyses of public administration and policies. It was founded on three basic ideas: that human action is based on a logic of appropriateness, that meaning is constructed through political and social processes and that institutions normally adapt slowly to their environments. This perspective is mainly formulated as an alternative to economic perspectives in political science and public administration, but can also be seen as elaboration on the theory of bounded rationality. A central hypothesis according to this perspective is that institutional features have a major impact on how public administration reacts to reforms and attempts at political control. March and Olsen emphasize that politics has both an instrumental and a symbolic or 'creation of meaning' side, and they stress the important distinction between aggregative and integrative processes in politics. In their latest book (March and Olsen 1995), the focus is more on the development of identity and the discretion for democratic governance. In this regard, they specifically emphasize the development of political capabilities, as well as political accounts and adaptiveness, thereby coming back to some important Weberian elements, but from a different angle.

Olsen (1988) outlined, as mentioned, different government or state models, of an instrumental and cultural flavour. Institutional-cultural theories, seeing public organizations as 'institutionalized organizations', have increasingly been used in empirical studies of public administration (Christensen and Lægreid 2001a; Christensen and Peters 1999). Another more social-constructive school has also inspired Norwegian researchers in their studies of public sector reforms. Often labeled the myth or fashion/fad perspective, these theoretical ideas focus on the 'institutional environment'. Røvik (1998) has especially been developing such a perspective on studies of changes in public administration and emphasizes that organizations are 'multi-standard organizations', combining institutional components from different 'organization fields'. Christensen and Lægreid (2001a) have developed and used a transformative perspective on public reforms, by discussing the dynamic relationship between environmental, structural and cultural factors. In a book on organization theory for the public sector, public administration scholars try to integrate an instrumental, a cultural and a myth perspective on public organizations, underlining the specific features of public sector organizations in contrast to private sector organizations (Christensen *et al.* 2007).

The development of theory on political and administrative institutions has increasingly been related to political theory and democratic theory and there has been an increasing interest in communicative rationality and deliberative and discursive aspects of politics (Eriksen 1993). An increasing interest in normative questions in public administration research has appeared, in discussions of the limits of governmental control and regulation, the question of identity building and the relation between state and society. Public administration research in Norway in this period has tried to supplement and challenge a one-sided economic analysis of public administration, politics and society. Instead the functioning of public administration has been characterized and analyzed on the basis of a democratic-political perspective, in which the value-, interest-, knowledge- and power-basis of the public sector has been emphasized.

Studies of administrative policies and politics have shown that reform processes in Norway have often been characterized by compromise and an apolitical rhetoric, creating incremental results. The link between talk and action (see Brunsson 1989) and between general attitudes, specific solutions and actual implementation, has not always been very tight. Even though general comprehensive programs of administrative policy have been formulated, a segmented public administration has to a large extent created segmented reforms. Compared to the political-administrative doctrines in effect in the central administration until the 1970s, with strong centralization, standardization and rule-following, studies have shown a development in the last decade towards relatively more devolution, increased flexibility, more management by objectives and results, and increased market-orientation. The result is a more complex and fragmented state. Now studies are emerging that show a reassertion of the center and increase emphasis on coordination (Christensen and Lægreid 2007).

In the last decade, more attention has been given to studies of the internationalization of political processes, understood as the development of more extensive networks of transactions and organizations among countries. Traditional studies of foreign policy decision-making processes have been supplemented by transnational policy perspectives and the idea that a fourth system level exists in addition to the traditional three characterizing domestic political processes. There is a growing interest in the implications of globalization and internationalization on public administration, and a central set of questions analyzed in the ARENA program includes to what extent and in what ways processes of Europeanization influence national institutions of governance in small countries like Norway (Egeberg 2006). The domestic, administrative institutions have adapted to European integration in an incremental and differentiated manner, and supranational allegiances have become supplements to domestic and national identities and role perceptions (Sverdrup 2000; Trondal 2001; Veggedal 2004).

The realization that it is impossible to understand the development of the Norwegian public administration from an internal, domestic point of view alone has led to a greater interest in comparative studies between countries. Examples here are studies of agriculture policy in Norway, Sweden and the United Kingdom (Steen 1988), studies of official statistics in Norway and Great Britain (Sangolt 1997), studies of environmental policy and of administrative policies in the Nordic countries, and studies of variations among OECD countries concerning administrative reforms and changes. Governance in Norway and USA has been studied comparatively, as well as the consequences of Europeanization on central public administration in the Nordic countries (Christensen and Peters 1999; Jacobsson *et al.* 2004). Christensen, Lægreid and associates (2001a) have compared New Public Management reforms in Australia, New Zealand, Norway and Sweden, and show variety in process and effects based on different combinations of environmental, political and cultural constraints.

In 1998 the Government launched a second study of Power and Democracy in Norway. This time, public administration research was more modest compared to the prominence it had in the first Power Study. The study concluded that the parliamentary chain of government is weakened, the state is transformed according to a liberalist program, and more fragmented, the local democracy is depoliticized and the traditional corporatist system is declining. All this leads to an erosion of the rule by popular consent and decline in the quality of representative democracy (Østerud and Selle 2006).

The increased theoretical variety in public administration research during this last period has resulted in more theoretical complexity that challenges the use of institutional theories in empirical research. The widening of the empirical focus has resulted in useful insights about the effects of the international and transnational context on our political-administrative system, which supplements internal perspectives. The price of more theoretical pluralism and more variety in the empirical area studied is more fragmented and less focused research programs.

Why the lack of focus on public management?

Compared to many European countries, and also the US, there is an evident lack of public management theories and studies in Norway. This is mostly connected with the early dominance of the integration of public administration theory with political science and democratic theory, and also the resulting dominance of research based on this theory. Early on, it was more natural to talk about political control and democratic aspects than public management and technical and economic aspects of public leadership. The institutional set-up, with PA theory and studies emanating more from the political science departments of universities and colleges than from business schools, also supported this. These departments have dominated the research done, produced the relevant textbooks and been behind the strong influx of political scientists (many PA-educated) into the central civil service. Another important aspect has been that Norway for a long time was a reluctant reformer, rather late in bringing the management terminology into the public eye.

When the modern reforms started to influence Norwegian public organizations, particularly from the 1990s, we saw some deviations from this pattern. Some political scientists in public administration research groups seem to warm more to the ideas of NPM, and use more economically related perspectives, without being actual rational-choice theorists of a genuine caliber, which is quite common in several political science or public administration departments in the US, for example. In the two business schools in Norway, we see however, a slow build-up of units, positions and study programs that are related to public management. These are composed of more rational-choice-oriented political scientists or economists. Relative to the public administration research at the universities, these groups are rather weak, but increasingly active (Johnsen 2006). An interesting observation is that some central professors in these groups headed several public committees during the Centre-Conservative government 2001–2005, driving different NPM-related reforms and furthering a normative agenda.

Main features and challenges in the future

In this chapter we have shown that the Norwegian central state apparatus was established nearly 200 years ago as a centralized entity, and has since then been both deepened and challenged by institutional, cultural-institutional and market-economic features. Likewise, the research on the central public apparatus started out in the 1950s, attending to a bounded rational model of analysis, well suited to analyzing the centralized state, but has since then been diversified and developed into institutional theories that can help us understand other developmental features of the modern Norwegian state. A systematic, cumulative and growing research effort has increased the knowledge base regarding the role of public administration in the Norwegian political-administrative system and contributed to clarifying the conditions that influence the actual behaviour, effects and changes in public administration. The special mixture of political science and organization theory has given Norwegian public administration research a relatively stronger theoretical profile than comparable research in many other countries. This theoretical basis has been used to formulate and conduct large empirical studies. March (1997) argues that these are all features that were typical in public administration research in the US until the 1960s, a tradition that was later lost.

A strong argument in the Norwegian research community in this field is that public administration plays a key role in the political-administrative system. Political processes and the content of public policy cannot be fully understood without considering the structure and practice of public administration (Christensen *et al.* 2002). Norwegian public administration research shows continuity through its focus on the political features and the democratic context of civil service, on formal structure, bounded rationality and internal processes. But it has also been characterized by a development from the intraorganizational approach to the interorganizational, to greater interest for comparative studies and internationalization of public administration. Static analyses have been supplemented by dynamic process studies and studies of effects, experiential learning and institutional change.

The criticism of theories of rational choice has gradually expanded; first emphasizing bounded rationality, then temporal logic, and finally the logic of appropriateness. If we make a distinction between analytical-descriptive studies (where the attention is directed towards how the central administration actually is working), prescriptive studies (which are more preoccupied with how public administration can function) and normative studies (focusing on how the public administration should or ought to work), we will conclude that the analytical-descriptive studies have had a dominant position in Norwegian research on public administration. However, the prescriptive and normative studies have been strengthened over time, especially in the last decade.

The development of public administration research in Norway is very much related to a few entrepreneurs and the tightly coupled network of researchers. The principal scholars are James G. March and Johan P. Olsen. Through their 40 years' cooperation and through the research unit Scancor at Stanford University, they have more than anyone else inspired Norwegian public administration research. This feature reflects Norway as a small country where coordinated research efforts are possible, the openness of the political-administrative system towards research, the willingness to give resources to such efforts, and the solid position of such research early on among decision-makers and public opinion. The cycles of the research indicated are related to the gradual maturing and development of the specific research field and the timing of entrepreneurship, but also reflect the increased complexity of the political-administrative apparatus. The Norwegian system is actually historically rooted in a combination of Roman law and traditions from continental Europe on the one hand, and Anglo-American influences on the other. This is also reflected in public administration research that has been oriented towards the state and collective-democratic values, but blended early on with theories coming out of research in the US with another cultural background. The strong and fruitful connection between March and Olsen, established in the late 1960s, and developed further through Scancor, has been very important for the development of the theoretical basis of PA research in Norway.

A central question in the future is what role the central public administration should and can play in the Norwegian political system. The national administrative institutions are being challenged by globalization, internationalization, Europeanization, communalization, devolution and marketization. This means that it is more necessary than ever to go beyond the internal focus of public administration and to study the role of interests, actors and forces outside the state as well as the challenges by multi-level governance and the need for horizontal coordination between sectors and policy areas (Jacobsen 2006). A special challenge is to bring together scholars studying local and central government. We have seen a change in the administrative policy from being a reluctant reformer to being a latecomer with increased reform efforts from the mid-1990s. This raises questions about the democratic implications of these trends and about whether there is a development towards qualitatively new complex and hybrid public structures, or maybe also a counter-reaction as indicated by the coming to power of the new centre-left majority government in 2005. To be able to answer these questions, it will be necessary to strengthen the comparative dimensions in public administration research, both concerning systematic comparisons over time and between countries, and with respect to the emphasis on the normative and constructive aspects and studies of effects. Rather than a single model, a repertoire of models of political-administrative actors and institutions are needed to understand the future challenges of public management, administration and governance (Olsen 2007).

There might be a need to revitalize the merger of organization theory and democratic theory, by bringing the discussion of democracy back in (Hernes 2004). It is important to recall that the fundamental purpose of public service is government, not management (OECD 2005). It is necessary to understand the changes in Norwegian public administration and management, where the role of democratic decision-making has been reduced. An important challenge for future public administration research, and one that is typical for the research tradition in Norway, will be to study the civil service in a wider democratic context, which implies that attention will be focused not only on economy and efficiency, but on how public administration attends to many other important considerations and influences values, interests, the knowledge basis and power conditions. A substantial democratic dilemma is how public administration can have enough autonomy to function effectively, but not so much freedom that it will be uncontrollable.

Notes

1 This section is mainly based on Christensen (2006).
2 This section is mainly based on Christensen and Lægreid (2004). The focus is here on central public administration. There is also an extensive research on Norwegian local government.

Bibliography

Brunsson, N. (1989) *The Organization of Hypocrisy. Talk, Decisions and Actions in Organizations*, Chichester: Wiley.
Brunsson, N. and Olsen, J. P. (1993) *The Reforming Organisation*, London and New York: Routledge.
Christensen, P. M. and Rommetvedt, H. (1999) 'From Corporatism to Lobbyism?', *Scandinavian Political Science*, 19: 195–222.
Christensen, T. (2003) 'Narratives of Norwegian Governance: Elaborating the Strong State Tradition', *Public Administration*, 81: 163–90.
Christensen, T. (2006) 'The Norwegian State Transformed?', in Ø. Østerud (ed.) *Norway in Transition*, London: Routledge.
Christensen, T. and Lægreid, P. (1998a) 'Administrative Reform Policy: the Case of Norway', *International Review of Administrative Sciences*, 64: 457–75.
Christensen, T. and Lægreid, P. (1998b) *Den moderne forvaltning* (The Modern Public Administration), Oslo: Tano Aschehoug.
Christensen, T. and Lægreid, P. (eds) (2001a) *New Public Management – the Transformation of Ideas and Practice*, Aldershot: Ashgate.
Christensen, T. and Lægreid, P. (2001b) 'A Transformative Perspective on Administrative Reforms', in T. Christensen and P. Lægreid (eds) *New Public Management – the Transformation of Ideas and Practice*, Aldershot: Ashgate.
Christensen, T. and Lægreid, P. (2001c) 'New Public Management – Undermining Political-Democratic Control?', in T. Christensen and P. Lægreid (eds) *New Public Management – the Transformation of Ideas and Practice*, Aldershot: Ashgate.
Christensen, T. and Lægreid, P. (2002) *Reformer og lederskap* (Reform and Leadership), Oslo: Scandinavian University Press.
Christensen, T. and Lægreid, P. (2003) 'Coping with Complex Leadership Roles: the Problematic Redefinition of Government-Owned Enterprises', *Public Administration*, 81: 803–31.
Christensen,T. and Lægreid, P. (2004) 'Public Administration Research in Norway: Organization Theory, Institutionalism and Empirical Studies in a Democratic Context', *Public Administration*, 83: 679–90.
Christensen, T. and Lægreid, P. (eds) (2006) *Autonomy and Regulation. Coping with Agencies in the Modern State*, Cheltenham: Edward Elgar.

Christensen, T. and Lægreid, P. (eds) (2007) *Transcending New Public Management*, Aldershot: Ashgate.

Christensen, T. and Peters, B. G. (1999) S*tructure, Culture, and Governance. A Comparison of Norway and the United States*, Lanham, MD: Rowman & Littlefield.

Christensen, T., Egeberg, M., Larsen, H. O., Lægreid, P. and Roness, P. G. (2002) *Forvaltning og politikk* (Administration and Politics), Oslo: Universitetsforlaget.

Christensen, T., Lægreid, P. and Roness, P. G. (2002) 'Increasing Parliamentary Control of the Executive? New Instruments and Emerging Effects', *Journal of Legislative Studies*, 8: 37–62.

Christensen, T., Lægreid, P., Roness, P. G. and Røvik, K. A. (2007) *Organization Theory and the Public Sector: Instrument, Culture and Myth*. London: Routledge.

Eckhoff, T. and Jacobsen, K. D. (1960) *Rationality and Responsibility in Administrative and Judicial Decision-Making*, Copenhagen: Munksgaard.

Egeberg, M. (1981) *Stat og organisasjoner. Flertallsstyre, partsstyre og byråkrati i norsk politikk* (State and Interest Organizations. Majority Government, Affected Parties and Bureaucracy in Norwegian Politics), Bergen: Scandinavian University Press.

Egeberg, M. (1994) 'Bridging the Gap between Theory and Practice: the Case of Administrative Policy', *Governance*, 7: 83–98.

Egeberg, M. (2003) 'How Bureaucratic Structure Matters: an Organizational Perspective', in B. G. Peters and J. Pierre (eds) *Handbook of Public Administration*, London: Sage.

Egeberg, M. and Lægreid, P. (eds) (1999) *Organizing Political Institutions. Essays for Johan P. Olsen*, Oslo: Scandinavian University Press.

Egeberg, M., Olsen, J. P. and Sætren, H. (1978) 'Organisasjonssamfunnet og den segmenterte stat' (The Organizational Society and the Segmented State), in J. P. Olsen (ed.) *Politisk organisering* (Political Organizing), Bergen: Scandinavian University Press.

Eriksen, E. O. (1993) *Den offentlige dimensjon* (The Public Dimension), Oslo: TANO.

Eriksen, S. (1988) 'Norway: Ministerial Autonomy and Collective Responsibility', in J. Blondel and F. Muller-Rommel (eds) *Cabinets in Western Europe*, London: Macmillan.

Gunvaldsen, J. A. and Karlsen, R. (1999) 'The Auditor as an Evaluator. How to Remain an Influential Force in the Political Landscape', *Evaluation*, 5: 458–67.

Hernes, G. and Nergaard, K. (1990) *Oss i mellom. Konstitusjonelle former og uformelle kontakter Storting – Regjering* (Among Us. Constitutional Forms and Informal Contacts between the Storting and the Cabinet), Oslo: FAFO.

Hernes, H. C. (2004) 'Public Administration in Norway: a Rejoinder', *Public Administration*, 82: 691–700.

Jacobsen, D. I. (2006) 'Enhet og mangfold – statsvitenskap og organisasjonsteori i Norge' (Unity and Diversity – Political Science and Organization Theory in Norway), in E. Døving and Å. Johnsen (eds) *Organisasjonsteori på norsk* (Organization Theory – the Norwegian Way), Bergen: Fagbokforlaget.

Jacobsen, K. D. (1960) 'Lojalitet, nøytralitet og faglig uavhengighet' (Loyalty, Neutrality and Professional Independence), *Tidsskrift for Samfunnsforskning*, 1: 231–48.

Jacobsen, K. D. (1964) *Teknisk hjelp og politisk struktur* (Technical Help and Political Structure), Oslo: Scandinavian University Press.

Jacobsson, B., Lægreid, P. and Pedersen, O. K. (2004) *Europeanization and Transnational States. Comparing Nordic Governments*, London: Routledge.

Johnsen, Å. (2006) 'Økonomiske organisasjonsteori og ny offentlig styring' (Economic

Organization Theory and New Public Management), in E. Døving and Å. Johnsen (eds) *Organisasjonsteori på norsk*, Bergen: Fagbokforlaget.

Lægreid, P. (1988) *Oljebyråkratiet. Om statsadministrasjonen i ein oljealder* (The Oil Bureaucracy. Central Civil service in the Oil Era), Oslo: TANO.

Lægreid, P. and Olsen, J. P. (1978) *Byråkrati og beslutninger* (Bureaucracy and Decisions), Bergen: Scandinavian University Press.

Lægreid, P. and Roness, P. G. (2000) 'Administrative Reform Programs and Institutional Response in Norwegian Central Government', in J. J. Hesse, C. Hood and B. G. Peters (eds) *Paradoxes in Public Sector Reform*, Baden-Baden: Nomos.

Listhaug, O. and Wiberg, M. (1995) 'Confidence in Political and Private Institutions', in H.-D. Klingemann and D. Fusch (eds) *Citizens and the State*, Oxford: Oxford University Press.

March, J. G. (1997) 'Administrative Practice, Organization Theory, and Political Philosophy: Ruminations on the Reflections of John M. Gaus', *Political Science and Politics*, 30: 689–98.

March, J. G. and Olsen, J. P. (1976) *Ambiguity and Choice in Organizations*, Oslo: Scandinavian University Press.

March, J. G. and Olsen, J. P. (1983) 'Organizing Political Life: What Administrative Reorganization Tells Us about Government', *American Political Science Review*, 77: 281–97.

March, J. G. and Olsen, J. P. (1989) *Rediscovering Institutions*, New York: The Free Press.

March, J. G. and Olsen, J. P. (1995) *Democratic Governance*, New York: The Free Press.

Martin, J. (1997) *Changing Accountability Relations: Politics, Customers and the Market*, Paris: OECD, PUMA/PAC.

Nordby, T. (2000) *I politikkens sentrum* (In the Core of Politics), Oslo: Scandinavian University Press.

OECD (2005) *Modernizing Government. The Way Forward*, Paris: OECD.

Olsen, J. P. (1978) 'Folkestyre, byråkrati og korporativisme' (Democratic Rule, Bureaucracy and Corporatism), in J. P. Olsen (ed.) *Politisk organisering* (Political Organizing), Bergen: Scandinavian University Press.

Olsen, J. P. (1982) 'Reorganisering som politisk virkemiddel og statsvitenskap som arkitektonisk disiplin' (Reorganization as a Political Instrument and Political Science as an Architectonic Discipline), *Statsviteren*, 4: 1–25.

Olsen, J. P. (1983) *Organized Democracy. Political Institutions in a Welfare State – the Case of Norway*, Bergen: Scandinavian University Press.

Olsen, J. P. (1988) 'Administrative Reform and Theories of Organisation', in C. Campbell and B. Guy Peters (eds) *Organizing Governance. Governing Organizations*, Pittsburgh: University of Pittsburgh Press.

Olsen, J. P.(1992) 'Analyzing Institutional Dynamics', *Staatswissenschaften und Staatspraxis*, 2: 247–71.

Olsen, J. P. (1996) 'Norway: Slow Learner – or Another Triumph of the Tortoise?', in J. P. Olsen and B. G. Peters (eds) *Lessons from Experience*, Oslo: Scandinavian University Press.

Olsen, J. P. (2007) 'Organization Theory, Public Administration, Democratic Governance' *Nordiske OrganisasjonsStudier* 9(1): 93–110.

Østerud, Ø. and Selle, P. (2006) 'Power and Democracy in Norway: the Transformation of Norwegian Politics', *Scandinavian Political Studies*, 29: 25–46.

Rommetvedt, H. (2002) *Politikken almengjøring og den ny-paluralistiske parlamentaris-*

men (The General Interest of Politics and the Neo-pluralistic Parliamentarism), Bergen: Fagbokforlaget.

Roness, P. G. (2006) 'Statsvitarfaget og organisasjonsutforming' (Political Science and Organizational development), in E. Døving and Å. Johnsen (eds) *Organisasjonsteori på norsk*, Bergen: Fagbokforlaget.

Røvik, K. A. (1998) *Moderne organisasjoner* (Modern Organizations), Bergen: Fagbokforlaget.

Sangolt, L. (1997) 'The Politics of Counting', PhD thesis, University of Bergen.

Self, P. (2000) *Rolling Back the State. Economic Dogma and Political Choice*, New York: St Martin's Press.

Simon, H. A. (1957) *Administrative Behaviour*, New York: Macmillan.

Slagstad, R. (1998) *De nasjonale strateger* (The National Strategists), Oslo: Pax.

Steen, A. (1988) *Landbruket staten og sosialdemokratene* (Agriculture, the State and the Labour Movement), Oslo: Universitetsforlaget.

Sverdrup, U. (2000) 'Ambiguity and Adaptation. Europeanization of Administrative Institutions as Loosely Coupled Systems', PhD thesis, University of Olso.

Trondal, J. (2001) 'Administration and Integration across Levels of Government', PhD thesis, University of Oslo.

Veggedal, F. (2004) 'Internasjonalisering og styring av matpolitikken' (Internationalization and the Steering of the Food Policy), PhD thesis, University of Oslo.

6 The study of public management in the Netherlands

Managing complex networks and public governance

Walter Kickert

Introduction

This chapter will show that the study of public management in the Netherlands to some extent reflects the particular institutional context of the Dutch state. Although the study of public administration and management for a long time more or less followed the North American example, in the 1990s some distinct Dutch approaches of public management developed, such as the internationally well-known approach of 'managing complex networks' (Kickert *et al.* 1997) and the perhaps less-known approach of 'public governance' (Kooiman 1995). To some extent these typical Dutch approaches to the study of public management seem related to the centuries-old traditions of Dutch politics, government and governance.

This chapter will follow the common format of this book by first describing the history of the Dutch state and administration, then looking at the development and current state of the academic study of public administration in the Netherlands, and finally giving an overview of the typical Dutch characteristics of the study of public management.

The historical exploration of the traditions of the Dutch state and style of governance will proceed backwards in time. We start with a review of the styles of governance after the Second World War and continue further back in time. The post-war styles of governance reveal some underlying continuity, that is, compromise and consensus. An account of the historical traditions of consensual corporatism reveals that apparently much older traditions exist beneath consensus and corporatism, which leads us to have a historical look at the prevailing style of governance in the seventeenth and eighteenth centuries in the Dutch Republic.

History of the state and administration

Origins of the modern state

Democratic Rechtsstaat

In 1848 the Netherlands adopted a liberal democratic constitution. The Dutch king, William II, at the time feared that the Paris revolution might spread over to his country, and therefore asked the Liberals to compose a new democratic constitution. The constitution formed the foundation of the Dutch 'decentralised unitary state'. The times of an absolute monarch personally ruling the state were over. Ministers were no longer personal servants to the king; they became accountable to parliament. The principle of ministerial responsibility was introduced and parliament became the highest sovereign authority. Legislation by parliament became the exclusive source of administrative actions. The administration could only take decisions that were based on the constitution, laws or regulations. Administration was based on the primacy of law. The Netherlands became a democratic *Rechtsstaat*.

In the nineteenth-century *Rechtsstaat*, the key tasks of state and administration were narrowed down to legislation and the execution of laws and regulations. Administrative law gained the monopoly of the only relevant expertise for the effective functioning of state and administration. This led to the *Juristenmonopol* within continental European states. State officials were predominantly lawyers, a situation that still holds true today in countries like Germany, Austria, Italy and Spain.

Expansion of welfare state and retreat

As in other north European countries, the dominance of legalistic thinking in the Dutch state and administration lasted until after the Second World War. In the Netherlands, the post-war reconstruction of the devastated economy and society required a strong state role. The creation and expansion of the welfare state led to an ever-increasing role of the central state in providing and paying for the welfare arrangements, and this role required more than simply juridical expertise. Besides legislation, planning and budgeting became major instruments. The state needed more than juridical scientific support for the rationalisation and improvement of its planning and policy-making.

The new welfare state was developed through rational government planning. The growth of policy sciences in the 1970s was explicitly aimed at offering a scientific rationale for government planning (Hoogerwerf 1978). The rise of government planning led to the establishment of planning bureaus for economic, spatial and social-cultural facets. In addition to these sectoral planning bureaus, the Scientific Council for Government Policy (WRR) was created for integral planning. Following the example of the North American Planning, Programming and Budgeting System (PPBS), in the Netherlands a similar interdepartmental commission for the development of policy analysis (COBA) was created. The growth of the welfare state during the 1960s and 1970s was enormous. The 1970s was the heyday of integral government planning. Bureaus for policy development and planning popped up like mushrooms at all ministries. The belief in the necessity for the state to plan and control the welfare society was strong.

The oil crisis, stagnating economy and soaring public budget deficits put an end to that period. The main objective became reviving the economy, reducing unemployment and downsizing the budget deficits. These were the days of retreat of the welfare state. The 1980s were the hard times of massive cutbacks throughout the public sector. The style of governance changed from government planning to the 'three Es' – economy, efficiency and effectiveness – and 'management' became the new credo.

Underlying continuity: compromise and consensus

Although different post-war periods – immediate post-war recovery, expansion of the welfare state, and retreat of the state – show different styles of governance – emergency management, government planning, public management – a closer look (Kickert 2004) reveals an underlying continuity. The post-war expansion of the welfare state led to a more active central state and to rational and integral government planning and top-down steering by central government, but that style did not last long. Likewise, the period in the 1970s of democratisation and politicisation seemed to herald the end of the traditional consociational way of wheeling and dealing between established interest groups 'behind the scenes'. Henceforth, the political decision-making should take place in public, an open debate between clear political standpoints instead of the eternal deliberation and compromises. However, that democratisation period was also only a short intermezzo; it was followed by a period in which the limitations of government steering were realised. Society should enhance its self-steering capacity and the state should be more a mediator than a leader. Although it was denied at the time that this meant a revival of the old consociational times of pillarisation, the more modest style of governance did show some resemblance. Even the subsequent period in which modern business management was embraced by the public sector as the panacea for cost-efficiency to a certain extent resembles the traditional pragmatic style of governance. Rather than the 'new Right' neo-liberal ideology that prevailed in Britain under Prime Minister Thatcher and in the United States under President Reagan, in the Netherlands the neutral technical term 'management' was preferred. The Dutch traditionally prefer pragmatic problem solving over ideological fighting. Deliberation, cooperation, compromise and consensus have always been, and still are, the main characteristics of the typical Dutch style of politics, government and governance. So let us have a closer historical look.

Pillarisation

A historical account of consensus democracy in the Netherlands is an account of 'pillarisation', that is, the division of society into separate population groups with different religions and their own confessional organisations. Lijphart (1968, 1969) has invented the model of 'consociationalism' in order to explain why, in a society which was fragmented into highly antagonistic population groups with different and separate cultures and institutions (the so-called 'pillars'), political stability could nevertheless exist. Lijphart's solution of this paradox was that the elites of the 'pillars' (in Dutch called '*zuilen*') reached consensus by making pragmatic compromises that were obediently followed by the rank and file. The 'pillarisation' (*verzuiling*) of Dutch society originated in the nineteenth century with the development of Protestant and Catholic 'pillars'.

In the second half of the nineteenth century, an orthodox Protestant movement arose, which united several churches into a new orthodox Protestant (Gereformeerde) Church, and led to a new (*Anti-revolutionaire*) political party. Although most descriptions of the Gereformeerde movement emphasise its confessional ideas and doctrines, it was also a social and economical emancipation movement for 'small people', craftsmen, labourers and fishermen, the lower classes. Within a few generations, the children of these 'small people' had become the new leading elite in the Netherlands.

The formation of a Catholic political party at the end of the nineteenth century was also an emancipation process of an underdeveloped population group. In the seventeenth- and eighteenth-century Republic, the Catholics had traditionally been oppressed. The Catholic population was, however, far from a minority group. In the southern provinces they even formed a majority. Catholics were, however, still excluded from political power; they could not fulfil public functions. So they had no choice but to unite politically and organise around their religion in order to obtain some influence (Kossmann 1986; Lademacher 1993).

The so-called 'school struggle' dominated Dutch politics in the second half of the nineteenth century. The Liberals wanted to improve education by creating state-subsidised schools. The orthodox Protestant politicians wanted confessional state schools. Parliament refused to subsidise (private) confessional schools. The Liberal position drove the orthodox Protestant party and Catholic party, which were fundamental (confessional) opponents, into a coalition. The school struggle was finally won by the confessionals, leading in 1917 to the constitutional freedom of education, that is, the recognition of legal (and soon afterwards also financial) equality between public state schools and private confessional schools.

Sociological studies of Dutch society show that pillarisation has nowadays almost ceased to exist, with some notable exceptions like education and broadcasting. Secularisation and individualisation were the continuing post-war trends (Ester *et al.* 1993). Nevertheless there is no doubt that the new multicultural Dutch society is more fragmented than ever before. Although coalition cabinets in Dutch politics are not (and have hardly ever been) 'grand coalitions' including almost all major parties, but simply parliamentary majority cabinets, they do indeed continue to be coalitions between more parties. In that sense the political science model of consensus democracy still prevails in the Netherlands.

Traditions underlying consensual corporatism

Neo-corporatism means that the state deliberates, consults and cooperates with a limited number of recognised interest organisations. However, deliberation and cooperation are centuries-old characteristics of Dutch state and society. It hardly makes sense to describe these centuries-old traditions with a term that originated in the early twentieth century as the Catholic response to the modern industrialised society. Neither does it make sense to describe these age-old traditions with a term that was rediscovered by some west European political scientists in the 1970s (Schmitter and Lehmbruch 1979, 1982). Apparently much older traditions exist beneath corporatism.

Similarly the question can be asked to what extent the political science model of consociational or consensus democracy (Lijphart 1968, 1969) differs from the age-old state traditions of tolerance, pragmatism and consensus. In the pre-democratic times of the Dutch Republic the ruling elite of wealthy municipal patrician regents did have to deal with different groups and ideas, the traditional difference being the one between Protestants and Catholics. The merchant elites were tolerant towards deviant ideas. They were pragmatic instead of dogmatic. Therefore they were capable of reaching compromises and consensus. Apparently much older traditions exist beneath consensus democracy (Kickert 2004).

So let us have a look at the typical characteristics of the regent's style of governance: tolerance, pragmatism, deliberation, persuasion, compromise and consensus.

Governance in the Republic

Governance by regents

Power in the Republic of Seven United Provinces (founded at the Union of Utrecht in 1579) was distributed across the provinces, which in turn were composed of many independent cities, quarters and estates. The state was fragmented and central authority in the Republic was hardly existent.

Power was in the hands of the wealthy merchant patrician families who governed the cities (Daalder 1974). Aristocracy played an important role in the poor eastern and southern provinces, but had hardly anything to say in the wealthy provinces like Holland, Zeeland and Groningen. There the patrician families (*regenten*) ruled the cities. Not the possession of land, owned by the aristocracy, but the possession of money was the base of power in the Netherlands. The origin of the wealth of these patrician families was usually from international trade (de Vries and van der Woude 1995; van Dillen 1970). Notwithstanding their sometimes gigantic private fortunes, regents did earn incomes from the governing positions they occupied. Especially in the larger and richer cities, top governing positions could yield substantial incomes.

In the Republic, the cities dominated regional and national politics. In the provincial estates most cities had a vote, and decisions had to be reached unanimously. All decisions taken by the Estates-General, which was the most important national government organ, had to be prepared in the provincial estates, and at local level in the city councils. In practice, the Republic was governed by some 2,000 municipal regents. Most of them were only involved in local government. A small elite of the most prominent regent families was responsible for national state affairs (Kloek and Mijnhardt 2001).

Positions in the administration meant respect, power and income for regents. Participation in the city administration was therefore crucial for the patrician regent families. It was their *raison d'être*. It was virtually impossible for someone not belonging to the recognised patrician families to acquire a position. The ruling elite of regents made sure that all governing positions remained in their own hands.

Tolerance and pragmatism

Tolerance and pragmatism were centuries-old traditions. The Dutch Republic was known to be a safe refuge for religiously oppressed and otherwise dissident groups.

The merchant elites' tolerance of other cultures and ideas represents the traditional double 'preacher-merchant' face of the Dutch state. On the one hand, the Protestant freedom-fight against the Catholic Habsburg tyranny formed the basis of the new Republic, and therefore Protestant preachers had an important say; most regents were active members of the Protestant church. But on the other hand, the state power was in the hands of the municipal patrician regents, who made sure that the preachers would not harm the economic trade interests. International trade implied the presence of traders from all over the world with many different religions and cultures and was the basis of tolerance and consensus and was based on the economic trade interests of the ruling elite. It was the calm, consensual pragmatism of the ruling regents versus the ideological, moralistic dogmatism of (some of) the Protestant preachers (Van Deursen 1996).

Persuasion and discussion

The tradition of deliberation and compromise can also be traced back to the origin of the Dutch Republic. The Republic of the Seven United Provinces was the result of a rebellion against the Catholic Habsburg Empire. Their unity served to win the war, the aim of which was to preserve the freedoms and privileges of the provinces. Maintaining their own rights and independence was the goal; united cooperation was the means. Governance in the Republic was an eternal search for the 'golden way' between unity and independence. Coercion and violence were impossible because the provinces were autonomous. Governing was a matter of wheeling and dealing, of deliberation. This art was called 'persuasion'. Concentration of power was also impossible within the provinces because the nobility and the cities remained autonomous and equal. Everywhere, power was divided. Government was always collegial; hierarchical command did not exist. Central authority was hardly existent, and certainly not in the hands of one single person. Decision-making was carried out in collegial bodies, which had to take many different interests into consideration.

Making compromises and reaching consensus was crucial in Dutch governance (van Deursen 1996).

Study of public administration

In its current multidisciplinary form, the study of public administration in the Netherlands dates from after the Second World War. The late 1970s until the mid-1990s witnessed a steady expansion and diversification of the Dutch PA sciences. Nowadays the subject of public administration is taught at 11 of the existing 13 Dutch universities. The strong growth of the first half of the 1990s is over. Student numbers have reduced, but stabilised at a substantial level, thus potentially consolidating the institutional position of PA departments in most universities (Kickert and van Vught 1995).

Table 6.1 sets out the establishment of the first Chairs in Public Administration. Gradually, other disciplinary backgrounds than Public Law started to dominate, some in social sciences, most in political sciences. In the course of the 1970s and 1980s, PA departments became increasingly separated from the background disciplines from which they had originated, both in an organisational and a substantial sense.

After the initial separation from administrative law, the post-war policy and administrative sciences in the Netherlands followed the multidisciplinary, strongly political-science-based example of the North American 'public policy and administrative sciences'.

Up until the 1970s, public administration study programmes were established as specialisations in disciplinary degree programmes in social science, political science and law. The first full-scale PA degree programme was established in 1976 at Twente University. This programme was based on the multidisciplinary concept of PA as the study of four separate disciplines: political science, sociology, economy and law. The second full-scale degree programme was established in 1984 as a joint venture between the universities of Leiden and

Table 6.1 Establishment of chairs in public administration up to 1976

Year	University	Disciplinary affiliation
1928	Economic Academy (Rotterdam)	Economics
1953	Institute for Social Studies	Social (Development) Science
1961	Free University Amsterdam	Political Science
1966	Erasmus University Rotterdam	Sociology
1969	University of Utrecht	Law
1970	University of Amsterdam	Political Science
1971	Technological University Delft	Law
1972	University of Leiden	Law and Political Science
1973	Catholic University Nijmegen	Political Science
1976	Interuniversity Institute Delft	Business Administration
1976	University of Groningen	Law

Table 6.2 Public administration programmes in the Netherlands in 2006

University	Position within the Institution
Erasmus University Rotterdam	Faculty of Social Sciences
University of Leiden	Faculty of Law and Faculty of Social Sciences
Technical University Twente	Faculty of Business and Public Administration
Catholic University Nijmegen	School of Policy and Governance
Catholic University Brabant (Tilburg)	Faculty of law and Faculty of Social Sciences
University of Amsterdam	Faculty of Political and Social-Cultural Sciences
Free University (Amsterdam)	Faculty of Social-Cultural Sciences
University of Groningen	Faculty of Law
University of Utrecht	School of Governance
Technical University Delft	Faculty of Systems, Policy and Management
Open University (Heerlen)	Faculty of Business and Administrative Sciences

Rotterdam and was modelled as a four-year, full-degree programme in PA, integrating the basic disciplines as an academic approach in itself. This joint enterprise lasted until the mid 1990s, when new government regulations made close inter-university cooperation virtually impossible, and the two programmes became independent.

Over the last few years, Utrecht and Tilburg have joined the ranks in terms of establishing full-fledged and independent PA degree programmes at BA and MA levels, in Utrecht closely related to the broader field of organisation studies, in Tilburg more geared towards applied and commissioned research. At the other institutions, PA is embedded in law, social, political or organisational studies degrees.

In the middle of the 1990s, the separate full-scale, regular degree programmes were together teaching some 3,000 students. The combined Leiden–Rotterdam PA department had well over 100 staff members (Kickert and van Vught 1995). By the early 2000s, the explosion in student numbers of the early 1990s was over. Social sciences as a whole underwent a remarkable decline in student popularity, particularly when compared to, for example, the popularity of business administration or psychology. It is probably fair to say that the growth of PA in the late 1980s, early 1990s was a by-product of the strong growth of higher education in the Netherlands in general, and the lack of broad liberal arts education at the undergraduate level within that system. The interdisciplinary conception of the PA field attracted many students interested in a broad study programme (Kickert and Toonen 2006).

Quality assessment

Science is self-referential. The quality of scientific results may only be assessed by the international scientific community. That is dangerous for progress and innovation, as the history of science shows, the more so in such a small academic community as Dutch PA. It is therefore crucial that quality assessment is judged by the international scientific community. That explains the importance that is attached to numbers of publications in international high-quality journals, and numbers of citations in those journals. Throughout the 1990s, the field pursued a rather deliberate internationalisation strategy, using European exchange schemes, but also by setting up a joint internationally oriented research school in political and administrative sciences: the Netherlands Institute of Government (NIG).

Assessing the quality of the field by exclusively looking at international publications would not do justice to the field. A remarkable feature of Dutch administrative sciences is its close relation with the practice of public administration, accounting for much of its sustained position from the second half of the 1990s onward, when the spurt in the academic growth cycle was over. The early generation of professors typically came from administrative practice. Currently, many professors and staff have close relations with public service, some leaving for, or coming from, top positions in administration. Several play an active role in local or national politics. Many are or have been members of major government advisory councils and temporary advisory committees. A relatively large number of research projects is financed as commissioned research by public and private organisations.

Internationalisation

The internationalisation of the field of PA at large and the subsequent need to mirror one's own identity to developments elsewhere, has contributed much to the self-awareness of the Dutch field. One's own identity becomes more and more visible through international contacts and cooperation. Dutch public administration discovered itself as a distinct branch within international PA.

Although the specificity of the object of study of administrative sciences, the national state and administration, implies that its study and science also depend on national characteristics – administrative studies in the 1970s and 1980s were mainly restricted to the territory of the Netherlands – the internationalisation trend in universities did not leave our field unaffected. The first initial attempts to internationalise Dutch administrative sciences were almost exclusively oriented towards our 'big brother' the United States. A self-respecting modern Dutch administrative scientist is supposed to be acquainted with the latest modern developments in the North American field. Until the beginning of the 1990s, the average Dutch administrative scientist, however, hardly knew anything that happened elsewhere in Europe, leave alone other regions of the world.

Yet, the last decade has shown a change in that one-sided orientation. State, politics, government and administration fundamentally differ between the United States and Europe; consequently, so does its study (Kickert and Stillman 1999). Administrative sciences in Europe cannot be a simple translation or mere copy of that study in the United States. Dutch administrative scientists have come to play a clear role in the European PA community. Dutch administrative sciences have developed into a separate field with their own academic status and their own institutional identity.

That situation does not hold in all western European countries. Why is it that, even compared to big nations like Germany and France, Dutch policy and administrative sciences are so relatively large and consolidated? Possible answers may be found in the Dutch academic educational system, with its high English proficiency, offering more rewards for publication in foreign academic journals, providing travel funds and research support for its top scholars, inviting foreign scholars into its universities, allowing more flexibility for new disciplines like PA to emerge. However, successful consolidation is no reason for conceitedness. The future of Dutch PA sciences will undoubtedly be turbulent and uncertain (Kickert and Toonen 2006).

Study of public management

We will not give an overview here of the scientific state of the art of Dutch policy and administrative sciences (Kickert and van Vught 1995; Kickert and Toonen 2006), but restrict ourselves to the subfield of public management. In the Netherlands, the study of public management is hardly carried out in departments of business administration, but mainly in departments of public administration. At the beginning of the post-war rise of Dutch administrative sciences, it more or less followed the North American example. Gradually a distinct Dutch approach of the study of public management has developed, of which we will describe three examples, that is, managing complex networks, public management reforms, and public governance.

Management and organisation

Attention in practice and science

The organisation and functioning of central administration have been the subjects of investigation by numerous advisory committees, some of which have commissioned supporting studies by Dutch scholars. The 1980 advice of the Vonhoff committee on the structure of the civil service was based on a number of background studies, some of which were carried out by administrative scientists. The 1993 report of the Wiegel committee on departmental reordering, which contained recommendations about the distinction between policy-making core-departments and executive agencies, was also partially based on contributions by administrative scientists.

In the United States, public management scholars since the early 1990s have succeeded in making a distinction between themselves and generic management and organisation sciences, and have developed a specifically public-sector-oriented approach (Bozeman 1989; Rainey 1997). In the Netherlands, an explicit school of thinking about public organisation and management has been lacking in the past. The department of public management of the Rotterdam business school, headed by Kooiman, used to be an exception. Another exception was the Leiden studies of the organisation and functioning of bureaucracy and civil service (van Braam 1986; Bekke 1990; van der Meer and Roborgh 1993). In the past, sporadic attempts were made to develop a distinct theory of managing public organisations (Kooiman and Eliassen 1987).

As the post-war rise of Dutch administrative sciences was intended to give scientific support to government planning, it is no surprise that in the beginning it had a strong policy-science orientation. As a consequence of this, during the 1970s and 1980s relatively little scientific attention was paid to management and organisation.

Attention in educational programmes

Educational programmes and training courses in public administration did pay attention to management and organisation. Following the North American public policy and administration sciences, the usual division in Dutch PA study programmes is that between policy process on the one hand, and organisation structure on the other. A university study programme in public administration therefore usually has a strong component of public management and organisation. Scientific attention, however, was not directed towards this area. It was, for instance, a long time before Dutch administrative scholars wrote their own course textbooks. In the 1980s a Dutch textbook on management and organisation would be a polytechnic-level book on generic organisation sciences (Keuning and Eppink 1985). University programmes therefore used English academic-level textbooks, usually also on generic management and organisation. Early Dutch specialists in organisation science, like Bekke in Leiden and van der Krogt in Twente, were organisation sociologists by origin. The first Dutch textbooks on organisation science written by public administration scholars (Kastelein 1985; Lemstra 1988; van der Krogt and Vroom 1989; Pröpper 1993) were introductory books on generic organisation science. It took much longer before specific public-sector-oriented textbooks on management and organisation appeared (de Bruijn and ten Heuvelhof 1995; de Wit *et al.* 2000; Noordegraaf 2004; Teisman 2005).

A survey of the current bachelor and master programmes in public policy and administration at Dutch universities shows that, at undergraduate level, introductory courses in management and organisation typically use the textbooks of Mintzberg (1980) and Morgan (1985). These two textbooks are generic and not public-sector-specific, and are also popular in introductory courses in business administration and social sciences. Master's courses in management and organisation at postgraduate level make use of a variety of textbooks, such as Rainey (1997), Pollitt and Bouckaert (2000), or Peters and Pierre (2004).

Dealing with complexity

Limitations of government steering

With the post-war creation and expansion of the welfare state, the planning role of government became increasingly important. Many social-welfare arrangements had to be built, extended and maintained, preferably in a coherent way, by means of integrated planning. Integrated government planning reached a peak during the 1970s. The oil crisis heralded the end of belief in planning. The economy could hardly be controlled, and despite all the beautiful plans, unemployment kept rising. Confidence in the beneficial effects of government planning faded. The planning euphoria of the 1970s was replaced by a planning aversion in the 1980s.

The developments within the Dutch academic community ran somewhat parallel. In the 1970s, planning theory attracted much scientific attention. Modern, refined, 'new' planning models and theories were invented (van Gunsteren 1976; in 't Veld 1982). The economic crisis and budget deficits led to a fundamental debate about the future, restricted steering role of government, and about the limits of governance. In the Netherlands, the debate on the limits of government steering arose in scientific as well as administrative and political circles. The Christian Democratic party launched ideas on the retreat of government and the revitalisation of social institutions in a plea for more self-responsibility of citizens in a 'responsible society'. In the Social Democratic party, doubts arose about the steering capabilities of government and the possibility and desirability of 'making and shaping' society. The Dutch Scientific Council for Government Policy (WRR) published a report on the inability of government to steer society as a *deus ex machina*, apart from and above society (den Hoed *et al.* 1983). These changing views on government steering led to an emphasis on the limitations and restrictions of the steering capacity of government in Dutch administrative research in the first half of the 1980s. The Nijmegen department of public administration was an outspoken representative of this school (in 't Veld 1982; Kickert *et al.* 1985; Snellen 1985). The Leiden Center for Societal Steering also played an important role in drawing attention to the study of the limits of governance (Bovens and Witteveen 1985).

Managing complex networks

At the end of the 1980s, as a reaction to the prevailing negative public and political opinion about the functioning of the public sector, another school of thinking emerged. Instead of mainly studying the limitations, boundaries and failures of government, research became more oriented toward exploring the possibilities of new forms of government steering. Within the limitations of complexity, new forms of governance were sought. Insight in complex and dynamic policy networks was considered as a possibility to improve government steering. This approach of 'managing complex networks' was adopted in the Rotterdam–Leiden research programme on governance in complex networks, first resulting in Dutch publications (Hufen and Ringeling 1990; Koppenjan *et al.* 1993). The later Rotterdam research programme 'Centre for Public Management' developed an international orientation (Kickert *et al.* 1997).

The Rotterdam research programme has developed a successful applied approach, particularly by advisory work and commissioned research projects in the infrastructure sector (Teisman 1992). Especially, the subject of 'interactive decision-making', also called 'co-production', has gained much attention. In the department of 'technical PA' in Delft, these ideas have been further developed into models of network management, process management, chain management and trajectory management and large-scale urban ICT infrastructures (de Bruijn and ten Heuvelhof 1995; de Bruijn *et al.* 1998; van Duivenboden *et al.* 2000).

The ideas of managing complexity have also led to the embracement of modern systems theories on complexity, chaos and order by some administrative scholars (Teisman 2005). Complexity theory has a rich scientific content based on contributions emerging from many disciplines, from non-linear systems theory to genetic biology, and from social networks to population ecology. The application of such concepts of complexity to administrative sciences seems theoretically promising.

Public management reform

The oil crisis and stagnating worldwide economy hit the Dutch economy hard. Unemployment grew, the economy stagnated, the budget deficit exploded. The 1980s were a period of downsizing the enormous budget deficits. The magic word in order to balance the budget, became cost-efficiency. Delivering the same services for less money, increasing productivity, efficiency and value for money. The refuge was sought in business administration, which was considered the panacea for efficiency. Since public management reforms in the Netherlands have been extensively described elsewhere (Kickert 2000), this account will be brief.

Local government reforms

By the mid-1980s, most middle-sized municipalities had carried out far-reaching reforms. They were simply forced into this measure because their budgets were in deficit, a situation that is legally prohibited for municipal government. Their options for increasing incomes were severely restricted; own incomes from local taxes and levies were relatively small (about 10 per cent of the municipal income), and changes in local taxes and levies were subject to strict national prescriptions. Municipalities therefore simply had to drastically downsize, terminate or privatise public tasks. The alternative was to increase productivity and efficiency.

The municipal reforms of the mid-1980s were dominated by two issues: a new financial 'planning and control system' and a new organisational 'concern-division' model. Result-oriented financial management and decentralisation of management responsibilities were the two main ingredients of the local reforms.

The municipal reforms were an almost prototypical example of what was later called 'new public management'. Actually the reforms in the city of Tilburg later became an example (the *Tilburg modell*) for German municipal reform in the early 1990s (*neues Steuerungsmodell*) and for Swiss local and regional reform in the mid-1990s (*wirkungsorientierten Verwaltungsführung*).

National government reforms

Although efficiency and management also became catchwords at national government level, one should realise that national administration itself, the ministerial departments in The Hague, was not as severely affected by reforms and reorganisations as local government. Downsizing public sector budgets affects the executive local level of schools, hospitals, housing corporations, etc., but affects much less the organisation and functioning of ministerial departments in The Hague. Managerial reforms at ministerial departments did of course take place during the 1980s but mainly started to get a real momentum with the so-called 'great efficiency operation' of the early 1990s.

A remarkable managerial reform trend of the early 1990s at national government level was the so-called 'autonomisation' of executive parts of ministerial departments, that is, the distinction between policy-making and execution, the organisational separation of executive task units from the policy-making core department and the increase in managerial autonomy of these executive units. 'Autonomisation' in the early 1990s took the form of special regime agencies (in Dutch *agentschap*), with contract management and a new administrative regime allowing more flexibility in financial and personnel affairs. The new special regime agencies were permitted an accrual accounting system. The British 'next steps agency' has been the model example for this special agency regime that was introduced in Dutch ministries in the early 1990s.

Downsizing the public sector and revitalising the private market sector were explicit government objectives. Privatisation was one of the government's instruments. So to some extent, neo-liberalism was a dominant ideology at the time. The two centre-Right Lubbers cabinets (1982–1989) included the conservative Liberal party that was an outspoken advocate of that ideology. To another, maybe much larger, extent, Dutch political decision-making is carried out without any ideology at all. Pragmatic compromises are reached according to the rules of consensus democracy. In the third, centre-Left Lubbers cabinet in 1989, the conservative Liberal coalition partner made place for the Social Democrats. Neo-liberalism ceased to be a dominant government ideology. The Socialist minister of finance and vice-premier reversed the ideological tide at his department, which played a leading role in those days of financial problems, to the more neutral term 'management'. Downsizing, realising the three Es, especially efficiency, could also be accomplished by adopting a neutral managerial style of governance without right-wing neo-liberal ideology. In a certain sense, Dutch public management rather looked like the age-old pragmatic style of governance.

Studying public management reform

Since the mid-1990s, Dutch administrative scholars have increasingly become involved in management reform studies, first at domestic level, later also international comparative. The drastic management reform in the city of Tilburg did not remain unnoticed in the academic community. The Tilburg-based administrative scientists Tops and van Vught (1998) extensively studied this municipal reform case. The interest of the German community in the Tilburg reform example for their own *neues Steuerungsmodell* led to German publications by Dutch scholars (Korsten 1995). The participation in international comparative research projects led to the increasing involvement of Dutch scholars in the international public management community (Kickert 2000; van Thiel 2003). An international 'civil service' project was launched as a cooperation between Leiden (Bekke, Perry and Toonen 1996; Bekke and van der Meer 2000), Indiana university (Perry) and Oklahoma (Raadschelders). And since Pollitt moved to Rotterdam Erasmus University, the Dutch PA community has housed one of the most distinguished authors on comparative public management reforms (Pollitt and Bouckaert 2000).

A distinctive characteristic of the Dutch study of public management reforms has been the critical stance toward 'new public management'. Although some international organisations, like the World Bank and OECD, propagate the universal convergence of worldwide government reforms toward one single public management model, the international academic community has gradually developed some counterbalance to this convergence belief. National characteristics of state, politics, government and administration do influence the national paths of reform (Pollitt and Bouckaert 2000). Public management reforms in Europe differ from those in the United States (Kickert 1997). Alternatives to the dominant Anglo-American public management approach have been proposed (Kickert 1997b).

The recognition that public management is different from private sector business management led to criticisms on the excessive belief in quantitative performance indicators (de Bruijn 2001). The inherent tension between management and professionalism, especially in professional organisations like universities, hospitals, judiciary, police, etc., has led in the Dutch administration and politics to some doubts about excessive applications of output and performance-oriented management techniques. The complaint by professionals is that such management techniques only lead to more regulations and bureaucracy. The Dutch national research school for political and administrative sciences has recently started a cooperative project on the tension between professionalism and public management.

Public governance

Governance in Dutch 'Bestuurskunde'

The Rotterdam approach of governance in complex networks has come to play a well-known role in the international scientific debate on 'public governance'. Governance has recently become an important theme in the international PA community. In the Netherlands, the notion of governance has a much longer tradition. The usual Dutch term for administrative sciences, *'bestuurskunde'*, literally means 'the art of governance'. Long before this notion was discovered in the international PA community, Dutch scholars were using it in the now internationally common sense of 'mutual steering relations between state and society' (Pierre 2000). Some decades ago, the term governance, let alone state steering, was unheard of in the Anglo-American PA community. This absence might be related to the difference in state tradition between the Anglo-Saxon world and continental Europe. Whereas the American administrative tradition is 'state-less' (Stillman 1990), strong state steering has of old existed in continental European states. The French Napoleonic state model, with a strong united central state, a highly centralised and hierarchical administration and a highly qualified and powerful civil service, or the German *Rechtsstaat* model, likewise highly centralised, hierarchical and professional, are examples of strong central state steering of society. It is no accident that the term 'etatism' originates from the French, and that the individual citizen in Germany is called '*Untertan*' (state subject, literally meaning submissive).

The retreat of the welfare state in the 1980s and 1990s has led to fundamental changes in the mutual steering relationships between state and society in many Dutch policy sectors. The liberalisation of the public housing sector, the introduction of market-like instruments in public health, the privatisation of the public utility sector and many other public organisations have given the concept of 'governance' a renewed high relevance. Many ministerial departments have been reflecting upon the new mutual steering relations with their policy sectors over the last two decades.

In the 1980s an explicit debate on the limitations of government steering took place in Dutch politics and administration (see earlier). This debate carried over into scientific circles. In the economic sciences, the poor state of the Dutch economy led to numerous publications. In the early 1980s, the debate among several professors of economics about scenarios for the future and proposed measures to save the economy and employment received much public coverage in newspapers and even on television. In the social sciences, considerable attention was paid to how the welfare state would develop. A series of publications with revealing titles by leading sociology professors hit the bookshelves, e.g. 'the stagnating welfare state' (van Doorn and Schuyt 1978), 'the declining days of the welfare state' (Idenburg 1983), 'the intervention state' (de Beus and van Doorn 1984). In public policy and administration sciences, the changing views on government steering led to an emphasis on the limits and restrictions of the steering and planning capacity of government. After this understandably negative reaction on the omnipotent state, scientific attention shifted toward an exploration of the possibilities of government steering within the limitations of complexity. Within the limits of complexity, new forms of governance were sought.

Besides the aforementioned approach of 'managing complex networks', the study of new forms of governance was also approached from other angles. Extensive studies into the changing governance relations between state and society were carried out by Godfroy and Nelissen (1993), both sociologists at the Nijmegen PA department. Their research group produced a number of books on renewal of governance (Nelissen *et al.* 1996) and governance capacities

(Nelissen *et al.* 2000), based on numerous studies of governance in various policy sectors.

The organisation sociologist Bekke (1990) in his works emphasised the importance of taking into account the external governance relations between public organisations and the political and societal context. Public management and organisation should be approached 'from-outside-to-inside', and pay explicit attention to the broader concept of governance. Another Dutch scholar in public management and organisation, Kooiman (1995, 2002), who also emphasised the importance of governance, used a modern systems theoretical approach of the subject. It is remarkable that the few early Dutch PA scholars in public management, all emphasised the importance of governance for public management and organisation (Kooiman 1995; Bekke 1987; Kickert 1993).

International debate on governance

The debate on governance contains substantial international variety. In the United States, major attention is paid to the issue of democratic governance, the response to the global public management revolution (Kettl 2000). In Great Britain, the concept of governance emerged from the studies of 'policy communities', from ideas on 'governance without government', governance in a complex interorganisational network (Rhodes 1997). This approach very much resembled the Dutch approach of governance and management in complex networks (Kickert *et al.* 1997). The German debate on *politische Steuerung* was highly influenced by systems theory notions on 'self-steering' and *autopoiesis* (Willke 1989; Luhmann 1984). The French etatist tradition of a strong central state led to pleas for a more 'modest' state (Crozier 1987).

The debate on governance also contains substantial theoretical variety. The 'complex networks' strand of studies can be distinguished as a number of distinct approaches: first, the interorganisational studies within the North American management and organisation sciences (Rogers and Whetten 1982; Gage and Mandell 1990); second, the network studies which emerged from the research into policy communities and subsystems in Great Britain (Marsh and Rhodes 1992; Rhodes 1997); and third, the Dutch studies of complex multi-actor and multi-rational policy networks (Kickert *et al.* 1997). Another strand of studies, which heavily relied upon cybernetics and systems theory, can also be subdivided. Both the ideas on 'collibration' of the British scholar Dunsire (1995) and the ideas on 'complexity, dynamics and diversity' of the Dutch scholar Kooiman (1995) relied on cybernetics and systems theory. The German ideas on 'self-steering' and *autopoiesis* relied on the particular interpretation of systems theory by Luhmann (1984). Governance can be approached from many more theoretical angles. In the Mediterranean administrative sciences, the juridical-institutional approach plays a dominant role. In modern political sciences, the historical neo-institutional approach (March and Olsen 1989) has gained a high popularity. Governance can also be approached with more traditional political science concepts like consociational democracy (Lijphart 1968,

1969) and neo-corporatist interest mediation (Schmitter and Lehmbruch 1979, 1982). Governance can also be considered from a socio-economical perspective of state interference in economy, or from a socio-cultural perspective on social values, culture and national identity.

Conclusions

Governance in complexity and underlying state traditions

In the post-war period, the Netherlands increasingly became a strong, central state. The 1970s were the heyday of rational central government planning. The economic crisis made the pendulum in the 1980s swing from the omnipotent state to the retreat of the welfare state. In the 1990s, that led administrative scholars to ideas about 'governance without government', about a society-centred, rather than state-centred, view on governance, about a state that cannot steer society from the top down, about governance in a complex horizontal network of social actors. The characteristic Dutch approach of 'governance in complex networks' is based on the rejection of strong central state steering in the past.

A historical account of the Dutch state and administration reveals that state steering in the past has not been so strong and central as was widely assumed, and that steering in a complex multi-actor and multi-rational network has, in fact, already existed in the past. History demonstrates that in the actual practice of Dutch state and administration, these allegedly novel insights are not at all new. In fact, this type of governance actually represents a centuries-old tradition of Dutch governance. Wheeling and dealing between different interdependent actors and compromising between different interests are age-old Dutch traditions, and steering by a strong central state has hardly ever existed in the Netherlands. Governance has almost always been a matter of deliberation, persuasion, compromise and consensus (Kickert 2004).

Of course, one should realise that deliberation, compromise and consensus between a multitude of various interests groups in order to reach broad societal support is different from compromises made by regents who were tolerant as long as it did not harm their vested interests and existing power positions. Regents were a very small elite, ruling the country as a closed shop, and excluding outsiders from political power. Governance in a complex network of many different social interest groups is different from governance by patrician regents.

Nevertheless one can conclude that it is no historical coincidence that Dutch administrative scholars became interested in managing complex networks. The centuries-old tradition of Dutch state steering in fact accounts for this specific approach in the study of public management.

Specificity in the study of public management

How specific is the study of public management in the Netherlands? The internationalisation of the Dutch field of public administration in general, of which the study of public management forms a part, implies that the latter cannot completely deviate from mainstream developments in the international scientific community, which is both quantitatively and qualitatively dominated by our colleagues in the Anglo-American world. The times when administrative studies were a purely domestic affair, only investigating Dutch cases and only conducted in the Dutch language, are over. So, nowadays, Dutch studies of public management show a clear resemblance to the international main trends and topics in that field. The rise of public management was also in the Netherlands clearly related to the necessity to economise and to increase effectiveness and efficiency in the public sector. Not surprisingly, Dutch studies of public management also deal with issues of financial management human resources management, and the various other worldwide similar issues, such as output budgeting, steering on results, client-orientation, agentification and the more.

The review of the Dutch field of public administration claimed that the internationalisation had led to a growing development of self-awareness and an distinct own identity, replacing the early strong and one-sided orientation towards our North American colleagues by an increasing orientation towards Europe. Growing maturity gradually leads to an own self-identity. That is not a reactionary attempt to defend own national traditions, culture and language in order to revive the old times of introvert domestic closeness, but an innovative attempt to find one's own place within the international field. Some Dutch administrative scholars have come to play a prominent role in the international and European community. Many others are developing in that direction. And many others proceed with their Dutch domestic affairs.

The claim of growing international self-identity in the Dutch field of public management ought to be nuanced. The discovery by administrative scholars that the state could not steer society top-down and that governance takes place in a complex network of social actors was hardly based on historical insight in the Dutch institutional traditions of state and governance. Many Dutch administrative scientists obviously lack historical awareness.

Bibliography

Bekke, A. J. G. M. (1987) 'Public Management in Transition', in J. Kooiman and K. A. Eliassen (eds), *Managing Public Organizations*, London: Sage, 17–32.

Bekke, A. J. G. M. (1990) *De betrouwbare bureaucratie. Over veranderingen van bureaucratische organisaties en ontwikkelingen in het maatschappelijk bestel*, inaugural address, Universiteit van Leiden.

Bekke, A. J. G. M. and Meer, F. M. van der (eds) (2000) *Civil Service Systems in Western Europe*, Cheltenham: Edward Elgar.

Bekke, A. J. G. M., Perry, J. L. and Toonen, Th. A. J. (eds) (1996) *Civil Service Systems in Comparative Perspective*, Bloomington: Indiana University Press.

Beus, J. W. and Doorn, J. A. A. van (eds) (1984) *De Interventiestaat*, Meppel: Boom.

Bovens, M. and Witteveen, W. (1985) *Het Schip van Staat*, Zwolle: Tjeenk Willink.

Bozeman, B. (1989) *All Organizations are Public*, San Francisco: Jossey-Bass.

Braam, A. van (1986) *Leerboek Bestuurskunde*, Muiderberg: Countinho.

Brasz, H. A., Kleijn, A. and in 't Veld, J. (1962) *Inleiding tot de Bestuurswetenschap*, Arnhem: VUGA-boekerij.

Bruijn, J. A. de (2001) *Prestatiemeting in de Publieke Sector. Tussen Professie en Verantwoording*, Utrecht: Lemma.

Bruijn, J. A. de and ten Heuvelhof, E. F. (1995) *Management in Netwerken*, Utrecht: Lemma.

Bruijn, J. A. de, ten Heuvelhof, E. and in 't Veld R. J. (1998) *Procesmanagement*, Schoonhoven: Academic Services.

Crozier, M. (1987) *État modeste, État moderne*, Paris: Fayard.

Daalder, H. (1971) 'On Building Consociational Nations: The Cases of the Netherlands and Switzerland', *International Social Science Journal*, 23: 355–71.

Daalder, H. (1974) *Politisering en Lijdelijkheid in de Nederlandse Politiek*, Assen: Van Gorcum.

Deursen, A. Th. van (1996) *De Hartslag van het Leven. Studies over de Republiek der Verenigde Nederlanden*, Amsterdam: Bakker.

Dillen, J. G. van (1970) *Van Rijkdom en Regenten. Handboek tot de Economische en Sociale Geschiedenis van Nederland tijdens de Republiek*, Den Haag: M. Nijhoff.

Doorn, J. A. A. van and Schuyt, C. J. M. (1978) *De Stagnerende Verzorgingsstaat*, Meppel: Boom.

Duijvenboden, H. van, Twist, M. van, M. Veldhuizen and in 't Veld, R. J. (eds) (2000) *Ketenmanagement in de Publieke Sector*, Utrecht: Lemma.

Dunsire A. (1993) 'Modes of Governance', in J. Kooiman (ed.) *Modern Governance*, London: Sage.

Ester, P., Halman, L. and de Moor, R. (eds) (1993) *The Individualizing Society. Value Change in Europe and North America*, Tilburg: Tilburg University Press.

Gage, R. W. and Mandell, M. P. (eds) (1990) *Strategies for Managing Intergovernmental Policies*, New York: Praeger.

Godfroy, A. J. A. and Nelissen, N. J. M. (eds) (1993) *Verschuivingen in de Besturing van de Samenleving*, Bussum: Countinho.

Gunsteren, H. R. van (1976) *The Quest for Control: a Critique of the Rational-Central-Rule Approach in Public Affairs*, London: John Wiley.

Hoed, P. den, Salet, W. G. M. and Sluijs, H. van der (1983) *Planning als Onderneming*, The Hague: WRR.

Hoogerwerf, A. (ed.) (1978) *Overheidsbeleid*, Alphen: Samsom.

Hufen, J. A. M. and Ringeling, A. B. (eds) (1990) *Beleidsnetwerken*, The Hague: VUGA.

Idenburg, Ph. A. (ed.) (1983) De *Nadagen van de Verzorgingsstaat*, Amsterdam: Meulenhoff.

Kastelein, J. (1985) *Modulair Organiseren Doorgelicht*, Groningen: Wolters Noordhof.

Kettl, D. F. (2000) *The Global Public Management Revolution*, Washington: Brookings Institution Press, 2000.

Keuning, D. and Eppink, D. J. E. (1985) *Management en Organisatie*, Leiden: Stenfert Kroese.

Kickert, W. J. M. (ed.) (1993) *Veranderingen in Management en Organisatie van de Rijksdienst*, Alphen: Samsom.

Kickert, W. J. M. (ed.) (1997) *Public Management and Administrative Reform in Western Europe*, Cheltenham: Edward Elgar.

Kickert, W. J. M. (1997b) 'Public Governance. An Alternative for Anglo-American Managerialism', *Public Administration*, 75: 731–52.

Kickert, W. J. M. (2000) *Public Management Reforms in the Netherlands*, Delft: Eburon.

Kickert, W. J. M. (2004) *The History of Governance in the Netherlands*, The Hague: Reed Business Information.

Kickert, W. J. M. and Stillman, R. J. (eds) (1999) *The Modern State and its Study*, Cheltenham: Edward Elgar.

Kickert, W. J. M. and Toonen, Th. A. J. (2006) 'Public Administration in the Netherlands. Expansion, diversification, consolidation', *Public Administration*, 81: 969–87.

Kickert, W. J. M. and Vught, F. A. van (eds) (1995) *Public Policy and Administrative Sciences in the Netherlands*, London: Harvester Wheatsheaf.

Kickert, W. J. M., Aquina, H. J. and Korsten, A. F. A. (1985) *Planning binnen Perken*, Zeist: Kerckebosch.

Kickert, W. J. M., Klijn, E. H. and Koppenjan, J. F. M. (eds) (1997) *Managing Complex Networks*, London: Sage.

Kloek, J. and Mijnhardt, W. (2001) *1800. Blauwdrukken voor een Samenleving*, The Hague: SDU.

Kooiman, J. (ed.) (1995) *Modern Governance*, London: Sage.

Kooiman, J. (2002) *Governing as Governance*, London: Sage.

Kooiman, J. and Eliassen, K. A. (eds) (1987) *Managing Public Organizations*, London: Sage.

Koppenjan, J. and Klijn, E. H. (2004) *Managing Uncertainties in Networks*, London: Routledge.

Koppenjan, J. F. M., de Bruijn, J. A. and Kickert, W. J. M. (eds) (1993) *Netwerkmanagement in het Opnebaar Bestuur*, The Hague: VUGA.

Korsten, A. F. A. (1995) 'Das Tilburger Modell oder Tilburg als neues Mekka der öffentlichen Verwaltung', in R. Kleinfeld and A. F. A. Korsten, *Konzern Stadt. Neue Steuerungsmodelle in den Kommunalverwaltungen*, Krefeld.

Kossman, E. H. (1986) *De lage landen, 1780–1980. Twee Eeuwen Nederland en België*, Amsterdam: Agon.

Krogt, Th. P. W. M. van der and Vroom, C. W. (1989) *Organisatie is Beweging*, Utrecht: Lemma.

Lademacher, H. (1993) *Geschiedenis van Nederland*, Utrecht: Spectrum.

Lemstra, W. (ed.) (1988) *Handboek Overheidsmanagement*, Alphen: Samsom.

Lijphart, A. (1968) 'Typologies of Democratic Systems', *Comparative Political Studies*, 1: 3–444.

Lijphart, A. (1969) 'Consociational Democracy', *World Politics*, 21: 207–25.

Lijphart, A. (1984) *Democracies. Patterns of Majoritarian and Consensus Government in Twenty-one Countries*, New Haven: Yale University Press.

Luhmann, N. (1984) *Theorie Sozialer Systeme. Grundriss einer algemeinen Theorie*, Frankfurt: Suhrkamp Verlag.

March, J. G. and Olsen, J. P. (1989) *Rediscovering Institutions*, New York: Free Press.

Marsh, D. and Rhodes, R. A. W. (eds) (1992) *Policy Networks in British Government*, Oxford: Clarendon Press.

Meer, F. M. van der and Roborgh, L. J. (1993) *Ambtenaren in Nederland*, Alphen: Samsom.

Mintzberg, H. (1980) *Structure in Fives*, Englewood Cliffs: Prentice Hall.

Morgan, G. J. (1985) *Images of Organizations*, London: Sage.

Nelissen, N. J. M. (ed.) (2000) *Bestuurlijk Vermogen*, Bussum: Countinho.

Nelissen, N. J. M., Godfroy, A. J. A. and Goede, P. J. M. van der (ed.) (1996) *Vernieuwing van Bestuur*, Bussum: Countinho.

Nelissen, N., Goverde, H. and Gestel, N. van (eds) (2000) *Bestuurlijk Vermogen*, Bussum: Coutinho.

Noordegraaf, M. (2004) *Management in het Publieke Domein*, Bussum: Countinho.

Peters, B. G. and Pierre, J. (2004) *Handbook of Public Administration*, London: Sage.

Pierre, J. (ed.) (2000) *Debating Governance*, Oxford: Oxford University Press.

Pollitt, C. (2003) *The Essential Manager*, Oxford: Oxford University Press.

Pollitt, C. and Bouckaert, G. (2000) *Public Management Reforms. A Comparative Analysis*, Oxford: Oxford University Press.

Pröpper, I. M. A. M. (1993) *Inleiding in de Organisatiekunde*, The Hague: VUGA.

Rainey, H. G. (1997) *Managing Public Organisations*, San Francisco: Jossey-Bass.

Rhodes, R. A. W. (1997) *Understanding Governance*, Buckingham: Open University Press.

Rogers, D. L. and Whetten, D. A. (eds) (1982) *Interorganizational Coordination: Theory, Research and Implementation*, Ames: Iowa State University Press.

Schmitter, P. C. and Lehmbruch, G. (eds) (1979) *Trends Towards Corporatist Intermediation*, London: Sage.

Schmitter, P. C. and Lehmbruch, G. (eds) (1982) *Patterns of Corporatist Policy-Making*, London: Sage.

Snellen, I. Th. M. (1985) *Limits of Government*, Amsterdam: Kobra.

Snellen, I. Th. M. (1988) 'De Grondlegger van de Nederlandse bestuurskunde', in A. F. A. Korsten and Th. A. J. Toonen (eds) *Bestuurskunde: Hoofdfiguren en Kernthema's*, Leiden: Stenfert Kroese, 57–69.

Stillman, R. J. (1991) *Preface to Public Administration*, New York: St Martin's Press, 1991.

Stillman, R. J. (1999) 'Public Administration in the United States', in W. J. M. Kickert and R. J. Stillman (eds) *The Modern State and Its Study*, Cheltenham: Edward Elgar.

Teisman, G. R. (1992) *Complexe Besluitvorming*, The Hague: VUGA.

Teisman, G. R. (2005) *Publiek Management. Op de Grenzen van Chaos en Orde*, Schoonhoven: Academic Services.

Thiel, S. van (2001) *Quangos: Trends, Causes and Consequences*, Aldershot: Ashgate.

Tops, P. W. and Vught, G. W. M. van (eds) (1998) *Zoeken naar en Modern Bestuur, het Tilburgs Model en de Logica van de Burger*, Alphen: Samsom.

Veld, R. J. in 't (1982) *Verandering en Bestuur. Pleidooi voor een Bescheiden Bestuurskunde*, inaugural address, Katholieke Universiteit Nijmegen.

Vries, J. de and Woude, A. van der (1995) *Nederland 1500–1815. De Eerste Ronde van Moderne Economische Groei*, Amsterdam: Balans.

Williamson, P. J. (1989) *Corporatism in Perspective*, London: Sage.

Willke, H. (1989) *Systemtheorie entwickelter Gesellschaften. Dynamik und Riskanz moderner gesellschaftlicher Selbstorganisation*, Munich: Juventa Verlag.

Wit, B. de, Meijer, R. and Breed, K. (2000) *Strategisch Management van Publieke Organisaties*, Utrecht: Lemma.

7 The study of public management in Switzerland

Wirkungsorientierten Verwaltungsführung

Kuno Schedler

Specific national features of state and public administration

Historical roots

Swiss historiography is characterised by a major issue that recurs throughout the centuries like a leitmotif: the independence of both private individuals and the community. This is how history is taught at school, and this is Swiss people's contemporary collective awareness, but it is actually also a long historical development.

A crucial date is the year 1291, when the first three states established the original confederation with an oath. As free citizens and farmers, and without any consideration of their descent and origins, they swore independence from all foreign rulers – and, at the same time, mutual respect for each other's own freedom. The foreign rulers they referred to were Burgundy (in today's France) and the Habsburgs (in present-day Austria), which governed the territory at the time. In the subsequent wars of independence, the Swiss defended their freedom and gradually attracted further states (today called cantons), which participated in the confederation as largely autonomous members of equal standing. The fundamental principle of the Swiss Confederation has always consisted of two elements: first, the intrinsically free private individuals, who in personal responsibility choose the path which strikes them as best for the community; and second, their acknowledgment of the confederation as a social principle, i.e. a cooperative society which alone is capable of securing peace and order without having to rely on a hierarchical – external – power.

All the states were involved in their own administration in a system of partnership, without any top-down organisation. This bottom-up involvement resulted in a new order which was unparalleled in a Europe led by the nobility and the clergy. Switzerland's valleys and mountains had provided an early home for all sorts of denominations and heretics since no central power was capable of bending them to its will there. Indeed, this territory was characterised by a profound mistrust of the exercise and abuse of power. Even as confederates, the individual cantons defended their independence from the others until in 1848 – at the time when the restoration of the monarchies was being embarked upon in Europe – the modern confederation was founded with its own constitution, thus providing the loose alliance of the cantons with an institutional umbrella. If, previously, the federal administration had been made up of one single full-time official, the Federal Chancellor, then it was to grow steadily and become more professional from 1848 onwards (Kupper 1929), since the customs service, the postal service and the mint were all delegated to federal responsibility.

A second crucial incident occurred in the fifteenth century when little Switzerland played at being a major military power in Europe. Swiss mercenaries were so notorious for their particular skilfulness and toughness in war that even the Pope and the French king decided to hire Swiss troops for their own protection, in the former case to this day, and in the latter until 1792. The Switzers' reputation spread so far that they were hired by all European rulers, until Switzers fought their own compatriots in one of the bloodiest battles of that time at Marignano (1515). The consequence of this Swiss bloodbath in foreign services was a shift in focus back on their own territory, combined with a deep-rooted military 'neutrality'.

The Reformation in the early sixteenth century confronted the young country of Switzerland, which then consisted of 13 cantons, with an ordeal. Several civil wars between the Protestant states of the Swiss midlands and the Catholic rural areas of central Switzerland prevented Switzerland from growing together in an organic fashion. This gave rise to a preference for thinking in terms of small areas, which in turn resulted in the pronounced 'federalism' still prevalent today.

In 1648 Switzerland was internationally recognised as an independent country by the big European powers. In 1798, with French help, the tables were turned on the old order: Swiss revolutionaries toppled the *ancien régime* and established a centralist Helvetic Republic. Based on the thinking of Pestalozzi and Rousseau, primary schools were set up in the spirit of the Enlightenment. It soon became clear that the Republic was not backed by the population, which is why the later French Emperor Napoleon imposed a federalist constitution on Switzerland. After Napoleon's fall from power in 1815, the newer ideas of equal rights gradually gained ground, and more civic rights were introduced in many cantons. Finally, Switzerland was obliged to retain its neutrality at the Congress of Vienna.

After a final civil war in 1847, in which the Swiss provided proof, not only of their newly acquired unfitness for war and their military inefficiency, but also of their far-sightedness and power of integration (Remak 1993), the modern confederation was founded in 1848. The template for the Swiss constitution was provided by the US constitution, which means that Switzerland has a bicameral system with the National Council (the House of Representatives), the Council of States (the Senate), and a cabinet (the Federal Council), but no president. In this latter respect, the independent-minded Swiss regarded the concentration of power in the USA as excessive, and so they decided to institute a collegial government, which would always have to make its decisions jointly. The federal government is elected by parliament, which always ensures that the political parties and the linguistic regions are adequately represented. In spite of many amendments and two total revisions, the essential provisions of today's constitution still reflect those of 1848.

Mistrust of political power, particularly if it was not regarded as 'one's own', is a distinctive feature of Switzerland's political culture and structures. People are always anxious not to have to serve under foreign rulers. Even today, it is still another community or another canton which is considered to be foreign, rather than another country or a supranational entity. Thus if someone moved to the capital of a canton, say, as an official, he was considered to have moved abroad. This applied even more if he moved to the federal capital, Berne.

Underlying state traditions in Switzerland

This brief historical outline makes clear why, in certain respects, Switzerland works differently from other countries. The profound mistrust of (foreign) political power serves to explain the three most important peculiarities of Swiss government organisation: federalism, the so-called 'militia principle', and direct democracy.

Federalism

The political concept of federalism in Switzerland is primarily an avowal of the autonomy of small territories. With just under 3,000 communities and 26 cantons ('states' in the US structure) for a population of seven million inhabitants, Switzerland is organised into distinctly small areas. In this context, communal autonomy is considered to be of very great political significance, and the cantons continue to conceive of themselves as the political centres which do not surrender any powers to the confederation unless this is done explicitly in an amendment to the constitution (Niedermann 1998). Anything that is not in the confederation's competence in accordance with the constitution is automatically a matter for the canton (Vatter 2002).

As a result of this, each canton has its own organisation in such vital political areas as education and health. As a rule, coordination between cantons is based on voluntarism, which is why harmony has become an important cultural phenomenon in Switzerland. In comparison with, say, their German neighbours, the Swiss are utterly addicted to harmony and try to avoid any open conflicts. Federalism is not least a means of mastering the great diversity in Switzerland, as it ensures that differences need not lead to open conflicts.

One way of preserving regional independence is a form of government that is based on concordance, coupled with the principle of collegiality. All the major political parties (four at federal level) are represented in this concordance system and, as a rule, the regions are also appropriately represented in the cabinets. The principle of collegiality means that resolutions of the government as a whole have to be publicly supported by all the federal ministers, even if they are in contradiction to individual ministers' personal convictions. This system results in an incisive self-control on the part of cabinets, since every government decision is already bound to be a compromise within the cabinet. An accumulation of political power in one person, one political party or one region is thus systematically prevented.

For the organisation of the administration (ie public management), this means that the normality of Switzerland is represented by an almost unmanageable diversity of solutions. The typical answer to the question, 'How do you solve this in Switzerland?' is invariably the same: it differs from canton to canton. Research into administration is therefore often a case study (i.e. an individual canton), or comparative in order to work out any differences or shared features. Switzerland, small as it is, represents an excellent field of research for the study of public management, since, owing to the high degree of the decentralised units' autonomy, all sorts of conceivable solutions evolve that can be analysed and compared with each other.

Nonetheless, Swiss public administration evolved in a more or less harmonised manner. The fact that hierarchical intervention on the part of the confederation remained precluded in many cases often resulted in the establishment of formal or informal networks of cantonal experts who agreed on certain guidelines. In the 1970s, this led to the recommendation to introduce full accrual accounting for cantons and communities (1978 Conference of Cantonal Finance Ministers). In the 1990s, the privileged status of public official was abolished in practically all German-speaking cantons and replaced by a status of unlimited employment with the generally applicable possibility of giving notice. New public management, too, owes its widespread application in (German-speaking) Switzerland to this exchange of ideas and experience.

Then again, federalism is a great opportunity for the Swiss public administration's innovation capacity. The decentralised development of new solutions to similar problems may cause redundancies which are economically inefficient, but the latent competition between the cantons is also an incentive for them to organise themselves better and more cleverly than the others. Thus federalism is a system of competing best practices, which in the long term leads to permanent improvement.

The so-called 'militia principle'

In the Swiss context, the term 'militia' is not limited to the notion of a citizens' army but simply stands for the opposite of professionalisation in all possible forms of organisation. Just as the Swiss army is a non-professional militia with only a small proportion of professionals (the instructors), Swiss parliaments at all levels are non-professional, i.e. their members also work in regular jobs (and thus naturally represent the interests of their profession). In keeping with the spirit of the intrinsic freedom of private individuals, these part-time parliamentarians enjoy such a high degree of autonomy that their membership of any parliamentary party is voluntary. They are not compelled to follow the party line when they vote in plenary sessions. In many communities, the members of the executive are also part-timers, and it is also a matter of course that Switzerland does not have a caste of officials who are appointed for life as in France or Germany. Swiss civil servants have always been appointed for a certain term of office in order to prevent the formation of a *classe administrative*. Brändli-Traffelet (2004) traces this fact back to a specifically Swiss notion of freedom, namely civic freedom: the freedom of the individual citizen has priority against all other requirements of the state. In contrast to Germany and France, which evolved into countries run by the civil service, Switzerland evolved into a country run by the people (*Volksstaat*) as opposed to a country that is dominated by an elite of civil servants and officials (*Beamtenstaat*).

In terms of the organisation of the civil service (for example, public management), this is tantamount to the evolution of an open administration, which has to remain sensitive to the concerns of the people. The Swiss have developed a particular phobia about bureaucracy and public offices, and they harbour a great mistrust of administrative processes that are not transparent. In this context it has never been possible to establish an institution dedicated to the education and training of civil servants along the lines of the French École Nationale de l'Administration or the German universities of administration. Swiss officials do not have to provide evidence of any specific training in administration in order to assume office, and positions of leadership are not infrequently filled by outsiders selected on the strength of their special technical knowledge. For the study of public management, this has a twofold significance. First, there is no evolution of self-contained, self-referencing knowledge societies of civil servants, such as can be found in Switzerland's neighbouring countries. Thus, public administration is constantly receptive to knowledge developed by nonstate organisations. Private sector management has a strong impact on the practice of public management. The mobility of the people involved also results in permeability for innovations in management. Second, public management is primarily a subject that has established itself in further education; when a manager's career points towards public administration, this requires specific administrative knowledge – which is not necessary at the regular levels of education. Thus, research in public management is distinctly aligned with the concrete requirements of practical working life, which are covered by executive education courses and consultation. The way in which academics in the field of public management conceive of themselves is also in line with practice; a direct involvement in reform projects is the rule rather than the exception, and the knowledge that is passed on to students is largely based on the professors' own practical experience.

Direct democracy

Although the ideals of equal rights for all citizens were cultivated in the Swiss Confederation from the very beginning, the fact remained that there were great social differences. In the nineteenth century, the interlacement of the economy and politics resulted in the development of a democratic movement which introduced the instruments of direct democracy in cantonal constitutions and, finally, in the federal constitution. The most important of these instruments are known as the referendum and the initiative. In a referendum, people are able to demand that a law, a constitutional amendment, a treaty or a major expenditure be subjected to a public vote. This requires a certain number of signatures; at federal level, this number is 50,000. With an initiative (100,000 signatures at federal level), people are able to demand the adoption of a new constitutional provision formulated by themselves.

Primarily, this has two consequences. First, a great number of political decisions are made directly by the people through their votes. Four weekends per year are regularly earmarked for public ballots in which people vote on federal, cantonal and communal business at the same time. In this manner, the people exercise a direct influence on political decisions made by the government and by parliament, thus massively limiting their power. Second, in practical politics, the threat of a referendum alone ensures that minority concerns are also enshrined in a bill – provided the minority has sufficient power to organise the necessary number of signatures. Every decision made by the executive and the legislative is therefore already a compromise.

In terms of the organisation of the civil service (for example, public management), this means that when it comes to preparing political decisions, the administration always has to take the people's mood into consideration. Every decision, every bill that is drafted must be able to survive a possible popular vote. Thus the bill must be worded in such a way that the people will be able to understand it, and the concerns must be well founded. This again prevents the formation of a high and mighty caste of civil servants; on the contrary, politicians and officials who are close to the people are greatly appreciated. The President of the Confederation for 2006, for instance, regularly commutes from Zurich to Berne by tram and train (about 90 minutes), and without bodyguards.

Above and beyond this, tried and tested consultation procedures among stakeholders ensure that new decisions are widely discussed even at the drafting stage. This prolongs the decision-making process but provides a high degree of legitimacy. This obligation of the state to involve people and the obligation of people to be involved in the state guarantee that public administrations always think further than their own concerns when, say, a federal provision is assessed by the cantons or when trade associations comment on the draft of a new social aid act.

Cultural differences

A final characteristic of Switzerland, which goes hand in hand with federalism, is a pronounced awareness of the regions' linguistic differences. Switzerland has four official national languages: German, French, Italian and Romansh. The language borders also constitute a kind of cultural border: the German-speaking Swiss (64 per cent of the population) are Alamans like the southern Germans, the French-speaking Swiss (20 per cent) are Burgundians like part of the French, and the Italian-speaking Swiss (6.5 per cent) are Langobards like the northern

Italians. Finally, the Romansh-speaking Swiss (0.5 per cent) are Rhaetians, who are descended from the Celts. Nine per cent of the Swiss population have native languages other than the four official ones. Swiss federalism does not only protect these regions and their differences from any encroachment by the others but actively promotes the cultivation of their languages and cultures.

In terms of the organisation of the civil service (for example, public management), this means primarily that it is not only the make-up of federal politics that is governed by the principle of parity but that the same applies to the federal administration, too (Germann 1997). In other words, it is the official employment policy of the federal administration that the linguistic regions be appropriately represented. Unofficially, the cantons also set great store by obtaining their share of federal administration jobs (at least in senior positions) in order to exercise their influence. Moreover, federal civil servants are generally expected to be fluent in German and French. Secondly, all the official documents in the confederation and in those cantons which have two or more linguistic regions are translated into the various national languages. This slows down the processes and may lead to interpretation difficulties but is not regarded as a serious problem.

Third, the different linguistic regions are not only separated by their language, but also by their societal and administrative culture. The administrative culture of French-speaking Switzerland takes its bearings from the statism of France, where government is called upon to solve the problems of society whilst at the same time, private individuals distance themselves from the same government authorities. In addition, the French-speaking part tends to cast more left-wing votes than the German-speaking Swiss. Conversely, the administrative culture of German-speaking Switzerland is characterised by the pragmatism of popular government, in which private individuals make their contributions towards the continuation of the community to the best of their knowledge and ability. The German-speaking Swiss neither expect nor like government institutions to regulate or actively influence too many social spheres. Sensitivity to problems, too, differs largely between the Romance and Alamanic areas. French-speaking Switzerland seems to tolerate government deficits rather more easily than German-speaking Switzerland. Economic arguments are accorded comparatively low significance in the public administration of French-speaking Switzerland; the public sector in French-speaking Switzerland seems to be less driven by the need to increase efficiency than is the German-speaking. The upshot of this was that New Public Management as the embodiment of an 'economisation of the political' (Pelizzari 2001) did not gain a foothold in French-speaking Switzerland, whereas it led to epoch-making changes in administrative structures and culture in the German-speaking part of the country (Lienhard et al. 2005).

The study of public management

To date, there has been no systematic summary of research and teaching in the field of public management, which is also lamented by Brändli-Traffelet (2004), who points out that it is particularly in the field of administration that political scientists and historians have failed to produce theoretical evaluations. Such works may at best be found in the legal sciences. Indeed, Schweizer (2001), for example, has been able to demonstrate that in Switzerland, developments in the administrative sciences have largely been shaped by the legal sciences.

Below, it will first be shown which topics of what is now called public management have been the focus of research over the years. Subsequently, a brief outline will be provided of the development of the institutions that have rendered services to the study of public management.

What is worth noting is the make-up of the fora in which public management research has been published. By far the largest number of publications on this topic are books in the German language, often works compiled by editors. The essays that have been analysed have also mainly been written in German. A result of this is the fact that, as a rule, Switzerland is not mentioned in comparative studies of public management (Pollitt and Bouckaert 2000). Moreover, the few authors who publish their works in English often remain descriptive, i.e. they sketch the peculiarities of the Swiss system without analysing it with the aim of arriving at generally valid findings. Some (Hofmeister and Borchert 2004) develop and publish recommendations for practical application.

Internationally relevant fundamental works on the basis of Swiss research have virtually only been published in the last few years (Rieder and Lehmann 2002; Schedler 2003; Chappelet 2004).

The study of public management as a disciplinary development

Dominance of law

Until after the Second World War, the development of the administrative sciences in Switzerland ran largely in parallel with that in Germany. As in that country, academic debates were almost completely controlled by lawyers, among whom an independent administrative science evolved around the turn of the century, not least under the influence of French developments. In contrast to private law, which is based on the equality of all the parties involved in a law case, the newly evolving administrative law submitted higher and lower orders in the relationship between government and citizens, from which it was derived that those who are subordinate to the law, i.e. the citizens, are in particular need of protection. This protection can only be ensured if any state action – which includes action taken by the private sector or, in today's terminology, by the productive state – is tied to a legal basis in applicable public law (Fleiner 1911). It is only this strong delimitation from private law, together with the creation of special institutions of an administrative judiciary guaranteeing the enforcement of public law, that protects citizens from administrative arbitrariness.

In Switzerland, unlike in Germany, it was the protection of citizens that enjoyed priority over the view that citizens are subordinated or subjugated by a magisterial state. Swiss administrative culture always appeared distinctly more purpose-oriented and less formalistic than its German counterpart, which may be both cause and effect of a more open administrative culture.

Even so, there were also formalistic endeavours in Switzerland, among others by leading exponents of administrative law (Giacometti 1960) who advocated a purely normative science of administrative law, which would not have to deal with empirical sciences. However, this view was strongly criticised (Grisel 1970), and from 1950 onwards, individual lawyers' research consciously refers to studies by other academics concerned with public administration (Eichenberger 1954; Schweizer 2001). It was Eichenberger, in particular, who increasingly turned to questions of the control of administration. He complained that a high-performance administration behaved in an increasingly overbearing manner and was more and more difficult to lead by government, which is why a reform of the state was required (Eichenberger 1989).

As the lawyer Schweizer (2001) explains, virtually all reforms of government and administration in Switzerland since the Second World War have been determined by the law. It was only with the increasingly economic world view of New Public Management that business-administrative concepts became dominant. Moreover, Germann (1997) emphasises that academic work on public administration in Switzerland was almost exclusively a matter for lawyers right up into the 1970s.

Political sciences

In Switzerland, it was only with the *Schweizerisches Jahrbuch für Politische Wissenschaften* – the 'Swiss Yearbook for Political Sciences' – from the 1960s that a theory of public administration evolved in Switzerland that took its motivation from the political sciences. This primarily consisted in analyses of the role of administration in certain policy fields, which was continued as policy analysis in the 1980s, in particular. Schweizer (2001) writes in this context that the many-faceted developments of American public administration theories from the 1930s onwards did not find any successors for a long time, with the exception of public finance, and that the important French *science administrative* only gained in significance from the 1960s onwards. In the 1970s and 1980s, the Swiss administration was recorded descriptively and its organisation and tasks in the confederation and the cantons were analysed (Neidhart 1974; Germann 1982). Subsequently, this type of publication was reworked repeatedly, with partially varying focal points (Germann and Weis 1995; Germann 1998; Neidhart 2002).

The 1970s and 1980s may in any case be regarded as the high-water mark of research into public administration from the point of view of political sciences. The 1970s were dominated by the discussions of the role and sociology of state officials (Klöti 1972) and the establishment of planning instruments for the state along the lines of the American Planning Programming Budgeting System (Linder *et al.* 1979). The 1980s were dominated by research into the role of public administration in the political process, into the growth of public administration (Du Pasquier 1986), and into the flood of legislation in Switzerland. After the planning euphoria had abated in Switzerland, and after the approaches of political analysis appeared unable to ensure that public administration could be controlled in technical terms (Knoepfel 1987), the political sciences largely withdrew from the discussion of issues that are now debated in the context of public management.

The emerging discussion of New Public Management in Switzerland occasioned few responses from the community of political scientists. An early criticism (Knoepfel 1995) drew parallels with political analysis and pointed out that similar approaches, such as control through technical solutions, had failed previously and would not prove successful in NPM either. Others (Bussmann 1995) criticised the economisation of the control of public administration. Only a handful of political scientists (Haldemann 1995) championed NPM and tried to introduce aspects of political science into the further formation of a Swiss New Public Management (Brühlmeier *et al.* 1998, 2001).

Other disciplines

Apart from the above-mentioned disciplines, it is particularly economics and sociology that have been concerned with public administration.

Economic issues that are related to the topics of public management are usually financial in nature: the division of functions between government levels (Buschor *et al.* 1993), public accounting and financial statistics, and the effects of certain subsidy and fiscal equalisation models. Frey (1995), for instance, anticipates that NPM and the reform of fiscal equalisation will complement each other favourably. NPM is internationally regarded as a model that is based on, among other things, New Institutional Economics. This ought to result in a situation whereby economists participate especially actively in the NPM discussion. Interestingly, economists in Switzerland are reluctant to comment on issues of the modernisation of public administration. Only Lane (2000) dealt with NPM in detail, but represents a highly neo-liberal position, which in the French-speaking environment has been regarded as proof that NPM is a strategy for the economisation of the state. Other economists criticise NPM for being based on an obsolete view of the agency theory (Kopp 1997) or for destroying civil servants' intrinsic motivation with the performance-pay concept (Frey and Jegen 2001).

Whereas economics and the management sciences often deal with conceptual issues and make use of empiricism as a test case for the concept, sociologists appear to pursue a completely different path. They often primarily consider the specifically observable effects which certain reforms have on employees or the organisation without first wanting to prove that the concept works. Mäder's (2000) research, for instance, prompts him to accuse NPM of pursuing a moral crusade. Varone (2003) convincingly explains that the introduction of political performance agreements for public administration has resulted in a reduction of the time horizon of administrative activities, since the fulfilment of performance agreements compels administrations to comply with political time frames. Ruflin (2006) demonstrates in a new publication that the technical innovative power of professional service providers will be in jeopardy if the management logic in performance agreements prevails in social non-profit organisations.

Management science

In modern Switzerland, public administration has always been the focus of business-administrative research, albeit sporadically. However, this did not evolve into an academic field of its own; rather, it reflected the observers' own logic and original fields. At the University of St Gallen, where a modern, holistic management model for the private sector had been developed under the aegis of Hans Ulrich, this was later adapted to serve the public sector as a 'small brother', as it were (Ulrich and Sidler 1977). In its core statements, however, this adaptation did not differ from the original.

In Switzerland, independent public management research of an academic nature only emerged in the 1980s. As late as 1977, Bischofberger (1977) lamented the lack of business-administrative research into public administration. Subsequently, however, a Swiss scientific community came into being which looked into the issues of public management in a more systematic fashion. Berchthold (1988), for example, explored the development of administrative structures from 1848 to 1988.

Jans and Meili (1988) used three case studies to examine the strategies for the rationalisation of public administration; at the time, this still relied on the method of indirect cost analysis and value analysis, which later proved to be rather less than successful. With NPM, research into public management increased both in quality and in quantity. An early publication on the model of outcome-based public management matched the zeitgeist of the 1990s to an unexpected extent and became a bestseller (Schedler 1995). Many excellent studies followed. A number of doctoral theses in public management provide evidence of this intensification of research. Thus, public management as an autonomous field of management research with a sufficiently broad basis in terms of personnel and institutions has been in existence since the 1990s. It must also be noted that contributions on Switzerland and from Switzerland have increasingly been published in English (Klöti 1988, 1994; Schedler 1997, 2000; Steiner 2000; Rieder and Lehmann 2002).

The interdisciplinary stage

The emergence of New Public Management paved the way for management science into areas of the politico-administrative system that had previously been the province of lawyers and political scientists. Outcome-based public management is a model that does not optimise the internal working order of the administrative apparatus alone, nor does it purely optimise certain selected functions, as was the case before. Rather, it aims to redesign the entire control mechanism of administration and of the politics that sets its course – and this neither in consideration of the previous detailed research of the traditional disciplines, nor with the use of their terminologies. It was clear to the reformers of public administration that this would provoke resistance. Up to a point, this provocation was intentional in order to spur the allegedly inflexible administrative lawyers into more creative thinking.

This is not the place to deal with the few vehement, partially offensive reactions and pamphlets from both proponents and opponents of NPM. What is more important is the fact that in the 1990s, a perfectly constructive dialogue was launched in Switzerland between lawyers, political scientists and exponents of public management (Mastronardi and Schedler 1998, 2005), which tackled the issues that it was necessary to discuss from the perspective of an orderly constitutional administration: the issue of the separation of powers in connection with NPM (Mastronardi 1999; Nuspliger and Kettiger 1999), the role of parliaments in NPM (Finger 2002), and the creation of legitimacy (Lienhard 2005).

In the wake of the evident changes caused by NPM in Swiss practice, important legal contributions were written which concerned themselves intensively with the publication of public management. In this context, two universities stand out. First was the University of St Gallen, where the lawyer Mastronardi joined the NPM debate with constructive criticism at an early stage (Mastronardi 1995, 1998) and even developed a new national policy concept in an interdisciplinary discussion with the local public management exponents (Mastronardi 2000). Next on the scene was the University of Berne, where it was Zimmerli and Lienhard (Zimmerli 1997; Zimmerli and Lienhard 2002; Lienhard 2003, 2005), in particular, who were actively involved in a further-reaching development of NPM in legal terms, reinforced by other legal practitioners from Berne (Bolz and Klöti 1996; Kettiger 2000, 2003; Bolz and Lienhard 2001). Today it may be assumed that the NPM discussion in Switzerland has made it possible to conduct an interdisciplinary debate on public management issues to a previously unknown extent because the scientific community that is actively concerned with NPM is still small in number and characterised by mutual respect.

Despite this new interdisciplinary nature of individual discourses, Mastronardi (2001) has noticed disciplinary representatives' inability to break through the barriers of their own logic.

Development of public management research in terms of subject matter

An analysis of the publications on the topics of public management in the narrower sense of the term makes clear that certain questions keep cropping up and are described as being in need of reform.

What is conspicuous is the recurring discussion of a modern accounting system for public administration. Early on, Zindel (1945), for instance, called for the public accounting system to the approximated to the private sector practice – at a time when Switzerland was still characterised by a bewildering heterogeneity of accounting systems as used by cantons and communities. However, it was not until the 1970s that a public accounting model was developed and recommended in Switzerland, which would now be described as accrual accounting (Buschor 1994). Ever since, and particularly under the influence of NPM, the accounting system has been further refined and adapted to the information requirements of public management (Schedler and Knechtenhofer 2002); indeed, the confederation and individual cantons have even resolved to introduce a high degree of compliance with the International Public Sector Accounting Standards (IPSAS).

A key notion in Switzerland's administrative landscape is that of the *service public*. This French expression might only cover a particular category of services (namely, the public services), but in Switzerland – as indeed in France – it describes a completely different concept from, say, the English-language 'public services'. In Switzerland, the *service public* is not merely a function, but primarily an institution. If Swiss people ask questions about the *service public*, they simultaneously ask questions about the functions of the state. The network of post offices is just as much a *service public* as the provision of telecommunications services and social security. The notion as such and its institutional implications have meanwhile been successfully elevated into a myth by the trade unions so that prominent representatives of the confederation's Personnel Office demanded that the *service public* would have to be further developed into a *service au public*, i.e. a service for the public (Blindenbacher *et al.* 2000).

Germann (1987) was one of the first exponents in Switzerland to draw attention to new forms of cooperation between public and private organisations (which today are described as 'public–private partnerships'). However, such a consistent implementation of PPPs as is known in other countries is lacking in Switzerland (Hofmeister and Borchert 2004). The reasons for this phenomenon are currently under investigation in a research project of the University of St Gallen (Ehrensperger 2007). It must be supposed that the Swiss communities' financial situation does not make it appear necessary to run the risk of partnerships with private organisations. Moreover, it would appear that there is a certain fear of getting tangled up with multinational companies in the field of the *service public* because this might result in uncontrollable dependence – an issue which already bothered the original confederates, who wanted to preserve their independence.

With only a short delay after NPM, a new wave of information and communication technologies was discussed in public management: electronic government. This discussion was again interdisciplinary, but this time predominantly between politics, management and technology. For many, e-government and the modernisation of the administration go hand in hand (Chappelet 2004; Summermatter 2006), the two aspects mutually promoting their respective developments (Schedler and Schmidt 2004).

Interestingly, hardly anything has been published about the nexus between public management and direct democracy. Although the issue has the highest degree of relevance for Switzerland both in cultural and in legal terms, there has been no research into the questions as to whether direct democracy leads to a particular form of public management – an assumption that would appear perfectly plausible. Thus it might be expected that the constant danger of a referendum being launched against a 'high and mighty' solution proposed by the administration would have to reinforce the administration's pragmatism and closeness to the people. Since direct democracy ensures that no *classe politique* can develop in Switzerland because politics always depends on the people's consent, public administration will not be able to find purely professionally perfect solutions as a *classe administrative* but will always have to measure them against the yardstick of popular acceptance. In comparison with France, this results in a tendency towards mediocrity as far as professionalism is concerned. Conversely, the constant pressure of having to explain themselves would give a considerable boost to the administration's closeness to the people.

As a political scientist, Möckli (1995) makes clear that direct democracy is a framework condition in Switzerland that will have a constitutive effect. Möckli is certainly right in saying that if NPM should limit democracy, then it would be doomed to failure in Switzerland. This is to say that not only will any reform model itself have to pass the litmus test of preserving direct democracy in Switzerland, but also the reform process will be significantly influenced by the permanent pressure of possible direct democratic interventions. Such considerations had an impact when an amendment to the constitution in favour of NPM was adopted in the canton of Solothurn, where, since 2006, the people may launch a referendum against performance agreements of the government for administrative offices. In this (single) way, not only does NPM not violate democracy, but indeed imbues it with additional strength, as the people can have a say even on the performance contracts the government is signing (Mastronardi and Stadler 2003).

From an economic angle, recent studies have proved that direct democracy tends to lead to more efficient government activities (Kirchgässner *et al.* 1999), which means that there is a case for it to be favoured.

Federalism is an issue which has been repeatedly examined and addressed throughout the period under observation, (ie 1900 to the present day), to begin with primarily from a legal point of view and with a descriptive tendency, and subsequently, for the newly emerging public management, also as a structural element of the Swiss context that cannot be disregarded. Klöti (1995), for instance, explains that interconnections in a federal state will not admit of such a simplifying separation of operative and strategic elements as is demanded by NPM of the first generation. Using the closure of regional railway stations and post offices as an example, he demonstrates that decisions that are of a purely operative nature at federal level can be of the highest strategic significance for the communities.

For the study of public management, federalism has the great advantage that it is eminently suitable for comparative studies. It comes as no surprise that this is exploited by practically all the disciplines. Recent outstanding work includes Geser's comparative study (1987), which compares 223 Swiss communities in terms of their organisation according to the so-called 'militia principle', that by Germann and Weis (1995), who systematically record and compare the structures of cantonal administrations, and that by Schedler and Summermatter (2005), who have regularly recorded and compared the development of e-government in Switzerland at all government levels ever since 2003.

It is interesting to note that the 'militia' system has not been examined a great deal from the point of view of public management. The publications that come closest to the issues of public management were usually written by political scientists and explore the role and influence of part-time politicians in cooperation with an administration that is increasingly professionalised (Albonico 1979). Berchtold (1988) alone outlined the development of administrative structures against the background of the 'militia' system. According to her, the increasing wealth of tasks transformed the erstwhile largely militia structures, with temporary committees that were advised by only a few civil servants, into more and more professional structures. However, those involved hesitated to decentralise things and divided them into different spheres of competence because they were afraid of a shift of the power centre from the legitimised area (ie the collegial government) to individual members of that collegial government and to their officials. Such administrative change was only possible with the intuitive feel and sensitive flair displayed by individual members of government and civil servants.

Human resources is decidedly a management function but – like the other questions – was for a long time dealt with from a legal perspective. This primarily concerned the terms and conditions of employment, and the fact that the job-for-life principle did not apply resulted in a detailed discussion of how the employment of officials can be terminated (Jud 1975). In terms of employment, there is a great difference between Switzerland and Germany. In Germany, employment is based on the so-called 'alimentation' of officials, i.e. the state undertakes to secure their material needs, while they have to place their full working power at the state's disposal. This rule has its historical roots in the relationship between prince and civil servant (Hattenhauer 1993). Thus it is not a specific performance that is required, but the officials' working time and work effort. In return, the state covers all their needs, including health insurance and pension after retirement. In Switzerland, however, a performance is defined and remunerated, and government officials have to assume personal responsibility for their material welfare like any other citizen.

Another important topic is the incompatibility of office and mandate, which appears to be a matter of course for Anglo-Saxon countries. When the Allies enforced a modernisation of personnel management after the Second World War, this included a ban on officials engaging in political activities. The occupation of an office (ie employment as an official) thus precluded the acceptance of a mandate (ie a parliamentary seat). Under pressure from the civil service, however, Adenauer relapsed into the old system of professional officialdom in 1950, so that it is not uncommon that present-day German parliaments have a majority of officials who are relieved of their office for the period of their mandate but have been guaranteed that they will be able to return to their previous employment at the end of their mandate (Hattenhauer 1993). In Switzerland, the incompatibility of office and mandate applies with only a few exceptions, so that a transition from administration into the politics of the same community is a great exception. In this respect, Switzerland also differs from France, which is characterised by a high degree of permeability between the two subsystems (Proeller and Schedler 2005). All in all, it may be said that the personnel management of government officials in Switzerland has been largely adapted to the conditions of the private sector, even though the context of personnel management continues to be distinctly different owing to the great influence of politics.

Questions regarding the performance and results measurement of government activities were addressed in two contexts in Switzerland. In the 1980s, political science first attempted to achieve a stronger objectivisation of performance control through politics with the help of policy analysis. In the 1990s, NPM introduced a very distinct performance orientation, not least through the implementation of performance-oriented funding systems for universities (Schenker-Wicki 2001) or for public transport.

Institutional development of public management research

The early stage of studies about public management was strongly influenced by discussions in Germany – at least in German-speaking Switzerland. Although early doctoral theses dealing with local circumstances were written in this country (Nievergelt 1916), the debate nonetheless leant heavily on Switzerland's big neighbour in methodological terms.

After the Second World War, the Schweizerische Studiengesellschaft für die rationelle Verwaltung (Swiss Study Society for Rational Administration) was established, which from 1946 onwards staged biennial conferences about issues that we would now describe as public management (e.g. in 1948). During the same period of time, first publications appeared at the St Gallen Graduate School of Commerce (today's University of St Gallen), which had set up a (legally focused) Swiss Institute for Administration Courses in 1938 and examined questions of administrative reform early on (1947).

In the 1970s, calls for an actual graduate school for administration science were growing louder. Thus Pius Bischofberger, an economics professor from Basel, noted in an essay on the state of administrative sciences in Switzerland that there was no discipline of public administration as a pendant to business administration, with the consequence that operational questions were invariably referred to a discipline whose suitability for public administration was limited.

In 1981, this pressure resulted in the establishment of the Institut des Hautes Études en Administration Publique (IDHEAP) in Lausanne, whose research was strongly aligned with political science and law. According to Pelizzari (2001), however, it was the creation of Switzerland's first – and until recently only – Chair of Public Management at the University of St Gallen in 1980, with Ernst Buschor as full professor from 1985, that was more important for the development of public management. This chair gave rise to lively research activities in the context of doctoral theses on public administration at the University of St Gallen. In addition, the Swiss Society of Administrative Sciences was set up in 1983, whose objectives included the promotion of an economical use of public resources in public administration.

A new, big wave of public management activities was triggered by the discussion of New Public Management, which has been known in Switzerland as outcome-based public management since 1993 (Buschor 1993; Schedler 1995). The wide practical application of this model resulted in an enormous demand for research, teaching and executive education. This motivated the so-called universities of applied sciences, which were established at about the same time, to profile themselves in the field of public management. It was not least the University of Berne which decided to set up its own Centre of Competence for Public Management to do justice to its special (administrative) location, so that academic work is now being done in 12 places: the Universities of Berne, EPFL Lausanne, Lugano, Basel and St Gallen, as well as the Universities of Applied Sciences of Berne, Chur, Lucerne, Solothurn, Valais, St Gallen and Winterthur.

Discussion

As in the neighbouring countries France and Germany, public administration is a topic that has been a debating point time and again in Switzerland. The literature on the topics of administration is wide-ranging and diverse but has only been moulded by a systematic conception of public management since the 1980s. An international dialogue which not only makes use of international sources but also provides the international scientific community with genuine research contributions has only been taking place for just under 20 years. Consequently, Switzerland will not be found as a research place for public management on any international map, although its finely faceted structures and the pragmatic make-up of its public administration should render it particularly receptive to the study of public management.

Much of what has been happening in Switzerland is comparable with processes in France and Germany, since their political systems are built on the same traditions and principles (Proeller and Schedler 2005). Like them, Switzerland is a constitutional state with its own public law and, as in Germany and France, the legacy of Napoleon still has a lasting effect. Nonetheless, Swiss public administration differs substantially from its German and French counterparts: officials have no longer been employed for life since the nineteenth century and, in the wake of NPM, even the limited terms of office for officials were abolished in German-speaking Switzerland. Following the tradition of popular government, civil servants are largely treated like 'normal' employees in Switzerland, with comparable terms and conditions of employment. This, too, has historical roots: on Swiss territory, clergymen were regarded as perfectly normal citizens without any formal privileges as early as the thirteenth century.

Switzerland's direct democracy is unique in Europe and results in a slow development of new policies in this country, since every change must be socially balanced and simple to communicate. This precludes an elite *classe politique* in Switzerland as much as it does Germany's permanent civil service or France's *grand corps*. The Swiss aversion to a concentration of power, combined with thinking in terms of small areas, results in a distinctive civic mentality – also in public administration. The remuneration of Swiss civil servants is therefore fairly moderate as they are governed by formal rules, and performance bonuses are on the modest side. Even decoration with orders is prohibited in Switzerland – a cost-effective possibility of recognition of which neighbouring countries make frequent use.

The practice of public management, which also has a substantial influence on the study of public management in Switzerland, is characterised by the permeability of the systems. Public advertisements for vacancies in public administration lead to a relatively large number of applicants from the private sector. It is this permeability and the wide-ranging possibilities of participation that other countries could learn from Switzerland. Since this climate prevented the formation of an elite caste of administration officials who run the risk of finally seeing no one but themselves, Switzerland's position on the continuum between *homo œconomicus* (agency theory) and *homo socialis* (stewardship theory) is likely to be closer to the latter. That is, NPM in Switzerland is less focused on individuals who maximise their economic benefit in rational decisions than on civil servants who are expected to be intrinsically motivated and to be responsible citizens with a social focus. In NPM, too, the relationship between politics and administration is characterised much less by accountability than by responsibility. Government officials are expected to be responsible citizens and to bear in mind the welfare of the whole community when they fulfil their tasks. This reform agenda that has evolved in Switzerland (Schedler and Proeller 2002) and which differs from that of the Anglo-American model countries (based on a concept of man that is closer to the *homo œconomicus*), may well be a reason for the fact that NPM is still being actively implemented and developed today, in 2006.

Another decisive factor in the success of NPM in German-speaking Switzerland may well reside in the fact that the public administration's closeness to the people and its pragmatism has always resulted in economic modesty. In this context, government resources have to be treated with particular care. New Public Management, which has created so much buoyancy for the study of public management in Switzerland, is therefore not just in tune with the zeitgeist. Rather, it is also in keeping with the culture of German-speaking Switzerland and its leading public administrators.

Bibliography

Albonico, R. (1979) *Nebenamtlich – Nebenbei? Selbstverwaltung in kleinen Gemeinden: eine Untersuchung über Möglichkeiten und Grenzen des Miliz-Systems auf Gemeinde-Ebene in Graubünden*, Fanas: Pro Alpina.

Berchtold, D. (1988) *Management in der öffentlichen Verwaltung der Schweiz. Verwaltungskultur und Führungsorganisation. Zusammenhänge des Kollegial- und Departementalsystems 1848–1988*, Bern: Paul Haupt Verlag.

Bischofberger, P. (1977) 'Regierungs- und Verwaltungsreform in der Schweiz. Stand und Chancen', *Öffentliche Verwaltung in der Schweiz*, S. V. f. P. Wissenschaft, Bern: Paul Haupt Verlag, 17: 33–56.

Blindenbacher, R., Hablützel, P. and Letsch, B. (eds) (2000) *Vom Service Public zum Service au Public*, Zürich: Verlag Neue Zürcher Zeitung.

Bolz, U. and Klöti, U. (1996) 'Parlamentarisches Steuern neu erfinden? NPM-Steuerung durch die Bundesversammlung im Rahmen des New Public Managements (NPM) – ein Diskussionsbeitrag', *Zentralblatt für Staats- und Verwaltungsrecht*, 97: 145–82.

Bolz, U. and Lienhard, A. (2001) 'Staatsrechtliche Kernfragen der wirkungsorientierten Steuerung in den Kantonen', *Schweizerisches Zentralblatt für Staats- und Verwaltungsrecht*, 102: 2–30.

Brändli-Traffelet, S. (2004) 'Verwaltung des Sonderfalles. Plädoyer für eine Verwaltungskulturgeschichte der Schweiz', *Revue Suisse d'Histoire*, 54: 79–89.

Brühlmeier, D., Haldemann, T., Mastronardi, P. and Schedler, K. (2001) *Politische Planung. Mittelfristige Steuerung in der wirkungsorientierten Verwaltungsführung*, Bern: Paul Haupt.

Brühlmeier, D., Haldemann, T., Schedler, K. and Mastronardi, P. (1998) 'New Public Management für das Parlament: Ein Muster-Rahmenerlass WoV', *Schweizerisches Zentralblatt für Staats- und Verwaltungsrecht*, 99: 297–316.

Buschor, E. (1993) *Wirkungsorientierte Verwaltungsführung – Referat an der Generalversammlung der Zürcher Handelskammer, Zürich 1. Juli 1993*, Zürich: Zürcher Handelskammer.

Buschor, E. (1994) 'Introduction: From Advanced Public Accounting via Performance Measurement to New Public Management', in E. Buschor and K. Schedler, *Perspectives on Performance Measurement and Public Sector Accounting*, Bern: Paul Haupt.

Buschor, E., Schedler, K. and Stäger, L. (1993) *Finanz- und Lastenausgleich im Kanton Zürich Gutachten zuhanden des Regierungsrates des Kantons Zürich*, Bern: Paul Haupt.

Bussmann, W. (1995) 'Wirkungsorientierte Verwaltung, NPM und Evaluationen', in P. Hablützel, T. Haldemann, K. Schedler and K. Schwaar, *Umbruch in Politik und Verwaltung*, Bern: Paul Haupt.

Chappelet, J.-L. (2004) 'e-Government as an Enabler of Public Management Reform: the Case of Switzerland', *Lecture Notes in Computer Science*, 3183: 283–8.

Du Pasquier, J.-N. (1986). *L'état englobé: l'insertion de l'état dans l'économie suisse 1950–1980*, Lausanne: Editions Réalités Sociales.

Ehrensperger, M. (2007) *PPPs in der Schweiz – Gründe für deren mangelhafte Umsetzung*, Bern: Paul Haupt.

Eichenberger, K. (1954). *Rechtssetzungsverfahren und Rechtssetzungsformen in der Schweiz: Bemerkungen zur Praxis der Rechtssetzung, insbesondere in der Gesetzgebung*, Basel: Helbing and Lichtenhahn.

Eichenberger, K. (1989) 'Hochleistungsverwaltung des entfalteten Sozialstaats', in U. Häfelin and W. Haller (eds) *Festschrift für Ulrich Häfelin zum 65. Geburtstag*, Zürich: Schulthess.

Finger, M. (2002) 'Dynamique de la Nouvelle Gestion Publique et Rôle du Parlement', Bellanger and F. T. Tanquerel, *Les Contrats de Prestations*, Geneva: Helbling and Lichtenhahn.

Fleiner, F. (1911) *Institutionen des Deutschen Verwaltungsrechts*, Tübingen: Mohr.

Frey, B. S. and R. Jegen (2001) 'Motivation Crowding Theory', *Journal of Economic Surveys*, 15: 589–612.

Frey, R. L. (1995) 'New Public Management und Finanzausgleich', in P. Hablützel, T. Haldemann, K. Schedler and K. Schwaar, *Umbruch in Politik und Verwaltung. Ansichten und Erfahrungen zum New Public Management in der Schweiz*, Bern: Paul Haupt.

Germann, R. (1982) *Regierung und Verwaltung beim Bund*, Lausanne: IDHEAP.

Germann, R. (1987) 'L'amalgame public-privé: l'administration para-étatique en Suisse', *Annuaire européen d'administration publique*, 25: 305–31.

Germann, R. (1998) *Der Staatsapparat und die Regierung*, Bern: Paul Haupt.

Germann, R. and Weis, K. (1995) *Kantonsverwaltungen im Vergleich*, Bern: Paul Haupt.

Germann, R. E. (1997) *Drei Essays zur schweizerischen Verwaltungsgeschichte*, Lausanne: IDHEAP.

Geser, H. (1987) *Milizorganisation und Berufsverwaltung. Vergleichende Untersuchungen in 223 deutschschweizer Gemeinden*, Bern: Paul Haupt.

Giacometti, Z. (1960) *Allgemeine Lehren des rechtsstaatlichen Verwaltungsrechts*, Zurich: Polygraphischer Verlag.

Grisel, A. (1970) *Droit administratif suisse*, Neuchâtel: Editions Ides et Calendes.

Haldemann, T. (1995) *New Public Management: Ein neues Konzept für die Verwaltungsführung des Bundes?*, Bern: EPA.

Hattenhauer, H. (1993) *Geschichte des deutschen Beamtentums*, Cologne: Carl Heymanns.

Hofmeister, A. and Borchert, H. (2004) 'Public-Private Partnerships in Switzerland: Crossing the Bridge with the Aid of a new Governance Approach', *International Review of Administrative Sciences*, 70: 217–32.

Jans, A. and Meili, R. (1988) *Rationalisierung der öffentlichen Verwaltung in der Schweiz*, Zürich: NZZ.

Jud, E. M. (1975) *Besonderheiten öffentlichrechtlicher Dienstverhältnisse nach schweizerischem Recht, insbesondere bei deren Beendigung aus nichtdisziplinarischen Gründen*, St Gallen: Schweizerisches Institut für Verwaltungskurse.

Kettiger, D. (2000) *Wirkungsorientierte Verwaltungsführung und Gesetzgebung. Untersuchungen an der Schnittstelle zwischen New Public Management und Gesetzgebung*, Bern: Paul Haupt.

Kettiger, D. (2003) 'Die Einführung von New Public Management aus gesetzgeberischer Sicht', *AJP/PJA*, 6: 641–54.

Kirchgässner, G., Feld, L. P. and Savioz, M. R. (1999). *Die direkte Demokratie: modern, erfolgreich, entwicklungs- und exportfähig*, Basel: Helbling and Lichtenhahn.

Klöti, U. (1972) *Die Chefbeamten der schweizerischen Bundesverwaltung: Soziologische Querschnitte in den Jahren 1938, 1955 und 1969*, Bern: Francke.

Klöti, U. (1988) 'Entrenching New Instruments for Government: The Case of Switzerland', C. Campbell and B. G. Peters, *Organizing Governance. Governing Organizations*, Pittsburgh: University of Pittsburg Press.

Klöti, U. (1994) 'Switzerland: Serving the State and Maximizing Income', C. Hood and B. G. Peters, *Rewards at the Top. A Comparative Study of High Public Office*, London: Sage.

Klöti, U. (1995) 'Auswirkungen des New Public Management auf den Föderalismus', in P. Hablützel, T. Haldemann, K. Schedler and K. Schwaar, *Umbruch in Politik und Verwaltung*, Bern: Paul Haupt.

Knoepfel, P. (1987) 'Probleme (international) vergleichender Politikanalysen', in R. Koch (ed.) *Verwaltungsforschung in Perspektive*, Baden-Baden: Nomos.

Knoepfel, P. (1995) 'New Public Management: Vorprogrammierte Enttäuschungen oder politische Flurschäden – Eine Kritik aus Sicht der Politikanalyse', P. Hablützel, T. Haldemann, K. Schedler and K. Schwaar, Bern: Paul Haupt.

Kopp, D. (1997) *New Public Management. Heil oder Segen? Möglichkeiten und Grenzen aus ökonomischer Sicht*, Basel: Wirtschaftswissenschaftliches Zentrum der Universität.

Kupper, E. (1929) *Die Besoldungspolitik des Bundes seit 1848*, Elgg: Büchi.

Lane, J.-E. (2000) *New Public Management*, London/New York: Routledge.

Lienhard, A. (2003) 'Verwaltung im 21. Jahrhundert: Versuch eines Ausblicks aus staatsrechtlicher Sicht', in R. J. Schweizer, C. Jeanrenaud, S. Kux and B. Sitter-Liver *Verwaltung im 21. Jahrhundert. Herausforderungen, Probleme, Lösungswege*, Freiburg: Universitätsverlag.

Lienhard, A. (2005) *Staats- und verwaltungsrechtliche Grundlagen für das New Public Management in der Schweiz. Analyse – Anforderungen – Impulse*, Bern: Stämpfli.

Lienhard, A., Ritz, A., Steiner, R. and Ladner, A. (eds) (2005) '10 Jahre New *Public Management* in der Schweiz. Bilanz, Irrtümer und Erfolgsfaktoren', Public Management, Bern: Paul Haupt.

Linder, W., Werder, H. and Hotz-Hart, B. (1979) *Planung in der Schweizerischen Demokratie*, Bern: Paul Haupt.

Mäder, C. (2000) 'Der moralische Kreuzzug des New Public Management in der Schweiz', *Sozialer Sinn: Zeitschrift für hermeneutische Sozialforschung*, 2: 191–204.

Mastronardi, P. (1995) 'Staatsrecht und Verwaltungsorganisation. Reflexionen am Beispiel des New Public Management', *AJP/PJA*, 4: 1541–53.

Mastronardi, P. (1998) 'Primat der Politik vor der Verwaltung? Das Verhältnis von Politik und Verwaltung – Wandel und Veränderungschancen', in B. Ehrenzeller, P. Mastronardi, R. Schaffhauser, R. Schweizer and K. Vallender, *Der Verfassungsstaat vor neuen Herausforderungen – Festschrift für Yvo Hangartner*, St Gallen/Lachen: Dike Verlag AG.

Mastronardi, P. (1999) 'Gewaltenteilung unter NPM', *Schweizerisches Zentralblatt für Staats- und Verwaltungsrecht*, 100: 449–64.

Mastronardi, P. (2000) 'Die staatspolitische Erweiterung des NPM-Konzeptes aus rechtlicher Sicht', *Verwaltung und Management*, 6: 222–7.

Mastronardi, P. (2001) 'Die Verwaltung im 21. Jahrhunder – eine Skizze', in R. Schweizer, C. Jeanrenaud, S. Kux and B. Sitter-Liver, *Verwaltung im 21. Jahrhundert. Herausforderungen, Probleme, Lösungswege*, Freiburg: Universitätsverlag, 369–400.

Mastronardi, P. and Schedler, K. (1998) *New Public Management in Staat und Recht – Ein Diskurs*, Bern: Paul Haupt.

Mastronardi, P. and Schedler, K. (2005) *New Public Management in Staat und Recht. Mit einem Kommentar von Daniel Brühlmeier und einer Stellungnahme von Daniel Kettiger*, Bern: Paul Haupt.

Mastronardi, P. and Stadler, P. (2003) 'Demokratietaugliche WoV: Das Solothurner Modell', *Schweizerisches Zentralblatt für Staats- und Verwaltungsrecht*, 8: 393–417.

Möckli, S. (1995) *Wirkungsorientierte Verwaltungsführung und direkte Demokratie*, St Gallen: Institut für Politikwissenschaft.

Neidhart, L. (1974) 'Aufbau und Wandel des eidg. Regierungssystems', *Schweizer Monatshefte*, 54: 419–29.

Neidhart, L. (2002) *Die politische Schweiz – Fundamente und Institutionen*, Zürich: Verlag Neue Zürcher Zeitung.

Niedermann, D. (1998) 'Zur Föderalismusreform – ein Diskussionsbeitrag aus kantonaler Sicht', in B. Ehrenzeller, P. Mastronardi, R. Schaffhauser, R. Schweizer and K. Vallender, *Der Verfassungsstaat vor neuen Herausforderungen – Festschrift für Yvo Hangartner*, St Gallen/Lachen: Dike Verlag AG, 697–712.

Nievergelt, J. (1916) *Beamtenrecht des Kantons Zürich*, Zürich: Dissertation Universität Zürich.

Nuspliger, K. and Kettiger, D. (1999) 'Gewaltenteilung und wirkungsorientierte Verwaltungsführung', *Schweizerisches Zentralblatt für Staats- und Verwaltungsrecht*, 100: 465–82.

Pelizzari, A. (2001) *Die Ökonomisierung des Politischen*, Konstanz: UVK.

Pollitt, C. and Bouckaert, G. (2000) *Public Management Reform: a Comparative Analysis*, Oxford: Oxford University Press.

Proeller, I. and Schedler, K. (2005) 'Change and continuity in the continental tradition of public management', in E. Ferlie, L. E. Lynn and C. Pollitt (eds) *The Oxford Handbook of Public Management*, Oxford: Oxford University Press.

Remak, J. (1993) *A Very Civil War: the Swiss Sonderbund War of 1847*, Boulder: Westview Press.

Rieder, S. and Lehmann, L. (2002) 'Evaluation of New Public Management Reforms in Switzerland. Empirical Results and Reflections on Methodology', *International Public Management Review*, 3: 25–43.

Ruflin, R. (2006) *Wohlfahrtstaatliches Kontraktmanagement*, Bern: Paul Haupt.

Schedler, K. (1995) *Ansätze einer wirkungsorientierten Verwaltungsführung*, Bern: Paul Haupt.

Schedler, K. (1997) 'The State of Public Management Reforms in Switzerland', in W. Kickert, *Public Management and Administrative Reform in Western Europe*, Cheltenham: Edward Elgar.

Schedler, K. (2000) 'Performance Measurement Challenges in Switzerland: Lessons from Implementation', *International Public Management Review* 1: 62–83.

Schedler, K. (2003) "And politics?" Public Management Developments in the Light of Two Rationalities', *Public Management Review*, 54: 533–50.

Schedler, K. and Knechtenhofer, B. (2002) 'Rechnungslegung in der öffentlichen Verwaltung', *Der Schweizer Treuhänder*, 76: 687–92.

Schedler, K. and Proeller, I. (2002) 'The New Public Management: a Perspective from Mainland Europe', in K. McLaughlin, S. P. Osborne and E. Ferlie, *New Public Management. Current trends and future prospects*, London, New York: Routledge.

Schedler, K. and Schmidt, B. (2004) 'Managing the eGov Organisation', in L. R. Jones, R. Mussari and K. Schedler, *Strategies in Public Management Reforms*, Cambridge: Information Age Press.

Schedler, K. and Summermatter, L. (2005) *Electronic Government Barometer. Bericht zum Stand von E-Government in der Schweiz 2004*, St Gallen: IDT-HSG.

Schenker-Wicki, A. (2001) 'Assessing the Impact of Federal Funding to Swiss Universities: a New Performance Audit Concept', *International Public Management Review*, 2: 70–87.

Schweizer, R. J. (2001) 'Verwaltung als Gegenstand sozialwissenschaftlicher Studien oder über den Diskurs unter den Verwaltungswissenschaften in der Schweiz', in R. Schweizer, C. Jeanrenaud, S. Kux and B. Sitter-Liver, *Verwaltung im 21. Jahrhundert. Herausforderungen, Probleme, Lösungswege*, Freiburg: Universitätsverlag.

Schweizerische Studiengesellschaft für rationelle Verwaltung (ed.) (1948) *Studientagung über die technischen Arbeitsmethoden in der Verwaltung*, Bern: EDMZ.

Schweizerische Verwaltungskurse (ed.) (1947) *Verwaltungsreform*, St Gallen SVK: Veröffentlichungen der Schweizerischen Verwaltungskurse der Handelshochschule St Gallen.

Steiner, R. (2000) 'New Public Management in Swiss Municipalities', *International Public Management Journal*, 3: 169–90.

Summermatter, L. (2006) *Einflussfaktoren der E-Government Entwicklung*, Bern: Paul Haupt.

Ulrich, H. and Sidler, F. (1977) *Ein Managementmodell für die öffentliche Hand*, Bern: Paul Haupt.

Varone, F. (2003) 'Le Temps Administratif et la Nouvelle Gestion Publique', in R. J. Schweizer (ed.) *Verwaltung im 21 Jahrhundert*, Freiburg: Universitätsverlag.

Vatter, A. (2002) 'Föderalismus', in U. Klöti, P. Knoepfel, H. Kriesi, W. Linder and Y. Papadopoulos, *Handbuch der Schweizer Politik*, Zurich: Verlag Neue Zürcher Zeitung.

Zimmerli, U. (1997) 'New Public Management und parlamentarische Oberaufsicht', *Der Schweizer Treuhänder*, 97/3: 185–8.

Zimmerli, U. and Lienhard, A. (2002) 'Rechtsgutachten zu FLAG – Genehmigung von Leistungsaufträgen durch das Parlament', Bern: Universität Bern, Kompetenzzentrum für Public Management, Institut für öffentliches Recht.

Zindel, W. (1945) *Neuzeitliche Abrechnungsmethoden im Rechnungswesen der öffentlichen Verwaltung*, Zürich: Kaufmännischer Verein.

8 The study of public management in Italy

Management and the dominance of public law

Marco Meneguzzo

Introduction

Public management research in Italy is a recent development, concurrent with the administrative reforms and the devolution process in place since the early 90s. The distinctive national characteristics of the study of public management in Italy are explained in this chapter by considering three main issues:

- the historical evolution of public administration in Italy, including an analysis of characteristics preceding and following the political and administrative unification in 1861;
- the coexistence of competing disciplines in the study of public administration and the traditional domination of the administrative law approach;
- the recent influence of the Anglo-American managerial approach, New Public Management ideas, and the Italian managerial theory *economia aziendale*.

The study of public management in Italy is strongly influenced by early administrative history and the coexistence of several disciplinary approaches including administrative, political and managerial sciences, sociology, law, and public economics.

First, we will examine a synthesis of historical texts on public administration before and after the unification in 1861, focusing on those historical trends which most influenced the path of public management and administration. This synthesis will help bring to light the principal causes of the current state of Italian public administration, including the heterogeneous performance of central, northern and southern Italy.

Next we will analyse public administration education in Italy while considering a survey of 42 Italian universities. The fourth section will explore the unique characteristics of Italian public management studies, highlighting both domestic patterns (ie the *economia aziendale* approach) and influences from abroad (namely the New Public Management wave). To this end, we will take a closer look at the aforementioned university survey. Finally, the closing section reviews the main features of public management research in Italy with a content analysis of the articles published in *Azienda Pubblica*, the most important academic journal on public management in Italy in the last decade.

History of the state and administration

One hundred and fifty years after unification, Italian public administration is relatively young when compared with the administrative systems of other European countries such as France, Spain, and the United Kingdom. Still, performance is disproportionately heterogeneous across regions, particularly when considering central, northern and southern Italy. Furthermore, the influence of pre-unification administrative systems on political, social, and civil society development merits exploration as it is not immediately obvious.

Italian public administration is the result of the cross-fertilization of different administrative cultures, including the *Rechtsstaat* tradition (Austro-Hungarian derived, Lombardia and Veneto), bureaucratic Napoleonic traditions (Piemonte and Sardinia), and weak-state models more similar to the Vatican State and the Two Sicilies realm (south Italy). These administrative cultures embody vastly differing visions of institutional and organizational models, and a diversity of relationships between public administration, citizens/civil society and other social and economic actors. These cultures further influence more minor themes such as public accounting and the management of public assets. This can be seen in northern regions, where attention was given to openness and clarity of bureaucratic processes and the delivery of basic public services such as waste and garbage collection, road maintenance, and public lighting. Here the philanthropy of the aristocracy and bourgeoisie played a strong role in the provision of social services and health care.

In contrast, the southern civil servants were known for their arbitrariness and free-riding behaviours which determined the low quality of public services and a greater distance between the government and the citizens. The *brigantaggio*, the rule of bandits, described the violent response from locals. This phenomenon lasted through most of the nineteenth century. However, in the *Sabaudia* realm, the French army had imposed Napoleonic institutions such as the *préfet*, with highly formalized careers and a strong hierarchy (Melis 1996).

While the Piedmont, in north-western Italy, played a leading role in shaping the unified administration, institutional modernization efforts took place earlier and more obviously in other pre-unified states. East of Piedmont, in the Lombardo-Veneto region, a social class of bureaucrats was developed following a formalized pattern fostered by the Austro-Hungarian empire, and featuring educational requirements for entry, career mobility, and ethical principles.

In the Naples realm and the Kingdom of the Two Sicilies, the main Bourbonic laws (1816 and 1817) were in line with the previous French tradition. There were differences between formal rules, based on professional bureaucracy and territorial mobility, and their real application (prevalence of personnel with aristocratic origins). In other states, such as the Vatican Kingdom, there was general lack of formal norms regulating the organization and functioning of public offices. On the eve of unification, the various administrations counted nearly 60,000 employees, of which about 25,000 were from the Kingdom of the Two Sicilies.

Prior to the political and administrative unification, the Italian states with the exception of Lombardo-Veneto, were converging towards the French administrative model. Still, in the years immediately following unification, there were many discussions about which administrative model to adopt at the national level. The two main options were the Lombardo-Veneto model, based on a contingency approach emphasising local specificities and considered highly successful, and the French-inspired Piedmont (Napoleonic) model, based on principles of organizational uniformity. The Piedmont model was selected hesitantly, considering the bureaucratic fragility of the southern administrative systems and the decentralization experienced under the Bourbon rule (Fedele 1998).

The new model aimed to centralize political accountability and unify policy-making and executive activities. The creation of the post of secretary general further linked the minister with the bureaucratic apparatus.

In the aftermath of unification, central government gained authority at the local level in almost every field, with the exceptions of defence and justice. First introduced in 1853 and then in the unified Italy in 1865, the main difference with the French model was the absence of inter-ministerial coordination. In Italy, the competences of the central government authorities operating at the local level were not integrated with those taken on by the prefects. Ministries were organized in general directorates, initially grouped as war, finance, and public works ministries, which expanded steadily during the following years. This induced a greater autonomy of the directors general from the minister. During the 1880s, liberal government revised this model, abolishing the post of secretary general and creating a deputy secretary general similar to the British parliamentary secretary. Yet at central level, the ministries-model, in a pure Weberian style, continued to exist until the 1990s.

During these years the number, size, and diffusion of the agencies and independent authorities fluctuated (Cassese 2003).[1] In terms of sub-national levels of government, Italy has elements of both centralized France and the regional state of Germany. Different from Germany, the Italian central government has peripherical administrations at the local level, which coexist with regions, communes, and provinces. Cassese (2003) estimated that in every province there were at least 100 peripherical offices of the state. Although local governments have been recognized as autonomous in the Italian constitution, it was only in 1990 that a thorough reform was undertaken, with constitutional revision only in 2001.

The Italian bureaucracy from the unification to 1900 was characterized by small size[2] and high uniformity, with most of the employees coming from the Piemonte administration. Career paths were mainly hierarchical, with high integration between bureaucrats and politicians. It was only in 1908 that a civil servants statute[3] was adopted, as a consequence of a major conflict due to the increasing size and function of the government, as well as the increasing social and cultural diversity of public employees, an increasing number of whom came from the former Kingdom of the Two Sicilies and the former Vatican State.

Public employment increased as a consequence of the expansion of the role of the state in the economy (Table 8.1). This increase in the number of public employees and functions did not happen in conjunction with political and administrative unification, as in other European countries, but four decades later in connection with the industrialization process. Here the state did not steer the economic development process as in France (Melis 1996). The increase in numbers of employees from south Italy – 'southernization' – was simultaneous with this expansion.

Selection and training were carried out by the administration itself, which brought about the isolation of bureaucracy. Administrative elites, such as those developed in France and the United Kingdom (Cassese 1983), were all but nonexistent, and the closeness of career paths did not allow the development of an education system similar to the ENA in France. Needless to say, Italy did not have established public administration education traditions such as the French *grands corps* or the English 'Oxbridge'. During the 1920s, the Giolitti government introduced a reform programme including privatizations and liberalizations of some public services, ministerial reorganization and merger, and modernization of civil service and public finance. It is important to note that, between the First and Second World Wars, many policies of public administration and public employment did not substantially influence the decision-making processes and way of working of Italian public administrations, which remained the same as when they were introduced during the 1920s.

The 1970s brought three important reforms: the reform of the health-care system, the reform of the fiscal system and the creation of regional governments. The decentralization process continued in 1977 and in 1998. Administrative reform launched in 1979–1980 (Giannini 1979) and remained idle until 1990.

The main thrust of this administrative reform included the adoption of scientific management ideas, the creation in each administration of a unit dedicated to the implementation of managerial techniques, and the privatization of public employment, with the exception of the higher civil service.

In 1990, the law on simplification and administrative transparency was approved and some of the most important independent administrative authorities were set up. A new agency was introduced in 1992 with the mission to coordinate the contractual bargaining process between the state and public-employee unions. This was followed by the reorganization of several ministries.

However, two decades after the reforms of the 1970s, innovations in administrative transparency remained unsatisfactory, as highlighted in an evaluation by the Agnelli Foundation. Less than 50 per cent of government offices had implemented governmental guidelines. This failure is even more pronounced in the areas of citizen relations and process management.

Table 8.1 The evolution of public employment after unification

	1861	1881	1891	1910(a)	1923(b)	1930	1941(c)	1975	1980	1997	2002
Public employees	50,000	64,992	126,343	376,777	509,145	527,769	1,139,774	1,995,834	2,145,960	3,102,727	3,546,507

Source: Based on data from Cassese, 1983; ISTAT, 2005.

Notes
Since 1910, figures include autonomous public enterprise; since 1923, judges; since 1932, teachers.

We can track the failures of transparency reform to several important factors, the most influential including fiscal and budgetary pressures, loss of citizens' trust, an ageing society, changes in the electoral system, and political vision and leadership.

Initially, budgetary pressures were the driving force for reform. A calamitous combination of a relatively low level of taxation, huge government debt, and poor quality and cost-transparancy of public services was magnified during European integration. This resulted in higher taxation and direct costs to citizens for certain public services.

A second driver is related to the low levels of citizens' trust in public institutions. While it was an overall trend, it is often exemplified by the massive popular protest against widespread corruption in the early 1990s, the so-called '*tangentopoli*' (the state of bribery), which led to many reforms aimed at improving the government–citizens relationship (Table 8.2). Several referenda during these years highlighted the positive attitude of citizens towards the abolishment of some ministries. The media in turn have placed enormous emphasis on the technical nature of managerial expertise as a sort of moral antidote to the degeneration of politics (Panozzo 2000).

A third factor in the failure of reform to yield the expected benefits is that demographic changes, in terms of the ageing of society and the growth of immigration, have led to many problems in the social, health, and pension systems.

Important changes to the electoral system introduced the direct election of mayors (1993), presidents of provinces (1993), presidents/governors of regions (2000), with the aim of strengthening the stability of local governments and public accountability mechanisms.

Influences from abroad were mainly visible in the greater focus on new management practices such as the performance orientation of budgeting and human

Table 8.2 Trust in the civil service (as a percentage)

	1981	1990	1999	2002
Austria		42	65	66
Denmark	47	51	50	60
Finland	53	33	43	43
France	52	49	44	45
Germany	32	38	43	45
Ireland	54	59	61	64
Italy	27	25	27	29
Netherlands	44	46	57	55
Portugal		36	44	47
Spain	39	35	39	43
Sweden	46	44	45	60
UK	47	46	44	48

Source: OECD/PGC, 2005; Eurobarometer, World Values Study.

resources management in what has been coined the 'Italian wave' of new public management.

Political vision and leadership were changed accordingly. It was only in the early 1990s, with the governments of Amato and Ciampi, that the modernization of the public sector became a central element with the public finances recovery programmes. More recently, regulatory reform became an area of focus for the Italian government. Policies of simple streamlining of individual practices and the introduction of the one-stop shops for businesses were followed by codified policies for specific areas and subjects.

Integrity and ethics in public service have also been addressed by initiatives aimed at fighting corruption and managing situations of conflict of interest. Law No. 3 of 2003 instituted the 'High Commissioner for preventing and fighting corruption' in conformity with the provisions of the International Convention against Corruption recently adopted by the United Nations. Another important area of reform focuses on implementing a shift from a procedures-based administration to a results-based administration. This was mainly achieved through the modernization of preventative legitimacy control systems, seeing them evolve to managerial controls focused on *ex post* evaluation of economic impacts, social impacts, efficiency, and effectiveness. A performance-oriented approach in the public sector has been introduced mainly through strategic planning initiatives, both at the central and the local and regional levels of government.

A key area of reform still under way is the devolution of powers from the central administration to the territorial administrations (ie regions, provinces, and municipalities). Future challenges in this area will be multilevel governance issues (particularly regulatory governance), integrated decision-making and the development of local-level competency in new functions.

Public management reforms in Italy have taken both a legislative and a top-down approach. While the contents of reforms are very much in line with the New Public Management principles and the experience of other OECD countries, the approach to implementation is particular to Italian reforms. These particularities include the implementation gap problem, problems of scope (namely, wide-ranging reforms), the varied speed and degree of modernization across geographical areas/types of administrations, and the lack of evaluation. While the Italian government has been very active in introducing new and all-encompassing laws for reform, it is particularly weak in implementation. The modernization paths of bodies such as the central and local governments, national and local public enterprises, and executive agencies are quite divergent. These differences are indicated by their varying innovation capacities. Still there has been no systematic evaluation of the public administration reform process in Italy.

The coexistence of different public administrations, the difficulties encountered in their integration and the effective establishment of a public administration system only in the past 50 years have without a doubt influenced the study, as well as the reform, of public management in Italy and produced significant consequences. It worth noting here the administrative and institutional dualism and the different speeds of the modernization process in the north and south

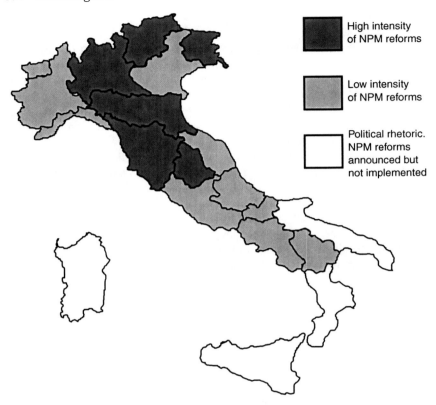

Figure 8.1 The adoption of NPM in different regions in Italy.

(Cammelli 2004; Dente 1999), the relationship between institutional performance and civil society (Putnam, Leonardi and Nanetti 1994) and the particulars
of public administration in the south (Mezzogiorno) in terms of political-
administrative relationships and the spread of free-riding behaviours (Dupuy
and Thoenig 1982; Rebora 1999). In illustration, Figure 8.1 presents the
varying rates of adoption of New Public Management across regions in Italy.

Public administration education, with a focus on public management

An analysis of public administration education programmes in Europe (Hajnal
2003) defines three clusters: a legal group of countries, where a strong emphasis
is put on administrative/public law; a public group, in which the public administration is recognized to have a unique public and political character; and a
corporate group, focused on business management techniques (see Table 8.3).

   Italian public administration has traditionally been dominated by administrative and public law, while hesitant initiatives aimed at introducing scientific

Table 8.3 Clusters in public administration education

Public	Legal	Corporate
Belgium	Greece	Denmark
Spain	Italy	Netherlands
France	Portugal	
Sweden		

Source: Adapted from Hajnal 2003 in van de Walle *et al.* 2004: 237.

management principles encountered obstacles related to a formalistic and juridical culture. Still we see the simultaneous presence of several disciplinary approaches in the study of public administration, each focused on different research areas. Among these are the administrative-sciences approach (developed inside the administrative law and public accounting areas), the organizational-sociology, the political-sciences, the public-policy-analysis and, finally, the *economia aziendale* approach. Still today the most consolidated approaches include both administrative law/science and political science. More recently, researchers have noted a convergence between these two areas which favours a multidisciplinary approach. This is exemplified in policy analysis and implementation research and the descriptive theory of public administration decision-making.

The current state of the study of public administration in Italy can be further analysed using a survey of 42 Italian universities,[4] which consisted of a web-based content analysis of the undergraduate and postgraduate programmes in the faculties of economics, law, political sciences, sociology, and science of communication. The sample of universities was determined by the necessity to compare these results with those of a 2004 survey on public management educational programmes to which the economic faculties of these 42 universities responded, an account of which is given later in this section.

Public administration degree programmes were found in 32 of the 42 universities. A closer look at these faculties exposes interesting aspects. The number of degree programmes on public administration is higher in political sciences faculties, followed by economic faculties and law faculties (see Table 8.4).

Table 8.4 Public administration degree programmes in different faculties in 42 Italian universities

Faculty	Number of programmes
Economic	26
Law	18
Political sciences	30
Sciences of communication	2
Sociology	1

Source: author, July 2006.

Table 8.5 MA programmes in public administration in different faculties in 42 Italian universities

Faculty	Number of programmes
Economic	19
Law	4
Political sciences	3
Sciences of communication	1
Sociology	2

Source: author, July 2006.

In the area of postgraduate education, there are 29 Master of Arts programmes and 12 doctoral programmes dedicated to public administration, as illustrated in Tables 8.5 and 8.6.

The pervasiveness of postgraduate courses related to public management in economic faculties can be explained by the demand competencies for expressed by public managers: in 2005 the Italian Department of Public Administration interviewed 1,588 senior civil servants, of which 99 per cent were felt to lack managerial competencies.

Academic departments dedicated to public administration issues are found in only six of the 42 universities, of which five were positioned inside economic faculties and one in a political sciences faculty. This feature, far from representing a strong influence of the New Public Management approach, can be explained by taking into account the *economia aziendale* approach, explained in the next section.

Regarding education programmes specifically focused on public management, a survey of *economia aziendale* carried out by the two state universities of Rome (Tor Vergata and Rome 3) on behalf of the Italian Academia has highlighted the steady expansion of graduate and postgraduate courses on public management in the 42 universities that responded to the survey. The survey found 149 graduate courses in public management (Bologna education model); 34 postgraduate master's programmes in public management, public policy

Table 8.6 PhD programmes in public administration in different faculties in 42 Italian universities

Faculty	Number of programmes
Economic	10
Law	0
Political sciences	1
Sciences of communication	0
Sociology	1

Source: author, July 2006.

Table 8.7 Undergraduate courses on public management in the 42 surveyed universities

Undergraduate courses	Number of courses
Public management (general)	64; 46%
Public accounting	24; 17%
Planning, budgeting and control	29; 21%
Other courses	23; 16%

Source: D'Alessio *et al.* (2004).

and management, and innovation and public management; and, four inter-university PhD programmes dedicated to public management. Of the 149 undergraduate courses on public management, 66 per cent were within triennial degrees, while 34 per cent were within the biennial specialist degrees of the Bologna system.

Twenty-one percent of the courses tackle issues of planning, budgeting, and control, compared with just 17 per cent of courses in accounting systems – which was earlier introduced in public management studies. The remaining courses are in areas of organizational and human resources management studies and public–private relationships. It should be noted that the increase in planning and control courses and the prominent role played by general courses in public management are a direct consequence of the impact of the New Public Management ideas on the study of public management in Italy.

Of the postgraduate degrees investigated, 34 are master of arts programmes. Futhermore, there are four doctoral programmes dedicated to public management at each of Rome Tor Vergata, Bocconi, Siena, and Salerno Universities.

Public administration and management research framework

The national characteristics of the Italian study of public management are the result of two main influences: the typical *economia aziendale* approach and the New Public Management wave. Although the development of *economia aziendale* dates back to the first decades of the twentieth century, it was thoroughly applied to public administrations only in the past two decades. The coexistence of several more dominant disciplinary approaches in the study of public administration, and

Table 8.8 Public management MA programmes in the 42 surveyed universities

MA programmes	Number of programmes
Public management and innovation	7; 21%
Focused on specific issues	27; 79%

Source: D'Alessio *et al.* (2004).

the development of its own disciplinary identity, are the main challenges faced by the *economia aziendale* researchers in Italy.

Economia aziendale is a theoretical framework developed in Italy for describing the strategies, behaviours, and operations of the private for-profit enterprises. It can be ascribed to the institutional approach to economics as opposed to the dominating technical and practical approaches. The main cornerstones and propositions of the framework are described in Pessina 2002 (see Box 1).

Box 1 The *economia aziendale* approach

A possible translation for *economia aziendale* may be business manage-ment or business administration, even if none of these terms satisfactorily captures its meaning, which corresponds to the German *Betrieb-swirtschaftslehre* (Borgonovi 1992).

Economia aziendale is the result of specific developments within the field of institutional economics, taking place in Italy, Germany, and central Europe. It is different from the analytical, model-based, and econometric focus of the Anglo-American approach (Borgonovi 1992) and also from the French *sciences de gestion*, since these studies are centred around the capitalist enterprise archetype, focused on individual profitability object-ives. Other differences concern the research method (inductive/deductive in the former, mainly inductive in the latter).

It is a positive, general theory of economics and of the management of all kinds of social-political entities. Also, it is holistic and interdisciplinary and oriented towards the guidance of managers in need of strong general principles and theories useful in understanding the contingent reality. Studies falling into this approach correspond to specific information needs relating to business management issues.

An organization, according to the *economia aziendale* approach, is an *azienda* if it obeys several guiding principles. It is seen as a social and economic unit with an autonomous existence that is unitary, evolutionary, enduring, and innovative.

Unitariness comes about when the decisions of corporate governance are mutually consistent and shared by the members of the organization. Autonomy means that, while taking into account legitimate external expectations, the organization must make its decisions freely and in the interest of its members. Furthermore, it means that the organization is not systematically dependent on third parties, in order to avoid having to submit to the will of such parties. In the absence of unitariness and auto-nomy, the organization loses the capability to make timely decisions ori-ented towards long-term development. Unitariness and autonomy are necessary conditions for efficiency (as a condition for institutional

---

equilibrium) and effectiveness. Whenever efficiency and effectiveness are not critical objectives (when the organization is allowed to operate in a protected environment), even unitariness and autonomy lose their relevance. Other principles relate to the integration and balances of interests, to equity, etc. (Airoldi *et al.* 1995).

The *economia aziendale* approach investigates simultaneously managerial (operational as well as strategic), organizational, and accounting aspects of every organization (of every *azienda*). It virtually breaks it up into three subsystems:

a   the management (or decisional) subsystem includes the design of production processes and the decisions aimed at making the best use of the resources;
b   the organizational subsystem comprises the organizational structures (units and relative functions) and the operative mechanisms (human resources management, planning and control, leadership style, etc.);
c   the information and control subsystem relates to auditing, accounting, and communication systems in place, aimed at satisfying the information needs of both internal and external stakeholders.

Source: With adaptations from Cepiku, Meneguzzo 2004; Pessina 2002. For literature in English on the *economia aziendale* approach, see Airoldi *et al.* 1995. See also Accademia Italiana di Economia Aziendale, online at www.aidea.it.

The main propositions of *economia aziendale* include the following (Pessina 2002):

- To satisfy their needs, individuals may create institutions, some of which perform economic activities.
- An institution is a durable entity, which includes individuals and resources (tangible and intangible), operating under a set of stable cultural norms and of behavioural rules and structures. It performs a set of coordinated activities with the final aim of satisfying human needs.
- Institutions include both public and private, for-profit and not-for-profit entities.
- Management theory and its general principles must cover all classes of institutions.
- The institutions of all classes share the following general features: they are guided by a dynamic vision; they are autonomous (although not independent); and they exist to satisfy human needs (which implies strategic effectiveness and operational efficiency). These are often referred to as *visione sistemica, autonomia ed economicità*.
- Management theory is the discipline that focuses on the economic dimension of institutions.

- Institutions include stakeholders and the governance structure, economic activities, organisational structure and mechanisms, human resources management, and physical and technical arrangements.
- Management theory considers the environment with specific reference to its economic dimension, which includes other entities having competitive, exchange, institutional, implicit, and liberality relations with the institution.

In public administrations and agencies the strengthening of the disciplinary identity of *economia aziendale* took place in the area of accounting as a reaction to the hegemony of administrative law, which highlighted the legal implications of national public accounting. Only now, decades later, a central issue in Italy has become the application of private business management (namely planning, accounting and control, decision-making) to the public sector.

The application of the *economia aziendale* paradigm to public administrations in Italy gained more space and interest during the starting phase of the New Public Management wave. The main developments are found in Borgonovi 1973; Rebora 1983; Borgonovi *et al.* 1984.

Table 8.9 lists the main levers of action ascribed to New Public Management reforms in Italy. Market-type mechanisms and managerial techniques in use in the private sector, particularly planning and control systems, are the areas receiving greater attention and higher visibility. There is a direct relationship between these New Public Management levers of change and the incidence of undergraduate courses in public management, in public accounting, and in planning, budgeting and control listed in Table 8.7.

Two issues here are noteworthy. First, the innovative experiences of management and organization preceding the New Public Management wave developed since the mid-50s have not received adequate attention from academia and the business administration researchers. Examples of this include the adoption of PPBS (Planning, Programming, and Budgeting Systems, in the 60s) and ZBB (Zero-Based Budgeting, in the 1970s) in central government. Another remarkable experience is the 1952 creation of an organizational unit dedicated to planning and project management in the municipality of Milan, which has multiplied since the 1960s. In 1982 the regions of Lombardy and Emilia Romagna also created units for planning and control and introduced systems for evaluating the impact of regional policies. The second issue is the adoption of managerial techniques in Italian public administration – in terms of both an institutional approach such as *economia aziendale* and the New Public Management approach. As previously mentioned, the success achieved by these later experiences varies significantly between different levels of government and between geographical areas.

The proliferation of graduate and postgraduate courses in public management in Italy is relative to a greater awareness of certain weaknesses of the *economia aziendale* approach to public administration. Among these are the low propensity

Table 8.9 Levers of public management reform in Italy

NPM levers of change	Public management reforms in Italy	New law/ regulations issued
Organizational change and downsizing	New organizational models at the macro level	1990
	New institutional arrangements (enterprises, foundations)	1993
		1997
	Fusion of ministries	
Public competition	Competition between public health-care organizations	1992
	Competition between other public agencies in allocating regional investment funds	
Market-type mechanisms	Contracting out to private profit and non-profit organizations	1990
		1996
	Contracting in	
Introduction of private management systems and techniques	Accrual accounting introduced in local government and health-care organizations	1990
		1993
	Responsibility centres and reorganization of budget items	1994
		1995
	Audit, control and budget systems (national health-care system)	1997
	Fixed-term contracts limited in time and new managerial positions (city managers, general directors in municipalities and health-care organizations)	
	More flexible HRM practices	
	Customer communication and orientation	
	Administrative simplification and transparency	
	Incentives and evaluation of senior civil servants	
Performance measurement and definition of result standards	Accrual accounting	1990
	Cost control and management planning (local governments)	1993
		1993
	Strategic planning, budgeting and auditing (public health-care organizations)	

Source: Meneguzzo, 1999.

towards interdisciplinary research and the lack of comparisons and confrontation with other disciplines, especially political sciences, sociology, and administrative law. Additionally, the approach gives limited importance to the study of public administration tendencies at the international level, including the pros and cons of the New Public Management experience and the emerging, now consolidated, paradigm of public governance.

Currently, some Italian universities (Bocconi Milano, Venice, Pisa, Siena, and Rome Tor Vergata), in partnership with the governmental units for modernization and innovation, are exploring international trends and beginning to overcome a vision of business administration limited exclusively to accounting with a movement towards developing a paradigm that integrates managerial, organizational, and strategic issues.

Key issues in public administration research

Though the Anglo-Saxon influence will remain strong, the institutional, political, social, and historical specificities will continue to play a role in the evolution of public management studies in Italy. Among the main future trends, we will see a movement towards other disciplinary approaches, such as sociology and political sciences (Cassese 1983), especially in the study of public governance (Cepiku 2005); strategic planning, performance measurement and evaluation (Rebora 1999); public policy impact evaluation; and, network management and governance (Kickert *et al.* 1997).

Themes such as the design and development of networks between public administration and both private and non-profit organizations are central to the current scientific debate, as well as important trends in the practice of public administrations. Considering the development of political entrepreneurship phenomena (mayors and presidents of regional governments) and the introduction of a spoils system model, another key issue concerns the relationship between political level and senior civil service. This trend, considering the duality and plurality of Italian public administrations, calls for an interdisciplinary approach to the study of public management.

Table 8.10 *Azienda Pubblica* articles classified by research issues

Research issue	Number of articles
Public procurement	3
Public value	3
Regulatory quality and simplification	4
e-Government	7
Government–business–ONP relationships	8
Administrative theories	10
Performance evaluation	10
Organizational change	12
Finance	12
Devolution, decentralization	12
Strategic management	15
Inter-organizational networks	15
Accountability and social, environmental reporting*	19
Local public services, privatization and liberalization	22
Marketing, quality, CRM, etc.	25
Public administration reform and innovation	35
Other issues	36
Planning and control	39
Leadership and HRM	40
Accounting	40

Source: author, 2006.

Note
*Special issue on accountability and social reporting included. Two special issues on accounting included.

Table 8.11 Azienda Pubblica articles classified by levels of government researched

Researched levels of government	Number of articles
International institutions	2
Cultural heritage administration	5
Non-profit organizations	5
Ministries	7
Health-care organizations	7
Other	10
Arm's length agencies	11
Regions	22
University and education*	24
Foreign administrations	30
Public sector in general	94
Local and provincial government	139

Source: Author, 2006.

Note
*Special issue on Universities included.

Table 8.10 to 8.12 illustrate the main issues addressed by articles published in the most important Italian academic journal on public management, *Azienda Pubblica*. Over 300 articles were analysed from 1996 to 2006 and classified according to the areas of research (Table 8.10), government levels addressed (Table 8.11) and research strategies (Table 8.12).

There is a direct relationship between the main levers of public management adopted in practice and postgraduate education and research in Italian universities. Public administration reform, innovation, planning and control, and accounting systems are the most recurrent issues in academic/scientific articles (114 articles). There are a surprisingly low number of articles addressing institutional decentralization and devolution (12), processes of interest in Italian public administration since 2000. Also of low frequency are articles referencing e-government and interdisciplinary issues, with only ten articles in ten years on administrative theories.

Table 8.12 Azienda Pubblica articles classified by research strategy

Research strategies	Number of articles
Literature review	113
Survey	59
Action research	15
Case study	90
Ethnography	3
Historical researches and longitudinal analysis	5
Simulation methods	3
Other research strategies	50

Source: author, 2006.

Other research issues, more in line with the current trends of public management and the progressive evolution towards public governance, are emerging: human resources management and leadership development, government–citizens relationships, public and institutional communication, public accountability and social/environmental responsibility, inter-institutional networks, and strategic management.

The analysis of publications in public management and administration in Italy offers other interesting information on the levels of government researched and the methodology adopted. Table 8.11 illustrates that regional and local administrations are the most analysed organisations (161 articles). The attention given to the local level of government is easily understandable by considering the higher innovation rate of these administrations, as exemplified by the various national and international awards (such as the four quality conferences of the European Union from Lisbon 2000 to Tampere in 2006). This is the direct effect of the greater managerial autonomy, the direct election of mayors and close contact with citizens. Furthermore, the type of activities included in local governmental functions – service delivery as opposed to the policy-making activities characterizing ministries and regions – may explain the viability of applying managerial principles (*economia aziendale* and New Public Management) and techniques.

Of the articles examined, 94 address the public sector in general, without reference to a specific type of public administration.

There is also a modest interest in the international context, with 30 articles dedicated to foreign experiences. Among the motivations for international public administration research, which is growing in recent years, is the limited access to Italian public funds as highlighted by Table 8.13.

Apart from the basic literature review, our research strategy also includes a review of case studies. The single-case approach (61 articles out of 90 adopting this method) is preferred to the multiple-case strategy. Highly relevant is the frequency of surveys, which are adopted more frequently than the methodologies of other disciplinary approaches such as ethnography (sociology), historical research (administrative sciences), simulation methods (managerial sciences). A final feature of Italian research on public management is represented by the predominance of qualitative research (324 articles out of 338).

Table 8.13 Internationalisation projects achieving financial support from the Ministry of Education

	2001–2003	*2004–2006*
Total projects attaining financial support	175	162
Of which projects on public administration	5	4

Source: author's elaboration on data from the Ministry of Education: (see online resource at http://interlink.miur.it).

Concluding remarks

The Italian experience of institutional, administrative, and managerial reform offers interesting ways to address the question, launched by Walter Kickert in his north–south comparison, 'How does the history of a state or administration affect the form and content of its administrative reforms?'

A historical perspective of Italian public administration cannot be restricted to post-Second World War, but must embrace the political and social unification process which was completed with the fall of the Vatican authority and the accession of several north-east regions after the First World War. Here, we have, herewith briefly reviewed the various institutional, political, and administrative cultures which gave birth to the unitary state, and analyzed the difficulties in their homogenization and the clarification of unitary and shared procedures in central and local administrations.

The coexistence of 'several Italys,' including the north–south dualism (well-known abroad) the three-Italys phenomenon (the territorial context of big firms in the north-west, and small-to-medium enterprises in the centre, north-east and *Mezzogiorno*) are without a doubt influenced by the underyling administrative and institutional cultures. These cultures have conditioned the orientation of public administrations to sustain industrial or service enterprises, and to promote the development of the civil society and public–private partnerships. This explains, in the perspective of administrative and business history, the creation of parallel models of administrations, the clientelism, the corruption, the weakness in the face of organized criminality and, especially, the different degrees of social and economic development, which are not immediately clear in the context of the country's history after the Second World War.

In order to overcome stereotypes, it is necessary to highlight some important characteristics of Italy when compared with other Mediterranean states. These issues include the difficulties of managerial reforms in breaking the legalistic monopoly, the ossified world, and the levels of collectivism mentioned by Walter Kickert, and should be dealt with by considering the innovations introduced by local governments before and during the New Public Management wave.

More generally, Italy demonstrates a particular dynamism and vivacity in its innovations in local public services delivery, in health care and social assistance, in education and cultural heritage management. In these sectors, the regional and local governments have developed important capacities in network management.

The capacity for innovation in service delivery activities is confirmed by several best practices well-known abroad, including the management of kindergartens in the *Emilia Romagna* region; mental health care in Trieste; cultural events management in Rome, Venice and Florence; and 'tele-heating' and co-generation in *Brescia*. More recently, innovations are being introduced in decisional processes and working methods. Examples of this are the 'network of strategic cities'[5] grouping over 100 municipalities adopting strategic planning and management, and the participatory planning and budgeting experiences of Florence and Rome. Italy, similarly to some Scandinavian countries and Germany, is experimenting and adopting public governance principles centred on networks among local governments and between health-care and cultural administrations, and public, private, and non-profit organizations.

The varying levels of innovation can be explained in part by the strong civic sense – an attention to the common good or administrative pride, which, in some territories (centre and north), developed historically and institutionally. This evolution was based on a pre-unitary state that was maintained and enforced systematically, from the socialist municipalities in the early 1900s to the 'good government' initiatives in some big cities and regions in the mid-60s.

The distinctive characteristics of Italy in comparison with the other southern European states include the diffusion and relevance of bottom-up innovation, important experiences of participatory planning and management, public governance principles in general and the enhancement of 'NIMBY' ('Not in my back yard') phenomena since 2005 on topics including high-speed rail lines, nuclear waste in the south, and US military base expansion in *Vicenza*.

In conclusion, in consideration of the Italian experience of the north–south comparative perspective, the three main reforms – namely professionalism and rationalization, democratization and modernization – should be applied to those administrative systems characterizing the country either at the institutional or at the territorial level.

A final remark concerns the ways in which universities, business schools, and the various national and regional civil servant training schools have addressed the specificities of Italy in reforming its public administration. As mentioned earlier, the New Public Management levers of change and the administrative reform/institutional decentralization processes have boosted the study and research on public management and administration in Italy.

The centrality of the legal culture and the juridification are progressively fading, although, as the survey presented here illustrates, undergraduate courses on public administration prevail in law, political sciences, and sociology faculties (49) and less so in economic faculties (26), the latter playing a dominant role in postgraduate programmes (master's and doctoral) in public administration and management. The strong development of postgraduate education in public management is mainly in the areas of performance measurement, planning, budgeting and control, and accounting, which play a central role in the New Public Management theoretical structure.

In the near future, once the managerial techniques introduced in the Italian public administrations are consolidated, it will be absolutely necessary to give great attention to promising areas of public governance. While, as shown by the analysis of academic articles, these areas already receive the consideration of researchers, Italian public administration will benefit from a recovered identity of public management and should adopt interdisciplinary approaches to integrate administrative history and international comparative analyses.

Notes

1 In the period 1861–1921, 100 organizations were created; during 1922–1940, this figure reached 260 (Cassese, 1983: 36). Their creation was motivated by different reasons including aims of technicality and efficiency in carrying out new functions of the welfare state (1910–1920); public intervention in economy (1930s); and aims of flexibility and independence in traditional areas (1940/1950s). See also Melis (1996).
2 In 1896, France had 38.5 million inhabitants and 416,000 employees the Austro-Hungarian empire 41.3 million inhabitants and 63,535 employees, and Belgium six million inhabitants and 47,880 employees, while Italy had 31 million inhabitants and 90,618 employees. See Melis (1996).
3 The statute differentiated between the regulations as applied to employees in public administrations and those applying to the private sector. It lasted until 1998, when the laws overcame the distinctions. This last reform is usually referred to as the 'privatization' of public employment in Italy.
4 The surveyed universities are 42 out of the 63 existent universities. The complete list can be found in D'Alessio *et al.* (2004), produced by AIDEA, a network that groups academics in the field of business administration from the economics faculties of Italian public and private universities.
5 Rete delle Città Strategiche (RECS). For more information, see the website at www.recs.it.

Bibliography

Airoldi, G., Amatori, F. and Invernizzi, G. (eds) (1995) *Ownership and Governance: the Case of Italian Enterprises and Public Administration*, Milan: Egea.

Borgonovi, E. (1973) *L'economia aziendale negli istituti pubblici territoriali*, Milan: Giuffrè.

Borgonovi, E. (1992) 'Continuity and Renewal in the Study of Public Administration', *Economia aziendale*, 6/5: 407–22.

Borgonovi, E., Fiorentini, G., Mazzoleni, M., Meneguzzo, M. and Zangrandi, A. (1984) *Introduzione all'Economia delle Amministrazioni Pubbliche*, Milan: Giuffrè.

Cammelli, M. (2004) *La pubblica amministrazione*, Bologna: Il Mulino.

Cassese, S. (1983) *Il sistema amministrativo italiano*, Bologna: Il Mulino.

Cassese, S. (2000) 'Lo stato dell'amministrazione pubblica a vent'anni dal rapporto Giannini', *Giornale di diritto amministrativo*, 1: 99.

Cassese S. (2003) 'The Age of Administrative Reforms', in J. Hayward and A. Menon, *Governing Europe*, Oxford: Oxford University Press.

Cepiku, D. (2005) 'Governance: riferimento concettuale o ambiguità terminologica nei processi di innovazione della PA?' *Azienda Pubblica*, 1: 105–31.

Cepiku, D. and Meneguzzo, M. (2004) 'Public Sector Networks: What Can We Learn from Different Approaches?', in S. P. Osborne, G. Jenei, K. McLaughlin and K. Mike, *Challenges of Public Management Reforms. Theoretical Perspectives and Recommendations*, IRSPM-Budapest University.

D'Alessio, L., Meneguzzo, M., Cepiku, D. and Gulluscio, C. (2004) 'Elaborazioni sugli insegnamenti attivati dalle Università censite: Progress report nr 4', Gruppo di Interesse AIDEA sull' Azienda Pubblica, unpublished.

Dente, B. (1992) *Le politiche locali nel mezzogiorno: Modelli di legittimazione e meccanismi di policy making*, Milan: Istituto per la ricerca sociale.

Dente, B. (1999) *In un diverso Stato. Come rifare la pubblica amministrazione italiana*, Bologna: Il Mulino.

Dupuy, F. and Thoenig, C. (1982) 'Revoir l'administration française de l'étude des structures à l'analyse des problèmes', *Sociologie du Sud-Est*, 33/34: 95–103.

Fedele, M. (2002) *Il management delle politiche pubbliche*, Rome: Laterza.

Giannini, M. S. (1979) *Rapporto sui principali problemi dell'Amministrazione dello Stato*, Rome: Tipografia del Senato.

Hajnal, G. (2003) 'Diversity and Convergence: a Quantitative Analysis of European Public Administration Education Programs', *Journal of Public Affairs Education*, 9/4: 245–58.

Kickert, W. J., Klijn, E.-H. and Koppenjan, J. F. (1997) *Managing Complex Networks*, London: Sage.

Lo Schiavo L. (1996) *Top Down Reform and Bottom Up Innovation. The Role of Evaluation in Two Italian Programmes on Public Service Quality*, Rome: DFP.

Melis, G. (1996) *Storie dell'amministrazione italiana*, Bologna: Il Mulino.

Meneguzzo, M. (1992) 'Metodologie di ricerca sulle aziende e amministrazioni pubbliche: un analisi comparativa degli studi di diversi paesi', in S. Vicari (ed.) *Metodo e linguaggio in Economia Aziendale*, Milan: EGEA.

Meneguzzo, M. and Lega, F. (1999) *From New Public Management to Government Modernisation: a Comparative Analysis of the Role of Innovation Awards*, 3rd International Research Symposium on Public Management, Aston Business School.

Meneguzzo, M., Mele, V. and Tanese, A. (2004) 'Strategies for Implementing Health Care Refom in Southern Italy: from Informal Relationship to Netwok Management', in L. R. Jones, K. Schedler and R. Mussari, *Strategies for Public Management Reform*, Oxford: Elsevier JAI.

Panozzo, F. (2000) 'Management by Decree. Paradoxes in the Reform of the Italian Public Sector', *Scandinavian Journal of Management*, 16/4: 357–73.

Pessina, E. A. (2002) *Principles of public management*, Milan: Egea.

Putnam, R. D., Leonardi, R. and Nanetti, R. Y. (1985) *La pianta e le radici*, Milan: Il Mulino.

Putnam, R., Leonardi, R. and Nanetti, R. Y. (1994) *Making Democracy Work: Civic Traditions in Modern Italy*, Princeton: Princeton University Press.

Rebora, G. (1983) *Organizzazione e direzione dell'ente locale. Teorie e modelli per l'amministrazione pubblica*, Milan: Giuffrè.

Rebora, G. (1999) *Un decennio di riforme. Nuovi modelli organizzativi.e. processi di cambiamento delle amministrazioni pubbliche*, Milan: Guerini.

Sepe, S., Mazzone, L., Portelli, I. and Vetritto, G. (2003) *Lineamenti di storia dell'amministrazione italiana (1861–2002)*, Rome: Carocci.

Walle, S. van de, Sterck, M., Dooren, W. van, Bouckaert, G. and Pommer, E. (2004) 'Public Administration', in Social and Cultural Planning Office of the Netherlands, *Public Sector Performance: an International Comparison*, The Hague: SCP.

9 The study of public management in Spain

An interdisciplinary and ill-defined terrain

Xavier Ballart

Introduction

Expertise in public administration (PA) and public management (PM) is claimed in Spain by scholars based in political science, economics, law and sociology. This is therefore an interdisciplinary field where the Spanish literature as a whole is quite ill defined. Specialists from political science may study public organizations (politics–administration relations, policy initiatives, implementation structures), substantive policy areas (education, health, social services) or processes (policy change, reform, influences). Other specialists from economics departments tend to focus on financial matters (budgeting procedures, accounting, auditing) or apply theoretical models to the analysis of the effects of institutional rules in the provision of public services (efficiency). Law students tend to write on regulations (procedure, civil service, public contracts) while sociologists may adopt different perspectives in the analysis of public organizations and their human resources (bureaucracy formation, organizational routines, power relations). Still there are transversal matters like administrative reform, modernization, participation, performance, etc., which appear in the studies of specialists with any of those backgrounds. The Spanish literature does not strictly distinguish between PA and PM but it does often refer to New Public Management (NPM), a family of ideas that over the past 20 years has meant a significant shift in the PM policy of some Anglo-Saxon countries (the UK, New Zealand, Australia). The term NPM is often applied to characterize market-oriented reforms (contracts, private provision, indicators), even if the administrative culture of Spain as a whole cannot be classified under this label.

This chapter will discuss studies of PA and PM in a broad sense, that is, both research intended to explain observed changes and argumentative papers debating management techniques and public sector reform proposals. The main objective is not to present the Spanish system of government or Spanish public administration. However, the thread of studies is closely associated with the historic evolution of Spanish public administration, the political discussion on the deficiencies of the public sector and the proposition of reforms, including actual public management policy.

One of the main questions in the study of public administration is how much change (in budget, civil service, organizational arrangements) eventually took place in a political era or after major historic reforms. Some of the studies, from a more general political or legal perspective, look at the process and outcomes of major administrative reform efforts. Other studies take an economic and managerial approach to discuss changes in policy tools (innovative instruments and practices intended to improve performance) or changes in the institutional structure of incentives (for example with the more recent division in the provision of health services).

There is a permanent question on the sociological characteristics of civil servants, their role and identity, the power of Spanish bureaucracy. In the background, there remains the question of the separation between politics and administration, political and bureaucratic roles, policy and management lines. Present issues in PA are the separation of policy-making and executive operational functions through executive agencies, the managerial role of public administrators, and political and administrative accountability in a decentralized state.

A part of the PA literature is fundamentally normative, since it is based on arguments about the way public administration should be organized or managed. Some of it is quite specific and looks at public management tools and practices. This more focused category of studies pays attention to instrumental reforms in the civil service, administration structures, budgeting procedures and decision-making, auditing and accounting functions. It is a different kind of literature, since it is more focused and at the same time looks more at international trends and their underlying doctrines than at the effectiveness of actual implemented changes with empirical data.

This is not done in a vacuum, given the influence of administrative traditions and culture and also of economic development and political change. Therefore, the paper starts with a short historical review of the administrative system in Spain and a description of the academic educational organization, since they both have a significant influence on the research and teaching of PA and PM. The chapter goes on to present studies of PA and PM in Spain according to the main approaches – legal, political, economic, sociological, management – mentioned before. The analysis of the literature shows that PA reflects institutional traditions which are associated with the study of law and sociology, but that, for some years now, an emerging literature is filling gaps and developing a variety of disciplinary approaches in the study of PA that are actually giving content to a more specific PM studies category.

A short historical view

There was a time, towards the end of the eighteenth century in Spain, when the public bureaucracy started to appear as an independent power. The transformation of the 'personal royal servants' into the first 'civil servants' developed the study of politics as a science of public administration. Along those lines, the innovations introduced in France, the United Kingdom and Prussia where followed by Floridablanca (the first Spanish acting prime minister), López Ballesteros (the main modernizer of public finances) and Bravo Murillo (the first modernizer of Spanish public administration), whose concern for the separation between politics and administration led to the rationalization of the structure of the administration of the time and to a proposal for the first civil servants regulations.

However, public administration studies were soon undermined by the development of constitutionalism in the nineteenth century. In this new context, the study of PA ceased to be perceived as a socio-economic political science similar to German cameralism, to come closer to the study of constitutional and administrative law. The mission of public administration was the execution of decisions taken in the political sphere according to public regulation, and civil servants were formally perceived as mere subordinates whose professional career depended on their political affiliation.

The centralized structure of Spanish public administration was completed with the creation of a territorial administration along the lines of the French administration. In 1833, De Burgos, a Minister of the Interior, implemented the division of Spain into 49 provinces. With regard to personnel, a statute approved by the Maura government in 1918 meant a qualitative change, since it put an end to the Spanish spoils system known as *'cesantías'* – the *cesantes* being those who lost their job with every change of government – and regulated civil servants as a professional body at the service of the state, organized in special corps according to different professional functions.

The main problem for the Franco regime after the Civil War was to maintain itself in power and this was only possible by the use of force. Spanish public administration went through a 'dark age', where offices were held by Falangists by virtue of party loyalty. The purges were dramatic and civil servants had to publicly declare their loyalty to the regime. It was not until the second half of the fifties and during the sixties that the internal battle for the control of the state between Falangists and Catholic Opus Dei technocrats was resolved in favour of the latter. Progressively, the authoritarian state followed a path of rationalization of patronage appointments and an increase in the number of the issues that were subject to objective rules.

A number of civil service reforms were approved in the first half of the sixties which created a professional administration dominated by elite corps. It was a career system where successful candidates to civil service positions entered posts reserved for the special or general administration corps of civil servants. Entry required specific educational requirements and a competitive selection procedure (*concours*). There was no recognition of professional experience from the private sector and civil servants had a public law appointment and contract for life.

On the whole, the number of studies produced in Spain before democracy was modest but there were a significant number of translations of management-oriented books which were politically neutral. Opus Dei technocrats were active in the promotion of the scientific study of PA with the creation of the Escuela Nacional de Administración Pública (founded in 1958, today Instituto Nacional de Administración Pública) or the journal *Documentación Administrativa*. López Rodó, a professor of administrative law and several times minister with Franco, was among the founders of the International Institute of Administrative Sciences, which for many years published its main journal in three languages, Spanish being one of them (López Rodó 1990).

More recently, and under the democracy after the death of Franco in 1974, the trajectory of the Spanish administration has been marked by the constitution of 1978, which set a plurality of power centres and administrations. The democratic governments at each level (central, regional and local) have developed their own public services on the basis of administrations which face a progressively more complex environment and are accountable to society through democratic elections. Spain has also been very active in maintaining a network of public administration institutes, similar to the Spanish INAP, in Latin America, where some of the PA and PM official studies produced in Europe and translated into Spanish are distributed.

With regard to administrative reform, the central government passed a civil service reform law in the 1980s which did not have a substantial impact on the general basis of Spanish PA but reduced the number of special corps, introduced job classification and regulated the conditions under which public employees could develop other professional activities outside public administration. These reforms contributed to changing the image of administration, particularly in the regulation of full-time dedication and the control of times of arrival and departure. Administrative reform followed a path of incremental change, with some difficulties in the regulation of issues that had a direct effect on the interests of top civil servants. For example, there was no agreement on the regulation of executive positions, since top civil servants wanted to preserve their benefits.

Top civil servants from 'special corps' – diplomats, finance and labour inspectors, state lawyers, university professors, judges and prosecutors – had a significant role during the transition, since they filled a gap in the management of the new democratic state. They continue to occupy the highest positions in administration under the political control of the government. But the Spanish administration is today a bureaucratic structure with less capacity to assert its own will, challenge the power of elected leaders or make special claims about representing the public interest than it had at the time of the transition to democracy. The fragmentation of power through decentralization, the reforms simplifying the number and regulations of 'special corps' and the politization by the two main political parties of top civil servants who are appointed for high-level positions like undersecretaries and general directors are factors that tend to weaken special corps' identity.

There has not been a well-defined public management policy in Spain with a clear vision of the situation that was desired. Both Socialist (PSOE) and Popular Party (PP) governments passed general plans of administrative modernization that were based on the idea of long-term cultural change towards a more client-oriented PA, diffusion of best practices with regard to efficiency, performance and quality and introduction of ICT. The major administrative change was induced by political decentralization and the creation of new public administrations at the regional level, which at present account for more than 50 per cent of public employees. The federal evolution of the Spanish government structure, together with the competitive nature of intergovernmental relations, has had a significant effect on all Spanish administrations, since the central administration had to adapt to the new democratic context, and both regional and local administrations expanded to assume the management of basic public services (education, health, police, prisons, taxes, etc.) and to respond to new problems and needs (such as ageing, immigration or housing).

Most of the new public employees in the regional and local administrations are not civil servants in a strict sense. And those who are civil servants do not always perform administrative duties; they often provide services (education, social assistance, health, police) or are hired as professional managers of public agencies, universities, institutes, consortiums, foundations and so on. None of those new public sector professionals correspond to the traditional image of the civil servant as a bureaucrat trained in law and formal procedures. Their demands on the academic system in terms of teaching and research are also different from those working in the core of the central public bureaucracy.

Brief description of the educational system in the field of PA/PM

The four dominant disciplines in the study of PA and PM are political science, economy, law and sociology. As represented in Figure 9.1, PA and PM can be defined as a 'second generation' discipline that is highly related to other, more specialized disciplines, such as administrative law (which used to be identified with PA), business management (more closely related to PM) or the study of public policies.

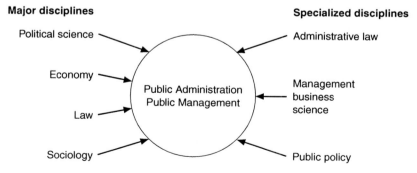

Figure 9.1 Related disciplines and PA-PM.

Since 1986, political science and administrative science were joined in Spain to create an official field of knowledge and give the name to one of the degree programmes which students pursue in the schools of political science and sociology (in some universities, social science or law schools). A few years later, a new first cycle (shorter degree) in public management and administration was created – the only one with PM in the name – for the training of the B personnel group of public administrations, with entry requirements and qualifications lower than top higher education studies. The term '*gestión pública*' – PM in Spanish – was therefore officially associated with a lower-rank type of studies.

However, the term PM was also used by a few public universities and at least one private business school in Barcelona – ESADE – to designate research groups and master's programmes in PM. In those cases, training programmes were aimed at professional managers in the public sector. Similar research and training initiatives were developed by the official training institutes of the central and various regional administrations. The demand for the development of management abilities in civil servants has had a significant impact on the effort to bring the field closer to the needs of practising public administrators.

Although economists are not officially trained in programmes under the heading of PA or PM, some economic departments in public universities have research groups with a public-sector orientation and offer courses to their students in public finance, budgeting and economic analysis of public services. One step forward in the training of economists has been the development of courses that may be identified as PM courses, where a bridge is made between the traditional training of economists in the area of public economy – based on the theory of public finance – and the more practical demands of analysis, evaluation and decision-making in relation to specific public services. The studies of PM from this perspective tend to be more instrumental – the objectives are given – with the distinctive economic concern for rationality and efficiency, to maximize the objectives in a context of restrictions.

It is less clear how sociologists or law students deal with PM as a distinct field from the traditional study of the sociology of civil servants and their regulations. They belong to PA studies but they did not have a significant stake in the development of a PM perspective if this is understood as a specific field, the aim of which is to change the public sector, the motivation of public employees, the reform of public organizations or their accountability. Public administration is the object of organization theory and administrative law. In the Spanish academic tradition, administrative law has been important numerically – the weight of law in relation to political science – and ideologically – the justification of differences between the public sector and the private sector. Public administrations continue to be the main arena for the study of the power relations between the social groups. The differential regulation of personnel, procedure and contracts in the public sector is also a key element in the training of both civil servants and social agents interacting with public bodies. Any student of law or sociology will have units on those issues in courses such as administrative law, public contracts, civil service regulations, sociology of organizations, but they do not provide the main justification for the existence of PA and PM as a field of study. Thus, the number of scholars and researchers specialized in PM is limited but significant, adding up economists, business specialists and political scientists with an interest in public management policy. There are also specialists from the Ministries of Public Administrations and Economy and Finance, or working as auditors in the public sector who publish works on spending planning and financial management, civil service and labour relations, contracting and procurement, public organizations and methods, auditing and evaluation. A few academics have worked on the analysis of government-wide policies and experiences that intend to produce sustainable changes in the ways the public sector is managed, guided, controlled and evaluated. Depending on the definition of the field and whether PA, not just PM, is considered, those numbers are bigger, since they can include, as mentioned before, specialists in public economy, administrative law or specific public policies.

In sum, since the creation in 1986 of the degree and area of studies called *Ciencias Políticas y de la Administración*, the study of public affairs and public policies is officially based on political science. There are no PA/PM departments or chairs independent from political science, and the universities that offer degrees in political science also offer courses in PA as part of the curriculum. Only a fraction of those universities (Complutense, Juan Carlos I and UNED in Madrid; Autónoma, Pompeu Fabra and ESADE in Barcelona) have consolidated research teams in PA or, more specifically, in PM.

Table 9.1 Public universities: political and administrative sciences degrees

University	Location	Institution	Since	Number of students 2004/5
UAB	Barcelona	Political Science and Sociology	1986	824
UAM	Madrid	Law	1993	49
UB	Barcelona	Social Sciences	1994	165
UBU	Burgos	Law	na	58
UCM	Madrid	Political Science and Sociology	1972	1,919
UGR	Granada	Political Science and Sociology	1988	na
UM	Murcia	Law	na	na
UMHE	Elche	Political Science and Sociology	na	281
UNED	Madrid	Social Sciences	1987	3,758
UPF	Barcelona	Social Sciences	1995	540
UPV	Bilbao	Political Science and Sociology	1989	352
USC	Santiago C.	Political Science and Sociology	1991	878
UV	Valencia	Law	na	na

Source: Report presented in 2005 by the Spanish universities to ANECA, the state agency in charge of the reform of university degrees and curriculum design.

State of the art in Spanish PA and PM research

In this section, a general review of Spanish studies is made, with the aim of presenting a research map and providing some references. The list of works is illustrative rather than comprehensive. It is organized according to a classification in four groups – administrative and civil service reform, politics and bureaucracy, governance and managerialism, economic and management studies – which partly follow the disciplinary perspectives presented above. Political scientists are more present in all kinds of studies, while jurists, sociologists and economists tend to follow a more specialized approach to the study of public administration.

Administration and civil service reforms

The first category of studies describes and analyses administrative reforms taken at different times in history and processes initiated with the rather vague aim of public administration modernization. The account of reform efforts in civil service or in organizational structures can look at content – measures taken by successive governments and relative success of the reforms in terms of actual change – or at processes – considering the reform of public administration as a continuum.

Most of the studies look at content and the actors behind the reform initiatives in the period under analysis. Beltrán (1994) looked at reform under the Franco regime, while Nieto (1988) Bañon (1994), Subirats (1990, 1994 and 1995) and Alba (1998) discussed reform initiatives in the 1980s and at the beginning of the 1990s. More recently, Torres and Pina (2004) compared reform initiatives in Spain that could be considered forms of NPM – customer focus, quality, service charts, ICT – with similar developments in the UK, with the aim of explaining differences in implementation and results on the basis of differences in culture and administrative tradition.

With regard to government organization, structures and procedures, there was a significant debate in the second half of the eighties after the creation of the Ministry for Public Administrations, with the specific mandate of addressing the need to modernize the state administration. MAP made attempts to conceptualize modernization and place it on the political agenda. The activities and debates of the time were the basis for the document 'Reflections the Modernisation of the State Administration', a paper which included proposals for a government-wide reform covering all the key management areas – structures, financial methods, contracting, civil service, auditing and evaluation. The document was published as a book in 1990 (MAP 1990) and was followed by a Delphi study on the modernization of public administration procedures (MAP 1991). The MAP strategy was not implemented across government structures but it was the origin of significant change processes, such as those experienced by the INSS – National Social Security Institute – and the Treasury, with the creation of an agency for tax administration.

A few studies analyze the policy process around public administration reform. Those studies give as much relevance to agenda-setting, alternatives specification and political context as to the description of the reforms. That is the case of the work by Gallego (2003), who applied a new form of institutionalism labeled 'processualism' that tries to capture the dynamics of change. This approach was initially developed by Barzelay taking an international comparative approach to the study of PM policy (Barzelay 2001). Ballart (2006) also uses this approach to explain the success of a public entrepreneur in breaking the public monopoly in the provision of primary health care in the Catalan region.

Closely associated with reforms in the civil service, there is literature on public sector human resources management (HRM) which describes and analyzes the Spanish civil service system, the main reforms in the regulations and the opportunities for improvement in various aspects of HRM, particularly in the selection of personnel (Jímenez Asensio 1989; Carrillo 1991; Férez 1993; Olías 1995; Rodríguez Fernández 1995; Longo 1995, 1996, 2004; Sánchez Morón 1996; Villoria and Del Pino 1997; Palomar 1997).

Politics and bureaucracy

One main category of actor in public administration reform is public bureaucrats. A key question is therefore the position of civil servants as a group with regard to political and administrative reform. Already in 1968, this had been studied by political sociologists like De Miguel and Linz. Beltran (1984) and later Villoria (1996) had this same concern in their studies of the role of the Spanish civil service during the transition and thus their position and contribution with regard to the modernization of the state.

Those studies are part of an important sociological tradition in the study of PA in Spain that goes back to the sixties and beginning of the seventies, when various professors in Madrid started to pay attention to bureaucratic theory, to analyze the characteristics of the Spanish public bureaucracy and the role of bureaucratic elites. García Pelayo (1974, 1977) wrote about the contemporary state and the role played by bureaucracies and technocrats. Other publications at the time followed this approach, looking at the relation between bureaucracy and economic development (Moya 1972), attempting to take a snapshot of Spanish public bureaucracy under Franco (Nieto 1976; Beltrán 1977; Información Comercial Española 1977; Pernaute 1978), or analyzing the relationship between the administration and the Cortes of the time (Bañón 1978; Baena del Alcázar and García Madaria 1979). A number of studies followed with the aim of describing and analyzing the bureaucratic elite (Baena del Alcázar and Pizarro 1983; Baena del Alcázar *et al.* 1984), the Spanish civil service and the characteristics of the Spanish bureaucracy after democracy was consolidated (Nieto 1984; Beltrán 1990a and 1990b). Along similar lines, some studies looked at the sociological characteristics of high-level civil servants and political appointees in the Basque Country (Mesa 1991) and Catalonia (Matas 1995). More recently, Baena del Alcázar (1999 and 2002) focused on power relations between interest groups in Spain.

Together with main textbooks in the field (Baena del Alcázar 1985; Ballart and Ramió 2000), the works cited above are representative of studies in the field of PA. The object of analysis and the approach is not the same as in PM studies, but it is certainly a significant part of the literature, based on the analysis of facts and events and clearly different from more normative studies or publications which either discuss reform proposals or management tools and techniques that are the object of international attention with regard to the management of the public sector.

Governance and professional managers

A third main category of studies observes and discusses what elected executives, managers and professional civil servants do and their relations. A recent research-based article by Brugué and Vallès (2005) on the evolution of the role of city councillors exemplifies this category. The word 'strategic' has become here a buzz-word and 'managing strategically' tends to refer to either the close relationship of public management with the political sphere – the source of support for new policies – or the need for public managers to engage in the analysis of their ideas – to determine how effective new policies might be. The emphasis on strategic governance is built on a few works (Brugué 1996) that defend the political nature of managerial work against the traditional concept of public administration as a rational and neutral executive instrument. Closely related to the issue of management professionalism, a few evidence-based studies on hiring practices of managers in public organizations – particularly in agencies, universities and local government – analyse the relations between this new category of public executives and civil service career public employees (Longo 1999).

Another category of works within this same group discusses political and managerial leadership (Natera 2001) and the distinctive nature of the senior executives' job in the public sector. Influenced by well-known international works, such as those of Mintzberg, a few business professors have written on the guiding job of public executives and on the transformation of public employees from bureaucrats to public managers (Losada 1999).

The underlying association of public administrators with entrepreneurs is also present in the studies referring to the 'new public management' paradigm. Some authors, like Torres and Pina in the article cited above, do not question NPM. Others associate this label with new developments in PA (Olías 2001) and a few express a critical view. The critical stance is based on cultural grounds – the inadequacy of implementing an NPM model in Latin administrations – or on arguments that tend to be more political, claiming to reflect a vision of public administration from the Left. The criticism towards NPM has been expressed in some papers in the context of the CLAD conferences – in Madrid 2004, Santiago 2005, and Guatemala 2006. Overall, however, there has not been much discussion on whether the hypothesis of convergence in administrative reforms towards one single model was applicable to the Spanish case.

Research efforts have also been directed to analysis of new forms of governance. The creation of networks between public, private and social agents for local development and the management of citizen participation in public projects is the object of the several studies, like the ones of Blanco and Gomà (2002). A closely related type of study is the one that looks into social policy, territorial exclusion and uncertainty associated with the emergence of new problems like immigration. The common element of this category of study is the concern for governance issues and the changes in organization structures from traditional hierarchical, top-down approaches to alternative, more flexible and horizontal network management structures. Some excellent studies, like the one on the transformation of the Raval neighborhood in Barcelona, are accessible through the web pages of sponsoring institutions (Subirats and Rius 2005), but not available through international journals.

A different perspective on governance is related to the transfer of power and resources to nationalities and regions. The decentralization process and intergovernmental relations have been the subject of much academic debate among constitutional and administrative law experts, but less so among political scientists and public administration scholars, with a few exceptions (Arenilla 1992; Morata 1995, 2001; Subirats and Gallego 2002).

At all three government levels – central, regional and local – one can observe similar administrative processes: creation of new agencies to manage services with a relative autonomy from the ministries; redefinition of the administrative units distributed in the territory (the central administration passed a law in 1997 changing the name and simplifying its representation in the provinces); and combination of public structures with private or third-sector organizations in the provision of public services through contracting out.

Some studies looked at the territorial administration of the central state (Arenilla 1992), while others described and analysed the development of the regional administrations and their tendency to build similar structures to those of the central administration (Ballart and Ramió 2000). Ramió is one of the few Spanish authors who takes an organizational approach to describe and analyze Spanish public administrations (Ramió 1999, 2002) while Agranoff goes beyond the legal and financial analysis of the Spanish regional system to take an intergovernmental relations perspective and analyse the dynamics of the Spanish multi-level government system (Agranoff 1999, 2004).

Economic and management studies

The category of economic studies includes those pieces of research that describe or analyze changes in policy tools and in the institutional framework for the provision of public services. This analysis is fundamentally economic and takes incentives and efficiency as its basic concern. In 1997, Albi, González Páramo and López Casasnovas, public finance professors, published a PM text book under this exact title, which includes analysis of regulated competition in the Spanish health insurance market, use of vouchers for the provision of education services, introduction of productivity bonuses for managers in top positions and use of incentive schemes for government contracts. This book is illustrative of a category of research study that has been well developed by economists and, less intensively, by political scientists studying major reforms in a policy domain. One example is the work by Gallego (2000) on the provision of public health services through third-sector and private hospitals.

Within the same category, some research has been devoted to innovative practices intended to improve performance. Again, the same economic literature (Albi *et al.* 1997) provides examples of cost accounting development in public organizations and use of cost-benefit techniques. In the 1980s, various publications examined the introduction of programme budgeting in the Spanish central administration (Zapico 1989), an issue which was later the object of argumentative studies cited below.

Spending procedures and financial rules had also been the object of debate and central government reforms. In 1984 the Ministry of Economy and Treasury introduced programme budgeting through pilot projects, a reform that was later generalized. As stated above, some studies analyzed this particular reform and considered it was not a success in terms of changing the decision-making process. This finding led to argumentative works where analysts introduced innovative concepts – like the 'three Ds' for 'diagnosis', 'design' and 'development', instead of the 'three Es' for 'economy', 'effectiveness' and 'efficiency' – and strategies that could be used for the successful implementation of reforms in budgeting (Zapico 1993).

A key concern in public management is 'performance'. This is a word which does not have an easy translation into Spanish but it is present in a few works in relation to budgeting reform (mentioned above), management control (López and Gadea 1992) and policy evaluation (Ballart 1992). The application of quantitative methods to the analysis of specific policies, as in the works of Ballart (1991) and Ballart and Riba (1995, 2002), is an example of a positivist approach that is not very common in the field.

More recently, one can find a few studies on management innovations in the areas of quality in the provision of public services (López and Gadea 1998; Muñoz Machado 1999; Sancho 1999), e-government and communication technologies (Torres *et al.* 2006), access to administrative information (Tornos and Galán 2000) and citizen participation in policy decision-making (Font 2001). Closely related are a few studies on ethics and corruption in public administration, an issue that receives increasing attention from the political-science side of PA studies (Villoria 2000, 2006).

A different kind of study has looked at the efforts to achieve better results in the management of public organizations and public bureaucrats through cases. One earlier example is the case study by Barzelay and O'Kean (1989) on a development agency created by the region of Andalucía in the south of Spain, which had the capacity to take a vague idea – endogenous development – and convert it into a successful programme that created enterprises and jobs around the production and commercialization of marble. Another example is the book published by Ballart in 2001 on innovation in public and private management, based on the stories of five successful Spanish managers with experience in both sectors, which analyzes the strategies and action plans they used to produce observable changes in the organizations they managed.

There is also older literature on management tools and techniques that public administrators should use in their day-to-day activities. One can find traces of this kind of literature in the efforts to import a management science before democracy, when the technocrats from Opus Dei were in control of the central administration. This literature evolved into a series of studies that argued in favour of the introduction of tools and techniques developed by the private sector into the public sector in order to improve management methods.

The literature on techniques is more sensitive to the passing of time than other categories of study. As early as 1975, one can find works that aim to present a general theory of administration (Jiménez Nieto 1975). In the eighties and the first half of the nineties, various publications presented management techniques for the modernization of the Spanish public sector (Paramés 1988; López González 1988; Mendoza 1990, 1993; Valero 1990, 1991). Others looked at European experiences in improving the public sector (Echebarría and Losada 1993; Echebarría 1993) or translated texts that were representative of international trends in organization theory (Ramió and Ballart 1993) and PM (Brugué and Subirats 1997).

Present situation

The present situation in the study of PA and PM in Spain can be characterized as incipient, constrained and fragmented. The PA/PM studies map described above can give an idea of the production and the extent to which a PM perspective is developed. If PA is considered in a wider sense, the number of scholars, studies and topics covered is significant. However, if PM is understood as a part of PA that looks at strategies, policies and practices that aim to change the management of the public sector, Spanish studies are less numerous.

There are studies of new policy tools and institutional reforms with the aim to improve efficiency in the provision of public services. This area is closely related to some studies of strategic leadership and new forms of governance through networks, particularly, in the provision of social services at the local level. There are also studies on the nature of managerial work and the relationship between managers and the political and professional civil service level. But these two categories need more development, from both an economic and political science perspective, since the number of studies is small and these are core categories in the study of PM.

There is continuity in the study of particular administrative reform and more ample modernization processes. A basic pillar in this category is the study of civil service reform which establishes a connection with more traditional PA studies of bureaucratic elites. There is also a tradition of argumentation in favour of management techniques – in the management science tradition – and reforms in structures, budgeting, performance evaluation, quality improvement, e-government, citizen participation, ethics and anti-corruption measures. But these two categories need to be further developed through research-based studies of PM policy, reform processes and outcomes that can be associated with the introduction of new tools and rules in public management.

The study of PA and PM is constrained by the 'official' categorization of the field and by the applied nature of the questions that are usually studied. As stated above, the label 'PM' has not been used to refer to a university degree, except for a lower-rank diploma which might disappear in the near future. PM has a practical connotation that makes it a less interesting option for economists or political scientists willing to make a career in academics. Students of PA and PM either pursue a PhD in political science or in economics and they are asked to investigate classic questions in those fields. If funding is considered, competitive basic research in the social sciences prioritizes projects with theoretical content, since applied research in PA is expected to get funding directly from the administrations. The demand for training in PM can at times be disturbing for more research-oriented projects, since that demand puts the emphasis on the introduction of approaches, methods and techniques that may be an innovation for public administrators, but has less appeal from the perspective of those interested in producing new knowledge or observing the relations between phenomenon.

Finally, studies in PA and PM are fragmented and there is a lack of coordination between specialists in the field, who belong to departments that respond to the logic of specialization in more consolidated disciplines. The connection between applied economics and political science is rather loose and needs to be developed. Within political science, those interested in policies, whether it is specific sector policies or policy process – policy formulation and implementation – rarely look at the effect of management in the policy and political process.

Conclusion

The evolution of studies of PA and PM in Spain is closely related to the historical institutional context. In the first place, the official field of knowledge combining political science and administrative sciences was not created until 1986. There was a tradition of PA studies that goes back to the Spanish Empire and the formation of the central state but it was not until the reorganization of official disciplines after the democratic transition that the new period of PA and PM studies began.

In the eighties, professors in administrative law and sociology were deeply influenced by their French and German colleagues. Spain had developed its state administration following the Napoleonic model and, at the time, France and Germany were the main destinations for postgraduate studies and researchers pursuing an academic career. In the last 20 years, both the Spanish administrative system and the academic field have changed significantly. Today, the study of PA and PM in Spain has a wider base, it is more plural in approach and it is more open to international influence than at any time before. The studies cited in this chapter – from the seventies until the present – give evidence of this process. Being still relatively small in numbers when compared with international production, the field integrates a diversity of studies. Still, there are a significant number of studies written in Spanish on Spanish issues and institutions. The topics and the perspectives resemble those of international and European colleagues but tend to take Spanish cases as the object of analysis.

The biggest change in Spanish public administration was induced by the strong political and administrative decentralization. The central state, which developed the welfare state in the eighties, when other European nations were already at a time of retreat, progressively transferred competences and personnel to regional and local administrations. This allowed a process of competition among administrations that put the whole public sector in a path of unplanned modernization and reform.

This is the 'Spanish' trait that is most distinctive. It has been intensively studied by jurists, economists and political scientists interested in federalism and intergovernmental relations, both in Spain and abroad. However, constitutional adaptation, public finances and the juridical distribution of powers have received more attention than the relation between administrations (Börzel 2002) or the reform in both central and sub-central administrations as a consequence of the redistribution of powers.

The Spanish field of PA and PM has undergone a quantitative and qualitative development in a short time and the evolution has not deviated from the mainstream developments taking place in the international scientific community. However, there is not a concept, approach or analysis that is genuinely Spanish. This should not cause concern, since innovative concepts and approaches are very much dependent on the production of an extraordinary individual or research group.

Nevertheless, one can conclude that there are a number of high-quality publications and some interesting research-based applications in each of the four categories of studies that were identified: analysis of reform policies and civil service, study of the politics–bureaucracy division and new forms of governance, effects of new policies and institutional rules, and new organization and management techniques, such as those related to performance, quality, e-government or citizen participation. Some of the authors are present in the international and European research community but there is not a distinct Spanish approach or contribution to the study of public management. The penetration of Spanish studies in international journals can be improved, given the size of the Spanish academic community in the field. Those working in PA and PM need to elevate the horizon of their perspective to enter into more international and comparative analysis.

Bibliography

Alba, C. (1998) 'Politique et administration en Espagne: continuité et perspectives', *Revue Française d'Administration Publique*, 86: 229–242.
Albi, E., González Páramo, M. and López Casasnovas, G. (1997) *Gestión Pública*, Barcelona: Ariel.

Agranoff, Robert (1999) 'Intergovernmental Relations and the Management of Asymmetry in Federal Spain', in R. Agranoff (ed.) *Accommodating Diversity: Asymmetry in Federal States*, Baden-Baden: Nomos.

Agranoff, Robert (2004) 'Autonomy, Devolution, and Intergovernmental Relations', *Regional and Federal Studies*, 14: 26–65.

Arenilla, M. (1992) *La modernización de la administración periférica*, Madrid: INAP.

Arenilla, M., Loughlin, J. and Toonen, T. (eds) (1994) *La Europa de las Regiones: una Perspectiva Intergubernamental*, Granada: Ediciones de la Universidad de Granada.

Baena del Alcázar, M. (1985) *Curso de Ciencia de la Administración*, Madrid: Tecnos.

Baena del Alcázar, M. (1999) *Élites y conjuntos de poder en España 1939–1992*, Madrid: Tecnos.

Baena del Alcázar, M. (2002) 'On the Nature of Power: an Examination of the Governing Elite and Institutional Power in Spain, 1939–92', *Public Administration*, 80: 323–38.

Baena del Alcázar, M. and García Madaria, J. M. (1979) 'Burocracia y élite franquista en las Cortes actuales', *Sistema*, 28: 23.

Baena del Alcázar, M. and Pizarro, N. (1983) *The Spanish National Elite, 1939–1975*, Florence: European University Institute.

Baena del Alcázar, Garrido, F. and Pizarro, N. (1984) 'La élite española y la presencia en ella de los burócratas', *Documentación Administrativa*, 200: 73.

Ballart, X. (1991) 'La evaluación de la actividad y el rendimiento de la policía', *Documentación Administrativa*, 224–5: 361–406.

Ballart, X. (1992) *¿Cómo evaluar programas y servicios públicos?*, Madrid: INAP.

Ballart, X. (2001) *Innovación en la gestión pública y en la empresa privada*, Madrid: Díaz de Santos.

Ballart, X. (2006) *Institutions, Processes and Policy Change: a Case in Primary Health Care*, in W. Genieys and M. Smyrl (eds) *Accounting for Change*, forthcoming.

Ballart, X. and Ramió, C. (2000) *Ciencia de la Administración*, Valencia: Tecnos.

Ballart, X. and Riba, C. (1995) 'Impact of Legislation Requiring Moped and Motorbike Riders to Wear Helmets', *Evaluation and Program Planning*, 18/4: 311–20.

Ballart, X. and Riba, C. (2002) 'Forest Fires: Evaluation of Government Measures', *Policy Sciences*, 35/4: 361–7.

Bañon, R. (1978) *Poder de la burocracia y Cortes franquistas*, Madrid: INAP.

Bañon, R. (1994), 'La modernizzazione dell'amministrazione pubblica spagnola. Bilanci e prospettive', in Vincent Wright and Sabino Cassese (eds) *La Riforma Amministrativa in Europa*, Bologna: Il Mulino.

Barzelay, M. (2001) *The New Public Management*, Berkeley: University of California Press.

Barzelay, M. and O'Kean, J. M. (1989) *Gestión Pública Estratégica: Conceptos, Análisis y Experiencias. El caso IPIA*, Madrid: Instituto de Estudios Fiscales.

Beltrán, M. (1977) *La élite burocrática española*, Barcelona: Ariel.

Beltrán, M. (1984) *Los funcionarios ante la reforma de la administración*, Madrid: CIS.

Beltrán, M. (1990a) 'La Administración Pública y los funcionarios', in S. Giner (ed.) *España, Sociedad y Política*, Madrid: Espasa Calpe.

Beltrán, M. (1990b) 'Sociología de la Administración Pública', S. Giner and L. Moreno (eds), *Sociología en España*, Madrid: CSIC: 107–15.

Beltrán, M. (1994) 'Política y administración bajo el franquismo: la reforma administrativa y los planes de desarrollo', working papers 1994/53, Centro de Estudios Avanzados en Ciencias Sociales, Madrid: Instituto Juan March.

Blanco, I. and Gomà, R. (2002) *Gobiernos locales y redes participativas*, Barcelona: Ariel.

Börzel, T. (2002) *States and Regions in the European Union: Institutional Adaptation in Germany and in Spain*, Cambridge: Cambridge University Press.

Brugué, Q. (1996) 'La dimensión democrática de la nueva gestión pública', *Gestión y Análisis de Políticas Públicas*, 5: 45–67.

Brugué Q. and Subirats, J. J. (eds) (1997) *Lecturas de Gestión Pública*, Madrid: INAP.

Brugué Q. and Vallès, J. M. (2005) 'New Style Councils, New Style Councillors: from Local Government to Local Governance', *Governance*, 18: 197–226.

Carrillo, E. (1991) *Gestión de los recursos humanos, presupuestación y hacienda local en España*, Madrid: Instituto de Estudios Fiscales.

De Miguel, A. and Linz, J. (1968) 'La élite funcionarial española ante la reforma administrativa', in AAVV, *Sociología de la Administración Pública Española*, Madrid: Centro de Estudios Sociales.

Echebarría, K. (1993) 'La gestión pública a través de agencias. Experiencias europeas', *Ekonomiaz*, 26: 170–97.

Echebarría, K. and Losada, C. (1993) *Institucions i mètodes per millorar el funcionament de l'Administració Pública*, Barcelona: Generalitat de Catalunya.

Férez, M. (1993) 'La igualdad, el mérito y la capacidad en el acceso al empleo público profesional', PhD thesis, Barcelona: Autonomous University of Barcelona.

Font, J. (2001) *Ciudadanos y decisiones públicas*, Barcelona: Ariel.

Gallego, R. (2000) 'Introducing Purchaser/Provider Separation in the Catalan Health Administration: a Budget Analysis', *Public Administration*, 78: 423–42.

Gallego, R. (2003) 'Public Management Policy-making in Spain, 1982–1996', *International Public Management Journal*, 6: 283–307.

García Pelayo, M. (1974) *Burocracia y Tecnocracia*, Madrid: Alianza Editorial.

García Pelayo, M. (1977) *Las transformaciones del Estado Contemporáneo*, Madrid: Alianza Editorial.

Información Comercial Española (1977) *La burocracia en España. Información Comercial Española*, 522, Madrid: Ministerio de Comercio y Turismo.

Jiménez Asensio, R. (1989) *Políticas de Selección en la Función Pública Española*, Madrid: INAP.

Jiménez Nieto, J. I. (1975) *Teoría General de la Administración*, Madrid: Tecnos.

López González, E. (1988) *Técnicas de control de ejecución en la dirección estratégica de la Administración Pública*, Madrid: INAP.

López Rodó, L. (1990) *Memorias*, Barcelona: Plaza y Janés.

López, J. and Gadea, A. (1992) *El control de gestión en la administración local*, Barcelona: Gestión 2000.

López, J. and Gadea, A. (1998) *Servir al ciudadano: gestión de la calidad en la administración pública*, Barcelona: Gestión 2000.

Longo, F. (1995) 'La reforma del empleo público: tótem o tabú', *Gestión y Análisis de Políticas Públicas*, 2: 5–15.

Longo, F. (1996) 'La gestión de recursos humanos en las organizaciones públicas de naturaleza profesional', *Boletín de Estudios Económicos*, 159: 489–503.

Longo, F. (1999) *Política y Gerencia Pública en los Gobiernos Locales, en Gobierno Local y Modelo Gerencial*, Barcelona: Fundación Pi i Sunyer.

Longo, F. (2004) *Mérito y flexibilidad*, Barcelona: Paidós.

Losada, C. (ed.) (1999) *¿De burócratas a gerentes? Las ciencias de la gestión aplicadas a la administración del Estado*, Washington: Banco Interamericano de Desarrollo.

MAP (1990) *Reflexiones para la Modernización de la Administración*, Madrid: MAP.

MAP (1991) *Jornadas para la Modernización de las Administraciones Públicas*, Madrid: MAP.

MAP (1992) *La formación de directivos para la Modernización de la Administración Pública*, Madrid: MAP.

Matas, J. (1995) *Els alts càrrecs: Política i Administració a la Generalitat de Catalunya*, Barcelona: EAPC.

Mendoza, X. (1990) 'Técnicas gerenciales y modernización de la administración pública en España', *Documentación Administrativa*, 223: 261–90.

Mendoza, X. (1993) 'Management público e indicadores de gestión: una perspectiva estratégica', *Ekonomia*, 26: 44–65.

Mesa, A. (1991) 'Datos de estructura y movilidad de los cargos de designación política en la administración autónoma vasca', in Instituto Vasco de Estudios de Administración Pública, *Jornadas de Estudio sobre el Estatuto de Autonomía del País Vasco*, Oñati: IVAP: 1573–1605.

Morata, F. (1995) 'Spanish Regions and the European Community', in B. Jones and M. Keating (eds) *The European Union and the Regions*, Oxford: Clarendon Press.

Morata, F. (2001) 'El Estado de las Autonomías: 20 años de rodaje', in M. Alcantara and M. A. Martínez (eds) *Política y Gobierno en España*, Valencia: Tirant Lo Blanc.

Moya, C. (1972) *Burocracia y Sociedad Industrial*, Madrid: Edicusa.

Muñoz Machado, A. (1999) *La gestión de la calidad total en la administración pública*, Madrid: Díaz de Santos.

Natera A. (2001) *El liderazgo político en la sociedad democrática*, Madrid: Centro de Estudios Políticos y Constitucionales.

Nieto, A. (1976) *La burocracia*, Madrid: Instituto de Estudios Administrativos.

Nieto, A. (1984) 'Funcionarios', in J. Linz and E. Garcia (eds) *España. Un presente para el futuro*, Madrid: Instituto de Estudios Económicos.

Nieto, A. (1988) 'Reforma administrativa y modernización de la administración: ¿Un problema pendiente?', *Modernización Administrativa*, Oñati: IVAP: 101–15.

Olías, B. (ed.) (1995) *La gestión de recursos humanos en las administraciones públicas*, Madrid: Universidad Complutense.

Olías, B. (2001) *La Nueva Gestión Pública*, Madrid: Prentice Hall.

Palomar, A. (1997) *Planificación de los recursos humanos en el ámbito público*, Madrid: McGraw Hill.

Paramés, C. (1988) *Introducción al management. Un nuevo enfoque de la administración pública*, Madrid: INAP.

Pernaute, M. A. (1978) *El papel de los cuerpos de burócratas en la organización administrativa española*, Madrid: INAP.

Ramió, C. (1999) *Teoría de la organización y administración pública*, Madrid: Tecnos-UPF.

Ramió, C. (2002) 'La Administración de las Comunidades Autónomas', in J. Subirats and R. Gallego (eds) *Veinte años de autonomías en España*, Madrid: Centro de Investigaciones Sociológicas.

Ramió, C. and Ballart, X. (1993) *Lecturas de teoría de la organización*, Madrid: INAP.

Rodríguez Fernández, A. (ed.) (1995) *Los recursos humanos en las administraciones públicas*, Madrid: Tecnos.

Sánchez Morón, M. (1996) *Derecho de la Función Pública*, Madrid: Tecnos.

Sancho, D. (1999) *Gestión de servicios públicos: estrategias de marketing y calidad*, Madrid: Tecnos.

Subirats, J. (1990) *Modernizing the Spanish Public Administration or Reform in Disguise*, Barcelona: Instituto de Ciencias Políticas y Sociales.

Subirats, J. (1994) 'La modernizzazione amministrativa in Spagna. Flessibilità, organizzativa e cambiamenti nelle procedure di attuazione della pubblica amministrazione: azioni intraprese', in V. Wright and S. Cassese (eds) *La Riforma Amministrativa in Europa*, Bologna: Il Mulino.

Subirats, J. (1995) 'La modernizzazione dell'amministrazione pubblica spagnola', in B. Dente (ed.) *Riformare la Pubblica Amministrazione*, Tcurin: Fondazione Giovanni Agnelli.

Subirats, J. and Gallego, R. (eds) (2002) *Veinte años de autonomías en España*, Madrid: Centro de Investigaciones Sociológicas.

Subirats, J. and Rius, J. (2005) *Del Xino al Raval: cultura y transformació social a la Barcelona central*, Barcelona: Centre de Cultura Contemporània de Barcelona.

Tornos, J. and Galán, A. (2000) *Comunicación pública. La información administrativa al ciudadano*, Madrid: Marcial Pons.

Torres, L. and Pina, V. (2004) 'Reshaping Public Administration: the Spanish Experience Compared to the UK', *Public Administration*, 82: 445–64.

Torres, L., Pina, V. and Acerete, B. (2006) 'E-Governance Developments in European Union Cities: Reshaping Government's Relationships with Citizens', *Governance*, 19/2: 277–302.

Valero, J. (ed.) (1990) 'Técnicas Gerenciales en Administración Pública', *Documentación Administrativa*, 223: 99–138.

Valero, J. (1991) 'La eficacia en la Administración: estrategia y factores de cambio', *Jornadas para la Modernización de las Administraciones Públicas*, Madrid: INAP: 96–124.

Villoria, M. (1996) *La modernización de la administración como instrumento al servicio de la democracia*, PhD thesis, Complutensa University Madrid.

Villoria, M. (2000) *Ética pública y corrupción. Curso de ética administrativa*, Madrid: Tecnos-UPF.

Villoria, M. (2006) *La corrupción política*, Madrid: Síntesis.

Villoria, M. and Del Pino, E. (1997) *Manual de Gestión de Recursos Humanos en las Administraciones Públicas*, Madrid: Tecnos.

Zapico, E. (1989) *La Modernización simbólica del presupuesto público*, Oñate: IVAP.

Zapico, E. (1993) 'Del presupuesto por programas al management estratégico del gasto público: nuevo papel del Ministerio de Hacienda', *Ekonomiaz*, 26: 66–93.

10 The study of public management in Hungary

Management and the transition to democratic *Rechtsstaat*

György Hajnal and György Jenei

Introduction

We are living in the decades of a worldwide trend of public management reforms. Hungary became part of these reform efforts from the very beginning of its transition to democracy. This chapter will show that, though located in central Europe, Hungary has been evolving similar management reform trends to the patterns of west European countries. We shall confirm that Hungary, as a new member of the European Union, has become an integral part of continental Europe, albeit with distinct Hungarian problems and approaches.

The study of public management and organisation in Hungary is a long process beginning in the Middle Ages, a plausible starting point being the reign of King Matthias in the second half of the fifteenth century. At that time, Hungary was an integral part of what is called western Europe today. Throughout the subsequent centuries, a series of what might be termed reforms of public administration and management were implemented. As a result, after a 150-year deviation from mainstream European development because of the influence of the Ottoman Empire, Hungary became part of the continental European *Rechtsstaat* tradition in the second half of the eighteenth century.

In the twentieth century, between the two world wars, the Anglo-Saxon approach to the study of public management had a growing influence in Hungary. After the Second World War, commitment to the communist ideology had a dominant role in public administration, and the role of managerial skills – apart from the ideological-political commitment of course – was emphasised only after the economic reforms of 1968.

In the beginning of the transition to a market economy and a liberal democracy from 1990 on, Hungarian public administration faced two simultaneous requirements:

- to renew the *Rechtsstaat* tradition;
- to increase the administrative capacities and raise the performance standards of the public agencies.

The main objective was, and is, to re-establish the institutionalised position of Hungary in the Euro-Atlantic world with membership of the World Bank and the European Parliament first, then entrance to the OECD and NATO. The process was completed with European Union membership in 2004.

Apart from that, the reforms had, and still have, to result in the improvement of international competitiveness and the stability of the newly established liberal democracy. At a lower level of abstraction, this means keeping a balance between legalism on one hand, and managerialism on the other, in order to reduce tensions between them through consensus and compromise.

Administrative practice and theory from the Middle Ages to 1990

The need for professional expertise in the pre-modern age

In the history of Hungary, the need for professional expertise in the public administration is connected to the absolutist efforts of the Hungarian kings.

The role of professionally educated civil servants was emphasised first by the Hungarian King Matthias Corvinus (1458–90) and it was related to the emergence of the Hungarian centralised state after 1471. King Matthias strengthened the role of the central government against the assembly of the nobles and the regional power of the nobility (*nobiles majores* and *nobiles minores*).

He established new organisations at the central level (Council of the King, different chancelleries) and he needed professionally educated people to run these offices. These chancellors, vice-chancellors and secretaries were educated mainly in different universities of Italy (Bologna, Padua) because at that time there were no higher education institutions in Hungary that could have provided this type and level of education (Magyary 1927: 149–61).

These people had one thing in common: they did not belong to the nobles. Rather, they were foreigners or they came from other social groups of Hungarian society. Based on their support, the king could counterbalance the power of the Hungarian nobles (Hóman and Szekfü 1936: 520–5).

The trend of growing importance of professional expertise in Hungarian public administration was continued and strengthened after the death of King Matthias. From 1490 on, the Hungarian kings increased the number of royal secretaries, first to ten then to 15. These secretaries' task was to deal with both foreign and home affairs, based on their professional expertise and high-level culture. All these officials had university degrees from different Western universities. Their role was dominant in the decision-making process of the royal council; at that time, the decision was not based on the majority principle but on the principle of *sanior pars* (part of more wisdom; i.e. the voting system favoured that part of the council that was deemed to be wiser than the rest) (Kubinyi 2006).

Second, the need for professional expertise emerged in the second half of the eighteenth century. It was connected partly to the emergence of the centralised state established by the Habsburg empress Maria Theresa and partly to the enlightened absolutism established by his son, Emperor Joseph II. Maria Theresa was not only Austrian empress but also elected Hungarian queen. She was convinced that the modernisation of Hungary required a substantial reform in public education and in public administration.

The development of the new Hungarian public administration from that point followed the continental pattern of the *Rechtsstaat* (*stato de diritto, droit d'État*). The reform process began in 1760 with the creation of the State Council. In the first stage, new public organisations were established, and then the influence of the merit system was strengthened (Magyary 1942: 59–61).

The substantial public education reform was outlined at the *Ratio educationis* issued by the queen on 24 August 1777 (Kosáry 1980: 407–13). Culturally, both reform trends were dominated by German and Austrian theories and practices.

Emergence of public administration education in the eighteenth century in Hungary

It became quite obvious that the development of the reforms outlined above required the establishment of public administration as a discipline in the curricula of universities and the creation of academies for the education of practitioners of the civil service.

The first attempt was the setting-up of a *Collegium scientiarum politico-oeconomico-cameralium* in 1763 at Szempc. It was a college where public finance and accountancy were taught. The building was burned down in 1776, which put an end to this historical experiment (Kosáry 1980: 495–6). The approach of *Kameralistik* appeared in a decree of the queen in 1776. This decree prescribed the creation of four academies in Hungary for the special education of Hungarian civil servants. These academies provided two different two-year programmes: one in philosophy and one in law.

The programme in law was a practice-oriented education following the needs of public institutions. The academies were supervised by the Faculty of Law of the Pázmány Péter University. The main subjects were Hungarian public law, international law, the history of Hungarian law, politics, state and public administration, commerce and public finance. The contents of the curricula were compiled on the theoretical basis of such scholars as Christian Wolff, Martini and Sonnenfels, who were well known and broadly accepted in the German-speaking areas of Europe (Kosáry 1980: 497–8). These academies provided civil servants with professional expertise for public administration.

The legalistic approach was supported at the university level by the extension of the curriculum of the Faculty of Law, Budapest with the subject of Hungarian public law. Moreover, a politico-Kameralistik subject was added to the curriculum, the so-called *Polizey und Kameralwissenschaften* (Máthé, 2003: 103).

The rationale behind these steps was the immediate practical needs of the administrative apparatus of the absolutist feudal state. The transition from the non-professional and feudal type of civil service to a professional system was strongly needed in order to be capable of dealing with the growing number of functions and tasks faced by the state. These new challenges stemmed on one hand from the devastation and general backwardness of the country as the heritage of more than two centuries of foreign occupation and a series of unsuccessful wars of freedom and on the other hand, from the enlightened absolutist ambitions of the Habsburg kings of the time. Adapting and measuring up to these new challenges made great demands on the education of professional civil servants, too.

In 1784 and 1787, the first legal regulations – concerned with the setting of minimum educational standards for different classes of civil servants – defined the legal degree as the highest in the field of public administration. Thus, from the beginnings of modern public administration, following the classical continental model of the *Rechtsstaat*, law as an academic discipline was considered the public administration science *par excellence* (*Verwaltungslehre* in German, *droit administrative* in French).

One can say, therefore, that the first period of PA as a field of systematic academic study in Hungary started around 1777. This period ended with the outbreak of the Hungarian revolution and freedom fight in 1848. At this time the day-to-day practice of public authorities was basically subject to two different influences: the legalistic approach and the politico-Kameralistik approach. The scientific background of PA was greatly dominated by the theories developed by scholars of the German-speaking part of Europe. The content of university study materials and that of professional publications was strictly specified and controlled by the Austrian absolutist monarchy. This also meant that even this early school of PA could exert its impact on Hungarian PA only with a specific Austrian 'interpretation'. The Napoleonic state model – with its modernisation efforts, rationality and effective public administration – had no special influence in Hungary at that time.

Development of legalistic approach after the fall of the freedom fight

The second period of PA in Hungary can be placed in the period between 1850 and 1930. The first decades of this period were characterised by the efforts of the emerging liberal capitalist state to limit and control the public administration of the *Polizeistaat* within universal and public norms. This movement for the creation of the rule of law had, by and large, similar characteristics to the parallel processes in other absolutist states of continental Europe.

This fact was reflected by both the fundamental characteristics – the professional composition, ruling culture, ethos and language, etc. – of the civil service of the period, and the legal regulations regarding entry requirements and career possibilities in public administration.

In this period, the scientific foundations of public administration education were essentially improved, and the Hungarian scholars succeeded in reaching European standards. Some names follow (Fazekas 2003: 98):

- Gyula Kautz in public economics and finance (Kautz 1868, 1911);
- Károly Kmety in public administration law (Kmety 1926–27);
- Győző Concha in constitutional law and the philosophy of the state. In his substantial and influential book (Concha 1905), he implemented the theory of Hans Kelsen (Kelsen 1927);
- Emil Récsi in constitutional and public administration law. Récsi wrote a 1,500-page textbook in public administration law;
- Móric Tomcsányi in public administration and financial law (Tomcsányi 1933).

This period saw the establishment and evolution of Hungarian public administration sciences. The basic approach of the Hungarian scholars followed the theories of Robert von Mohl (*Polizeiwissenschaft nach den Grundsätzen des Rechtsstaates* 1832) and of Otto Mayer, professor of the University of Strasbourg (*Theorie des französischen Verwaltungsrechts* 1886 and *Deutsches Verwaltungsrecht* 1895/6).

The beginning of the managerial approach

After the First World War, the independent Hungarian kingdom was established, having, instead of a King, a governor in the top political position. In the 1920s, the legalistic approach remained dominant but the establishment of the Faculty of Economics opened up the opportunities for public agencies to employ economists in different positions. But their role in the public agencies remained peripheral.

The short period of 1930–45 can be described as a very progressive era in the history of Hungarian PA. As a foretaste of this era, a public administration programme was launched at the University of Economic Sciences, indicating that, in the era of post-war economic crises, disciplinary approaches different from that of administrative law were needed to cope with the challenges.

The new school of PA, endorsed by the name of Zoltán Magyary, started a new direction in the development of the discipline. A widely quoted sentence of Magyary, himself a professor of law at the University of Budapest, is emblematic: 'You can't protect the country against flood with laws.' The new movement, focused around the Hungarian Institute of Public Administration Science, reflected the latest achievements of US and western European PA, scientific management, political science and sociology. This broad and theoretically well-grounded approach to PA, along with Magyary's personal professional integrity and quality, had a great impact on PA science and, to a lesser extent, PA programmes of the era.

Zoltán Magyary and his school formed a scientific movement aimed at the rationalisation of public administration. In the year preceding the Second World

War, the school of Zoltán Magyary was influenced by the American mainstream movement of public management orientation. In the USA the movement used the phrase, 'economy and efficiency of public administration'. Zoltán Magyary and other scholars implemented a managerial approach – instead of the legalistic dominance – which was outlined by internationally well-known and accepted US results such as the Report of the Brownlow Committee, or the work of such authors as F. W. Willoughby, the director of Brookings Institution, Leonard D. White, professor at the University of Chicago, Luther Gulick, professor at Columbia University and director of the Institute of Public Administration, New York.

In the 1930s, local governments in the US had greater autonomy than local governments in Europe. Gulick and White also developed the city sciences ('*Kommunalwissenschaften* in German) with a public administration orientation. The American scientists also influenced European scientists, not only in Hungary but in other countries as well (for instance William A. Robson in Great Britain and Karl Jeserich in Germany). In Hungary, research results in city sciences were published in the periodicals of the Institute of Hungarian Public Administration and in the journal of public administration science in the 1930s.

Public management studies in the communist era

The fourth era of PA is characterised by its relationship with socialism. After 1949, an entirely new, totalitarian power structure emerged. The dominance of this structure and of the communist ideology and the immediate practical interests of the regime prevented the practitioners of public agencies from creating even a crude theoretical basis for the new, socialist public administration until the sixties. Nevertheless, the primary focus of PA both as an academic discipline and as different university degree programmes became – or, since Magyary's pre-war approach never became institutionalised, one could rather say 'remained' – predominantly administrative law. By the academic year 1953/4 a unified programme of state and legal studies was created and it was implemented in all universities that had law faculties.

But the surrounding societal reality, primarily the dominant mode of rule of the Communist Party, meant that a formerly unimaginably large proportion of economic and societal functions became centralised, and a system of detailed and totalitarian economic planning was built up. In this context, the primary tool and focus of power were inevitably arbitrary actions, which started slowly to erode only in the sixties.

From this time on, Communist Party power was gradually more exercised by means of legal norms and written party regulations of a similar nature. State decisions and intentions towards the lower levels of a unitary hierarchy – including not only public administration organs but also the dominant proportion of the productive sphere – were increasingly transmitted in this vein. It is no wonder that, if public administration is nothing else than applying law, PA was equal to administrative law.

Nevertheless, from the late seventies on, efforts were made to differentiate between administrative law and public administration. Pragmatically reflecting some of the changes in the surrounding societal reality, the new emphasis was on administration as a specific element in PA not sufficiently dealt with by the classical study of administrative law. Prior to this, from the 1950s, a new type of post-secondary-education institution was launched in the field of local and regional public administration (the so-called 'council academy').

In 1977 a new educational institute named the College of Public Administration was created. The college awarded bachelor-level degrees to future officials of public administration, primarily (but not entirely) to those of territorial and local administration. The curricula of the college tried to strike a balance between administrative law, (public) management, and basics in social sciences like political science and sociology.

Although graduate programmes in the field of PA maintained a dominantly legal approach, academic and other research centres often applied their efforts on a more interdisciplinary basis. The same trend could be observed in the day-to-day reality of public administration, especially in some sectoral ministries and specialised deconcentrated state organs. Here, the dominance of law professionals as the most competent generalists of the administration of the state was less marked.

In 1968 a series of economic reforms was launched in Hungary. These reforms gave more emphasis to market incentives and mechanisms in the framework of a centrally planned economy. Due to the reforms – first in agriculture, and later in commerce and industrial firms – enterprises acquired a new, albeit limited autonomy in decision-making. The extension of the economic reform was not continuous and there were controversial elements and intentions in the economic system. But it had a great importance and by the end of the 1980s, market incentives had a significant influence in the framework of a planned economy in Hungary. The consequence was a growing importance of economic sciences in the state enterprises and, increasingly, in a number of public agencies, especially in those sectoral ministries and central bodies that dealt with economic planning/administration.

Therefore the basic task of the transition – which had started already, as a much more modest attempt to reform the existing system, in 1987–8 – was somewhat different from that of other former socialist states. A transition took place from a planned economy interspersed with some market-type elements to a basically market-oriented economy, less and less controlled by the power centre, and gaining more and more impetus from autonomous, non-state actors. Due to these circumstances, some elements of the legal framework of a market-type economy were already established before the political changes of the transition. A new company code – allowing the creation of privately owned enterprises and limited companies – and modern income tax and value added tax systems were introduced already in 1988.

In the Hungarian political system, there was also limited cultural autonomy. Based on this autonomy, the Hungarian Socialist Workers' Party was not as homogeneous as other ruling parties in the region. In the political system, the articulation of the interests of different groups was also possible in a limited way. There were ideological taboos of course, which could not be touched. This autonomy created a genuine demand for a real transition in Hungary. The majority of the population had experience of how to express their interests using institutionalised and legal forms and opportunities, but Hungary was far from the political pluralism that had been emerging in Poland in the 1970s and 1980s.

That is the reason why the Hungarian (and, for that matter, the Polish) transition was evolutionary, which contrasted sharply with the experience of other countries in the region, such as the 'velvet revolution' of Czechoslovakia or, even more evidently, the 'bloody revolution' in Romania. Because of the existence of a degree of political tolerance, a single nationwide election in 1990 established a market economy and a pluralistic democracy in Hungary.

These Hungarian special conditions had their influence on the role of the management sciences. Since the directors of public enterprises had more – albeit limited – economic and political autonomy than in other CEE (central and eastern Europe) countries, the need for the improvement of managerial skills was officially accepted and emphasised. Hence different management sciences were taught in different universities and postgraduate training centres established and managed by different ministries.

Reforms and modernisation: the practice of contemporary public administration

It is evident that the transition from command economy to market economy and from totalitarian state to pluralist, multiparty democracy is not only a transition but rather a process of transformation and it requires essential reforms in the basic functions and institutions of the state (König 1992).

In general, the feasibility of PMR initiatives – or, rather, the lack thereof – has clearly been a key issue throughout the entire period. First of all, a number of institutional factors played a crucial role in blocking PMR. The liberal democratic constitution entrenched practically all major institutional arrangements by protecting them with a qualified (two-thirds) majority voting procedure. Although these arrangements were originally intended to serve only on a provisional basis, the government very rarely managed to reach a political consensus strong enough to make the necessary changes that would give more room for shaping the government machinery.

An important aspect of the institutional arrangements is the role of the Constitutional Court in policy-making. The constitution grants the Hungarian Constitutional Court very powerful rights; moreover, these rights were significantly broadened by the court in the course of the past 16 years. Examples of the court's decisive role in blocking PMR include the nullification of some major elements of the Bokros package aiming at the restriction of certain welfare services on the basis that these measures would have violated the acquired rights of welfare recipients.

In addition to institutional obstacles, there are other types too, such as the lack of relevant expertise and the (related) lack of real demand for public management expertise (and, more generally, for the reforms themselves).

It is convenient to break up the process of administrative reform into various sections. In the following discussion, the process will be considered in three phases, the first lasting from 1989 to 1992, the second from 1993 to 1997, and the third from 1998 to the present time.

The three phases of modernisation

In the first phase, there were fundamental changes in the economic, political and legal environment of the public administration. In economic terms, the basic thrust has been to move away from a centrally planned, so-called command economy towards a market-oriented economic system. In political and legal terms the principal development has been the collapse of a totalitarian political system and the emergence of a pluralistic, multi-party system based on a constitutional state and liberal democratic political institutions. These fundamental changes required basic shifts in the functions of the state and comprehensive reform of public administration. The most important elements of public sector reform include:

- creating the institutional and legal foundations of democratic (in the case of armed forces, civilian) political control over the state apparatuses, with a special emphasis on the creation of a loyal and competent civil service;
- devolution of political power and the creation of an administrative capacity capable of serving the needs of autonomous local and regional self-government;
- privatisation programmes and contracting-out activities;
- decentralisation of decision-making to the regional and local level, providing genuine legal and financial autonomy for local institutions;
- deregulation reforms that make the long, complicated laws and regulations understandable to the public;
- transforming and flattening organisations so that they are not only relative, but also proactive in connection with changes in public requirements and demands;
- changing procurement policy, financial, human resource management and information systems in public organisations so that government agencies can work more effectively to develop new forms of cooperation with the nongovernmental organisations and the private sector and give more attention to the citizens they serve;
- measuring the performance and the outcomes of public sector activities by reviewing and monitoring, rather than by commanding and controlling.

After the first phase of the modernisation, the performance of the public sector became a progressively more crucial factor in Hungary. It was increasingly accepted that public sector performance was one key component of the overall performance of national economies, not only because of its direct impact as a buyer and seller of goods and services but also because of its indirect effects on product and labour markets. Poor administration and inadequately conceived or unnecessary regulations could substantially burden the private sector and voluntary activity of non-profit organisations. From that point of view, the improvement of infrastructure, the quality of public services and the performance of public administration became key long-term factors of economic recovery and modernisation. In the second phase, institutional capacity-building was the core requirement of the reform, resulting in an increasing necessity for a managerial approach.

In the third phase, it has become quite obvious that the performance level of the civil service has had a decisive impact not only on economic competitiveness but also on political stability. Thus there are many pressures and challenges facing public administration. For instance, people are losing confidence in all institutions, while at the same time every institution is faced with pressures on its resources and budgets. There is also a continuing push for more direct democracy, as well as more opportunities for participation. These trends are accompanied by decreasing respect for traditional instruments of 'representative' democracy. Under these circumstances, reacting in an oppressive way or trying to minimise problems will only serve to harm the credibility of public administration, an institution already viewed with considerable scepticism (Jenei 1999).

Apart from that, the implementation of the standards and values of the European Administration Space has brought great challenges for Hungarian public administration. These administrative principles are not formalised *acquis*, but more than a code of ethics. They are legally defined, containing a certain set of civil service standards and values, transmitted by law (constitution, acts of Parliament or by-laws). They are considered to be common trends and features, not a particular, national organisational model of the civil service.

In the implementation of the administrative principles, there are day-to-day tensions between:

- professional integrity, political neutrality and professional loyalty;
- autonomy, discretional decisions of civil servants and the rule of law (*Rechtsstaat, État de droit*);
- legalism and managerialism.

The results of the administrative transformation

With regard to the first phase of administrative reforms – that is, institutional reforms aiming at the creation of the administrative preconditions of a liberal democratic political system operating in a capitalist socio-economic context – it has been more or less successful. It was especially so in the first few years of the transition period, when Hungary featured as the forerunner of administrative transformation in many respects; for example, the country was the first to create a fully European local government system in 1990, or a similar civil service law in 1992.

The results of NPM-style reforms at the central-government level were, and are, much more controversial. This controversy does not lie in their effects. On the contrary, out of the central-government-level initiatives implemented since the mid-nineties it is difficult to find any with a significant main effect – either positive or negative. However, their side effects are, on some occasions, significant, such as the amount of resources spent on implementation, or the cumulative process of discrediting any sort of reform, irrespective of its intentions or content.

Nevertheless, there have been, especially in the last one to four years, constant efforts to produce some kind of visible result in creating a customer-friendly administrative service. Concepts like one-stop shopping and e-government measures seem to figure the best in this regard. However, there are strong indicators that in experiments with fancy NPM techniques, even the very basic classical bureaucratic virtues are often missing from large segments of the central government machinery. For example, basic coordination and information tasks are not carried out, and structures and processes are often largely chaotic and anarchistic, reflecting the temporary interests and aspirations of different, conflicting (micro-) political and, more typically, personal power centres. Moreover, even the most basic lines and mechanisms of bureaucratic accountability are often missing on multiple levels of the system.

The study of public administration and public management in contemporary Hungary

The previous sections gave an overview of the practice and the study of day-to-day government in a historical perspective; in this section we offer a picture of the scholarly field of the present day. The more one approaches the present, however, the more difficult it becomes to delineate, with an acceptable level of conceptual validity and empirical clarity, what exactly constitutes Hungarian public administration/public management as a field of study.

This difficulty is mainly rooted in two factors:

a   First, Hungary is one of those countries of Europe where the practical as well as the scholarly issues of government/administration have been for a long time, and to a significant extent still are, viewed through the conceptual lens of (administrative) law. So far, this has been one of the idiosyncrasies of Hungarian development. However, when it comes to the internationally comparative research of the topic, this distinct difference from the international mainstream means that one has to avoid the comparison of apples with pears;

b   Second, the lack, or at least weakness, of the field's disciplinary identity – and the resulting disciplinary and institutional vagueness – is also remarkable.

Thus it is also difficult to locate the subject from a more formal, institutional perspective.

The study of the more practical aspects of government, whatever it is called in various academia, languages and historical epochs, is present in practically all politico-administrative systems. However, the terms 'public administration' and, possibly even more, 'public management' are deeply rooted, and can only be easily operationalised, in the professional, institutional and discursive context of contemporary Anglo-Saxon and, increasingly, European countries. This difficulty is well illustrated by the fact that a relatively recent, large-scale survey of European governance programmes (Verheijen and Connaughton 1999; Verheijen and Nemec 2000) identified no academic programmes called 'public administration' in at least three, and no university programmes entitled 'public management' in about eight to ten (current) member countries of the EU.

This picture is, to a significant extent, characteristic for Hungary too. A statistical analysis of PA-related academic programmes in 23 European countries identified three distinct clusters of countries: one characterised by a predominantly legalistic, one by a management-oriented, and a third by an interdisciplinary approach to teaching PA. This analysis put Hungary, along with a number of central/eastern European and Mediterranean countries, definitely into the group of countries characterised by an overwhelmingly (administrative) law-based approach to PA (Hajnal 2003). Therefore, it may be misleading to assume the problem-free transferability of such concepts as 'a PA degree programme' – and, more generally, the concept of Public Administration or Public Management – from a North American or western/northern European context to the Hungarian (or, for that matter, to a southern or eastern/central European) one.

This discrepancy exists in the realm of terms used to denote the concept of PA. The Hungarian equivalent of the term 'public administration' – and, much more so, 'public management' – is actually rarely used in reference to the respective fields of academic study. Instead, a number of other concepts and corresponding terms are often used, such as 'state and legal science' or 'state/public administrative law'. Moreover, even in cases where the term 'administration' is used, it usually refers to the legal aspects of public administration. It may be interesting to note that, likewise, most CEE languages do not have a term for 'public policy' (or have started to create one only very recently).

Another common feature of the 'legalist' group of countries mentioned above is that the disciplinary identity of public administration (let alone public management) is traditionally weak or even non-existent. The following subsections attempt to delineate and describe the study of public administration by approaching the problem from the three more-or-less distinct aspects of (i) administrative practice (more specifically, the patterns of civil servants' academic background), (ii) scholarly work, and (iii) higher education programmes.

Public management as practice: the academic background
of civil servants

As already mentioned, throughout the past decades, mainstream PA in Hungary has maintained a dominantly legal approach, although academic and other research centres have operated on an increasingly interdisciplinary basis, especially in the past two decades. This trend can be observed in the everyday reality of public administration, too. Here the unquestioned dominance of law professionals as the most competent generalists of public administration still exists, but exhibits a decreasing tendency.

Table 10.1 gives an insight into this process by charting time series data on the educational background of territorial and local public administrators having a higher-education (or similar) degree.

There are two remarkable features of this data. One of them is related to the dramatic changes since the seventies and the eighties: the shrinking proportion of College of PA and council academy degree holders among civil servants. It is important to note that, notwithstanding their titles and their intention to base PA education on a more interdisciplinary (as opposed to purely legal) approach, these programmes remained predominantly law-oriented. The other interesting feature is the remarkably stable proportion of lawyers, which remained practically constant over a period of 30 years. Although this 10–13 per cent seems to be a modest proportion, there are some circumstances that shed more light on the true importance of lawyers in Hungarian public administration:

• First, lawyers are strongly (by about 100 per cent in 2005) over-represented in subsets of higher importance, such as (i) among civil servants in managerial

Table 10.1 Academic background, of civil servants in local and regional administration 1975–2005

	College of PA/council academy	Law	Economics	Finance	Engineering/ technical
1975	66%	13%	1%	0%	2%
1985	54%	13%	3%	0%	3%
2005	23%	10%	10%	12%	19%

Source: For the 1975 and 1985 data: Gajduschek (2006); for the 2005 data: a survey (questionnaire interview) of a nationally representative sample of civil servants (*n* = 1000); the research was designed by György Gajduschek and György Hajnal.

Notes
Time series data available both before and after the transition are extremely rare. Therefore the comparability of data is less than perfect (reply categories had to be 'matched' to one another across the different surveys).

Percentages for any single year do not add up to 100 per cent. The reason for this is that only the key reply categories are included in the table, and some minor/insignificant response categories were omitted.

positions and (ii) in ministries (authors' calculation). It is particularly telling that in the senior civil service, consisting of the highest-ranking civil servants, 57 per cent have a degree in law (Gajduschek 2006: 605);

- Second, legal regulations make it clear that, in practice, lawyers are definitely perceived as the most competent generalists of administration. Examples include the exemption rules for the so-called 'specialised examination system' of civil servants, compulsory for a large majority of administrators: only lawyers are exempted from the obligations of passing this – mostly legal-type – exam. The situation is similar with the General Basic Public Administration Examination scheme (Gajduschek and Hajnal 2001).

In sum, there are serious arguments that, in the discursive context of Hungarian public administration practice, PA still refers much more to administrative law than to anything else – the latter including meanings attached to the term in the mainstream international discourse. Still, in order to ensure comparability, the next subsection describes relevant Hungarian scholarly outputs according to this international mainstream conceptualisation of PA.

Hungarian PA/PM in the view of scholarly work

This subsection gives a brief overview of PA/PM-related publications authored by Hungarian researchers. Although all such classifications are necessarily imperfect, we have grouped them in order to ease their presentation. This thematic classification is made for mostly didactic purposes, as there are no distinct schools of PA/PM.

Internationally comparative contributions published for the international audience

The broad and – in the light of arguments presented earlier – vague field of study sometimes referred to as 'PA' (or, much more rarely, 'PM') has undergone remarkable development since the transition. The most important and visible change is the increasing internationalisation of scientific practice. One aspect of this is of a technical nature: the increasing presence of theories, topics, methodologies and academic standards characteristic of international practice. In addition, the technical and organisational/financial possibilities of international scientific cooperation have dramatically improved in comparison to the previous decades. Another aspect of this development relates to the increasing presence of international comparative work on the research agenda. An important factor underlying the shift towards internationally comparative topics may be, besides the actual importance of this type of work, the international 'marketability' of comparative studies involving, for example, other countries of the post-communist region.

In addition to its sheer volume (relative proportion in overall research output), the key importance of international comparative work in Hungarian academic research stems from the fact that this is the leading field that demonstrates some convergence towards the theoretical and methodological approaches and quality standards characteristic of the Western academic community.

In the vast majority of cases, comparative research meant an involvement in international comparative projects by authoring piece(s) related specifically to Hungary (for example, Balázs 1993; Szabó 1993; Verebélyi 1993; Hajnal 2000, 2003; Newland *et al.* 1999). In some distinctly unusual cases, Hungarian authors were involved in international comparative research at the central node, i.e. as the initiators/designers of the research. While a few of these research efforts had an overwhelmingly academic, theoretical ambition (Hajnal 2003, 2005), most of them had a relatively practical orientation (Gajduschek and Hajnal 2003; Horváth 2000; Horváth and Péteri 2004; Soós *et al.* 2002; it is important to note that the last four of these projects were run under the auspices of the Open Society Institute's Local Government and Public Service Reform Initiative in Budapest).

Other contributions to the international discourse on PA/PM

Most elements of this group are 'stand-alone', article-length contributions to the international discourse on various PM topics. The majority of these contributions deal with the broad problem area related to regional and local government (Horváth 1997; Jenei *et al.* 2005; Jenei and Szalai 2002; Pálné *et al.* 2004). Contributions in some other fields include Ágh (1999) and Gajduschek (2003).

Significant publications in Hungarian

Many works from this category are concerned with the dissemination and, to a varying but usually modest extent, adaptation of already existing and 'canonised' Western results in various subfields of PA, PM or public policy. These works usually take the form of well-structured books, showing that they were fundamentally intended as training/course materials in university education. Some of these books have a predominantly comparative focus, such as Horváth 2002 and Lörincz 2006. Other, non-comparative works are exemplified by Gulyás and Jenei (1999), Hajnal and Gajduschek (2002), Horváth (2005), Jenei (2005), and Zupkó (2002).

In trying to conclude the above rough and mostly quantitative overview, it should be said that in an international perspective, notwithstanding the existence of certain important results, Hungarian scholarly work definitely seems undeveloped. Of course it is not an easy task to supply substantive arguments supporting such a general and – possibly – harsh statement. Although they are admittedly far from being compelling arguments, some telling indicators of this weakness of the field are as follows.

• For the time being, there is no scholarly journal of PA/PM in Hungary. Although there is a monthly journal titled *Magyar Közigazgatás* (Hungarian Public Administration), it doesn't have an academic ambition; moreover, even this journal is likely to cease to exist in the coming months. There are some other journals (such as *Comitatus*) conforming more to the ideal of a scholarly journal, but the definite majority of their articles fall outside the disciplinary realm of PA/PM.

- There is no scientific association of the field in Hungary (such as a Society of PA, PM, Evaluation, Policy Studies, etc.).
- There is only a sporadic appearance of Hungarian authors in the mainstream international literature. For example, in the period of 2001–5 only about half a dozen papers (co-)authored by Hungarian authors appeared in five prominent journals of the field (*Public Administration, Public Administration Review, Public Management Review, Governance* and the *Journal of Administrative Research and Theory*).
- The institutional infrastructure of the field is also relatively weak. Again, it is possible to give only some rough quantitative indicators supporting this statement. One such indicator is the lack of departments of PA/PM; although there are a number of universities offering a degree in PA (see the next sub-section), there are only a very few – about three to four – departments of public administration, or of public management. Moreover, as already mentioned, even some these actually conduct administrative law studies. Another indicator is the scarcity of other, non-university-based research centres. Although there are a small number of research institutions involved to some, usually marginal, extent in PA/PM research (such as the various Centres of Regional Studies of the Hungarian Academy of Sciences), there is only one institute primarily dealing with research in PA/PM (the Hungarian Institute of Public Administration).

PA/PM in the view of higher education programmes

Although, as we mentioned earlier, the essentially legalist concept of public administration has not changed fundamentally since 1990, the emergence and relatively rapid development of other disciplinary approaches to PA in academic education has become increasingly visible. These new approaches are, in practice, transferred from the Anglo-Saxon and, to a lesser extent, other European countries' academia and administrative practice.

A 1999 survey of the field (Hajnal 2000) identified two types of programmes relevant in the field of public administration (see Table 10.2). One of them was the traditional MA in law. Their inclusion was justified by the circumstances outlined on the previous pages; that is, the fact that the daily reality – the legal regulations as well as the ruling culture of public administration as a field of practice – identified (and, to a large extent, continue to identify) lawyers as the public administration professionals *par excellence*. Importantly, law programmes were, and still are, taught at faculties of state and legal sciences, which reflects the still-prevailing ambition of the legal discipline to cover issues of administering/controlling the governmental sector.

Table 10.2 Composition of the PA higher education field in Hungary in 1999

Programme type	Number of programmes	Number of HE institutions
Law programmes	7	7
PA/PM (i.e non-law) programmes	5	3
Total	12	10

Source: Hajnal 2000.

The other type of programmes was PA, in the international/Western sense of the word. (Note that the proportions apparently implied by the data are somewhat misleading, since enrolment in law programmes was higher than enrolment in PA/PM programmes by about one order of magnitude.)

In the last five to seven years, the situation has changed in some important respects. These changes include the restructuring of the Hungarian higher education system, and the increase in size and number of 'real' PA programmes.

As for the restructuring of the higher education system, one of the major developments was the amalgamation process of higher education institutions. This was initiated, by the government under the pressure of a large World Bank conditional loan, in order to realise economies of scale. An evaluation of this reform is outside the scope of this work; therefore it is noted only briefly that, to many observers inside and outside academia, the main result seems to be only changes in the institutional banners and some further growth in the complexity, opacity and irrationality of the system.

The other structural development was the introduction of the Bologna system in higher education programmes. It is not our intention to reflect on these changes here either. However, from the point of view of analysing today's university programmes, this creates a technical problem, since programmes that are due to cease within a few years are coexisting with those just started at the time of writing of this paper. The solution chosen here is that only new programmes – i.e. those conforming with the Bologna system – are included in the overview below.

Table 10.3 shows university programmes related to at least some segments or aspects of public administration from 2006 onwards. Those programmes that most resemble generic PA/PM programmes in the West are set in bold; from all subsequent analyses by PA/PM programmes we refer only to these ones. At the first glance, the table might suggest that PA has by now been sufficiently embedded in the Hungarian higher education system; narrowing down our analysis to the 'real' PA programmes (ie public administration and public service), the figures on these programmes are comparable with, for example, those given by Kickert (in this volume) on the Netherlands.

These 'real' PA/PM programmes are in general characterised by a relative heterogeneity of relevant disciplines such as (public) management, political and applied political sciences, administrative law, public policy studies, etc.

Table 10.3 Summary of Hungarian civilian undergraduate programmes related to public administration or public management, starting in 2006

Title	Number of programmes	Total enrolment*
Administration and ICT in agriculture policy	3	524
Administration of international affairs	2	250
Administration of labour affairs and social security	3	595
Administration of justice	3	1,100
Cadastral administration	1	60
Health management	5	670
International studies	12	2,122
MA in Law	8	5,062
Public Administration	3	1,468
Public service	7	1,429
Total	47	13,280

Source: based on OFIK (2006).

Notes
*Enrolment figures are based not on actual but on planned numbers. Real enrolment is likely to be somewhat smaller than planned.

However, the so-called public administration programmes have a legal character that would be outstandingly strong in the western/northern European context; about 35 to 50 per cent of compulsory courses taught in these programmes definitely belong to the legal discipline. Another illustrative point is the composition of the faculties teaching core courses. As an example, in the state/public administration department at one of the largest PA programmes, close to 100 per cent of the faculty have a background in law; the situation is similar with the other two programmes.

It is clear, nevertheless, that PA/PM education is 'on the move'; the status quo of traditional legalism is impossible to maintain. Still, it is not possible to say that a clear and decisive convergence, let alone catching up, with mainstream Western thinking has happened. A telling sign of the chronic vagueness of PA identity is the official location of PA university programmes in the system of disciplines. The Hungarian Accreditation Committee – the public entity responsible for the accreditation of university programmes – created a classification system of programmes. Each programme submitted for accreditation has to fit into one of the programme categories, examples of which include the public administration and public service programmes highlighted in Table 10.3. These programme categories are then classified into higher-level academic branches reflecting the disciplinary status of the given programme. A review of this classification results in some peculiar findings. The programme in public administration is classified into the academic branch of legal and administrative studies, together with, e.g., MA in Law; whereas the programme in public service is classified into academic branch of economics, along with such programmes as economic analysis (econometrics) and applied economics. At the same time, in the academic branch of social sciences, where such programmes are located as sociology, political sciences, and social and international studies, nothing like PA/PM can be found.

This weird institutional structure has a twofold significance. On the one hand, it reflects the pre-existing institutional structure of higher education, having been formed in part by the legalist historical traditions of PA education referred to earlier, and in part by chance events and contingencies related to the inter- and intra-organisational micropolitics of influential players of the field. On the other hand, however, it exerts a significant impact on how PA as a field of study is perceived and taught. Clearly, the fact that PA programmes are primarily affiliated to faculties of state and legal sciences or faculties of economics is likely to have a decisive, lasting and probably damaging effect on the institutional, epistemological and professional identity and status of the field.

Table 10.4 Compulsory courses at the largest representatives of Public Administration and Public Service programmes

Programme	Courses
BA in PA, Budapest Corvinus University	Basic institutions of PA**; History of Hungarian constitution and PA**; Statistics; Political theory; Social psychology; Economics; Applied mathematics; Applied ICT; Administrative law; Logic; Urban administration*; Communication; Sociology; ICT in the public administration; Administrative procedure**; Hungarian constitutional law**; Civil law**; Organisation and management; History of philosophy; Social and cultural administration**; Hungarian constitutional law**; Environmental law**; Administrative organisation; Tax law**; Economic administration**; Administrative criminal law**; Theory of state and law**; Administrative technology; International law**; Economic administration of public organs**; Local governments**; Police administration**; Civil service law**; Accounting of public organs*
BA in Public Service, Budapest Corvinus University	Basics of mathematics; Economic mathematics; Statistics; Introduction to accounting; ICT; Microeconomics; Macroeconomics; International economics; Finance; Corporate economics; Corporate finance; Constitutional theory*; Introduction to EU integration; Economic law**; Social policy; Introduction to public policy; Organisation and management; Public household and finance; Public finance; Research methods; Public choice; Introduction to public management; Market structure; Ethics in PA; Economic and social statistics; History of economic theories

Notes
*Subject with significant legal content.
**Predominantly or wholly legal subject.

Table 10.4 lists the core (compulsory) courses of the largest programme in public administration and the largest one in public service. The table well illustrates the points made in the previous paragraphs. The public administration programme consists of mostly legal subjects; subjects with an entirely or overwhelmingly legal character amount to 17 courses out of the 35 (49 per cent; note that this figure doesn't contain the more modestly legal courses marked with '*'). This fundamental bias towards legalism makes this type of programme distinctly different from what, in the international discourse, is called a programme in public administration. Unfortunately, however, the public service programme is also – albeit less strongly – distorted if measured according to mainstream Western standards. It is particularly notable that barely any political science subjects are included in the core curriculum. On the other hand, economic and related subjects are over-represented, which reflects the programme's institutional affiliation to the economic discipline.

Thus, it seems that Hungarian education in PA, let alone PM, is still quite far from being on track. Although a distinctly new programme type emerged that represents a clear departure from the legalism traditionally present in Hungarian PA/PM, this new approach is also characterised by significant and dysfunctional deviations from the concept(s) of PA/PM to be found in any western European country. It would be interesting to attempt to account for this strange phenomenon. Doing so lies, unfortunately, beyond the ambition and scope of this paper. A few probable factors that are, however, worth mentioning are (i) the weakness of Western-like academic communities around PA/PM, (ii) the strong ability of particularistic interest groups to pursue their own agenda, and (iii) the minimal ability of governmental policy centres to think and act strategically.

Conclusions

In the communist era, the basic nature of political power was arbitrariness, and the practice of administration consisted mostly of the execution of laws. Legal norms and regulations, in addition to the informal and omnipotent power of the Party that was manifested in non-legal regulations of similar character to that of the legal ones, transmitted all state decisions and intentions towards the lower levels of a unitary hierarchy, including the dominant proportion of the productive sphere.

It is important to notice that this legalism of public administration differed from the legalism of traditional, Weberian bureaucracies of the liberal democratic systems in one important respect. Namely, while administrative apparatuses of liberal democratic political regimes had, historically, an important role in both preparing and executing laws (cf. Kickert in this volume), the role of administrative apparatuses was restricted to execution only; all important policy decisions were prepared by strictly separate Party organisations.

Nevertheless, if public administration was nothing else than applying law, PA as a field of study became – or, in the light of the prehistory outlined earlier in this chapter, remained – almost equal to administrative law.

In central and eastern European transitional countries such as Hungary, public administration has had to face special challenges because the creation of a liberal democracy and the implementation of the principles of efficiency and effectiveness have become crucial tasks of modernisation at the same time. Since the early 1990s, more fundamental changes have been introduced in public administration in terms of private management methods and the commencement of an overall effort to reduce the scope of the state. This has resulted in a completely new situation. The increasing economic, political and social pressure on public administration has forced bureaucrats to consider the requirements of legalism and managerialism at the same time. This has resulted in tensions and uncertainties within Hungary.

Even in the EU countries, there are tensions between the administrative principles. There is a broadly discussed tension between the principles of professional integrity and professional loyalty. And a well-known consequence of customer-orientation, quality improvement and application of management techniques is the tension between legalism and managerialism. In the EU, the development of the rule of law and the introduction of New Public Management was a sequential process. (Even in this development, tensions are wellknown.)

In the Hungarian context, these dilemmas and issues boil down to two sets of conclusions, one dealing with the narrower subject field of PA/PM as a field of study, the other referring to the practice of administrative transformation.

PA/PM as a field of study

The question of what actually constitutes the Hungarian study of PA/PM in the current, mainstream Western sense of the term is far from being trivial. This difficulty is a historically evolved, common feature of countries currently characterised by a predominantly (administrative) legal approach to problems of public administration in most southern and central/east European countries. Moreover, not only the concepts and terms but also the professional identity and the institutional boundaries of the field are vague.

As a consequence, and unlike much of the northern/western European and North American academic communities, it is not meaningful to differentiate between PA and PM in today's Hungary. The discipline is still very much in the process of departing from the study of administrative law – a process that took place in the aforementioned countries several decades earlier.

With regard to the substantive features of the PA/PM field, two observations deserve attention. First, starting from a level close to zero in 1990, the discipline has become increasingly visible in terms of both scholarly work produced and higher education programmes available in the field. International scientific cooperation has significantly helped this process. Second, the professional/disciplinary identity of the field and its practitioners is still much weaker than in most western/northern European academic communities. This is accompanied and underpinned by such problems as serious misconceptions, manifested even in institutional structures, regarding what PA/PM as a discipline actually is, and a relative quantitative and qualitative weakness of research. As a result of these difficulties, it does not seem meaningful to position Hungarian PA/PM on the international landscape of contemporary scientific schools of PA/PM.

The practice of administrative transformation

Compared to western European countries, there is an essential difference in Hungary and, more generally, in the CEE countries. Namely, in the early 1990's these countries had just established the legal and organisational framework of a *Rechtsstaat*, and shortly after this they also had the challenge of introducing managerial systems and techniques in the public sector. Essentially the development of the rule of law and of the New Public Management have become a parallel process; moreover, this duality and the dilemmas involved clearly correspond to those detected in the realm of scientific ideas with regard to the legalist vs multidisciplinary/managerial approach to public administration. This means that the real danger in the region is not a tension between legalism and managerialism, but fragmentation.

Creating a legal–organizational framework for a *Rechtsstaat* does not mean that the reformed system is already a fully functioning legal state based on firm Weberian principles. But without a functioning Weberian democratic system, without the regulative and monitoring power of the state, the initial steps of New Public Management can strengthen corruption.

On the other hand, without adopting some forms of NPM concepts and practices, CEE countries cannot increase the competitiveness of the public sector, which is an essential component of the economic, social and political modernisation processes of these countries.

Are we really in a trap situation? Is it a dilemma which cannot be solved? The only solution is that the CEE countries should not try to avoid the Weberian phase of development. A functioning *Rechtsstaat* is a necessity in the course of modernisation but you have to add to this development the application and implementation of the Western models and techniques as well. What these countries seem to need is a balanced position, and public administration needs a stable political background and strong consensus of the political parties in supporting this process.

Another precondition of the transferability of public management reforms is that the CEE region – and, within that, each CEE country – should find its own way in solving its particular problems. Instead of imitation, their experiences should be assimilated in a way that reflects the local circumstances. Making an eclectic selection from the experiences of different models risks producing a combined mistake instead of a relevant synthesis. This is a central challenge of the coming years, not only for the practitioners but also for scholars of public administration.

230   *G. Hajnal and G. Jenei*

Bibliography

Ágh, A. (1999) 'Europeanization of Policy-making in East Central Europe: the Hungarian Approach to EU Accession', *Journal of European Public Policy*, 6: 839–54.

Balázs, I. (1993) 'The Transformation of Hungarian Public Administration', in. J. J. Hesse (ed.) *Administrative Transformation in Central and Eastern Europe*, Oxford: Blackwell.

Concha, G. (1905) *Politika II,* Volume: 'Közigazgatás', Budapest: author's publication.

Fazekas, M. (2003) 'A politico-cameralis tudományok oktatásának 225 éve' (225 years of teaching politico-cameralis sciences), *A jogászképzés múltja, jelene és jövője*, Acta Congressiuum. 10, Budapest: ELTE ÁJK.

Gajduschek, G. (2003) 'Bureaucracy: Is It Efficient? Is It Not? Is That the Question?', *Administration and Society*, 34: 700–22.

Gajduschek, G. (2006) 'A közszolgálat harminc éve' (Civil service in Hungary. Trends in the past thirty years), unpublished research report, Budapest: MKI/Hungarian Institute of Public Administration.

Gajduschek, G. and Hajnal, G. (2000) *Evaluation of the Hungarian General Civil Service Training Program*, Budapest: OSI/LGI Publications.

Gajduschek, G. and Hajnal, G. (2003) *Civil Service Training Assistance Projects in the Former Communist Countries: an Assessment*, Budapest: OSI/LGI Publications.

Gulyás, G. and Jenei, G. (1999) *Bevezetés a közpolitikába* (Introduction to Public Policy), Budapest: BKE Közszolgálati Tanulmányi Központ.

Hajnal, G. (2000) 'Public Administration Education in Hungary', in T. Verheijen and J. Nemec (eds) *Building Higher Education Programmes in Public Administration in CEE Countries*, Bratislava: NISPAcee.

Hajnal, G. (2003) 'Diversity and Convergence: a Quantitative Analysis of European Public Administration Education Programs', *Journal of Public Affairs Education*, 9: 245–58.

Hajnal, G. (2003) 'Hopes and Reality: the First Decade of the Hungarian Local Government System in the Eyes of the Public', in P. Swianiewicz (ed.) *Public Perception of Local Governments*, 2nd edn, Budapest: OSI/LGI Publications.

Hajnal, G. (2005) 'The Spirit of Management Reforms: towards Building an Explanatory Model of NPM', *Public Management Review*, 7: 495–513.

Hajnal, G. (2006) 'Public Management Reforms in Hungary', Ljubljana, Slovenia: NISPAcee 14th Annual Conference, May 2006.

Hajnal, G. and Gajduschek, G. (2002) *Hivatali határok – társadalmi hatások. Bevezetés a hatékony közigazgatás módszertanába*, (Introduction to the Methodology of Efficient Public Administration) Budapest: Magyar Közigazgatási Intézet.

Hesse, J. J. (ed). (1993) *Administrative Transformation in Central and Eastern Europe,* Oxford: Blackwell.

Hóman, B. and Szekfü, G. (1936) *Magyar Történet* (The History of Hungary), vol II, Budapest: Királyi Magyar Egyetemi Nyomda.

Horváth, M. T. (1997) 'Decentralization in Public Administration and Provision of Services: an East-Central European View', *Environment and Planning C, Government and Policy*, 15: 161–75.

Horváth, M. T. (ed.) (2000) *Decentralization: Experiments and Reforms*, Budapest: OSI/LGI.

Horváth, M. T. (2002) *Helyi közszolgáltatások szervezése* (Managing Local Public Services), Budapest-Pécs: Dialóg Campus.

Horváth M. T. (2005) *Közmenedzsment,* (Public Management) Budapest-Pécs: Dialóg Campus.

Horváth, M. T. and Péteri, G. (2004) 'Threats of Transformation Failures. Local Public Utility Sector in Central and Eastern Europe', *Society and Economy,* 26: 295–324.

Jenei, G. (1999) 'Public Service Management and the Transition Process in Hungary', in D. Braiunig and D. Greiling (eds) *Stand und Perspektiven der Öffentlichen Betriebswirtschaftslehre,* Berlin: Arno Spitz Verlag.

Jenei, G. (2005) *Közigazgatás-menedzsment* (Public Management), Budapest: Osiris Kiadó.

Jenei, G. and Szalai, Á. (2002) 'Modernizing Local Governance in a Transitional Nation', *Public Management Review,* 4: 367–86.

Jenei, G., Kuti, É., Horváth, Á. and Palotai, Z. (2005) 'Local Governments, Civil Society Organizations and Private Enterprises – Partnerships in Providing Social Services: The Case of Eger, Hungary', *Journal of Comparative Policy Analysis,* 7: 73–94.

Kautz, G. (1868) *A nemzetgazdasági eszmék fejlödési története és befolyása a közviszonyokra Magyarországon* (The History of National Economics and its Influence on Public Affairs in Hungary), Pest: Heckenast.

Kautz, G. (1911) *A nemzetgazdasági eszmék története Magyarországon,* (The History of Theories of National Economics) Budapest.

Kelsen, H. (1927) *Az államélet alapvonalai* (Basics of State Functioning), Szeged.

Kmety, K. (1902) *A magyar pénzügyi jog kézikönyve,* (Handbook of Hungarian Financial Law) Budapest: Politzer.

Kmety, K. (1926–7) *A magyar közigazgatási és pénzügyi jog kézikönyve,* (Handbook of Hungarian Public Administration and Financial Law) Budapest.

König, K. (1992) 'The Transformation of a "Real-Socialist" Administrative System into a Conventional Western European System,' *International Review of Administrative Sciences,* 58: 147-61

Kosáry, D. (1980) *Müvelödés a XVIII. századi Magyarországon* (Culture and Education in Eighteenth-Century Hungary), Budapest: Akadémiai Kiadó.

Kubinyi, A. (2006) 'A Jagelló-kori Magyar állam. 1490–1526' (The Hungarian State in the Age of the Jagello Royal House), *História,* 27: 1–4.

Lörincz, L. (ed.) (2006) *Közigazgatás az Európai Unió tagállamaiban. Összehasonlító közigazgatás* (Public Administration in the EU Member States. Comparative Public Administration), Budapest: Unió.

Magyary, Z. (1927) *A magyar tudománypolitika alapvetése* (Foundations of Hungarian Science Policy), Budapest: Királyi Magyar Egyetemi Nyomda.

Magyary, Z. (1942) *Magyar Közigazgatás* (Hungarian Public Administration), Budapest: Királyi Magyar Egyetemi Nyomda.

Máthé, G. (2003) 'Az önállósult közigazgatási szakemberképzés' (Educating Public Administration Professionals in Hungary), in *A jogászképzés múltja, jelene és jövöje,* vol 10, Budapest: Bibliotheca Iuridica, Acta Congressuum, ELTE ÁJK.

Newland, C., Jenei, G. and Suchorzewski, L. (1999) 'Transitions in the Czech Republic, Hungary and Poland: Autonomy and Community among Nation-States', in W. J. M. Kickert and R. J. Stillmann (eds) *The Modern State and its Study: New Administrative Sciences in a Changing Europe and United States,* Aldershot: Edward Elgar.

Pálné Kovács, I., Paraskevopoulos, C. J. and Horváth, G. (2004) 'Institutional "Legacies" and the Shaping of Regional Governance in Hungary', *Regional and Federal Studies,* 14: 430–60.

President's Committee on Administrative Management (1937) 'Report with Special Studies', Washington: United States Government Printing Office: 384.

Soós, G., Tóka, G. and Wright, G. (eds) (2002) *The State of Local Democracy in Central Europe*, Budapest: OSI/LGI Publications.

Szabó, G. (1993) 'Administrative Transition in a post-Communist Society: the Case of Hungary', in J. J. Hesse (ed.) *Administrative Transformation in Central and Eastern Europe*, Oxford: Blackwell Publishers.

Tomcsányi, M. (1933) *Magyar közigazgatási és pénzügyi jog. Különös (szakigazgatási) rész* (Hungarian Administrative and Financial Law. Specific Provisions), Budapest: author's publication.

Verebélyi, I. (1993) 'Options for Administrative Reform in Hungary', in J. J. Hesse (ed.) *Administrative Transformation in Central and Eastern Europe*, Oxford: Blackwell Publishers.

Verheijen, T. and Connaughton, B. (eds) (1999) *Higher Education Programmes in Public Administration: Ready for the Challenge of Europeanisation?*, Limerick: Centre for European Studies, University of Limerick.

Verheijen, T. and Nemec, J. (eds) (2000) *Building Higher Education Programmes in Public Administration in CEE Countries*, Bratislava: NISPAcee.

Zupkó, G. (2002) *Közigazgatási reformirányzatok az ezredfordulón* (Contemporary Schools of Public Administration Reform), Budapest: Századvég.

11 The study of public management in the United States

Management in the New World and a reflection on Europe

Laurence E. Lynn, Jr

Introduction

From their beginnings, American administrative thought and practice have evinced a managerial spirit. First alluded to by Alexander Hamilton as 'energy in the executive', American managerialism was authoritatively endorsed by Leonard White in his seminal 1926 textbook *The Study of Administration* and by President Franklin Roosevelt's Committee on Administrative Management. The scientific management movement originated in the United States, and among the most successful of American administrative reforms is the city-manager form of local government. Government run with business-like efficiency has been a goal of American presidents from Theodore Roosevelt through Franklin D. Roosevelt, Ronald Reagan and George W. Bush. It is understandable that American public administration and management are often viewed as a manifestation of the business-corporate style that enjoys a favored place in the American practical imagination.

Overlooked in this narrative, however, is another, equally important Hamiltonian precept. To ensure that citizens enjoy 'safety' from tyranny, administration must, said Hamilton, exhibit a 'due dependence on the people in a republican sense, ... a due responsibility'. The authors of America's Declaration of Independence had complained that '[King George] has erected a multitude of new offices and sent hither swarms of officers to harass our people and eat out their substance'. America's Founders were determined that the new nation not recreate European-style central institutions that might threaten liberty and property. Instead they created a formal separation of powers and a de facto system of checks and balances, including a form of federalism in which the national government exercises enumerated and implied powers and all remaining powers are reserved to the states and to the people.

Public administration and management in America are, therefore, fundamentally Madisonian in that they are a resultant of the dynamics of constraining faction and power in order that government and its managers may always exhibit a due dependence on citizens, who express themselves through representative institutions, and a sense of responsibility to America's constitutional principles. While corporate-sector ideas and practices have often been influential in thought and practice within the field of public administration – as have the ideas originating in academic research, the nonprofit sector, and the practices of other levels of government – the discussion below will show that the story of public management in America is about implementing a complex constitutional scheme that is contrary in spirit and practice to corporate-style governance. However much business-inspired ideas such as scientific management, strategic planning, continuous quality improvement, and performance measurement might have appealed to policy makers, the influence of such ideas on managerial practice is determined by the centrifugal forces of America's polycentric institutions.

It is America's constitutional scheme of governance that explains why Dwight Waldo believed European administrative thought and practice to be inappropriate for the emerging American administrative state and why Walter Kickert and other Europeans argue that American administrative thought and practice are not automatically transferable to European and other non-American contexts, a point discussed more fully below.

Emergence of the American administrative state[1]

It is notable that the American revolutionaries' indictment of British colonial rule primarily concerned the abuse of administrative powers (Wilson 1975; Nelson 1982). However, the Founders were clearer about what they did not want – the possibility of such abuse by their own government – than about what they did want in their institutional arrangements.

An aggregate, not a unit

The first attempt at sovereign government following the Declaration of Independence was a confederation of 13 colonial states called the United States of America. The Articles of Confederation that governed America's first republic established a 'league of friendship and a perpetual union' between and among the thirteen former colonies, reflecting their wariness of a strong central government. Unlike the Jacobin democracy that emerged from the French Revolution, American democracy is 'primarily an aggregate and only secondarily . . . a unit' (Small 1909: 586). Moreover, whereas European states 'began with the nation-state and worked downward . . . in the United States the progression was reversed' (Mosher 1975: 8). The American administrative state would perforce be founded on its primordial democratic principles.

Meeting to overcome the incapacity of their new national government, the Founders were determined to prevent the emergence of a European state of dangerously unaccountable executive power (Stillman 1999; Waldo 1984), and so a formal separation of powers, checks and balances, and federalism constituted America's second (and enduring) republic. Initially, the result was the America observed by de Tocqueville. According to Dwight Waldo, 'the lack of a strong tradition of administrative action . . . contributed to . . . public servants acting more or less in their private capacities' (Waldo 1984: 11) rather than as agents of central authority.

Following the election of President Andrew Jackson in 1828, a spoils system – to the victor belong the spoils or privileges of office – of rotation in office replaced the largely aristocratic personnel practices of the Federalists. In E. N. Gladden's account (1972), the Tenure in Office Act of 1820, which limited to four years the terms of office of officials handling moneys, 'endorsed a principle that was to gain increasing support thenceforward' (1972: 309). The spoils system dominated nineteenth-century selection and control of administrators, and the oversight of administration exercised by legislators, political parties, and the courts was haphazard (Lynn 2001).

Though credited with creating the spoils system, Jackson at the same time inaugurated the beginnings of bureaucratic government in America (Crenson 1975; Fesler 1982; Nelson 1982). The key idea, argues Nelson, was Jackson's notion that federal jobs 'admit of being made' so simple that any intelligent person could do them. Thus there arose the need to restrain corruption among office-holders unsocialized by specific education or by *noblesse oblige*. The result was the creation of agencies with significant internal checks and balances to prevent thievery. As Nelson notes, 'agencies organized to avoid evil became that much less able to do good' (1982: 763). To citizens, however, these checks and balances often looked like red tape. Ironically, nineteenth-century political parties had little incentive to curb bureaucratic power when they might instead mobilize it on behalf of their own interests. As a result, bureaucrats had – and in fact continue to have – every incentive to develop political bases of support.

A positive state

Jacksonian traditions were more quintessentially American than the European-inspired institutions that replaced them beginning late in the nineteenth century. In his famous 1887 essay, Woodrow Wilson memorably condemned the 'poisonous atmosphere of city government, the crooked secrets of state administration, the confusion, sinecurism, and corruption ever and again discovered in the bureaux at Washington' (Wilson 1997 [1887]: 16). Contemporary American managerialism grew out of a reform movement that reflected 'a fundamental optimism that mankind could direct and control its environment and destiny for the better' (Mosher 1975: 3; Davy 1962). Following the Civil War, industrialization, urbanization, and immigration began to transform American society and to strengthen middle-class elites, who, with Wilson, viewed spoils-ridden government as corrupt, incompetent and an impediment to prosperity. Promoted by intellectually oriented activists, the emerging administrative state reflected a number of currents in American thought: a progressive political agenda, the growing authority of science and of the idea of management, the professional development of administrative law and a spirit of pragmatic empiricism.

The groundwork for change at the federal level was laid by the civil service reform movement, the milestone of which was the Pendleton Act of 1883, which initiated the trend toward merit-based civil service. Thus, argues Stephen Skowronek (1982: 165), '[w]ith the legitimacy of the early American state under attack from all sides, government officials finally made the pivotal turn down the bureaucratic road', a road which was already being traveled in Great Britain and was something of a superhighway in continental Europe. All levels of government began an inexorable expansion, initially into regulating the private sector but ultimately, as in Europe, into the service and public works agencies of what would become the American welfare state.

The result of these various transformations at local, state and federal levels of government was dramatic, wrote Harold Laski in 1923 in the new British journal *Public Administration*: 'A state built upon *laissez-faire* has been transformed into a positive state. Vast areas of social life are now definitely within the ambit of legislation; and a corresponding increase in the power of the executive has been the inevitable result' (1923: 92). In the same year, John Gaus noted that:

> [t]he new administration includes a wide share of policy formulation; it requires a large measure of discretion on the part of the civil servant; it claims wide exemption from judicial review of its findings of fact; in brief, we are seeing a development somewhat akin to the rise of the administration in the days when the Tudors and the great monarchs were welding together the modern national state.
>
> (1923–4: 220)

Noting that American reformers often suggested that European 'administrative technology' be imported and adapted, Dwight Waldo nonetheless insisted that 'no substantial, systematic, transfer was possible. European administrative technologies were intimately related to the social, economic, and governmental systems in which they had evolved, and could not be simply copied in America' (1984: xxxii). Historian Barry Karl argues that '[t]he American adoption of systematic methods of management being developed in Great Britain and Germany had to take place in a political environment, the democratic rhetoric of which could always render the very concept of management suspect' (Karl 1976: 491). While the influence of British and continental public administration on American reform thinking is demonstrable, what was to emerge from a century of Madisonian politics was a model of public administration that was distinctively American.

The basic difference was America's separation of powers, which, Frank Goodnow (1900) was perhaps first to recognize, creates a discontinuity in the constitutional scheme such that the people cannot be fully assured that their wishes will be carried out or enforced. The problem is one of coordination between law and implementation – the central, multi-branch relationship in American public management – without creating unaccountable power in executive agencies. It was also recognized, however, that '[t]he traditional dogma of the separation of powers is an over-simplification of the governmental process as it actually takes place and as it is recognized by the courts' (Hart 1925: 38). The fact remains, argued John Fairlie, 'that there is a broad twilight zone between the field of what is distinctly and exclusively legislative and what is necessarily executive in character; that courts have recognized that matters within this "no man's land" may be expressly authorized by statute for administrative action; and if neither of these steps is taken such action has been, under some circumstances, assumed as an inherent executive or administrative power' (Fairlie 1920, quoted by Hart 1925).

Executive government

Just as the Founders had to confront the disadvantages of a weak government, evolving ideas about constitutional administration a century later coalesced around a particular idea: the need for strong 'elected' executives. Argued Frederick Cleveland (1919: 252), 'we have purposely deprived ourselves of responsible executive leadership for fear we shall not be able to control it'. The question was whether elected executives had the capacity to administer the rapidly expanding scope and reach of the their expanding governments. The seminal development was the Budget and Accounting Act of 1921, which institutionalized the executive budget. But the 1937 Report of President Franklin Roosevelt's Committee on Administrative Management (termed the 'Brownlow Report', after its chair, Louis Brownlow), became 'a landmark statement of "managerialism" in public administration' (Hood and Jackson 1991: 135; cf. Dunsire 1973; Merkle 1980). 'The President needs help', proclaimed the committee in presenting its solution.

The solution to weak executive control over a bureaucracy swelling with New Deal programs 'is couched in terms of a more centralized top-down reporting structure based on a private business management analogy, with a large general staff apparatus around the chief executive' (Hood and Jackson 1991: 136). The president should be in a position 'to coordinate and manage the departments and activities [of the government] in accordance with the laws enacted by the Congress' (PCAM 1937: iv), achievement of which would require an expanded White House staff; stronger management agencies; a strengthened and expanded civil service system; a subordination of independent agencies, administrations, authorities, boards, and commissions to major executive departments; and an independent post-audit of the fiscal transactions of an executive with complete responsibility for accounts and current transactions. 'There is nothing [in this program]', Roosevelt insisted, 'which is revolutionary, as every element is drawn from our own experience either in government or large-scale business' (PCAM 1937: iv).

Though the Brownlow Report rapidly faded to political obscurity owing to opposition by a rancorous Congress, the most basic of the reorganization proposals was nonetheless achieved in 1939, when Congress passed a bill authorizing creation of the Executive Office of the President, which recognized the executive role of the president and the concept of administrative management, 'the most profound contribution in our generation to the progress of administrative science' (Emmerich 1950: 80). In the immediate aftermath of World War II, however, Congress struck back at a presidency perceived to have grown so powerful that it threatened to reduce Congress to irrelevance (Rosenbloom

2000). In a series of legislative enactments, the most prominent of which was the Administrative Procedure Act of 1946, Congress effectively restored legislatively centered public administration, albeit vis-à-vis a now strengthened federal executive.

With the Cold War in full swing, and confronted with an accelerated pace of social and economic transformation reminiscent of the Progressive era and the New Deal, American government began to be inundated by what Paul Light (1997) has called 'tides of reform', some initiated by the executive branch, some by Congress, some by the courts, all reflecting the competitive dynamics of the separation of powers. Presidential initiatives in the form of John F. Kennedy's New Frontier, Lyndon B. Johnson's Great Society and Richard M. Nixon's New Federalism brought changes in administrative technologies. Though American public management reforms such as the Planning–Programming–Budgeting System (PPBS) and Management by Objectives (MBO) were often viewed as imitating the private sector, in fact they were political strategies to strengthen the executive branch, although ultimately they left the system basically unchanged except for increased numbers of analytical specialists in staff positions (Derlien 1987).

In Francis Rourke's synoptic view of developments in governance during the latter decades of the twentieth century,

> the growth of national bureaucracy in the United States since the 1930s has been a far less important phenomenon than the simultaneous emergence of new ways by which the traditional institutions of American national government – the presidency, Congress, and the courts – have been able to meet and contain the challenge of a bureaucracy that many people prior to World War II anticipated would actually become a fourth branch of government in the post-war period.
>
> Rourke 1987: 218

These adjustments included a collegial or collective presidency of the president and the White House staff to preserve executive hegemony over bureaucracy, and the increased utilization of experts from the private sector to advise policymakers and managers; expansion in the size and proficiency of legislative staffs, an enhancement of the legislature's capacity to do its job; judges becoming 'major actors in the policy process, largely as a result of statutes that provide broader opportunities for private parties to challenge the decisions of executive agencies in the courts' (Rourke 1987: 226); and the proliferation of iron triangles and issue networks linking bureaucrats, interest groups, legislative staff members, and others with a stake in governmental outcomes.

The precursors of reinvented government

If what became widely known beginning in the 1990s as New Public Management did not produce the frisson in America that it did in much of the rest of the world, the reason is that most, if not all, of its features had already become widely used tools of government as tides of reform updated American public management. Charles Schultze's 1977 *The Public Use of Private Interest* assayed the possibilities of performance contracting, and the several varieties of new tools were soon labeled 'third-party government' by Lester Salamon (1981) for their dependence on lower levels of government and the private, especially the non-governmental, sector. Donald Kettl (1988) called attention to the increasing reliance of the federal government upon a variety of intermediaries – nonprofit organizations, hybrid entities, other levels of government, the proprietary sector (including banks and insurance companies) (in effect, a 'quasi government') – to implement national policies. Specifically:

- The US federal government began systematically to privatize public services, using such instruments as contracts, user charges, vouchers, and alternative delivery systems, beginning in the mid-1950s, a practice pursued with even greater enthusiasm by state and local governments (Ott, Hyde and Shafritz 1991: 110);
- A concurrent development was the deinstitutionalization of state and county hospital and other institutionalized populations, reflecting the growing concern for the civil rights of dependent people and the development of drugs and treatment approaches permitting community-based care for those with chronic conditions;
- The accelerating popularity of hybrid organizations beginning in the 1960s – examples included ComSat, the Manpower Development Research Corporation, the Corporation for Public Broadcasting and the Synfuels Corporation – reflected several factors: federal budget controls, which force agencies to seek new sources of revenue; evasion of general management laws such as statutory ceilings on personnel and compensation; the popularity of generic, business-focused values and, in particular, the belief that entity-specific laws and regulations facilitate management flexibility, 'even at the cost of accountability to representative institutions' (Moe 2001: 291);
- In the aftermath of the Nixon-era Watergate scandals, the Civil Service Reform Act of 1978, in a historic departure from 'protection' as a principle of public personnel administration, abolished the Civil Service Commission and reorganized its functions. The Act also created a Senior Executive Service of experienced career managers who might be assigned wherever needed by an administration. That the act failed to accomplish its goals largely reflects competitive politics of controlling the bureaucracy; Congress and the courts largely vindicated the protection principle and thwarted the Act's purposes.

Finally, in a continuing effort to maintain control over administration, Congress enacted a number of provisions, including the Budget and Impoundment Control Act of 1974, the Congressional Budget Office, and the Foreign Intelligence

Surveillance Act, intended to ensure presidential accountability to Congress, measures which were later to be sharply contested by the administration of President George W. Bush on behalf of its 'war on terrorism'.

New public management in America

A weakened economy and fiscal stress were pushing politics rightward, however. With a kindred spirit, British Prime Minister Margaret Thatcher, providing an inspiring example, President Ronald Reagan attempted to initiate a new era in American public administration when he embarked on his 'war on waste', with the goal of shrinking the size and increasing the economic efficiency of government. Although neo-liberal in spirit, Reagan's reform strategy was quintessentially American and bore little resemblance to what, as Thatcher's initiatives evolved, was soon to become known as New Public Management.

Reagan's chosen instrument, a throwback to the kinds of initiatives launched by Presidents Theodore Roosevelt and William H. Taft early in the twentieth century, was the President's Private Sector Survey on Cost Control in the Federal Government, known as the 'Grace Commission' after its chair, businessman J. Peter Grace. The commission's objective was to demonstrate how the intrinsically superior methods of the private sector might save billions of dollars by eliminating waste, fraud and abuse (Downs and Larkey 1986; Grace 1984). Its 1984 report called for measures straight out of the business community playbook, such as objectives-based management, goal clarification, better planning, and the development of performance measures, without, however, acknowledging that prior reforms of a similar character had not accomplished much (Downs and Larkey 1986). This particular report generated no legacy of sustained reform activity and no new ideas.

Reinventing government

Less-ephemeral American contributions to the public management reform movement were the publication in 1992 of two influential books. David Osborne and Ted Gaebler's best-selling *Reinventing Government* and Barzelay and Arunajani's *Breaking Through Bureaucracy*. With its universal 'steer, don't row' prescription and canonical principles, *Reinventing Government*, reinforced by Michael Barzelay's proclamation of a post-bureaucratic paradigm of governance, was to provide the text for a new generation of reform-minded activists, including officials associated with the Clinton administration's National Performance Review (NPR) – later renamed the Alliance for Reinventing Government – and the practitioner-dominated National Academy of Public Administration.

Beginning in 1993, Vice President Al Gore led an eight-year effort, popularly known as 'Reinventing Government', to create a federal bureaucracy that was smaller, cheaper, and more effective. Its four themes were:

- cutting red tape, including streamlining the budget process, decentralizing personnel policy, reorienting the inspectors general, and empowering state and local governments;
- putting customers first, including demanding that service organizations compete, and using market mechanisms to solve problems;
- empowering employees to get results, including decentralizing decision-making power, forming a labor-management partnership, and exerting leadership;
- cutting back to basics, including eliminating programs, investing in greater productivity, and re-engineering programs to cut costs.

'[T]he people who work in government are not the problem', proclaimed Osborne and Gaebler, 'the systems in which they work are the problem'. Echoed Vice-President Gore, 'The Federal Government is filled with good people trapped in bad systems: budget systems, personnel systems, procurement systems, financial management systems, information systems. When we blame the people and impose more controls, we make the systems worse' (Gore 1993: 2).

It is important to note, however, that while the American reinvention movement was managerial in its ideological orientation (Aberbach and Rockman 2004), it placed far less emphasis on the kinds of neo-liberal, market-mimicking reforms that had already become popular in America, especially with state and local governments. Reinvention-inspired reforms instead employed strategies emphasizing the liberation management theme of managerial deregulation, quality improvement, employee empowerment, and managerial entrepreneurship. Moreover, as Guy Peters (1997: 255) notes, '[p]erhaps the one defining feature of reinvention is a disregard of some of the conventions associated with traditional public administration and an associated desire to rethink government operations from the ground up'. Peters continued (1997: 255): 'The deregulatory movement differs from the widespread use of market models in Europe in part by not having any clear substitute for the rules and hierarchy that are being abolished by reform'.

Joel Aberbach and Bert Rockman (2004) argue that, while some NPR recommendations were unarguably good ideas, the main thrust comprised slogans and nostrums that could not withstand critical scrutiny. For example, they note that, although many of the inefficiencies and restrictive rules decried by NPR were legislatively mandated, NPR largely ignored the need for legislative reforms, de-emphasizing the role and importance of Congress. As for successes, they cite NPR claims concerning

> more contracting out, streamlining the hiring process, use of various devices to gauge agency customer opinion and respond to it, greater and more effective use of information technology, streamlining some aspects of procurement, and attention to a variety of internal agency management reforms.
>
> (31)

The one initiative that was clearly NPM-inspired failed to make more than minor inroads on the status quo. The reasons are instructive. The Clinton administration sought to imitate Great Britain's Next Steps reform by promoting the creation of Performance-Based Organizations (PBOs). As Andrew Graham and Alsdair Roberts note (2004: 146), however, the separation of powers meant that 'an influential third party – Congress – threatened to complicate negotiations over the content of annual performance agreements'. Regarding funding predictability, performance agreements required commitments to budgets for the period covered by the agreements, but future Congresses cannot be bound by the decisions of a sitting Congress. Terms restricting the termination of chief operating officers for other than performance-related reasons failed because Congress 'may not limit the ability of the President to remove appointees, unless those appointees exercise quasi-legislative or quasi-judicial functions that require some independence from the administration' (147). The three PBOs that were created were denied the kinds of flexibilities that Ms Thatcher could achieve virtually by fiat.

Supporting pessimistic views of reinvention is the fact, noted by Lombard (2003), that in 1994 Congress, at the administration's request, amended the Government Employees Training Act of 1958 to change the legal purpose of government training from training related to official duties to training to improve individual and organizational performance. Also, in compliance with administration directives, the Office of Personnel Management (OPM) reorganized and cut its staff by 50 percent, abolished many mid-level positions, reduced personnel in its training policy, procurement, information technology, financial management, and human resources functions, closed many of its field offices, and privatized its nationwide training and investigation programs (Lombard 2003). Interestingly, Congress, in typically American fashion, stepped into the vacuum and began to manage training resource allocations and operations by statute. Unfortunately, as Lombard (2003) notes, private sector trainers turned out to lack the special skills needed in federal appropriations, personnel, ethics, and procurement law. A net loss of administrative capacity was the result.

The Government Performance and Results Act

The more important, and surviving, American public management reform of the 1990s was initiated by Congress. The Government Performance and Results Act (GPRA), enacted in 1993 largely on the initiative of conservative Congressional Republicans, is now a routine aspect of public management at the federal level and a key building block of America's expanding practice of performance management at all levels of government (Radin 2001). The Act requires each federal agency, in cooperation with Congress and in coordination with the budget process, to formulate forward-looking performance plans and to conduct performance evaluations using agreed-upon performance measures. John Rohr (2002: 84) sees GPRA as an example of traditional legislative pre-eminence within the American separation of powers: 'By law it requires nothing less than close cooperation between executive branch agencies and congressional subcommittees, first in developing goals and plans and then in evaluating performance measured against these same goals and plans'. The US Government Accountability Office (GAO, formerly known as the General Accounting Office), an agency of the US Congress tasked with monitoring implementation of GPRA, was less than pleased after a decade of executive branch effort, viewing with concern the less-than-whole-hearted use of performance information in government-wide or agency management (USGAO 2004).

The President's Management Agenda

In the most recent of America's uncoordinated public management reforms, this time initiated by the executive branch, the just-elected administration of President George W. Bush promulgated the President's Management Agenda (PMA) in 2001, which emphasized performance-driven, outsourced management in federal departments and agencies. Little publicized by the administration and only slowly acknowledged by the professional field, the Bush administration's approach features the quarterly scoring of all federal agencies against PMA priorities and other administration initiatives and use of a Program Assessment Rating Tool (PART) to evaluate individual program accomplishments in coordination with preparation of the president's annual budget. Evidence concerning the effects of the PMA was accumulating slowly, especially with regard to higher-order objectives. The PART process, however, appeared during Mr Bush's second term to be having some influence on incremental budgetary allocations, if not on the overall shape and size of the budget, where Republican-led 'big government conservatism' was enlarging the federal budgets and payrolls. The GAO somewhat haughtily declared that PART assessments are 'not a substitute for GPRA's strategic, longer-term focus on thematic goals, and department and government crosscutting comparisons' (USGAO 2004, summary), yet another example of the separation-of-powers tensions that pervade American public management.

The Bush administration's distinctly Thatcherite hostility to the traditional civil service was further demonstrated in its insistence that the permanent personnel of the new Department of Homeland Security be exempt from most civil service rules and managed toward the goal of performance, a model it intended to extend to the entire federal government. In typically American fashion, however, many Bush administration personnel reforms were stymied by the rulings of federal courts in response to lawsuits filed by federal employee unions.

From Theo Toonen and Jos Raadschelders' vantage point, American reforms such as the ones just described represent a continuation and refinement of earlier attempts to improve government by professionalizing the policy process (1997). Reinventing government, in their view, represented a rediscovery of classical American public administration. What was new with reinventing government was its pro-government spirit as against what went before, especially in the Reagan administration. Ezra Suleiman (2003) sees the same reforms as a landmark in combining sweeping scope with an anti-government agenda associated with the political right wing: '[A]t the heart of the reinvention-of-government movement lies a skepticism about the existence of a public-service institution' (Suleiman 2003: 47; cf. Frederickson 1996). These conflicting assessments only highlight the difficulty of appraising public management reform in polycentric, ambiguous America.

The study of politics and administration

Accompanying the rise of the American administrative state, and usually following in its wake, has been the emergence of the systematic study, by academics and by other research institutions and consultancies, of politics and administration, coalescing into the American field of public administration and, in recent decades, into the related field of public management.

The emergence of a professionally and scientifically aware public administration early in the twentieth century led initially, as noted earlier, to a consideration of European precedents. Americans educated on the continent were attracted to the idea of separating administration from politics to insulate service delivery from the corrupting influences of often virulent political partisanship. Attractive as well was the continental tradition of applied administrative science, adaptations of which might enhance the legitimacy of increasingly bureaucratized American government in the eyes of Americans enamoured of scientific achievement but sceptical of governmental power. While both ideas have retained their ideological appeal, the study of administration and politics in America has, in contrast to Europe, necessarily evolved in pragmatic response to growing competition among legislatures, elected executives and the judiciary for control of an increasingly powerful administrative state.

The new administration

The systematic study of public administration originated in the reform movements that began in the nation's large cities and spread within a generation to state and national governments. Early ideas – 'scientific' management, a politically neutral civil service, unity of command – were elements of reform agendas intended to empower governments to meet the challenges of a growing, industrializing, urbanizing, and diversifying society, codified by reform organizations such as the bureaus of municipal research and W. F. Willoughby's Institute for Government Research into actionable administrative programs. Ideas now (inaccurately) regarded in America as the rigid credos of a bureaucratic paradigm (Lynn 2001b) were in their time pragmatic Madisonian responses to problems of governance arising at federal, state, and municipal levels of government, devised by men and women of affairs, advocates of administrative reform, and public officials, together with the reform-minded organizations they founded, led, or advised.

These early developments, Laurence O'Toole (1984) has argued, did not represent an effort to blend European and American ideas. Rather, they constituted a reaction against European formalism, which used abstractions, deductive systems of logic, and formal coherence as initial principles. 'Anti-formalism proposed action and reform was the stance of the activist' (O'Toole 1984: 145). O'Toole continues:

> [o]ur administrative tradition was developed by individuals who were hostile to doctrine, who have banked on experience, who have exaggerated the defects of previously proposed solutions and the probable beneficial consequences of the currently fashionable ones, and who were simultaneously held in thrall by the imperatives of technique and the goal of democracy.
>
> O'Toole 1984: 149

Early teaching and research on public administration emerged in association with administrative reform movements, with only reluctant and limited involvement by American universities. The first systematic training was provided by the private bureaus of municipal research, and academic research was sponsored by the nonprofit Social Science Research Council. The rapidly growing role of government during and following the New Deal, however, brought university-sponsored teaching and scholarship fully into the picture, shortly followed by the formation of the American Society for Public Administration. The largely pre-scientific functional and organizational study and instruction in public administration, featuring formal/legal, descriptive, and prescriptive frameworks, began to yield to an increasingly analytical academic enterprise, largely within political science, based on the scientific study of organizations, decision making, and political behavior, although not without significant tensions between positivist and normative schools of thought that persist to this day.

The managerialism that John Gaus had christened 'the new administration' in the early 1920s had in a single generation become institutionalized in thought and practice.

Scientific management

In advocating a science of administration, Woodrow Wilson had observed in 1887 that one already existed but that it was wholly European, originating in the work of French and German professors to meet the needs of a centralized state. To be of use in America, he argued, such a science would have to be Americanized, a task made inherently difficult when the sovereign is popular opinion rather than a monarch (Dunsire 1973). Scientific management was to flourish during Wilson's presidency (from 1913 to 1921) – Frederick Taylor's immensely influential book, *The Principles of Scientific Management*, was published in 1911 – but it reached the field of public administration primarily via developments in the industrial sector.

Concurrently with the emergence of 'the new administration', a contemporaneously identified 'management movement' (Person 1977 [1926]) had been gathering strength in the industrial sector, reflecting primarily the thinking of engineers such as Henry R. Towne, Henry Metcalfe, and Taylor (George 1972; Person 1977 [1926]). The initial focus of what became known as 'the scientific management movement' was on efficient use of labor and on costs and cost systems. From those concerns there arose a more general concern for organization and coordination. Under the banner of Scientific Management, the generic concept of management (Church 1914) was to gain a following among those concerned with the reform of public administration.

The relationship of public administration to management was most famously expressed by Leonard White (1926, viii), who, rejecting formal legalism, insisted that 'the study of administration should start from the base of management rather than the foundation of law'. However, argues Andrew Dunsire (1973: 93), the scientific management movement 'meant by "science" something more than the eighteenth- and nineteenth-century writers on "administrative science" (or indeed "economic science" or "political science") had meant by the word – something like "disciplined study"'. Taylor aimed to replace hunch with observation and measurement, traditional practices with calculation and rational methods. He fervently believed that scientific management was humane, good for society, and likely to promote friendship between worker and employer. The rest is history. '[M]uch of modern American business and public administration', argues Judith Merkle (1980: 294), 'is, for various historical reasons, the heir to the Scientific Management movement'.

The appropriation of Scientific Management by the creators of 'the new administration' (or what Leonard White later termed 'the new management') exemplified the pragmatic spirit of the emergent American field rather than any embrace of ideology, however. Indeed, the field of business administration was also in its formative stages and offered no coherent ideologies to imitate. 'Scientific Management', both as a method and as a body of principles, was attractive to reform-oriented public administrators because, owing to its business origins, it promised legitimacy for administration in the face of congenital American scepticism of the kind of bureaucratic power associated with recently experienced American 'bossism'.

Of particular significance is that the ethos of management reflecting scientific analysis became even more influential within the academy through the work of Herbert Simon and the Carnegie School, which featured the behavioral study of organizations and decision-making, the policy analysis movement, and neoclassical managerialism reflected in public-choice theories. The implications of this kind of scientific analysis included strengthening the public executive in setting priorities and in making and enforcing policies, employing analytic methods to vet the efficiency and other consequences of alternative policies. The other social sciences were evincing a growing interest in politics and bureaucracy and bringing powerful intellectual and empirical tools to bear on their study.

The cumulative effect of this flourishing scientific heterodoxy of theories, concepts, and empirical applications was, ironically, a growing sense of intellectual crisis within the field of public administration, still only entering its third generation. A particular vexation was the developing interest in public management within the public-policy schools that had formed at several of America's leading research universities in a distinct challenge to the intellectual and pedagogical authority of public administration.

The study of public management

As noted above, within traditional American public administration beat a managerial heart, albeit incorporated within a Madisonian body. Some scholars saw no need to distinguish between the terms 'administration' and 'management'. However, although Luther Gulick had asked in 1937, 'What do managers do?' – his famous answer was 'POSDCORB' – public administration scholars, with important exceptions, paid little attention to the craft of actually managing agencies and programs (Bertelli and Lynn 2006), a vacuum public-policy schools were eager to fill.

Public management as craft

The systematic and sustained study of public management as a species of human action began inauspiciously enough as an academic and curricular innovation. Policy implementation in general and the phenomenon of third-party government in particular were among the early staples of what was emerging as a public management movement. When choosing to complement technocratic training in policy analysis with an emphasis on policy implementation as a subject for research and teaching, faculties at the public-policy schools spawned by the PPBS movement, such as those at Harvard University, Princeton University, Duke University and the University of California at Berkeley, rebuked 'traditional public administration' for having too little regard for the public manager as a strategic political actor. In creating an emphasis on public management that paralleled the emphasis on policy analysis, these schools were concerned with defining how public managers could 'realize the potential of a given political and institutional setting' (Moore 1984: 3), that is, on public management as statecraft, a product of skill and psychological fitness.

Craft-oriented pedagogy and scholarship in the policy schools was designed to prepare a new breed of trained professional for service in advisory and managerial capacities at the highest levels of federal, state, and local governments, primarily, although not exclusively, in the executive branch. The new curriculums featured experiential learning such as client-oriented workshops, internships, and the extensive analysis of teaching cases. The goal was identifying best practices and universal principles (based now, however, on 'experience' rather than 'science'), rules, and checklists for effective public management conceived as a craft (Bardach 1987; Majone 1989). Works that distill managerial principles from personal experiences and case analyses have subsequently become one of the most popular genres in the field, in academic publications, in the prescriptive management literature of consultancies, and in government reports such as those of the Government Accountability Office. Examples of this literary genre include works by Eugene Bardach (1998), Robert Behn (1991), Stephen Cohen and Howard Eimicke (1995), Richard Haass (1999), Phillip Heymann (1987), Moore (1995), and Robert Reich (1990).

Although this largely unhistorical, 'institutions are givens' approach to public management drew criticism from traditional public administration scholars and political scientists, eventually it caught the wave of popularity enjoyed by the best-practices perspective in business management literature initiated by the success of the 'Japanese management' movement (Pascale and Athos 1982) and of Thomas Peters and Robert Waterman's *In Search of Excellence: Lessons from America's Best-Run Companies* (1982). The latter book's no-nonsense principles – a bias for action, close to the customer, productivity through people, simple form, lean staff – inspired numerous public-sector-oriented imitators motivated to arrest government's declining popularity following the Nixon-era Watergate scandal, the economic crises of the 1970s, and the ineffectual presidency of Jimmy Carter. The analogy to the earlier, faddish popularity of Scientific Management in public administration cannot be missed.

Public management as governance

Despite its popularity, public management is a sharply contested idea which, like the term 'administrative management' before it, may yet fail to achieve permanent status as a paradigm of scholarship and practice. For some critics (e.g. Carroll 1995; Gilmour and Jensen 1998; Suleiman 2003), public management is irredeemably associated with managerialism viewed as ideologically motivated effort to substitute corporate-sector values and instrumental notions of efficiency for an ethical commitment by the state and its officers to service and collective justice, in the process transforming active citizens into passive consumers. For others (e.g. Dobel 1992), public management invites an undue focus on actors in managerial roles to the exclusion of the organizations, institutions, and systems that constrain and enable managerial behavior. For still others (e.g. Wildavsky 1985), for whom government is about politics and policy, public management is nothing more than traditional public administration with a fashionable new label, a domain for technocrats and mavens of government operations – the public sector equivalent of industrial engineering.

The ambiguous standing of public management is one reason why a new term, 'governance', began coming into use to characterize the domain within which both traditional public administration and the new public management might coexist. This term has already achieved wide popularity with American and European scholars as well as with international organizations, who view it as encompassing administrative arrangements that envelop, or even lie outside, traditional governmental hierarchies. Many within the field have begun to embrace the idea of governance as an organizing concept (Garvey 1997; Heinrich, Hill, and Lynn 2005; Kettl 2000, 2002; Peters and Pierre 1998; Rhodes 1996; Salamon 2002). The momentum behind this idea has reached the point that George Frederickson and Kevin Smith (2003: 225) can suggest that governance had become 'a virtual synonym for public management and public administration'.

Public sector governance has been defined as 'regimes of laws, rules, judicial decisions, and administrative practices that constrain, prescribe, and enable the provision of publicly supported goods and services' through formal and informal relationships with agents in the public and private sectors (Lynn, Heinrich and Hill 2001: 7). This definition links constitutional institutions with the realities of policy-making, public management, and service delivery. Underlying this concept is recognition that governance involves means for achieving direction, control, and coordination of individuals or organizational units on behalf of their common interests (Vickers 1983; Wamsley 1990; Lynn, Heinrich, and Hill 2001). This general approach to the conceptualization of public governance is not new (Forbes, Hill and Lynn 2006). For example, Kiser and Ostrom (1982) distinguished among 'three worlds of action': constitutional choice, collective choice, and operational choice. Toonen elaborates,

> [t]he three worlds approach ... opens up an understanding of public admin-istration that goes very much beyond the organization. The three levels do not refer to different layers within a formal structure. Rather, they have to be understood as nested systems and subsystems of public policy, adminis-trative behavior, or institutional macro structures.
>
> Toonen 1998: 235

In general, reference to a logic of governance encompassing interactions between different levels is a reminder of the interdependence of complex governance processes and facilitates empirical research that illuminates its significance. Toonen (1998: 248) argues that Kiser and Ostrom's three-worlds 'framework clarifies, for example, that reform and change at one level of analysis presupposes certain conditions at other levels of analysis'. Another advantageous feature of the three-worlds approach, in Toonen's (1998) view, is that it can accommodate 'more subtle and differentiated conceptualizations which allow us to go somewhat deeper into the actual operation of the system instead of simply scratching the surface' in comparative public administration research (237).

Public management as values

In the face of what often appears to be a vacuum of governing values, many public administration and management scholars have been prone to invoke idealizations of public service values, from equity to individual rights to demo-cratic participation to constitutional trusteeship to business-like efficiency. A classic example is Norton Long (1952: 811), who argued that 'important and vital interests in the United States are unrepresented, under-represented, or mal-represented in Congress. These interests receive more effective and more responsible representation through administrative channels than through the legislature'. A bureaucracy representative of the citizenry, in this view, becomes an alternative and independent forum for Madisonian governance. Policy politics, in Evelyn Brodkin's (1987) term, takes place inside bureaucracies rather than in legislatures.

A normative/prescriptive bent is strong in American public administration and management. As early as 1942, Egbert Wengert urged administrators to facilitate communication, learning, and consensual relations with citizens, and David Levitan, decrying ideological neutrality among civil servants, endorsed deeply rooted personal beliefs as a basis for public service. A 1968 conference at Minnowbrook proclaimed yet another new public administration dedicated to social equity, a perspective later updated by H. George Frederickson in his *The Spirit of Public Administration* (1997), who endorsed a form of bureaucratic disobedience to policies that undermined equity. Other scholars issued the Blacksburg Manifesto, urging broad and direct citizen participation in administration, a view – the democratic ethos – endorsed by Peter and Linda deLeon (2002). Guy B. Adams and Danny Balfour (1998) admonished public administrators to abjure administrative evil, defined as inflicting pain and suffering on other human beings.

In practice, however, the values governing American public management must comport with the constitutional separation of powers, and that scheme is founded on managerial discretion that is premised on an ingrained and selfless responsibility to republican institutions. Those officials who attempt to distance themselves from 'a due dependence on the people in a republican sense', Hamilton's precept, are likely to find themselves either under increasingly detailed statutory restraint, perhaps nullifying their ability to manage effectively, or cast as defendants in institutional reform lawsuits, brought by classes of citizens against those who act in their name, whose objective is to curb official autonomy and capacity to abuse their discretion. In America, the separation of powers rules.

Public management's glasnost

American intellectual leadership in public administration and management has brought organized and detailed attention and a high degree of academic prestige to the evolving field worldwide (Lepawsky 1949; Dunsire 1973; Kickert 1997). According to Theo Toonen (1998: 231), '[b]y the end of the 1970s international [public administration] was largely still American [public administration]'. 'The orientation of Dutch, German, British and Scandinavian [public administration] scholars on the Northern American study of Public Administration is striking', observed Walter Kickert (1997: 28). American scholarship and managerial practices have given legitimacy to ideas and methods that European legalism has tended to regard with scepticism (Rugge 2004).

The popularity of New World administrative thought in the Old World prior to the 1980s is somewhat mystifying on its merits, however. In a very real sense, the American administrative state is an extension of the legislative branch

(Roosenbloom 2000), but not only that. Public managers, as noted earlier, must also cope with continuing competition among all three branches of government for control over the extent and uses of managerial authority and discretion. Public managers exercise little 'independent' influence within this scheme unless given legitimacy by elected officials and courts. In Europe, in contrast,

> the legislature is largely dominated by the executive. Legislatures in France, Germany and Britain do not initiate legislation to any significant degree, they are peripherally involved in the budgetary process and party cohesion and institutional limitations serve to restrict the scope of powerful scrutiny of executive actions by the legislatures.
>
> Page 1992: 89

Managerial theories and ideologies tailored to the pluralistic American context, therefore, were not obviously appropriate for state-centered Europe.

But circumstances have changed in recent decades. Just as public management was evolving into a distinct field in America beginning in the 1970s, so, too, was managerialism emerging in European thought and practice (Kooiman and Eliassen 1987; Aucoin 1990; Kickert 1997; Löffler 2003; Lynn 2005, 2006; Pollitt 1990). While perhaps most obviously inspired by the economic crises of the mid-1970s, in which expenditure and revenue trajectories began to diverge sharply, the broader background of the new managerialism in Europe includes the complex challenges of sustaining the post-war welfare state, the conservative re-assertion of the market as an ideal institution for social resource allocation, ongoing decentralization and deconcentration of national administration not associated with managerialism but affecting it, and the effects on national administrations of the policies of the European Union. These factors have brought about an internationalization of management policy discourse and scholarship first under the portmanteau concept of New Public Management and increasingly under the rubric of governance.

American and European perspectives

Old Public Administration, in Johann Olsen's view (2003: 510), 'assumes that the core of political life is law-making, interpretation, implementation and enforcement'. Public managers are governed by rules and hierarchy and by the public service values of reliability, consistency, predictability, and accountability to legislatures and courts in executing and maintaining the rule of law (constitutional, administrative, jurisprudential) or the principles of *Rechtsstaat*, all on behalf of the common good or the public interest. In contrast, New Public Management implies that 'the public sector is not distinctive from the private sector' (Olsen 2003: 510). The original assumption of NPM was that introducing relatively uniform, market-like incentives – competition and rewards proportional to performance – would produce more accountability than the rule-bound bureaucracies of the Old Public Administration. It is tensions between the Old and the

New that have dominated public management reform processes on both sides of the Atlantic.

The tensions have even deeper sources. From an intellectual perspective, Aucoin (1990) sees two distinct sets of ideas underlying the new emphasis on public management in Europe and, it would seem, in America as well: managerialism, which establishes the primacy of managerial principles over bureaucracy, and public choice theory, which establishes the primacy of representative government over bureaucracy. These two sets of ideas, Aucoin argues, are having 'a profound impact' on governance structures despite their being in sharp tension; managerialism requires a separation of administration from politics, whereas public choice theory repudiates such a separation. Aucoin's insight warrants elaboration.

Christopher Hood and Michael Jackson provide a contrasting analysis to that of Aucoin. In many ways, they argue (1991: 179), 'NPM can be seen as a development of the international scientific management movement, with its concern to eliminate waste and measure work outputs as a precondition for effective control'. While traceable to Frederick Taylor and, farther back, to Jeremy Bentham's ideas about public administration, its origins are even older, in seventeenth- and eighteenth-century European cameralism. In essence, cameralism assumed that the foundation of the state lay in economic development which, in turn required active management by governments whose administrators should, therefore, be trained and loyal to a strongly led state. Cameralism and NPM are similar in their use of the term 'public management' (*Staatswirtschaft*, *Haushaltungskunst*); stress on administrative technology; separation of policy-making from its execution; the emphasis on thrift; avoidance of direct state management of complex processes; centralization; and acceptance of the existing social and economic order. NPM could, in Hood and Jackson's view, be called a 'new cameralism' (Hood and Jackson 1991: 182).

In contrast to America, where, as noted above, the idea of management has infused public administration from its beginnings, managerialism in Europe, despite its historical roots, was a less familiar concept, a fortuitous fusing of ideological, practical, and scientific ideas (Kooiman and van Vliet 1993).[2] Whereas Europeans could and did draw on American ideas concerning the application of business management techniques to government as well as on America's public choice and public administration intellectual traditions (Kickert 1997), European approaches to public management also tended to reflect the indigenous traditions of administrative science and public administration (Pollitt and Bouckaert 2004).

Thus public management and managerialism in Europe have come to mean something different than in the United States, a fact not always recognized in cross-national discourse. In Europe, public management refers primarily to the delivery of public services and to the organizations responsible for service delivery – in effect to those organizational and functional aspects of government that, because they entail repetitive tasks, are most business-like or could be made to be so. Many Europeans tend to view public management as quite distinct from public administration, with its broader orientation to statecraft. In America, managerialism tends to be more strategic and political than operational, and Americans are less disposed to view public administration and public management as conceptually and practically different from one another (Lynn 2005). In effect, Europeans tend to emphasize public 'management', Americans tend to emphasize 'public' management.

Varieties of policy and practice

Despite the convergent rhetoric of managerialism, public management reform remains primarily a national (and constitutional) matter (König 1997; Rohr 2002). This fact is underscored by the essays in this volume: Germany evolves only slowly from its *Rechtsstaat* and corporatist traditions, France combines old and new traditions, albeit in some tension with one another; the emergence of managerialism in Napoleonic Spain is embryonic; and the United Kingdom, the most aggressive NPM reformer, may be breaking ground for a new public governance paradigm. While New Public Management 'continues to exert widespread fascination', according to the editors of *The Oxford Handbook of Public Management*, 'each country makes its own translation or adaptation' of its core ideas owing to differences in constitutions, institutions, administrative cultures, and economic circumstances (Ferlie, Lynn and Pollitt 2005b: 721).

The reality of historically conditioned national variation is evident to many European scholars. Jos Raadschelders and Theo Toonen (1999: 60) argue that European public management reforms illustrate 'how more or less uniform challenges may result in rather different responses and solutions' and thus in considerable national variation. The post-World War II expansion of European welfare states, they argue, has been redirected, not terminated. (Vincent Wright [1994] similarly notes that many states seek to modernize, not denigrate and dismantle, themselves.) They continue,

> Public sector reforms generally leave the existing state and administrative institutional structure intact. They do not, and probably cannot, fundamentally alter the constitutional principles upon which the welfare state could be built. In a globalizing world governmental response to social change will resort to familiar avenues until the citizenry decides it is time for fundamental changes. And only then the functions of the state rather than its tools will be subject to evaluation.
>
> Jos Raadschelders and Theo Toonen 1999: 60

Wright notes that in terms of the style of national reforms, 'there are marked differences ... between the evolutionary and internally motivated program of the Germans, the reformist and negotiated program of the French ... and the imposed radicalism of the British' (Wright 1994: 117). Pollitt and Bouckaert (2004: 147) add the insight that Anglo-Saxon regimes are more inclined toward managerial reforms because the instruments of the state are held in lower esteem than in continental Europe. In the meantime, they argue, states proceed by trial and error, gradually, incrementally, which constitutes the best practice and produces the most sustained results.

In its narrow, corporate-mimicking manifestations, managerialism's variations will reflect the forces of increasingly pluralist European democracies. This is true in significant part because managerialism has typically lacked democratic legitimacy. 'Rarely if ever', say Roger Wettenhall and Ian Thynne (2002: 7),

> have governments consulted their electorates about whether to embark on privatization programs or adopt other elements of NPM-type reforms. Managerialism has generally appealed to political and commercial elites, and has been introduced by them as *faits accomplis* presented to mostly passive publics.

In the same vein, Carsten Greve and Peter Jasperson (1999: 147) argue that 'the concepts of citizen, citizens rights and citizen participation are almost non-existent in NPM debates'. Public dissatisfaction with such reforms has in fact led to electoral reversals in a number of countries. The most recent reforms have shifted attention to improved citizen access and participation.

Perhaps, then, Wettenhall and Thynne (2002: 9–10) are prescient when they aver that

> as we settle into the new century, the thrust of things to come will be away from NPM-type initiatives towards a system that might be described as 'enlightened public governance', a system which will even more clearly than NPM recognize the great value of flexibility and diversity, while at the same time appreciating that responsiveness to market forces must be conditioned and complemented by a commitment to enhancing the role of civil society.
> Wettenhall and Thynne 2002: 9–10

They continue, 'Overall, both existing and new means of control and accountability will be invoked to ensure the openness and legitimacy of state action and of the various associated initiatives involved in the management of public affairs' (10). Stephen Osborne (2006) argues in a similar vein that the New Public Management represents a transition stage linking traditional public administration with what he calls the emerging 'New Public Governance'.

A global profession

Impressed by the apparently global scope of public management reform initiatives and by the family resemblance of its justifications, new international forums for professional discourse on the subject have emerged.[3] These include the International Research Society on Public Management, the International Public Management Network, the European Group of Public Administration, and the increasingly internationalized Public Management Research Association and the Association for Public Policy Analysis and Management in the United States. Klaus König (1997: 226) observes that management has become the . . . lingua franca in an increasingly internationalized administrative world. It signals that public administration implies planning and coordination, staff recruitment and development, personnel management and control, organisation, and so on, and that allowances must be made in all these respects for the scarcity of resources.

American scholarship, with its social-scientific foundations, has made significant contributions to the emergence of public management as an international academic field through export of its theories and methods. For example, a recent edited volume, *Public Service Performance: Perspectives on Measurement and Management* (Boyne *et al.* 2006), presents the efforts of American and UK researchers to contribute jointly to empirical analysis of a topic of increasing international importance. Further, Melissa Forbes, Carolyn Hill and Laurence E. Lynn Jr have shown that American and non-American public management scholars tend to agree that 'the determinants of government performance are multifarious and are to be found at multiple hierarchical levels of governance that are interrelated in complex ways' (Forbes, Hill and Lynn 2006: 269). Far more emphasis is given by both groups of scholars to hierarchical, rather than network or consociational, influences on government performance.

International differences in scholarly approach are, like differences in managerial institutions, likely to persist, however. As Fred Thompson (2006) notes of the international roster of *The Oxford Handbook of Public Management* authors, Americans tend to be more empirical and positivist and affiliated with public affairs schools, Europeans more social constructionist and affiliated with management schools. Forbes, Hill and Lynn (2006) note, moreover, that non-American investigators favor more linear managerial hypotheses, linking policies and structures directly to outcomes, whereas American investigators are more inclined to explore the polycentrist, multi-level nature of governance.

Notwithstanding the plain fact of national differences of administrative thought, research, and practice, the subject of public management can now be intelligibly studied and discussed by academic and practicing professionals of widely different national experiences and disciplinary and professional orientations. National differences in institutions and practices may be inimical to reaching consensus on universal principles of public administration and management, a goal of recent scholarship (for example, Aucoin and Neintzman 2000; Raadschelders and Rutgers 1999). But such differences – viewed as variance – are the lifeblood of scientific inquiry and thus well serve the project of creating the theories and empirical understanding that can sustain a professional field on a global scale (Forbes and Lynn 2005; Forbes, Hill and Lynn 2006). While their orientations to disciplines, theories, methods, and national agendas will differ (Stillman 2001), these professionals, including the authors in this volume, are coming to have in common a grasp of larger issues that transcend the descriptive particulars of national regimes or tenets of disciplinary training. Public management has become a global profession.

Notes

1 Much of the discussion in the remainder of this paper is adapted from material in the following sources: Laurence E. Lynn, Jr, *Public Management: Old and New* (London: Routledge 2006) and Anthony M. Bertelli and Laurence E. Lynn, Jr, *Madison's Managers: Public Administration and the Constitution* (Baltimore: Johns Hopkins University Press 2006).
2 It is worth noting, however, that English civil servant Desmond Keeling's insightful *Management in Government* (1972) appeared when the renewed emphasis on public management in America was still in its infancy. Toonen (1998: 236–7) notes, moreover, that 'a tradition of "governance" does not preclude an abundant use of managerial practices at the operational level of government' and that many continental countries 'have strong managerial traditions of their own, particularly at decentralized, local levels of government. Public administration as a discipline often started out at these levels', as was the case in the US. Management could be seen as 'a new way of conducting the business of the state' (Pollitt and Bouckaert 2004: 12).
3 Pollitt notes, however, that '[t]he most active participants [in discursive reform] have been the Anglophone countries, the Netherlands and the Nordic group. The others (for example, Germany, France, the Mediterranean states) have been much more cautious, even at the talk stage' (2002: 489). Within the Anglophone group, reform decisions have been noticeably more radical and far-reaching in New Zealand, Australia, and the UK than in Canada and the USA.

Bibliography

Aberbach, J. D. and Rockman, B. A. (2004) 'Reinventing Government or Reinventing Politics? The American Experience', in B. G. Peters and J. Pierre (eds) *Politicians, Bureaucrats and Administrative Reform*, London: Routledge.

Adams, G. B. and Balfour, D. (1998) *Unmasking Administrative Evil*, Thousand Oaks: Sage.

Aucoin, P. (1990) 'Administrative Reform in Public Management: Paradigms, Principles, Paradoxes and Pendulums', *Governance*, 3: 115–37.

Aucoin, P. and Neintzman, R. (2000) 'The Dialectics of Accountability for Performance in Public Management Reform', *International Review of Administrative Sciences*, 66: 45–55.

Bardach, E. (1987) 'From Practitioner Wisdom to Scholarly Knowledge and Back Again', *Journal of Policy Analysis and Management*, 7: 188–99.

Bardach, E. (1998) *Getting Agencies to Work Together: The Practice and Theory of Managerial Craftsmanship*, Washington, DC: Brookings Institution.

Barzelay, M. and Armajani, B. J. (1992) *Breaking Through Bureaucracy: A New Vision for Managing in Government*, Berkeley: University of California Press.

Behn, R. D. (1991) *Leadership Counts: Lessons for Public Managers from the Massachusetts Welfare, Training, and Employment Program*, Cambridge: Harvard University Press.

Bertelli, A. M. and Lynn L. E. Jr (2006) *Madison's Managers: Public Administration and the Constitution*, Baltimore: Johns Hopkins University Press.

Boyne, G. A., Meier, K. J., O'Toole, L. J. Jr and Walker, R. N. (2006) *Public Service Performance: Perspectives on Measurement and Management*, Cambridge: Cambridge University Press.

Brodkin, E. Z. (1987) 'Policy Politics: If We Can't Govern, Can We Manage?' *Political Science Quarterly*, 102: 571–87.

Carroll, J. D. (1995) 'The Rhetoric of Reform and Political Reality in the National Performance Review', *Public Administration Review,* 55: 302–12.

Carroll, J. D. (1998) Book Review, *American Review of Public Administration,* 28: 402–7.

Church, A. H. (1914) *Science and Practice of Management,* New York: Engineering Magazine Co.

Cleveland, F. A. (1919) 'Popular Control of Government', *Political Science Quarterly* 34: 237–61.

Cohen, S. and Eimicke, W. B. (1995) *The New Effective Public Manager: Achieving Success in a Changing Government,* San Francisco: Jossey-Bass.

Crenson, M. (1975) *The Federal Machine: Beginnings of Bureaucracy in Jacksonian America,* Baltimore: Johns Hopkins University Press.

Davy, T. J. (1962) 'Public Administration as a Field of Study in the United States', *International Review of Administrative Sciences,* 28: 63–78.

deLeon, L. and deLeon, P. (2002) 'The Democratic Ethos and Public Management', *Administration and Society,* 34: 229–50.

Derlien, H.-U. (1987) 'Public Managers and Politics', in J. Kooiman and K. A. Eliassen (eds) *Managing Public Organizations: Lessons from Contemporary European Experience,* London: Sage Publications.

Dobel, J. P. (1992) Book Review, *Journal of Policy Analysis and Management,* 11: 44–7.

Downs, G. W. and Larkey, P. D. (1986) *The Search for Government Efficiency: From Hubris to Helplessness,* New York: Random House.

Dunsire, A. (1973) *Administration: The Word and the Science,* New York: John Wiley & Sons.

Emmerich, H. (1950) *Essays on Federal reorganization,* University: University of Alabama Press.

Fairlie, J. A. (1920) 'Administrative Legislation', in *National Emergency. Hearings before the Special Committee on the Termination of the National Emergency of the United States Senate 93rd Cong., 1st sess., Part 3-Constitutional Questions Concerning Emergency Powers*: 675–830, November 1973.

Ferlie, E., Lynn L. E. Jr and Pollitt, C. (2005a) 'Afterword', in Ferlie, Lynn and Pollitt *The Oxford Handbook of Public Management,* Oxford: Oxford University Press.

Ferlie, E., Lynn, L. E. Jr and Pollitt, C. (2005b) *The Oxford Handbook of Public Management,* Oxford: Oxford University Press.

Fesler, J. W. (1982) 'The Presence of the Administrative Past', in J. W. Fesler (ed.) *American Public Administration: Patterns of the Past,* Washington: American Society for Public Administration.

Forbes, M. A., Hill, C. J. and Lynn, L. E. Jr (2006) 'Public Management and Government Performance: An International Review', in Boyne *et al.* (eds) *Public Service Performance: Perspectives on Measurement and Management,* Cambridge: Cambridge University Press.

Forbes, M. K. and Lynn, L. E. Jr (2005) 'How Does Public Management Affect Government Performance? Evidence from International Research', *Journal of Public Administration Research and Theory,* 15: 559–84.

Frederickson, H. G. (1996) 'Comparing the Reinventing of Government with the New Public Administration', *Public Administration Review,* 56: 263–70.

Frederickson, H. G. (1997) *The Spirit of Public Administration,* San Francisco: Jossey-Bass.

Frederickson, H. G. and Smith, K. B. (2003) *The Public Administration Theory Primer*, Boulder: Westview.

Garvey, G. (1997) *Public Administration: The Profession and the Practice*, New York: St Martin's Press.

Gaus, J. M. (1923–4) 'The New Problem of Administration', *Minnesota Law Review*, 8: 217–31.

George, C. S. Jr (1972) *The History of Management Thought*, Englewood Cliffs: Prentice-Hall.

Gilmour, R. S. and Jenses L.S. (1998) 'Reinventing Government Accountability: Public Functions, Privatization, and the Meaning of "State Action"', *Public Administration Review*, 58:247–58.

Gladden, E. N. (1972) *A History of Public Administration*, Volume II: 'From the Eleventh Century to the Present Day', London: Frank Cass.

Goodnow, F. J. (1900) *Politics and Administration; A Study in Government*, New York: Macmillan.

Gore, A. (1993) *From Red Tape to Results: Creating a Government that Works Better* and *Costs Less: Report of the National Performance Review*, Washington. US Government Printing Office.

Grace, J. P. (1984) *Report of the President's Private Sector Survey on Cost Control*, Washington: US Government Printing Office.

Graham, A. and Roberts, A. (2004) 'The Agency Concept in North America: Failure, Adaptation, and Incremental Change', in C. Pollitt and C. Talbot (eds) *Unbundled Government: A Critical Analysis of the Global Trend to Agencies, Quangos and Contractualisation*, London and New York: Routledge.

Greve, C. and Jespersen, P. K. (1999) 'New Public Management and its Critics: Alternative Roads to Flexible Service Delivery to Citizens?', in L. Rouban (ed.) *Citizens and the New Governance: Beyond New Public Management*, Amsterdam: IOS Press.

Haass, R. N. (1999) *The Bureaucratic Entrepreneur: How to be Effective in Government, the Public Sector, or Any Unruly Organization*, Washington: Brookings.

Hart, J. (1925) *The Ordinance Making Powers of the President of the United States* reprinted in *Historical and Political Science* (Johns Hopkins University Studies in), Vol XLIII, 3: 1–359, Baltimore: Johns Hopkins Press.

Heinrich, C. J., Hill, C. J. and Lynn, L. E. Jr (2005) 'Governance as an Organizing Theme for Empirical Research', in P. W. Ingraham and L. E. Lynn, Jr (eds) *The Art of Governance: Analyzing Governance and Administration*, Washington: Georgetown University Press.

Heymann, P. (1987) *The Politics of Public Management*, New Haven: Yale University Press.

Hood, C. C., and Jackson, M. W. (1991) *Administrative Argument*, Aldershot: Dartmouth Publishing Company.

Karl, B. D. (1976) 'Public Administration and American History: A Century of Professionalism', *Public Administration Review*, 36: 489–503.

Keeling, D. (1972) *Management in Government*, London: Allen and Unwin.

Kettl, D. F. (1988) *Government by Proxy: (Mis?)Managing Federal Programs*, Washington: Congressional Quarterly Press.

Kettl, D. F. (2000) *The Global Public Management Revolution: A Report on the Transformation of Governance*, Washington: Brookings Institution.

Kettl, D. F. (2002) *The Transformation of Governance: Public Administration for the Twenty-First Century*, Baltimore: Johns Hopkins University Press.

Kickert, W. J. M. (1997) 'Public Management in the United States and Europe', in W. J. M. Kickert (ed.) *Public Management and Administrative Reform in Western Europe*, Cheltenham: Edward Elgar.

Kiser, L. L. and Ostrom, E. (eds) (1982) 'The Three Worlds of Action: A Metatheoretical Synthesis of Institutional Approaches', in E. Ostrom, *Strategies of Political Inquiry*, Beverly Hills: Sage.

König, K. (1997) 'Entrepreneurial Management or Executive Administration: The Perspective of Classical Public Administration', in W. J. M. Kickert (ed.) *Public Management and Administrative Reform in Western Europe*, Cheltenham: Edward Elgar.

Kooiman, J. and Eliassen, K. A. (eds) (1987) *Managing Public Organizations: Lessons from Contemporary European Experience*, London: Sage Publications.

Kooiman, J. and van Vliet, M. (1993) 'Governance and Public Management', in K. Eliassen and J. Kooiman (eds) *Managing Public Organizations. Lessons From Contemporary European Experience*, London: Sage.

Laski, H. J. (1923) 'The Growth of Administrative Discretion', *Journal of Public Administration*, 1: 92–100.

Lepawsky, A. (1949) *Administration: The Art and Science of Organization and Management*, New York: Knopf.

Levitan, D. (1942) 'The Neutrality of the Public Service', *Public Administration Review*, 2: 317–23.

Light, P. C. (1997) *The Tides of Reform: Making Government Work, 1945–1995*, New Haven: Yale University Press.

Löffler, E. (2003) 'The Administrative State in Western Democracies', in J. Pierre and B. G. Peters (eds), *Handbook of Public Administration*, Newbury Park, CA: Sage.

Lombard, J. M. (2003) 'Reinventing Human Resource Development: Unintended Consequences of Clinton Administration Reforms', *International Journal of Public Administration*, 26/10–11: 1105–33.

Long, N.E. (1952) 'Bureaucracy and Constitutionalism', *American Political Science Review*, 46: 808–18.

Lynn, L. E. Jr (2001) 'The Myth of the Bureaucratic Paradigm: What Traditional Public Administration Really Stood For', *Public Administration Review*, 61: 144–60.

Lynn, L. E. Jr (2005) 'Public Management: A Concise History of the Field', in E. Ferlie, L. E. Lynn, Jr and C. Pollitt (eds) *Handbook of Public Management*, Oxford: Oxford University Press.

Lynn, L. E. Jr (2006) *Public Management: Old and New*, London: Routledge.

Lynn, L. E. Jr, Heinrich, C. J. and Hill, C. J. (2001) *Improving Governance: A New Logic for Empirical Research*, Washington: Georgetown University Press.

Majone, G. (1989) *Evidence, Argument, and Persuasion in the Policy Process*, New Haven: Yale University Press.

Merkle, J. A. (1980) *Management and Ideology: The Legacy of the International Scientific Management Movement*, Berkeley: University of California Press.

Moe, R. C. (2001) 'The Emerging Federal Quasi Government: Issues of Management and Accountability', *Public Administration Review*, 61: 290–312.

Moore, M. H. (1984) 'A Conception of Public Management', in *Teaching Public management*, 1–12, Public Policy and Management Program for Case and Course Development, Boston: Boston University.

Moore, M. H. (1995) *Creating Public Value: Strategic Management in Government*, Cambridge, MA: Harvard University Press.

Mosher, F. C. (1975) 'Introduction: The American setting', in F. C. Mosher (ed.) *American Public Administration: Past, Present and Future*, 1–10. University, AL: The University of Alabama Press.

Nelson, M. (1982) 'A Short, Ironic History of American National Bureaucracy', *Journal of Politics*, 44: 747–78.

Olsen, J. P. (2003) 'Towards a European Administrative Space?', *Journal of European Public Policy*, 10: 506–31.

Osborne, D. and Gaebler, T. (1992) *Reinventing Government: How the Entrepreneurial Spirit is Transforming the Public Sector*, Reading: Addison-Wesley.

Osborne, S. P. (2006) 'The New Public Governance?', *Public Management Review*, 8: 377–87.

O'Toole, L. J. (1984) 'American Public Administration and the Idea of Reform', *Administration and Society*, 16: 141–66.

Ott, J. S., Hyde, A. C. and Shafritz, J. M. (eds) (1991) *Public Management: The Essential Readings*, Chicago: Lyceum/Nelson-Hall.

Page, E. C. (1992) *Political Authority and Bureaucratic Power: A Comparative Analysis*, Hertfordshire: Harvester Wheatsheaf.

Pascale, R. T. and Athos, A. G. (1982) *The Art of Japanese Management*, London: Alan Lane.

Person, H. S. (1977 [1926]) 'Basic Principles of Administration and of Management: The Management Movement', in H. C. Metcalf (ed.) *Scientific Foundations of Business Administration*, Easton: Hive Publishing Company.

Peters, B. G. (1997) 'A North American Perspective on Administrative Modernisation in Europe', in W. J. M. Kickert (ed.) *Public Management and Administrative Reform in Western Europe*, Cheltenham: Edward Elgar.

Peters, B. G. and Pierre, J. (1998) 'Governance Without Government? Rethinking Public Administration', *Journal of Public Administration Research and Theory*, 8: 223–44.

Peters, T. J. and Waterman, R. H. (1982) *In Search of Excellence: Lessons from America's Best-Run Companies*, New York: Harper & Row.

Pollitt, C. (1990) *Managerialism and the Public Services: The Anglo-American Experience*, Oxford: Basil Blackwell.

Pollitt, C. (2002) 'Clarifying Convergence: Striking Similarities and Durable Differences in Public Management Reform', *Public Management Review*, 4: 471–92.

Pollitt, C. and Bouckaert, G. (2004) *Public Management Reform: A Comparative Analysis*, 2nd edn, Oxford: Oxford University Press.

President's Committee on Administrative Management (PCAM) (1937) *Report of the Committee with Studies of Administrative Management in the Federal Government*, Washington: US Government Printing Office.

Raadschelders, J. C. N. and Rutgers, M. R. (1996) 'The Waxing and Waning of the State and its Study: Changes and Challenges in the Study of Public Administration', in W. J. M. Kickert and R. J. Stillman (eds) *The Modern State and its Study: New Administrative Sciences in a Changing Europe and the United States*, Cheltenham: Edward Elgar.

Raadschelders, J. C. N. and Toonen, T. A. J. (1999) 'Public Sector Reform for Building and Recasting the Welfare State: Experiences in Western Europe', in J. L. Perry (ed.) *Research in Public Administration*, Greenwich: JAI Press.

Radin, B. A. (2001) 'Intergovernmental Relationships and the Federal Performance Movement', in D. Forsythe (ed.) *Quicker, Better, Cheaper? Managing Performance in American Government*, Albany: Rockefeller Institute Press.

Reich, R. B. (1990) *Public Management in a Democratic Society*, Englewood Cliffs: Prentice-Hall.

Rhodes, R. A. W. (1996) 'The New Governance: Governing without Government', *Political Studies*, XLIV: 652–67.

Rohr, J. (2002) *Civil Servants and Their Constitutions*, Lawrence: University Press of Kansas.

Rosenbloom, D. H. (2000) *Building a Legislative-Centered Public Administration: Congress and the Administrative State, 1946–1999*, Tuscaloosa: University of Alabama Press.

Rourke, F. E. (1987) 'Bureaucracy in the American Constitutional Order', *Political Science Quarterly*, 102: 217–32.

Rugge, F. (2004) Personal communication.

Salamon, L. M. (1981) 'Rethinking Public Management: Third-Party Government and the Changing Forms of Public Action', *Public Policy*, 29: 255–75.

Salamon, L. M. (ed.) (2002) *The Tools of Government: A Guide to the New Governance*, Oxford: Oxford University Press.

Schultze, C. L. (1977) *The Public Use of Private Interest*, Washington: Brookings Institution.

Skowronek, S. (1982) *Building a New American State: The Expansion of Administrative Capacities, 1877–1920*, New York: Cambridge University Press.

Small, A. W. (1909). *The Cameralists: The Pioneers of German Social Polity*. Chicago: University of Chicago Press.

Stillman, R. J. II (1999) 'American versus European Public Administration: Does Public Administration Make the Modern State, or does the State Make Public Administration?', in W. J. M. Kickert and R. J. Stillman (eds) *The Modern State and its Study: New Administrative Sciences in a Changing Europe and the United States*, Cheltenham: Edward Elgar.

Stillman, R. J. II. (2001) 'Toward a New Agenda for Administrative State Research? A Response to Mark Rutgers's "Traditional Flavors?" Essay', *Administration and Society*, 33: 480–8.

Suleiman, E. (2003) *Dismantling Democratic States*, Princeton: Princeton University Press.

Thompson, F. (2006) Book Review, *Journal of Policy Analysis and Management*, 26: 201–4.

Toonen, T. A. J. (1998) 'Networks, Management and Institutions: Public Administration as "Normal Science"', *Public Administration*, 76: 229–52.

Toonen, T. A. J. and Raadschelders, J. C. N. (1997) 'Public Sector Reform in Western Europe', Background Paper for Presentation at the Conference on Comparative Civil Service Systems, School of Public and Environmental Affairs (SPEA), Indiana University, Bloomington, IN, April 5–8, 1997. Online, available at www.indiana.edu/~csrc/toonen1.html (accessed 20 December 2005).

US Government Accountability Office (USGAO) (2004) *Performance Budgeting: OMB's Program Assessment Rating Tool Presents Opportunities and Challenges For Budget and Performance Integration*, Washington: GAO-04-439T.

Vickers, S. G. (1983) *The Art of Judgment: A Study of Policy Making*, London: Harper & Row.

Waldo, D. (1984) *The Administrative State: Second Edition with New Observations and Reflections*, New York: Holmes & Meier.

Wamsley, G. L. (1990) 'The Agency Perspective: Public Administrators as Agential Leaders', in G. L. Wamsley (ed.) *Refounding Public Administration*, Newbury Park: Sage.

Wengert, E. S. (1942) 'The Study of Public Administration', *The American Political Science Review*, 36/2: 313–22.

Wettenhall, R. and Thynne, I. (2002) 'Public Enterprise and Privatization in a New Century: Evolving Patterns of Governance and Public Management', *Public Finance and Management*, 2: 1–24.

White, L. D. (1926) *Introduction to the Study of Public Administration*, New York: Macmillan.

Wildavsky, A. (1985) 'Professional Education: The Once and Future School of Public Policy' *Public Interest*, 79: 25–41.

Wilson, J. Q. (1975) 'The Rise of the Bureaucratic State', *Public Interest*, 41: 77–103.

Wilson, W. (1997 [1887]) 'The Study of Administration', in J. M. Shafritz and A. C. Hyde (eds) *Classics of Public Administration*, 4th Edition, Stamford: Wadsworth/ Thomson Learning.

Wright, V. (1994) 'Reshaping the State: The Implications for Public Administration', in W. C. Muller and V. Wright (eds) *The State in Western Europe: Retreat or Redefinition?*, London: Frank Cass.

Index

Wilson, W. 234–5, 245
wirkungsorientierte Verwaltungsführung
   10, 134, 144
World Bank 136, 209, 224
WRR (Dutch Scientific Council for
   Government Policy) 123, 133

zeitgeist 154, 161
Zero-Based Budgeting 180
Zürich 149

eBooks – at www.eBookstore.tandf.co.uk

A library at your fingertips!

eBooks are electronic versions of printed books. You can store them on your PC/laptop or browse them online.

They have advantages for anyone needing rapid access to a wide variety of published, copyright information.

eBooks can help your research by enabling you to bookmark chapters, annotate text and use instant searches to find specific words or phrases. Several eBook files would fit on even a small laptop or PDA.

NEW: Save money by eSubscribing: cheap, online access to any eBook for as long as you need it.

Annual subscription packages

We now offer special low-cost bulk subscriptions to packages of eBooks in certain subject areas. These are available to libraries or to individuals.

For more information please contact webmaster.ebooks@tandf.co.uk

We're continually developing the eBook concept, so keep up to date by visiting the website.

www.eBookstore.tandf.co.uk